FUTURE OF THE PROPHETIC

FUTURE OF THE PROPHETIC

ISRAEL'S ANCIENT WISDOM RE-PRESENTED

MARC H. ELLIS

Fortress Press
Minneapolis

FUTURE OF THE PROPHETIC

Israel's Ancient Wisdom Re-presented

Cover image: Joel Carillet/iStock/Thinkstock

Cover design: Rob Dewey

Library of Congress Cataloging-in-Publication Data

Print ISBN: 978-1-4514-7010-9

eBook ISBN: 978-1-4514-7237-0

The paper used in this publication meets the minimum requirements of American National Standard for Information Sciences — Permanence of Paper for Printed Library Materials, ANSI Z329.48-1984.

Manufactured in the U.S.A.

This book was produced using PressBooks.com, and PDF rendering was done by PrinceXML.

To my sons

Aaron

*"See I place you in the role of God to Pharaoh,
with your brother Aaron as your prophet."*

Isaiah

*"Whom shall I send? Whom will go for us?"
And I said. "Here I am; send me."*

Once again, the dynamic that was so extraordinarily characteristic of Kafka, a dynamic that shaped and energized him, was set in motion. It was the dynamic of catastrophe. A letter that arrived late or a slight cough in the room next door made him falter, yet a world that was falling apart appeared to offer him boundless new resources.

It was as though Kafka were determined to try out everything that narrative traditions have to offer–parables, fables, fairy tales, reports, lists, monologues and dialogues, flashbacks and background stories, first-person and third-person perspectives–and swirl them together. He blended all that tradition had yielded and emerged with an extraordinary new synthesis, turning lead into gold.

Reiner Stach

CONTENTS

Acknowledgements

With gratitude–for Isaiah Ellis and his wonderful Index; Santiago Slabodsky, Keren Batiyov, Sara Roy and Roger Sanders for standing by me; Ildikó Bodolósz and Susanne Scholz for supporting me; Philip Weiss and Adam Horowitz who offered me a daily publishing platform to carry on.

Introduction

During the 1950s and early 1960s, America was opening to Jews. We also created our own openings. Even so, the idea of a Jewish political force was still in the future. Religiously, we remained in the ancient rabbinic framework of interpretation. We mined ancient precepts to cope with modern realities.

The Holocaust hovered in the background, as yet unnamed. We knew, of course, of the slaughter of European Jews in World War II. It followed us like a shadow that moves as the day unfolds. Like our political opportunities, the Holocaust had yet to become the dominating force—*the* Holocaust—as it is known today.

In 1948, the state of Israel was created. Unlike the Holocaust, Israel had a name but the content of the state was yet to be determined. At least in America, Jews thought of Israel as a small, pioneering community far from our shores. International travel was still in its infancy. Over the years, the Holocaust and Israel grew together. Although they were separate historical events, over the next decades they became twinned in the Jewish historical imagination. Twinned, they grew to be almost mythic in their reach and power. The turning point was the 1967 Arab–Israeli war when Israel, feeling threatened, routed the Arab world in a lightning-fast, six-day campaign. Shortly after the war, the Holocaust and Israel became as central to Jewishness as the rabbis had been for centuries.

After the 1967 war, the Holocaust was named as the epitome of Jewish suffering. Israel was named as the response to that suffering. Ancient texts and the ancient Jewish God were thrust into the background, and our immediate Jewish history took precedence. The remnants of the past that survived did so only in the wake of the drama of contemporary Jewish life.

Time passed. The Holocaust and Israel took on more and more significance in Jewish life until there was little else to speak or think about. It was a heady time for Jews. We were becoming prime movers and shakers in America on all fronts. The Holocaust was one of our tickets of admission in America; the state of Israel, with its military prowess, emboldened us. As Jews, we stood tall.

The state of Israel itself was complicated. It lived on a razor's edge, strong but vulnerable, defiant yet anxious. For American Jews, Israel served as a symbol of our arrival as a proud and powerful people. Israel is hardly a symbol to itself, however. Israel is real to Israelis. They talk the talk and walk the walk. They live the Jewish drama in peace, on the threshold of war, and in war. For decades, Israel seemed perpetually on the verge of peace. As I write, and despite the peace initiative headed by U S Secretary of State John Kerry in 2013-2014, its arrival date remains uncertain. Here one must add justice to peace, for the various frameworks of peace offered over the decades, including Secretary Kerry's proposals, have lacked the justice needed for a real resolution to the Israeli-Palestinian conflict.

Israel was founded as a small state in a larger and complicated Middle East. After the 1967 war, Israel expanded its borders, annexing the eastern part of Jerusalem she had conquered in the war and began building Jewish settlements in the Golan Heights, West Bank, and Gaza territories, also won in the war. Many thought that the settlements and Israel's occupation forces in the territories would be temporary. They weren't. Some thought that after the 1967 war, the region, including Israel, would forsake war. Peace would be right around the corner. It wasn't.

Years continue to pass. American Jews are more deeply entrenched in the Holocaust and Israel than ever before. Israel is more deeply entrenched in wars, settlements, and occupation. Meanwhile, Palestinian voices have been gaining an audience especially in the growing movement equating the Israeli occupation of Jerusalem and the West Bank with South African apartheid. The boycott, divestment and sanctions movement (BDS) that helped end apartheid in South Africa is now being applied to Israel's occupation.

The support for the Palestinian cause around the world has increased exponentially. For American Jews who came of age before the 1967 war, their story was largely unknown. When it became known, many Jews thought that Palestinians only opposed Israel because they opposed Jews. The Holocaust was the epitome of antisemitism. In opposing Israel, it seemed that Palestinians were continuing that history. After all, who could oppose Jews having a state of our own?

Israelis know Palestinians like the back of their hand—that is, as conquerors know the people they conquer. Many Israeli families had gone through the Holocaust. Countless family members had been murdered. For those who had survived, Israel was their refuge. Any challenge to that refuge had to be met with force.

Israelis know the Holocaust close-up. They also know their nation close-up. For Israelis, the Holocaust is existential. Their wars are real. Their occupation of Palestinians is real. Unlike American Jews, Israelis have their boots on the ground.

When I say Israeli boots on the ground, I mean Jewish boots on the ground. First, because the Israelis who serve in the Israeli Defense Forces are overwhelmingly Jewish, and second, because Israel is an icon in the Jewish community in America and among Jews around the world. The state of Israel comes from the suffering in Jewish history and has been enabled through the political advocacy and financial support of Jews living outside of Israel. Jews in Israel and in the Diaspora make a huge investment in Israel's success, an investment that stems from Jewish solidarity in the face of the Holocaust. Jews everywhere have said, "Never Again."

Today, many Jews in and outside of Israel realize that "Never Again" means more than Jewish survival. Historically, it meant the displacement of Palestinians and Palestine in the creation of the state of Israel. That displacement continues today through settlements in Jerusalem and the West Bank. More and more Jews believe that the Jewish ethical tradition has been outsourced. It exists in a conceptual universe that bears less and less relation to the facts of Jewish life.

While Jewish leaders emphasize Jewish suffering, the great majority of Jews live in a world where Jewish life is secure and strong. The shattering of the Jewish ethical tradition has consequences. It means that the substance of the Holocaust and the possibility of a renewed and just Jewish presence in Israel-Palestine are disappearing from view. Over time, the ground of resistance for Jews begins to give way. The ethical sources of Jewish life are becoming distant. Increasingly, Jewish youth throw up their hands in despair. Apathy becomes the norm.

Some movements among Jews on college campuses point in another direction. Recently, students have revolted against mandates by the campus Jewish organization, Hillel, that speakers with strong criticisms on Israel be severely restricted. Jewish students at Swarthmore and Vassar have declared themselves independent of these directives. They have renamed themselves "Open Hillel."

There are other voices of dissent. An example is Jewish Voice for Peace. In this organization justice for Palestinians is spoken boldly. As part of Jewish Voice for Peace, there is a Rabbinical Council where rabbis identify themselves as supportive of Palestinian rights. Severely criticizing Israel in public is new in Jewish life. Jewish voices of dissent are becoming more serious and committed.

Nonetheless, over the decades, Jewish life has become increasingly militarized. There is less tolerance for Jews to ask questions about the direction of our communal life. More Jews are asking if Jewish history comes down to this: Having suffered, are we as Jews to cause others to suffer?

This question should occasion the short and simple answer: "No." But, as often is the case with Jews in light of Jewish history, what seems simple is more complex. This is true especially after the Holocaust and the state of Israel.

My book is an attempt to explore questions and answers, angles and interpretations relating to contemporary Jewish identity. This hardly means that I am neutral. As every Jew, I have a stake in Jewish history. I have spent my adult life trying to understand what is up for grabs in Jewish life and what stands I need to take in relation to Jewish history.

By some accounts, contemporary Jewish life in America and Israel is flourishing. It is time to celebrate. By other accounts, contemporary Jewish life in America and Israel is in steep ethical decline. It is time to mourn.

For more and more Jews, Jewish life has reached a tipping point. Whereas in earlier times, the struggle revolved around whether the Jewish ethical tradition could bend Jewish power toward justice, these last decades have introduced a new question. Is there anything ethical left in Jewish life worth saving? Israel has gone so far in its occupation of Palestinian land and settlement building in Jerusalem and the West Bank, that the possibility of two states, Israel and Palestine, standing side by side in peace and harmony seems a charade. Some engaged Jews and much of the international community think that through a continuing occupation and extensive settlements, Israel has foreclosed the possibility of the two-state option. The dream of Israel living side by side with a full, real state of Palestine in peace and harmony has become just that—a dream.

Today there is only one state—Israel controlling the territory stretching from Tel Aviv to the Jordan River—but with millions of Palestinians within those borders. That is why many dissenting Jews look askance at the most recent peace process. Frameworks and principles that grant Israel almost everything it already has conquered, occupied and settled finalizes the diminishment of Palestine. Dissenting Jews want more than an Israeli victory that seals the fate of the Palestinian people. Dissenting Jews want justice—for Jews but also for Palestinians.

Thus my description of Jewish life tilts toward the mourning side of the equation. Or, rather, my account explores the soft underbelly of achieving Jewry in advanced modernity in a time where Israel, with an enabling world Jewry, has permanently conquered another people. In my view, then, our glory days are shadowed by more than complexity. They are shadowed by culpability.

A soft underbelly is common to every community, nation, ideology, and religion. But for Jews, that vulnerability is also the place where our strength—Jewish ethics—is strongest. "Jewish ethics" is the modern way of conceptualizing an ancient and more profoundly troubling foundation of Jewish identity. I believe this ancient and troubling foundation is the prophetic.

There is much talk today about essentializing tradition or identity, an academic classification for refusing to posit a core as immutable. We are rightly cautioned against essentializing any entity or idea as it discloses itself. Essentializing terminology like "Jew," "Jews," "Jewish," as if these labels are static, is taboo.

In modern understandings, such identifiers have little meaning in and of themselves. Essentializing leads to errors in definition and categorization. Those who are essentialized can become targets, as "Jews" have been. Essentializing can lead to a warrior mentality against the Other—"we" against "them." This is part and parcel of Israel's targeting of Palestinians.

I attempt to address this long and involved story in the pages that follow. I take this caution against essentialism seriously. I leave it to each individual and community to decide where they stand on the issue. Obviously, much of Jewish history, including Jewish life in the twenty-first century, is evolving, mixed, and contextual. Jewish identity is impossible to define in a single brushstroke.

Nonetheless, and with the warning against essentialism taken on, I believe there is something unique and essential about being Jewish. Rather than simply assert this belief, in these pages I attempt to explore aspects of both uniqueness and essentiality. I want to understand the core of Jewishness. I desire to approach that core. I want to embody it.

I lay out this core as foundational to Jewish history, to Jewish life, to being Jewish, to the very definition of "Jew." This does not mean that all Jews think the same as I do or want what I define as the essence of being Jewish.

In these pages, I travel against the grain of how many Jews perceive their lives and the life of our community. Nonetheless, as a Jew I am far from alone. In an age of unparalleled Jewish success, there are many Jews who travel against the grain of what "Jewish" has come to mean.

The pages ahead lay out the "essentials" of Jewish life as I understand them. Here is my confessional backdrop to those essentials: I believe that ancient Israel gave the prophetic to the world. Of the gifts to the world, there are few that can rival it. Without the prophetic, there is no meaning in the world. There in fact may be no meaning in the world. The prophet embodies the possibility of meaning in the world.

It is easy to dismiss this formulation, especially by those outside the Jewish tradition who embody the prophetic and correctly rail against claims of difference that might to lead to claims of superiority. I agree with their dissent. I do not claim that Jews should be privileged. I do not think that Jews are superior. Moreover, history is a hodgepodge of influences, borrowings, and mixing. Jews embody a mix of peoples, histories, traditions and cultural influences. Nonetheless, the world knows the prophetic through the Jewish tradition.

Although the Jewish prophetic is distinctive, it is now found throughout the world. One of the themes I explore is that the prophetic today is in some ways stronger among non-Jews than it is among Jews. Jews are in the peculiar situation of being re-presented the prophetic from outside.

This re-presentation has many facets but the primary shift it embodies is central. For more than a thousand years Christianity and Islam have re-presented the Jewish tradition to Jews. Too often this re-presentation has been negative, as if having absorbed the Jewish witness, Christians and Muslim stand as the triumphal successors to Jews and Judaism. Today, many Christians and Muslims—as well as their secular counterparts—seek a solidarity with Jews. They are grateful for what they have inherited from the Jewish tradition. Instead of denigrating Jews and Judaism, others who carry the prophetic wonder where the prophetic witness of Jews and the Jewish community have gone. They seek out Jews in a gesture of solidarity and work with Jews who retain the prophetic. Instead of demeaning Jews, Jews and others are forging a new interfaith and inter-communal solidarity.

The prophetic is lauded by Jews and others. The prophetic is vilified by Jews and others. Either way, there is no way around the prophetic. The prophetic stalks the world. For better and for worse, Jews are the people who embody the prophetic as an ancient tradition in the modern world.

The consequences of the prophetic are enormous. As gift and burden, there is nothing in the world more powerful. Open warfare is declared against the prophetic.

The prophetic is the unraveling of righteousness assumed. Innocence assumed. Affluence assumed. Progress assumed. Civilization assumed.

I believe that what we Jews have accomplished in the post-Holocaust era stands under prophetic judgment. Our newfound power stands under prophetic judgment. Our memorialization of the Holocaust stands under prophetic judgment. The state of Israel stands under prophetic judgment.

Prophetic judgment comes from a variety of locations. Palestinians judge the militarized behavior of Israel. Nations outside of Europe and America judge the American-Israeli alliance as colonial and imperial. Those on the bottom of the income and status ladders in the United States judge both Jewish economic success as well as the success of Jews in trumpeting our history of suffering as worthier than theirs.

All of these locations have their say in my writing. Yet I primarily write about the inner workings of the prophetic and Jews wondering out loud about the direction of Jewish life to which others, too, are pointing. My writing is about Jewish particularity, about Jewish history, where we have come from, where we are. And what is to be done.

These pages are about the unraveling of Jewishness in our time. I seek to clarify the elements of that unraveling by separating aspects of Jewish history and examining how we as Jews look at and dwell within the world. I want to separate the dream of Jewishness and the reality of it. In tracing this unraveling, I struggle to clarify what is mysterious and baffling about contemporary Jewish life.

I would love to solve our predicament, lay aside our bad behavior, and practice justice, but obviously I alone cannot change our direction. With other Jews, however, I can witness to our predicament. I can be present to our contradictions. I can surface Jewish voices to condemn what is wrong. I can attempt to write our hope.

The Jewish unraveling is likely to continue for decades. Just when we think we have reached rock bottom, we sink to another level. When Jews occupy another people, what can be expected other than a loss of ethical bearings? What is hopeful within this dark saga is that there are Jews—sometimes Israeli soldiers themselves in organizations like Breaking the Silence—who call out the behavior they once participated in. There are also Israeli organizations—like B'Tselem—that document the human rights abuses of the Israeli military and settlers.

Yet, even here, we enter a most difficult issue. Are these soldiers and human rights workers documenting abuses that will be corrected so that Jewish life will right its course and begin a new process of justice-seeking and reconciliation with the Palestinian people? Or has Jewish life reached a terminus where their testimony and documentation is less a clarion call for change than it is becoming a historical archive that details the end of Jewish history as we have known and inherited it?

Without a two-state solution to the Israeli-Palestinian conflict, that is, two real states where Palestinians control all of the West Bank and East Jerusalem with a link to a free Gaza, or a one-state solution where Jews and Palestinians participate in governing themselves as equal citizens without restriction according to religion or ethnic identification, then Jewish life as we have known it with an ethical base is over.

Previous peace processes have held out a glimmer of hope for the possibility of a two states solution. The Kerry initiative is sorely lacking and in some ways is even worse than previous attempts. Overall, Kerry's proposals involve a significant permanent Israeli settlement and population presence in East Jerusalem and the West Bank. For the most part it is silent on Gaza. Even the Palestinian Authority's floating proposals of Israeli military troops in the Jordan Valley and an American-led NATO military force throughout Jerusalem and the West Bank to guarantee the demilitarization of Palestine as a state and placate fears of Israel of an independent Palestine is wanting. Foreign military troops stationed in Palestine is another form of occupation. Such proposals deny Palestinian sovereignty. As well, allowing hundreds of thousands of Israeli settlers on Palestinian land is to accept a permanent diminishment of Palestine. The Palestinians would exist as a ghettoized population in perpetuity.

In the struggle for justice in Israel/Palestine more and more Jews and Palestinians are coming together. Within this struggle, Jews and Palestinians are increasingly critical of the political authorities who speak in their name. Crossing the boundary into solidarity with Palestinian freedom is a potent signifier of the possible future of Jewish and Palestinian life together. Is it too late?

This hardly means that those Jews and Palestinians who argue for justice agree on all matters. Nor does it signify that others in the international community who have joined the quest for justice for Palestinians are in solidarity with Jews as individuals, as a community and with the Jewish tradition. As in any movement, complexity is important to identify and surface. Surely some Jews privilege Jewish flourishing over others. Some Palestinians would like a Palestine—which includes for them the state of Israel—without Jews. Clearly, the international community has mixed feelings about Jews, Jewish influence in politics and Jewish empowerment.

Some one-state theorists who champion BDS do so at the expense of the possibility that, in the post-Holocaust world and with the history of anti-Semitism, Jews might deserve and need a collective political dimension to survive and flourish. Unfortunately, Jewish support for the state of Israel and Israel's behavior itself has poisoned the waters of reflection. Though the life of any community is complex and in need of negotiation, Jewish establishment pronouncements on antisemitism in the world have made nuanced arguments more and more difficult.

Whatever the complexities and the need for thoughtful reflection, the situation is beyond grave. We may be at the end of Jewishness as we have known and inherited it. At the end, there may be a beginning. There may not be. Yes, Jewish history will endure. At issue is what direction it will take since Jewish history has had many trajectories. Surely there is no way back to our previous celebration of Jewish life. Speaking of Jewish life and the state of Israel as innocent is disingenuous. It is willful deceit.

My exploration is primarily about the foundations of the Jewish journey and how the present can be seen in the past. But to stop there would be to fall short. In the pages that follow, I explore the interaction of the Jewish past and the present so that contemporary Jewish life may shed its fated sensibility.

Jews are not fated to suffer. Nor are we fated to be oppressors. There is a middle ground of being empowered and being unjust—of feeling the deep embrace of Jewishness without feeling that we are alone—of being at home in an increasingly interconnected world—of paying attention to our particularity while affirming the particularity of others.

When I embrace my Jewishness, I embrace the world. It is for others to learn how, by embracing the world, they can also embrace Jewishness.

Chapter 1 discusses how what we dream and what we experience in reality defines individuals and communities. Jews have ancient dreams of a homeland. We have spent most of our history outside that home. The homeland promised by God as the people Israel left Egypt looked much different upon arrival. The land may have been flowing with milk and honey in Israel's dream. What the Israelites found and did there cast them into confrontation with God's promise and with God. Soon the Israelites were out of the land and into exile.

The promise of a homeland has resurfaced in Jewish life continuously, in an almost mythic pattern. Jews first began to settle again in the land in the late nineteenth and early twentieth centuries. When the Nazis appeared and then took hold of Europe, Jews settled in Palestine in greater numbers. The ancient homeland, a dream of rescue, now materialized in the crucible of history, but the reality of Palestinian life on the land collided with the dream some had of a modern Jewish state. To realize that dream in the ancient homeland meant the cleansing of hundreds of thousands of Palestinians from their homeland. The founding of the state of Israel gave rise to the Nakba, the Palestinian catastrophe.

Was the founding of Israel also the birth of another catastrophe for the Jewish people? There were different types of dream returns for Jews. One was a Jewish state where Jews would dwell alone. This state would be like any other state. Another dream was of a homeland within, among, or next to a homeland for Palestinians in Palestine. Here Jews would recover part of their central focus on language, education, and social experiments. It is important to consider the two dreams side by side so we know that what became—and continues to be—the state of Israel is not fated. We cannot restore the past. There are no do-overs in history. However, we can open our imagination to a different kind of future.

In chapter 2, I explore the internal workings of ancient Israel as they apply to the ongoing struggle within the Jewish community about the place of empire in Jewish history and beyond. I find that Jews have been on both sides of the "empire divide" since time immemorial. The biblical witness is important here. Ancient Israel flees empire on the wings of a liberating God, or so the biblical story narrates. The Israelites are special, chosen by God, and have a destiny to be a light unto the nations. What is that light? Light is about creating a just society and a way of life that stresses community over empire. Once in the land, however, empire desires surface. Soon Israel has its own earthly king.

To create and sustain empire an Other has to be created, more or less like the Other ancient Israel had been in Egypt. But unlike in Egypt where the Other, Israel, critiqued the empire, Egypt, in the promised land the divide is internal, within Israel itself. The thrust against empire is within the same community that now struggles to attain empire. This early division marks Jewish history in a primordial way. Within this division, the prophets arrive. The prophets proclaim that the movement from community toward empire is a betrayal of God's own being.

The prophets accuse Israel of turning its back on God. How do we know this? The biblical account—and judgment—is rendered compactly: Israel is recreating Egypt in the land. Later, as Jews sojourn among the peoples of the earth, the prophetic accusation is hurled outward on behalf of universal justice. The empires of the world are on notice. Yet the prophetic retains its internal bite. It resurfaces periodically and with special force in the modern period when Jews enter the struggle for an emancipated Europe. Then, in an emancipated Europe, the Holocaust inscribes Jews with unimaginable suffering.

The prophetic voice is chastened. Yet in the midst of an unexpected, almost miraculous empowerment, the prophetic voice reappears as a critique of Israeli power used unjustly against Palestinians. Few could have predicted this resurgence. I doubt it is a coincidence that the Jewish prophetic voice reappears as Jews finally get back on their feet and began to strut on the world stage for the first time in two millennia.

Jewish history is marked by a prophetic instability. When Jews right their ship, it is upended with ethical questions that come from within. This brings us back to Israel's God. Could this instability come from an ancient relationship with a fascinating and unstable God?

Chapter 3 moves our exploration to modern America. The uphill struggle of Jews for stability becomes golden in America. For the first time in history, Jews are accepted fully as citizens. Jews participate equally in the political and economic life of the nation. At home in America, Jews identify as American. Still, America has its own complexities for Jews. Over the centuries, America has become an empire. Jews flourish in and are protected by American empire, as is the state of Israel, which has become its own empire in the Middle East.

It is difficult to hear the prophetic voice when the community's life is so intertwined with power. Jews in America and Israel are dependent on America's power. Jews have also become a power unto themselves. Yet it is curious that even with this newfound power and connections to it, Jews have a sense of being alone. How can this be?

The dream and reality are joined. I question whether the power Jews want and need after the Holocaust make Jews more or less secure. For example, if Jews dwell alone, even if it is only in the Jewish imagination, Europe as it was—as a Jewish graveyard during the Nazi period—is essential to maintain. If we dwell alone, even if it is only in our imagination, Israel as it is—a besieged rescue point for a perpetually unwanted Jewry—is essential to maintain as well.

A sense of aloneness coupled with power makes communities and nations do strange things. From the outside, these actions may seem irrational and against their own best interests in the long run. This is occurring in the Jewish world. We strategically position our aloneness as a form of strength and unaccountability. Yet aloneness becomes a self-fulfilling prophecy. Empires are not immune from the reality that what goes around, comes around. Jews have suffered under empire. When others suffer at the hands of Jews we should expect pushback. What happens to Jews when the empire boomerang hits home?

In the first chapters, I circle the question of Jewish identity. In chapter 4, I explore this issue more closely. What does it mean to be Jewish? In every generation, the question arises. Does Jewish identity change generationally, or beneath some of its contextual exteriors does it remain essentially the same? In surveying the historical landscape, Jewish identity has mostly formed in the Diaspora rather than in the land. In interaction with other cultures, elements of Jewish distinctiveness have remained. Jewishness has likewise contributed to and absorbed elements of other cultures.

Although biblical texts and Jewish prayers pine for the promised land, the majority of Jews, even when return to the land is possible, remain outside.

Despite admonishing texts and haunting prayers, Jews prefer distance from the land. Perhaps this is because the demands on the people are too great in the land. Israel has suffered expulsion from the land multiple times. Why live with that threat constantly hanging over you?

Although Israel prays for God's blessing and leadership, Jews seem to savor their distance from God as well. In exile, God is far away. Even in biblical times, Jews are a rebellious lot. Being rebels, Jews also prefer autonomy. Once more we have a difference between the dream—being in the land with God—and the reality. For many Jews, exile from the land is tolerable, perhaps even preferable.

Jews long for stability, even in exile. They long to banish the prophetic. Without the prophetic, Jews are autonomous. They are free to pursue their lives in peace and can, to their benefit, align themselves with injustice. Without the prophetic, Jews are unaccountable. Adopting the Holocaust and the state of Israel as formative, as unstable as both these events are, might be a way that Jews once again try to distance themselves from the unreasonable demands of being a light unto the nations. If the Holocaust and Israel are named and defined as formative , they ultimately function as a way of shielding Jews from yet another round of inconvenient, even dangerous, accountability.

With the cornerstone of Jewish identity as the prophetic, seeking and maintaining distance from God is a full-time effort. To distance themselves from God, colonial and imperial endeavors on behalf of Jewish memory and empowerment must be continuously augmented. To accomplish this goal with the resources it requires, colonial and imperial outreach must move outside Jewish life. Yet what exists outside ultimately comes to reside within Jewish identity as well. It is an oxymoron to believe that empire outside does not demand empire within.

Like any powerful group, Jews cover over their empire connections with an argued innocence. Conversely, we could choose to listen to the world and the prophetic voice within the Jewish community. Instead of deflection, Jews could instead share our suffering, our dreams, and our hopes with other struggling communities, binding us to them and them to us, in a new solidarity.

Chapters 5 and 6 take us deeper by way of Jewish and Palestinian commentary on the sixtieth and sixty-fifth anniversaries of Israel's founding in 2008 and 2013, respectively. Anniversaries are times to take stock. We look back and ahead while pausing to view where we have arrived. On Israel's sixtieth anniversary, we find that the narrative of contemporary Jewish history and possibility that we usually hear is far more complicated. When we expand our view outside the tried and true the state of Israel's history is found to have many dark edges. There are far fewer voices on Israel's sixty-fifth anniversary, which is telling in and of itself.

In these chapters, I explore Jewish and Palestinian dissident groups, writers, and activists, of which there are many. An Israeli group, Zochrot, enjoins Jews in Israel to remember what happened to Palestinians as the state was founded. Jeff Halper, an American-born Jewish Israeli, wants Jews to recognize that whatever the hopes were for Israel at the beginning of its existence, Israel has developed an apartheid system much like the one that ruled South Africa. Mazin Qumsiyeh and Joseph Massad are Palestinian thinkers and activists who are critical of Jewish dissidents for the limitations of their analysis. They fight against a Judeocentric view of Palestine and proffer their own perspective of the struggle against Israel's expansion and destruction of Palestinian life.

Other commentators on Israel's anniversaries include the Holocaust survivor Elie Wiesel. His and other commentaries, found in *Time* magazine, reflect a more mainstream American understanding of Israel. Not surprisingly, *Time* only asked Jews to contribute. In turn, the Jewish contributors mention Palestinians only in passing, often in a negative way. I finish with an Orthodox Jew, Yakov Rabkin, who portrays anti-Zionism and opposition to a state of Israel as fundamental to Judaism. He even broaches the understanding among some Orthodox that the Holocaust may have been a punishment from God as Jews had strayed from the true faith. At least, the discussion is joined and moves beyond the mainstream presentation of Jewish identity and the Jewish future.

In chapter 7, I return to the beginning and explore what I call the "eternal trauma." The eternal trauma for Jews begins in the formative event of Exodus and all that flows from that experience. This includes the prophetic as the center of Jewish life, history, and identity, the same prophetic that Jews carry through history. Trauma is commonly understood as ordeal, disturbance, and distress—which the Exodus, Israel's entry and existence in the land and the prophetic are—but it also represents possibility. Once experienced, our lives are determined by what we do with trauma. We can succumb to trauma, using it to cause pain to others. Or we can take trauma and mold it into a positive contribution to our lives and the lives of others.

How a people can carry an original trauma of pain and possibility through history is difficult to explain. Since trauma cannot be passed down through history as a biological force, how is it that Jews are marked so clearly by their origins? Perhaps it is simply a cultural phenomenon. Jews are formed by narratives that emphasize these original traumas. There could be a presence that shadows Jewish history beyond culture. Regardless of one's take on the transmission of trauma, the historical drama remains and is taking on a new and explosive power in our time.

The God of Israel is a peculiar God. At times, God accompanies Israel; at other times, God disappears. In our time, God seems to have left the scene altogether. Yet the prophets remain. They continue to haunt the Jewish people in the time of Jewish empowerment. The biblical prophets are commissioned by God. Can the prophetic persist without God? On the face of it, this is a theoretical question. But, as with the ancient prophetic, it remains tangible. Today the Jewish prophetic exists for the most part without God.

Within empowerment there are prophets who have emerged on the scene from the most unlikely of places—the state of Israel. This is unexpected for a variety of reasons, not the least of which is that Israel is seen as the vanguard of Jewish empowerment after the Holocaust. To have Jewish Israelis break with that power, and to do so for the sake of Palestinians, is startling. Some Jewish Israelis take their critique so seriously that they leave the state of Israel entirely. Having returned, they once again enter into exile.

Just as startling, many of these Jewish Israelis no longer identify as Israelis or even as Jews. Yet their protest is so prophetic, so Jewish. That is why I refer to these prophets as Still/Former Jewish/Israelis. They have lived the dream and reality of the Jewish return to the land. They have been the Jewish boots on the ground. Now, at least for them, it is over. I ask what this growing number of disaffected Still/Former Jewish/Israelis have to say to the Jewish community about Jewish identity and the Jewish future. Is the Jewish future to be determined by how many Jews inside and outside of Israel become (un)Jewish? Is becoming (un)Jewish in our time precisely the way to embrace the deepest sense of what it means to be Jewish?

In chapter 8, I explore the way the designation of the Jewish dead of the Holocaust as martyrs has directed establishment Jews to assume power without accountability. Jewish empowerment assumes an almost religious sensibility. Not only is power exercised without restraint, but other options of an interconnected empowerment are diminished or derided. The chapter begins with an exploration of the two Jewish museums in California, one of which, the Judah L. Magnes Museum carried the name of the homeland Zionist, Judah Magnes, without examining his life's work in Palestine. Or, rather, only certain parts of Magnes's work in Palestine are emphasized, such as his role as founding chancellor of Hebrew University in Jerusalem. Deemphasized is that Magnes was a homeland Zionist who encouraged the settlement of Jews in Palestine while remaining adamantly opposed to the formation of the state of Israel.

Another erasure in Jewish history is taken up by Timothy Snyder in his book *Bloodlands*. Snyder offers a bold analysis of what happened in Europe during the years 1933 through 1945. Jews would immediately recognize these as the Holocaust years, but Snyder is interested in reconstructing that history beyond what has become defining. Snyder finds that what is commonly known as the Holocaust was a clash between the empire hopes of Germany and the Soviet Union, with millions of Jews and non-Jews caught in between both empire-hungry entities. Snyder's analysis is devastating. The human carnage he portrays is even worse than the Holocaust suggests. At the same time, he forces a reconsideration of Jewish suffering as unique and singled out.

I then return to our Still/Former Jewish/Israelis. Since the Bloodlands of Europe contained Jews and non-Jews, and the state of Israel has also been involved in war after war that includes Jews and non-Jews, have Jews gone from one Bloodlands in Europe to another in the Middle East? If we strip away a Judeocentric view of Israel and look at the broader Middle East since Israel's founding, is the Middle East a new Bloodlands? Jews who leave Israel and live in a prophetic exile may thus witness to the hope that the Bloodlands—wherever they are—comes to an end.

It is difficult to underestimate the importance of what it would mean if Jews realized that the Holocaust, as horrific as it is narrated, was actually shared with others historically and therefore the memory of the Holocaust must be shared. Sharing the Holocaust in history and memory undermines a central part of Jewish identity and thus is dangerous to those who see the Jewish community as immune to internal and external criticism. Yet deconstructing Jewish aloneness in the Holocaust might become a place of healing for Jews and others. This could also preface a redirection of Jewish politics within and toward a just peace in Israel and Palestine.

Chapter 9 connects the dots of our journey. Jews carry a lot of historical baggage. We also carry a conceptual sensibility in the contemporary world. "Jewish" means something. But to do something positive with "Jewish" in the world means we will have to move from where we are to where we need to be. The first step has to do with how we teach our children and the children of others about the Holocaust. Through Snyder's *Bloodlands*, we understand that what Jews assume about ourselves and what we narrate to the world is partially true. It is also skewed for our benefit—or detriment—since teaching the Holocaust as we have taught it isolates Jews, allows the Holocaust to function to enable power, and ultimately places Jews in danger.

The death camp, Auschwitz, has become a symbolic marker in Jewish history. Holocaust memorials dot the European and American landscapes. The

Holocaust landscape has become central to Jewish self-definition. To allow the Holocaust to transition into a broader arc is a challenge to Jewish self-definition. This is certain to happen with the passage of time, but contemporary history is forcing this upon us in an accelerated time-frame. For a community that has invested itself so heavily in the Holocaust, the prospects are daunting. Thus the desire to hold onto the Holocaust as exclusive to Jews is understandable. Nonetheless, the Holocaust is in transition. It will be taught differently to the next generation of Jews and others.

With the Holocaust shifting, the Jewish sense of and commitment to the state of Israel will change. It already is changing. But the pace of historical events is much faster than changes in narrative discourse. A cognitive dissonance between facts on the ground in Israel-Palestine and the use of the Holocaust to remain unaccountable for injustice grows daily. At issue is whether Jewish dissidents, including our Still/Former Jewish/Israelis, will remain connected to the Jewish community. They are the vanguard of the Jewish future. Will Jewish dissenters be lost to the Jewish community?

Is it antisemitic to criticize Israel? If it is possible to criticize Israel, how far can one go in that criticism? If, as a Jew, or a non-Jew for that matter, you believe that Israel is an apartheid state, is that antisemitic? Or if you do not believe that any nation-state should privilege one ethnic or religious group over another, not even for Jews in Israel? Forces within and outside the Jewish community seek to blunt criticism against Israel by branding such views as hate speech. Does supporting BDS against Israel for its policies toward Palestinians constitute such a crime?

Chapter 10 comes back to the beginning: the prophetic voice. There are some who believe that Jewishness is a prison, an identity from which some Jews want to escape. Jews want to be among others without distinction. Especially with the absence of God, why identify as Jewish? Yet non-Jews define Jews as Jews and other Jews identify Jews as Jews—there seems no escape. Being bound within one's Jewishness can lead in variety of directions. Sometimes the external pressure on being Jewish is enormous. Other times the pressure is internal. If Jewish identity has a prison-like reality to it, this is also the place from which the prophetic springs. This is yet another part of Jewish life that begins in the Bible. Often, the prophets chosen by God want out of that designation. Yet it is within the prophetic that Jews find their core.

The prophetic is an action. It is also a performance. By performance, we do not mean an actor on a stage, as in a play written by someone else. However, the prophet has a stage and, in the end, performing the prophetic has its own patterns of speech and delivery. What is amazing is how similar performing the prophetic today is to its ancient prototype. Of course, the prophetic is hardly limited to Jews. Through the spread of this ancient vocation through Christianity and Islam, today the prophetic is performed around the world. Though it is usually unrecognized, what is of great importance is how the prophetic is being re-presented to Jews in the time of Jewish empowerment. Through this re-presentation, can Jews as a community reclaim what it once gave to the world?

One example is the boats that carry supplies to the Palestinian of Gaza who are under siege. These boats are real—they carry medical and other needed supplies—but they are also symbolic. They seek to advise Israel and the broader Jewish community that the prophetic is, at root, the conscience of humanity and that root, residing in the heirs of ancient Israel, is atrophying among Jews today. Could exercising the conscience of humanity in Israel-Palestine bring a deeper reckoning for justice on the world scene and especially among Jews?

Closing out the prophetic in its more universal search, I explore two Jewish women, Naomi Klein and Adrienne Rich. Klein is the author of *Shock Doctrine*, where she explores the latest phase of "Disaster Capitalism," a global get-rich-quick scheme that feeds off the misery and oppression of others in need. Israel is part of this equation as Israel benefits in a myriad of ways from the occupation of Palestinians, as well as from global insecurity after 9/11. Although broad in her reach, Klein focuses more specifically on Israel-Palestine when she signs on to the BDS movement that seeks to force Israel to end their occupation of Palestinian lands.

Adrienne Rich is the late Jewish poet who, because of her mixed parentage, had to choose Jewishness as her primary identity. Like Klein, Rich supported the BDS movement and, like Klein, was a searcher for connections within and among people of conscience. Rich's evocative poetry and poetic cadences are ripe for the expansion of the prophetic in our time as she seeks to be a Jew "without borders." In this search, Rich explores the boundaries of the prophetic as a Jew, a woman, and a lesbian. What she finds is that by telling the truth, we create more truth. The opposite is case as well. When we limit that outreach, we begin a cascade of lies that ultimately makes the truth inaccessible.

I close with a meditation on whether Jews—or anyone, for that matter—can be just when injustice reigns. The prophetic is a wager made against the odds and at a personal sacrifice. This is Israel's ancient wisdom. It is a wisdom exploding in our time.

1

Dream and Reality

In the seventh decade of the Israeli–Palestinian crisis, is there anything left to say, think, or do? Although many feel the possibilities for a solution to the crisis are exhausted, diplomacy continues. Yet diplomatic missions come and go. The Arab Spring has come and gone or, more to the point, has morphed into an almost fascist dictatorship in Egypt and mind-boggling violence in Syria. Israel-Palestine remains more or less the same. Or worse.

When we think that the situation cannot get any worse, it does. Even when peace is "necessary," "urgent," and "right around the corner," the plight of the Palestinians worsens. For years now, Palestinians on the West Bank have been refused entry into Jerusalem. Jerusalem's Palestinian population continues to be evicted as Jewish settlers in East Jerusalem increase. Ostensibly temporary, the Apartheid Wall encircles the Palestinian population of the West Bank as a permanent boundary. Even the Palestinian Authority has offered a continuing Israeli military presence in Palestine's Jordan Valley, along with a permanent stationing of American-led NATO military throughout the West Bank—all in hopes of gaining some limited autonomy. Hamas-led Gaza is often referred to as a vast prison camp. It is absent from the peace process. Gaza's borders are rigorously controlled by Israel and Egypt. Even international aid has difficulty being delivered there.

Israel is triumphant, almost defiant, yet continues to fear for its safety and security. Israel lives crisis to crisis. Some believe that the crisis atmosphere benefits Israel's plans to continue its expansionist policies at the expense of Palestinian sovereignty. Others believe that Israel would hardly know how to live if its borders were settled and peace reigned with its neighbors.

Israel is one of the strongest nations in the world, yet continues to depend on the United States to guarantee its security. With this guarantee, Israel stands strong. Yet beneath this exterior, dependence breeds anxiety. What if the United States commitment to Israel turned in another direction?

The Israel-Lebanon war in 2006 demonstrated Israel's vulnerability. Lebanon was burning, as was Israel. Israel's 2008 invasion of Gaza hardly made Israel more secure. Though a nuclear power, Israel threatens Iran because of its nuclear program. Iran threatens Israel—so Israel claims. Israel lives on the edge.

Fundamental issues lie at the heart of the Israeli-Palestinian crisis. Yet the foundational issue of the conflict, the 1948 war that founded Israel and dispossessed the Palestinians, remains outside the parameters of Jewish thinkable thought. At the same time, binational and homeland alternatives to state Zionism, exemplified in the work of Jewish luminaries such as Martin Buber, Judah Magnes, Hannah Arendt, and Albert Einstein, are buried. The silence surrounding the founding of Israel is connected with the silence on the historic alternatives offered to state Zionism.[1]

The past is the path to the present. The past may also open us to an alternative future. What options were there in the founding of the state of Israel? What choices were made during that time period? If the past related to Israel's founding is virtually unknown to many Jews and non-Jews alike and the present is an emergency situation with dangers on all sides, a sense of fate pervades. The future unfolds with a logic that makes choices about the future seem naïve, even foolhardy.

To approach this subject of Israel is challenging. Every issue is fraught. Emotion and suffering color the pages of Jewish history. The passage of time limits haunts us. On 2013's sixty-fifth anniversary of Israel's birth and the ensuing Palestinian catastrophe, the lay of land and the political and intellectual discourse that survives was so different from what it was decades before that appeals to memory appeared out of place. In some quarters, such appeals were deemed irresponsible. On the seventieth anniversary, the passage of time will be acute.

Time passed is time lost. Still, in lost time there are messages for the present. Thinking through the past brings us back to the origins. The origins signal choice for the future. In the Middle East it is time to begin again. How can we break through the stalemate, anger, violence, and numbness that envelop Israel and Palestine?

---

1. For our purposes, diverse understandings of non-state Zionism—including those Zionists who saw a binational reality—will be gathered under the rubric "homeland Zionism." For a current discussion of the diversity of Zionism, see Judith Butler, *Parting Ways: Jewishness and the Critique of Zionism* (New York: Columbia University Press, 2012). An example of non-state Zionism during the founding of the state of Israel can be found in Hannah Arendt, "To Save the Jewish Homeland: There Is Still Time," in *Hannah Arendt: The Jewish Writings*, ed. Jerome Kohn and Ron H. Feldman (New York: Schocken, 2008), 388-401.

Each people and community has a right to be at home. Home is part of the human quest. Peace, too, is a common aspiration, a necessary one. Our lives orient in the direction of home and peace. Despite great similarities with other cultures and communities, the Jewish journey features specific trajectories that set Jews apart. Jewish history claims an ancient origin and journey that begins with a world created by God and God's choice of the people Israel to be God's people.

In the biblical narrative, the main line of Israel's journey unfolds. Through Abraham, the people Israel are called into being to inhabit a certain terrain. Israel descends into slavery in Egypt, is liberated with a promise of land, enters the Promised Land, settles there, and becomes a kingdom. When, through abuse of political power, injustice reigns, the prophets appear. Israel is chastened by the prophets. Exile from the land is penalty for this abuse.

Through repentance, Israel returns to the land, is exiled again for backtracking on its promised repentance, returns, and is exiled once more. Israel then begins an almost two-thousand-year sojourn outside the land. Israel is dispersed among the nations, its anchor being the ancient formative events that inspired it.[2]

Jews are commanded to remember their narrative prehistory as a clarion call to a unique destiny. Jewish destiny combines religious, national, political and cultural aspects of peoplehood—in the land and outside of it. The Jewish dream is birthed, struggled for, found, lost, returned to, lost again, seemingly forever. During that loss home is prayed for, often without a realistic hope of retrieving the dream and with much anguish. Many questions arise during this journey. Jews are shadowed by the land of promise that is beyond their grasp.

Questions facing Jews multiply with the passage of time. Why do Jews exist as a people through history? Why is the promise of land important, especially when most Jews live outside the land? Is there a specific Jewish destiny and is that destiny intertwined with this specific "promised" land? How do Jews fulfill their destiny in the land? How do Jews fulfill their destiny outside the land? What are the ends of Jewish history? Is there a bridge between the dream of the land and the reality of dispersion?

We know that fate does not have the last word. Destiny, however interpreted, is open. Changes of direction are possible. All religions invoke transformation as achievable. Judaism is no exception. The challenge is to act

---

2. My rendition of the biblical narrative takes into account the scholarly literature critical of any overall historical sense of the biblical canon. Nonetheless, at the end of deconstructing the canon, the canon itself remains a force to be reckoned with, and not only in a critical way.

individually and in concert with others. Do I—do we—act as if transformation is possible?

In 2012, Jewish Voice for Peace, a dissident Jewish group and its Rabbinical Council, issued a Passover Haggadah that hopes for a collective effort by Jews to alter the direction of the state of Israel. Taking the tradition of breaking the middle matzah and hiding one half, to be found later as the afikomen, the Haggadah notes that once the matzah is broken it cannot be repaired completely—"irreparable damage has been done."[3]

Nonetheless, the broken pieces can be reunited. The Jewish Voice for Peace Haggadah relates that reunification within past brokenness is possible in the present: "As we break the middle matzah we acknowledge the break that occurred in Palestinian life and culture with the establishment of the State of Israel in 1948 when hundreds of villages were destroyed and hundreds of thousands of people displaced. This damage cannot be undone—but repair and return are possible."

How does repair begin? First, Jews have to understand the history behind the present brokenness. There is no better season to explore this than Passover, when Jews relate their brokenness in slavery and delight in their liberation from bondage. The Jewish Voice for Peace Haggadah counterpoints Jewish liberation then with Palestinian dispossession now. Can Jewish liberation be celebrated today without the end of Palestinian enslavement?

Jews are commanded to place ourselves in the telling of Passover as if we *are* there—in slavery, in Egypt. But we are also supposed to be here, in the now. The subtitle of the Jewish Voice for Peace Haggadah is "Israeli and Palestinian: Two People, One Future." The dating is 2012 and, with the long arc of Jewish history in mind, 5772.

Distance always exists between dream and reality. This is true for every community and religion. However, the issue remains as to how Jews bridge this distance. We long for a time when the dream of liberation and the reality of liberation, for Jews and for others, will become one.

The covenant at Sinai is the culmination of the liberating actions of God in forming and promising to be with the people Israel. As well, the biblical narrative evolves after God and Israel embrace the covenant. Inherent in the covenant is a back and forth between God and Israel, which unfolds during the course of Jewish history. It is evident in the Bible. It is true today.

3. Passover Haggadah, 2012/5772, Jewish Voice for Peace, http://jewishvoiceforpeace.org/sites/default/files/hagadah_jvp_final_2012.pdf. For the blog of the Rabbinical Council see http://palestiniantalmud.com/

From the beginning, ancient Israel is faced with recurring possibilities and pitfalls. In turn, archetypes emerge in Jewish history that continues to define the Jewish journey today. Listing a bare outline of these archetypes speaks of a significant history of interpretation and contestation. The embrace of the covenant, the commandment of remembrance, and mining the ancient canon for meaning and purpose—all are ancient and ongoing. Also included is the ability of Jews to argue with God—in essence, to contest God's will—as well as the quest for justice on earth.

These contemporary Jewish concerns are already present in the Bible. Most importantly, in the Bible, wherever injustice rears its head, but especially among the people Israel, the haunting shadow of the prophets appears. The prophetic haunting of Jewish life has renewed itself in our post-Holocaust world.[4]

The pursuit of justice in and outside of the land is present from the beginning in the biblical text. There we find a canonical reading of justice-seeking in the dynamic interplay of the Sabbath, Sabbatical year, and the Jubilee. As well, there is a cycle of settlement, exile, and return revolving around the land. These are primal markers for the Jewish people.

In the Bible, we discover that the prophetic is indigenous to the people Israel. We know that the prophetic sensibility comes before the land and has priority over it because injustice judges Israel's sojourn there. Through God, the prophets judge Israel's record of justice. When the prophet's judgment is damning and Israel refuses to repent, Israel suffers grievously. The Bible records the constancy of the prophetic—when it is convenient for Israel and especially when it is inconvenient.

All of this is foreground to contemporary Jewish life and the Israeli-Palestinian conflict. Is it relevant today? Many think that religion simply mucks up what is already a complicated issue. The entire world cannot bring the crisis of Israel-Palestine to closure. One doubts the Bible can.

From the beginning of Jewish history there is promise of a homeland. The homeland is the Land of Israel. In the biblical story, the Land of Israel remains the Jewish homeland whether Jews are physically present in the land or not. When Jews are not in the land, they are dispersed. The Diaspora is defined over against the Land of Israel—dispersion as exile, (un)home.

Exile from the land is bitter. Yet the Diaspora is the birthplace of Judaism. Judaism is the religion of Jews that emerges primarily outside the land. During

4. For archetypes in Jewish history, see Efraim Shmueli, *Seven Jewish Cultures: A Reinterpretation of Jewish History and Thought* (Cambridge: Cambridge University Press, 2008). For a post-Holocaust take on these archetypes, see David Roskies, *The Literature of Destruction: Jewish Responses to Catastrophe* (Philadelphia: Jewish Publication Society of America, 1989).

the Roman occupation of Jerusalem in the first century of the Common Era, Jews revolted against Rome. They were defeated. The subsequent dispersion of the Jewish people from the land ends Israelite religion.

Israel's religious law and obligations revolved around the land and the Temple in Jerusalem. Without either, Jews needed a new religion that, though connected to the old, responded to the reality of dwelling outside the land without access to the now-destroyed Temple. A new religious system, what we know as Judaism, responded to the historical catastrophe that befell ancient Israel.[5]

Judaism forms in the Diaspora. Over the last two thousand years, for the most part Jewish history takes place in the Diaspora. In Judaism, the longing remains for the land. In 1948, that dream becomes reality. The state of Israel is born. Some Jews feel that the rebirth of a Jewish state is the fulfillment of the longing of a dispersed and suffering people. Then again, promise often loses luster when reality intrudes. The backdrop to this return is ominous—the Holocaust.

To sketch the "dream" backdrop to the reality of 1948 is to enter an uneven history. In Jewish history, dream follows nightmare, nightmare follows dream. Often in Jewish history dream and nightmare are intertwined. It is complicated to untangle them. Should we try?

Even though the Hebrew calendar extends the time of the birth of Jewish history back to creation, in modern historical terms the time of ancient Israel to 1948 spans roughly three thousand years. This history is uneven. In the last two thousand years, for example, Jews have been accepted by and lived in harmony with their neighbors. Jews have been assaulted and forced to flee their native lands. At times, Jews who were forcefully expelled from lands are later welcomed back. Centuries later the heirs of Jews welcomed back were slaughtered. In Jewish history, hope and anguish encircle each other.

The Holocaust years arrive. For many Jews, the Holocaust is a *novum* in Jewish history. It is true that Jews suffered before. But after every disaster that befell the Jewish people, hope returned. Now the numbers—and geographical reach—multiply. The Holocaust is a global assault. Every living Jew is targeted. After the Holocaust, the prospect of hope is shadowed by the specter of mass death. Hope after the Holocaust is almost unbearable.

---

5. Sholmo Sand disputes these historical renderings in his, *The Invention of the Jewish People* (Brooklyn: Verso, 2010) and again in *The Invention of the Land of Israel: From Holy Land to Homeland* (London: Verso, 2012).

What should Jews do after the Holocaust? If there is hope, does hope need to be redefined? "Hope" after the Holocaust. "Liberation" of the death camps. The meanings of words change.

Downward Spiral

What does liberation mean—*after*? The "liberation" of the death camps seems an odd, if almost blasphemous, bonding. What is hope in light of the millions murdered and in the face of the starving survivors? Our vision has to readjust. What can the survivors of the Holocaust hope for? Jews had faced this dilemma before but not at this level. Systematic mass death is different than pogroms and expulsions. Exile is preferable to Auschwitz.

Because of this transposition of meanings, placing the Jewish journey in perspective is demanding. It is becoming more difficult for Jews with each passing day. On the international scene because of its policies toward Palestinians and the government's bellicose pronouncements on world affairs, it is almost impossible to speak in positive tones about the state of Israel. But, even more alarming, it is increasingly challenging to speak in affirmative ways about Jews and Jewishness.

This awkwardness has to do with how Jews and Jewish history are interpreted in light of the creation and expansion of the state of Israel. What happened to Palestinians during the creation of Israel and, as much, what is happening to Palestinians today, colors the discussion of Jews and Jewishness. Because of the injustice done to Palestinians by Israel, for increasing numbers of Jews and non-Jews alike, the ancient promise of the Jewish people, as well as the dislocation and destruction of European Jewry, is consigned as a fading and irrelevant history.

Far worse, though, is when the defense of Israel becomes a slogan to mobilize Jews against others. Mobilizing Jews for Israel's defense further denigrates Palestinians. It also denigrates the Jewish ethical tradition. Movements spring up to "rebrand" Israel, "defending" Israel and Jews against the "propaganda" of its enemies. Yet the rebranding of Israel as a positive force in the world is strongly contested by the facts on the ground that Israel is creating in its continuing occupation of Palestinians.[6]

6. One example of the rebranding is the publicity campaign arguing Israel's liberality on gay and lesbian issues over against the more conservative Arab world. Even here, seemingly on safe ground, the claims are increasingly contested by Jewish gay and lesbian activists who do not want to trade one injustice for another. On "Pinkwashing," see Sarah Schulman, "Israel and 'Pinkwashing,'" *New York*

Mostly because of the plight of the Palestinian people, the world is becoming less and less interested in Jews and Jewish discourse about itself and the state of Israel. Mobilizing Jews deflects from the confrontation needed within Jewish history. Rather than addressing the issues at hand, mobilizations for Israel in the Jewish community deepens the abyss that many Jews seem unwilling to confront.

In the contemporary discussion of the Middle East, Jews and non-Jews who oppose Israel's policies toward the Palestinians are disparaged in public. To silence dissenters, the Holocaust is invoked. Jewish leaders especially warn that the Holocaust is part of the Jewish future rather than confined to history. In their view, weakening Israel inevitably leads to another Holocaust. In many quarters, the defense of Israel is akin to a religious commandment. The commandment has to be obeyed by Jews even if criticism of Israel is justified.

Dissenters against Israeli policies are lumped together. It hardly matters whether dissenters are Jewish or non-Jewish, American or European, Israelis who dissent within their own country or Palestinians who resist their dispossession. At one time, the Jewish establishment saw the threat to Israel as mainly coming from the Palestinians and Arab nations. At another time, the threat emanated from Lebanon and then Iraq. Then it was the Arab Spring. Now it is Iran. Separately or together, they are part of a second, seemingly eternal, another-Holocaust chorus.[7]

In turn, vilified Jews and non-Jews sometimes denigrate the promise and hope of ancient Israel. These critics single out for particular attention the use of violence in pursuit of that dream, at least as narrated in the Bible. The state of Israel is perceived as repeating the biblical pattern of ancient Israel cleansing the land of its indigenous inhabitants. Forgotten is that other ancient and contemporary histories are similarly filled with violence. A few scholars who think that the history of ancient Israel is connected to the present-day violence of Israel demand that the parts of the biblical scriptural narration be condemned. Israel's narrative of its origins is transposed into modern history and judged from a contemporary vantage point.[8]

Times, November 22, 2011. Also see her *Israel/Palestine and the Queer International* (Durham: Duke University Press, 2012).

7. Events such as September 11th also set off this discussion of antisemitism. For an interesting example of this genre see Gabriel Schoenfeld, *The Return of Anti-Semitism* (New York: Encounter Books, 2004).

8. Unfortunately, some of these works veer into historically antisemitic areas, in this case defined as vilifying Jewish texts as Jewish though historically used by Christians in their violence against others. The late Michael Prior is an example. See his *The Bible and Colonialism: A Moral Critique* (Sheffield: Sheffield Academic Press, 1997).

Disentangling the ancient and the modern, weaving and unweaving the tapestry of Jewish history and hope that can be embraced and acted upon in solidarity with others, is clearly a challenge. After the Holocaust, and after what Israel has done and is doing to the Palestinians, this task is even more challenging. Yet the challenge must be met forthrightly. Otherwise, the ethical history of the Jewish people will be consigned to the unspeakable. Antisemitism will also have its say.

As the situation in Israel and Palestine continues its downward spiral, mythic claims about Jews and Jewish history return. Once again, Christian antisemitism and Enlightenment suspicions about Jewish particularity fill the air. While the Jewish establishment exaggerates and exploits these fears for its own advantage, denying negative feelings about Jews is hardly the right response. Rather, sorting out truth and fiction is important.

Ancient conspiracy theories about Jews are being modernized. Jews are accused of controlling the media and the global economic system. The U. S. Congress is felt to be beholden to Jews. Some believe American Jews and Jewish Israelis orchestrated the tragedy of September 11th, 2001, to further Jewish interests. The list goes on.[9]

The debate about ancient Israel and its application to the modern world is also spiraling downward. Jewish history represents an important trajectory in world history. The attempt to demean and denigrate this history is misplaced. Instead, it is important to follow ancient Israel and the Jewish people through the complex maze of history. We glean positive lessons of a destiny Jews internally embrace and project in the world. Instead of demeaning, we should struggle to encounter Jews and Jewish history in a constructive way. In this encounter we are neither passive bystanders nor superficial critics. As Jews and non-Jews we come into a critical solidarity with the unfolding of Jewish life.

Solidarity means that all sides refrain from romanticizing embraces or demonizing cheap shots. The challenge is to enter into a people's journey while maintaining a certain distance from it. Being with and outside of a people's journey, as an insider or outsider, provides a vantage point to learn about the struggles of other peoples as well. Over the course of any history, no community, religion, or nation is innocent. Nor should any community be demonized. Entering into relation with others, a critical solidarity is necessary. Can it be any different with Jews?

The increasing inability to reason about contemporary Jewish life is worrisome. Jews are culpable in this difficulty precisely because the narrative of

9. For a more measured analysis on the history of antisemitism to contemporary times, see David Nirenberg, *Anti-Judaism: The Western Tradition* (New York: Norton, 2013).

Jewish history is often presented as one of innocence. This innocence is then coupled with the right to aggress against others, as if aggression is also innocent. Aggression is redefined. Aggression isn't aggression.

This "Jewish aggression in Israel against the Palestinians that isn't aggression, thus Jews as innocent" bundle is presented as essential to secure Jewish survival in light of an ill-defined Jewish destiny. By constantly referring to suffering in the Holocaust—as if only Jews have suffered in history—*and* pretending to innocence in Jewish empowerment in Israel, Jews, most especially Jewish leadership, appropriate a narrative justification to use power over against the Palestinian people without accountability.

The Jewish establishment enables violence in the name of destiny, all the while claiming innocence. Others have used destiny as their *raison d'etre* to demean and slaughter Jews. They, too, claimed innocence in their pursuit of Jews, a claim that since has been convicted within the communities that once claimed it. Can Jews escape that very same judgment by others and even by Jews themselves? One day will Jews indict themselves in regard to the violence done to the Palestinian people?[10]

To get behind this narrative of innocence is important. Parsing Jewish culpability and the different choices that could have been taken is important. We can do this by paying attention to history. In this regard, a brief survey of the origins of the Zionist movement is fruitful. In the Zionist movement, we find innocence as well as an intense realism. We discover patterns of Jewish history as well as a people in need.

As the twentieth century dawned, the religious and secular wings of the Zionist movement began to settle Jews in Palestine. For Zionists, Palestine was the Land of Israel. In their settlements in the land, Zionists found fulfillment of their dream of return. The exile that seemed indeterminate and was increasingly dangerous might be coming to an end.

A minority of the Jewish settlers were religious. They sought an "ingathering" of Jews as a harbinger of messianic times. Most of the Jewish settlers were secular. They sought a safe haven that augured a "normalization" of the Jewish condition wherein Jews would be safe, secure, and self-governing. Dwelling among others had been dangerous. In the land of their own, Jews would determine their own fate.[11]

---

10. See one of my early books that references this theme: *Beyond Innocence and Redemption: Confronting the Holocaust and Israeli Power* (San Francisco: HarperSanFrancisco, 1990).

11. On a history of Zionism, see David Vital's multivolume work, *The Origins of Zionism* (Oxford: Oxford University Press, 1980); *Zionism: The Formative Years* (Oxford: Oxford University Press, 1982); and *Zionism: The Crucial Phase* (Oxford: Oxford University Press, 1987).

A small majority of religious Zionists were Orthodox Jews. They looked askance at the prospect of normalizing the Jewish condition. The Orthodox believed Jews were singled out for a specific destiny that would be fulfilled when Jews returned to the biblical land God promised to Jews. Settling in the Land of Israel was a commandment. The rest was left to God. Orthodox Jews believed that only God could initiate the messianic era. Religious Zionists had little desire to change the social, economic, or political conditions of Palestine itself.

Secular Zionists had a different vision. For secular Jews, normalization of the Jewish condition was the hope. Secular Zionists did not want to be set apart any longer. Their idea was to change the concrete material and political conditions of European Jews. In their Palestine, Jews would breathe free and develop their own way of life.

Secular Jews wanted to be free of Christian power and religion. They also wanted to be free of Jewish religion and the authority of the rabbis. To become free, Jews needed a state. Secular Zionists wanted a Jewish state for Jews like France was for the French and England was for the English. Since a Jewish state did not exist, it would have to be built—by Jewish hands.

Although Zionism was a minority position in the Jewish world, the energy surrounding the movement grew as the twentieth century unfolded. During these years, the pros and cons of Zionism were debated. Zionism became an organizing principle for Jewish uplift and self-sufficiency.

There was significant opposition to Zionism. Many Jews sought peace, freedom, and security in the lands where they lived. They viewed Zionism as a retrograde movement that sought a return to an outdated nationalism. It might even be dangerous for Jews. Jews were scattered all over the world and, at that, were a small minority of the world's populations. Would the world tolerate a Jewish state and, in the end, what benefit would a Jewish state accrue to Jews who remained minorities in other nations?[12]

In the first decades of the twentieth century, Zionism's ultimate direction and success was in doubt. There were contentious disputes within Zionism as to what Zionism should hope to attain. What would a successful return to the land mean in relation to Jewish identity for Jews who lived in the land and for those who continued to live elsewhere? If there was a return, how should Jews govern themselves? Should Jews live in the land with others or should there be a Jewish state? Should Jews go it alone in the land or Jews need a colonial sponsor?

---

12. One case study of dissent against Zionism is found in Thomas Kolsky, *Jews Against Zionism: The American Council for Judaism, 1942-1948* (Philadelphia: Temple University Press, 1992).

Homeland Zionism was a dissenting form of Zionism. Unlike Zionists that wanted a Jewish state, homeland Zionists saw their mission as the development of an educational, spiritual, cultural, and linguistic center in the land for Jewish people everywhere. In their vision, some Jews would live in the Jewish homeland. Many Jews would continue to live in the Diaspora. Although homeland Zionists favored a homeland for Jews, the Land of Israel would be shared with the Palestinians. Palestinians would also have their own homeland there.

Homeland Zionists were against the creation of a Jewish state for a variety of reasons. They feared a state would corrode the ideals of Judaism and Jewish destiny. A Jewish state would create enmity with Arabs already living in Palestine. A Jewish state would need protection against outside forces, including the Palestinian Arabs, who would suffer from its establishment. A Jewish state would, of necessity, be militarized.

A Jewish state would become like any other state. In numerous ways, Jews would be recreating the states they lived within. Would such a state be an advance for Jews? Would Jewish energies outside the state also have to be devoted to the state for no other reason than its survival?

For state Zionists, homeland Zionists were idealists. Their ideals would recreate the instability of the Diaspora they were trying to escape. Homeland Zionists would exist within another alien environment, surrounded now by Arabs rather than Europeans. Since most Jewish settlers were European, the animosity of the Arabs might be even greater than the non-Jewish Europeans from which the Zionists were trying to remove themselves. Besides, as Europeans, state Zionists were trying to recreate the Europe they were escaping, this time under protected Jewish auspices.

State Zionists were interested in the Land of Palestine because of its Jewish roots. As Westerners, they had a colonial sense of the backwardness of the East and of Arab culture. State Zionists wanted Europe in the Middle East. The thought of being Arabized filled them with foreboding.[13]

Enthusiasm within the various forms of Zionism increased as the Ottoman and British Empires diminished in power and authority. Enthusiasm increased further in the 1920s and 1930s as the world plunged into economic depression. With the ascension of the Nazis to power, and then the ensuing world war that culminated in the Holocaust, the Zionist movement coalesced. In 1948, just three years after the end of World War II, the state of Israel was born. State Zionism became the state of Israel. Homeland Zionism faded from history.

13. For a view of non-European Jews on the state of Israel, see Ella Shohat, *Taboo Memories, Diasporic Voices* (Durham: Duke University Press, 2006), 201-232, 320-58.

THE BIRTH OF ISRAEL AND THE PALESTINIAN CATASTROPHE

The disjunction of the Jewish dream and the reality is central to the state of Israel's birth. It is impossible to approach this chasm of Jewish distinctiveness and normalization and the reality of Jewish life in Europe and Palestine without the perspective of Jewish history. Likewise, it is impossible to approach it without the prior history of those already in the land, the Palestinians.

With the creation of Israel, the Jewish dream of a state and the reality of Palestinian existence clashed. The collisions of two histories began. Each anniversary of the state of Israel also marks an anniversary of the Nakba, the Palestinian catastrophe. The creation of the state of Israel and the ethnic cleansing of Palestinian Arabs from their land go hand in hand. Historically, they cannot be separated.[14]

Zionism predated the Holocaust, the Jewish catastrophe. Nonetheless, the Holocaust provided the last push that brought fledgling Jewish settlements into a state formation. From the beginning, the clash of Jews and Palestinians was a catastrophe in motion. One catastrophe led to the other. Now they exist side by side.

The Holocaust, the creation of Israel, and the Nakba are beside one another. They cannot be separated. Nor is there an end in sight for their joint journey. We do not yet know whether Jewish Israelis or Palestinian Arabs will be the ultimate victims of this joining of catastrophes and state building—or even if there will be an ultimate victim.

Perhaps the original Jewish and Palestinians catastrophes will be transformed into a mutual justice that transcends the suffering of both peoples. Jews and Palestinians may one day develop a mutual solidarity that diminishes the catastrophes that befell both peoples. Absent a Palestinian state, though, another larger catastrophe might be in the offing. Both peoples may go down together.

As Jewish forces fought for a state in the wake of the Holocaust, the demise of the British Empire left the Middle East segmented and weak. The international community took note of Jewish suffering and supported the creation of Jewish state. There was also an awareness of the Palestinian question. This is evidenced in the United Nations Partition Plan and the subsequent involvement of the United Nations in the ongoing Israeli–Palestinian conflict.[15]

14. For a recent perspective on the Palestinian Nakba, see Nur Masalha, *The Palestine Nakba: Decolonising History, Narrating the Subaltern, Reclaiming Memory* (London: Zed Books, 2012)

Jews on the ground were immersed in building and expanding Jewish settlements as their hope for the future. They were less interested in the borders the United Nations or other international actors proposed. After the dust of war cleared, Israel was born as a Jewish state. Jews had now become state actors themselves. The state of Israel conducted itself in the manner it saw fit.

During the war that gave rise to Israel, some 750,000 Palestinians were driven out of the boundaries of what became the declared Jewish state, leaving a Palestinian Arab minority of 150,000 or so within Israel's borders. The Palestinian Arabs became citizens of Israel, though their citizenship is of a second-class nature, a further reminder that they are but a remnant in the land they once had lived as a majority. Along with the population, the geographic territory of historic Palestine also diminished. Thus was born the Palestinian refugee crisis. Today, Palestinian refugees number in the millions. Israel continues to expand its population and borders. Historic Palestine is disappearing.[16]

Like the refugee crisis, the reduction of Palestine has evolved over time. Yet the original question about the ethnic cleansing of Palestinians remains. How could Israel be a Jewish state if the majority of its citizens were non-Jews? The Palestinians were cleansed from what became Israel for that reason. But the formation of the state of Israel is still more complex.

There are various interpretations of the formation of the state of Israel. What happened on the Jewish and Arab sides during the war that surrounded Israel's creation is hotly debated. One debate revolves around who accepted and did not accept various borders offered by the international community. Yet another debate centers around the issue of which side aggressed, invaded, or defended.

Although the debate continues, the result of the 1948 war is clear. Israel emerged the victor. Palestine was divided. A majority of the Palestinian population became refugees. The United Nations Partition Plan was overwhelmed and ignored by Israel's victory. Subsequent United Nations resolutions with regard to the needs of the Palestinians have been disregarded by Israel. Israel has continually increased the size of its territory since its founding. The wars over the borders of Israel and the Palestinians continue. So, too, do the wars with Israel's Arab neighbors. Since the formation of Israel, wars have

15. For an interesting take on the international community and the formation of Israel, see *The Palestine Question in International Law*, ed. Victor Kattan (London: British Institute of International and Comparative Law, 2008)

16. See Ilan Pappe, *The Ethnic Cleansing of Palestine* (London: One World, 2007).

been constant. With advances in modern technology, they are increasingly dangerous.

Despite the various peace plans offered, today Israelis and Palestinians are farther away from a "just" solution to the Israeli-Palestinian conflict than ever before. Continuing Israeli expansion in Jerusalem and the West Bank has led many Middle East experts to believe such a solution is foreclosed. The situation is so dire that some fear a new and unexpected uprising or, worse, a catastrophe of unimaginable proportions. Then all the players in the Middle East would have to find a solution to the impasse. But who hopes for a new beginning that might reduce Israel, the Palestinians, and the Middle East to a smoldering heap of ashes?

Whatever the Jewish dream, 1948 introduced a significant level of aggression, insecurity, and destruction in the Middle East which continues today. For many Jews, the 1948 war was a defensive war to create the Jewish state, and Israel has been engaged in a defensive strategy ever since. The Arab side of the Israel narrative is viewed through a different lens. Whatever the Arab world would have become without Israel, the cycle of underdevelopment and destruction that occasioned Israel's creation and expansion has been extreme.

The Israeli perspective on the perpetual Arab and Palestinian opposition to the state of Israel is simple. The only reason to oppose Israel is a retrograde hatred of Jews. Therefore, it is counterproductive for Israel to search with Palestinians for a way beyond the nightmare that has evolved. This diminishes the argument among some that the Israeli-Palestinian crisis can only be seen through the aftermath of the Arab-Israeli 1967 war and the settlements that have been built in Jerusalem and the West Bank since. For these interpreters, Israel has been and will continue to be under assault by Palestinians and the surrounding Arab states simply because Israel is a Jewish state.

In Palestinian "terrorism," Israel sees a conflict between the forces of light and darkness. Some Jews who live outside Israel agree with this analysis. Some do not. Within Israel there is an ongoing debate about this line of demarcation. Could it be, though, that resistance to Israel has to do with the dispossession of Palestinians and Israel's continual expansion? Separating political grievances from antisemitism is almost impossible for many Jews.

Deflecting political grievances by charging antisemitism mobilizes Jews and others in the West to uncritically support the state of Israel. The Holocaust is used in this deflection as well. If Palestinian political grievances are reduced to threats of another Holocaust and antisemitism, the Palestinians are, by definition, antisemites. Why listen to the grievances of antisemites? Palestinians are further defined as the new Nazis. The logic unfolds: Why listen to destructive myths of the Palestinians when we know where that led during the Nazi era?

Regardless of where Jews stand on the trajectory of contemporary Israel, most Jewish analysis precludes the origins of conflict. Yet the reality of 1948 must be reckoned with. It is the time and place where dream and reality collided. What ensued is a cycle of violence and atrocity as yet without end.

Nonetheless, for some Jews concentrating on the establishment of the state of Israel begs the question. History is history, why revisit it? Move beyond the impasse. Start where we are. The facts on the ground are where we should begin.

By making 1948 the starting point, however, a different set of "facts" is placed in motion. In 1948, two suffering peoples exist at a historic crossroads. Their paths are possible to reconcile. Even today, Jews and Palestinians still live in proximity to each other. Israelis number more than five million. Within the territory controlled by the state of Israel—a territory that today stretches from Tel Aviv to the Jordan River—three remnant Palestinian populations remain. The first remnant comprises over a one-and-a-half million Palestinians who live with Jews within the state of Israel proper. The second remnant is more than two-and-a-half-million Palestinians who live with Jews in Jerusalem and the West Bank. The third remnant is in Gaza where more than a million-and-a-half Palestinians live. Because Jews and Palestinians are close in numbers and proximity there is still time to rectify the impasse and begin again. 1948 is long ago. 1948 remains present.

Too often, the catastrophe that befell Palestinians is obscured. The rhetoric of parts of the Jewish community in Israel and America makes sure that this continues. Obscuring rhetoric comes from a Holocaust consciousness that emphasizes how weak Jews were—which rhetorically posits that this weakness remains in the present. Obscuring rhetoric tells us how much Jews suffered because of that weakness—which rhetorically posits that Jews are either suffering today or will suffer in the near future. Ironically, but without the hint of irony, this argument is made in an era of unparalleled Jewish empowerment.

Holocaust consciousness views Jews as innocent in suffering and in power. It also perceives Israel as the bulwark against renewed suffering. Israel is Jewish redemption after the Holocaust. Israel is the state that keeps the Holocaust from recurring. An array of institutions, think tanks, media personalities, and academics spread this message of innocence and redemption. In what way, then, could Israel be culpable in 1948 or after?[17]

Keeping together what is defined in opposition is a challenge. On the one hand, the need for a Jewish safe haven after the mass killing of European Jews can be upheld. It is difficult to pass judgment on the survivors who made a home in what became the state of Israel. On the other hand, Palestinians have a right to object to the very idea of a Jewish state. There is no way around Jewish complicity in the ethnic cleansing of Palestinians.

When catastrophes happen in history, questions of what is to be done in their aftermath take on urgency. With regard to Jewish suffering in the Holocaust, some Jews question whether Israel makes the world safer for Jews or more dangerous. Israel has certainly made the world more dangerous for Palestinians.

Yet the Jewish dream and the reality of 1948 remain largely unaddressed. This has to do with the desire not to rehash history and the inability to undo what has occurred. It also has to do with obscuring the reality of 1948 and emphasizing the Jewish need for a secure place to live after the Holocaust. Still, whether done purposely or not, the neglect of the formation of the state of Israel makes it more difficult to reconcile the wrong done to Palestinians. Without this recognition, Jewish culpability remains unaddressed. Jewish identity is built on a fractured foundation. What kind of Jewish future does this portend?

REMEMBERING HOMELAND ZIONISM FOR THE FUTURE

Obscuring the catastrophe that befell the Palestinians limits the choices Jews have to change the present reality of Israel/Palestine. If Jews are without culpability, Jews have little reason to listen to those we harmed. If Jews are innocent in the creation of Israel, how can Palestinian justify their struggle to be free?

With the reality of 1948 obscured, Israel is viewed as defending itself against those Palestinians and the Arab world who seek to harm Jews. Palestinians and Arabs do not have a legitimate grievance against Israel. Nor do they have a legitimate grievance against Jews outside of Israel who offer unquestioned allegiance and aid to Israel's policies. Instead, Palestinians pursue Israel and Jews because they are antisemitic. They become the heirs of Hitler, the new Nazis who seek to finish Hitler's work. Do Jews really believe this?

The leaders of Jewish life today form an establishment. This establishment is Constantinian in form. "Constantinian" refers historically to Christianity when it was a minor and maligned religious community in the first centuries

---

17. On the development of Holocaust Theology, one variant of Holocaust consciousness, see my *Toward a Jewish Theology of Liberation*, 3d and Expanded Edition (Waco: Baylor University Press, 2004), 13-28.

after Jesus. In the fourth century, the Emperor Constantine had a vision of Jesus shielding his forces in battle. Henceforth, he adopted Christianity as a viable religion. Under his successors, it became the religion of the empire.

Constantine's Christianity entered into a working relationship with the government, ultimately becoming beholden to the government for property and a monopoly on religion. In return, Christianity did the empire's bidding. The empire blessed Christianity. Christianity blessed empire.[18]

As with other Constantinian establishments before it, Constantinian Judaism links to power and empire. Although there are many differences with Christianity in its Constantinian formulation, the Jewish establishments in America and Israel have made their own empire deal. Jews are blessed in America. America blesses Israel. What is good for one is good for the other. For the protection American foreign policy offers Israel, Jews offer their support to the American government.[19]

A major desire of the Constantinian Jewish establishment is to obscure Israel's present actions against the Palestinians. By obscuring Israel's actions—and intentions—Israel remains above criticism. The Holocaust is used as a shield. So is antisemitism. The aim is to depoliticize Palestinian grievances, rendering them as unjustifiable emotional and irredentist lashing outs against Jews. In turn, the Holocaust and antisemitism are mobilized and politicized. They become the guardians of Israel's innocence.

There are Jewish critics of the Constantinian Jewish establishment. They respond that Israel has done wrong but limit that wrong to the occupation and settlement of Palestinian lands after the 1967 war. This analysis is that of the Progressive Jewish establishment, with Michael Lerner and the Jewish journal *Tikkun* leading the way through the 1990s, but with the recent addition of a political lobbying group, J Street, now in the forefront. By limiting their critique to the post-1967 war period, Progressive Jews maintain Jewish innocence and the possibility that the state of Israel is redemptive. If only the sins of the post-1967 occupation of Jerusalem and the West Bank can be expiated, then Israel's policies and trajectory can be righted.[20]

18. Though Constantine started the evolution of Christianity into a state religion, it would become the state religion with the Edict of Thessalonika in 380 ACE after Constantine's death. For our purposes, however, we use the known terminology, Constantinian Christianity and apply it as a type to a Jewishness benefitting from and supporting state power. See James Carroll, *Constantine's Sword: The Church and the Jews: A History* (Boston: Houghton Mifflin, 2001).

19. For a take on Constantinian Judaism as well as their relationship to Progressive Jews, see my *Judaism Does Not Equal Israel* (New York: New Press, 2009).

Progressive Jews find it difficult to address 1948. Like the Constantinian Jewish establishment, they declare it an act of treason to do so. Progressive Jews obscure the real problematic Jews need to confront. Wherever Progressive Jews move along the ever-changing Israel-Palestine crisis fault lines, they continue to avoid or minimize 1948. They cloak the same reality the Constantinian Jewish establishment does. Because of this, increasing numbers of analysts view Constantinian and Progressive Jews as fellow enablers of the dislocation of Palestinians and the destruction of Palestine.

At issue is freedom for Jews and others to think outside the structures that the Constantinian and Progressive establishments deem "authentically" Jewish. Progressive Jews define antisemitism and Jewish self-hate in similar terms to the Constantinian Jewish establishment. When Jews or non-Jews question the formation of the state of Israel or are insistent on the crimes committed against the Palestinian people, their integrity is questioned.

Jews criticizing Israel are open to harsh judgment. But who draws the red line and what interests are served when this line is drawn? On whose authority is the line drawn? If the red line moves one way or another, and the once condemned are now affirmed, who repairs the reputation of those that were so summarily disparaged?

Progressive Jews resent their pairing with Constantinian Jews. They see themselves in fierce opposition to Constantinian Jews. But their differences are often exaggerated. At the foundational level, what is allowable for Jews and non-Jews to think, speak, and act upon is similar. A return to the origins of the state of Israel in 1948 spells trouble. Too harsh a criticism of Israel means antisemitism is at play. The similarities between the two establishments are as important as their differences. It is best to think of Progressive Jews as the left wing of Constantinian Judaism.

There is another group of Jews—Jews of Conscience—who break with the Constantinian and Progressive Jewish establishments. Jews of Conscience recover both the dream and the reality of 1948. In doing this, they reject the notion of Jewish innocence in the creation of the state of Israel. They also reject the assertion that Israel is redemptive of the Holocaust and an answer to Jewish powerlessness. Instead, Jews of Conscience seek to understand the reality of 1948 and Jewish power in its various dimensions. This includes the catastrophe that befell the Palestinians and the Jewish establishment's link with American power. Jews of Conscience view the catastrophe that befell the Palestinians as

20. A good snapshot of the strength and limitations of Progressive Jews is found in Michael Lerner, *Embracing Israel/Palestine: A Strategy to Heal and Transform the Middle East* (Berkeley: North Atlantic Books, 2011).

a catastrophe for Jews as well. They question what the linkage with American empire bodes for the Jewish future.

Jews of Conscience analyze the ideologies and theologies that obscure what is happening in the present. Revisiting the ethnic cleansing of Palestinians in 1948, Jews of Conscience understand the continuing dislocation and displacement of Palestinian population and land after the establishment of the state of Israel as a continuity of settler policies. Thus the aftermath of the 1967 war was a continuation of the wrong done to Palestinians. A truncated freedom in a further diminished Palestine is hardly the appropriate response to this historical wrong.

The Palestinian catastrophe is thus placed in a broader framework. Not only was Israel culpable in its origins, the central thrust of Israel today retains that culpability. The Palestinian trauma of dislocation and displacement is laid squarely at the feet of the Jewish establishments in Israel and America posing an urgent question. Since the Palestinian Nakba continues, Jews of Conscience ask what Jews are to do about this enduring injustice that is foundational to Israel's existence.[21]

Jews of Conscience are horrified by the continuing war against the Palestinians. They believe that Israel's behavior after the establishment of the state is best understood by coming to grips with the founding of Israel itself. The occupation of East Jerusalem, the West Bank, and Gaza after the 1967 war has a "before." The "before" is the original settlements on the coast, then their expansion into the interior as Palestinians were cleansed from the land. The growth of the settlements in Jerusalem and the West Bank is continuous with Israel's founding, present, and future. "Before" is crucial to understanding the future trajectory of the state of Israel.[22]

Jews of Conscience believe that re-visioning alternatives to Zionism in its statist formulations—even the original opposition to Zionism itself—is crucial for the future of Jews and Palestinians. Without making a definitive judgment with regard to the historical moment of Israel's founding, thinking through the variety of Jewish life at that time is crucial to imagining a joint life beyond the present divisions. Besides, all of these alternatives exist among some Jews in the

21. The analysis of a radical Jew of Conscience can be found in Ronit Lentin, *Co-Memory and Melancholia: Israelis Memorialising the Palestinian Nakba* (Manchester, UK: Manchester University Press, 2010). For an interesting and controversial take on life within Israel and the occupied Palestinian territories by a Jew of Conscience see Max Blumenthal, *Goliath: Life and Loathing in Greater Israel* (New York: Nation Books, 2013.)

22. This continuity of settlements is discussed in Rafi Segal and Eyal Weizman, *A Civilian Occupation: The Politics of Israeli Architecture* (Brooklyn: Verso, 2003).

present. One kind of view, state Zionism, has become dominant. Other points of view have to surface for an alternative and inclusive future to be envisioned.

Whereas after the Holocaust, a majority of Jews were soft Zionists, ranging from mildly supportive to indifferent to the movement, for Jews of Conscience it is important to remember homeland Zionism as an alternative to state Zionism. Alongside Judah Magnes and Martin Buber, two other important homeland advocates were Hannah Arendt and Albert Einstein. All were active in alternative Zionist movements before the state of Israel was created and continued in their opposition to state Zionism afterward as well. Magnes, who died as Israel became a state, spent his last years lobbying Secretary of State Marshall and President Truman against recognizing the declaration of Israel's statehood and the partition of Palestine. Buber, Arendt, and Einstein continued their search for an alternative to state Zionism after Magnes's death.[23]

Although they lost the battle in the political arena, homeland Zionism continues as a critique of the more militant policies of the state. It may stimulate thought about Israel's future. Just as reckoning with 1948 forces Jews to understand that Arab and Palestinian opposition to Israel is more than a form of antisemitism, resurfacing the homeland option within Zionism reminds Jews that life in the land could have taken different directions.

By remembering homeland Zionism's proposals for the Jewish community in Palestine, other avenues in the present come into view. The daunting question is whether there is the time and will within Israel and among its supporters to reconfigure the trajectory of the state toward justice and an ethical future. It may be too late.

Israel has conquered Palestine. The challenge is how the Jewish and Palestinian populations will live within this expanded Israel. On the seventieth anniversary of Israel in 2018, what relationship will Jews and Palestinians have? Will they be living together in justice or injustice? Divided as antagonists or united in a new project of mutuality and reconciliation?

If a massive transfer of Palestinian population from the three remnants of Palestinian life under the control of Israel is avoided, a reconfigured understanding of how Jews and Palestinians exist together in the land will have to be created. If more decades of occupation are to be avoided and a further ethnic cleansing of Palestinians to be circumvented, homeland Zionism needs a second look if only to open alternative modes of thinking.[24]

---

23. Magnes is quite interesting here. For a biography of him, see Daniel P. Kotzin, *Judah L. Magnes: An American Nonconformist* (Syracuse: Syracuse University Press, 2010). For more on Magnes and his interaction with the American recognition of Israel as a state see John B. Judis, *Genesis: Truman. American Jews and the Origins of the Arab/Israeli Conflict* (New York: Farrar, Strauss and Giroux, 2014).

What does homeland Zionism look like when glimpsed through the lens of Holocaust consciousness and Israeli statehood? The Holocaust obscures the origins of the state of Israel and alternative approaches to Zionism as the state came into being. A comprehensive historical approach is needed here but, like the 1948 war and the ethnic cleansing of the Palestinians, a general overview is enough to suggest future possibilities.

Homeland Zionism included binational, confederation, and federation approaches to Jews living in neighborly relationships with the Palestinian and the surrounding Arab countries. It emphasized the Jewish longing for a home in its place of birth and as a center for the Jewish people. As important, a Jewish homeland sought to renew life in the Jewish Diaspora. The Diaspora would have a center from which it could draw nourishment and strength.

Homeland Zionism envisioned the rebirth of Hebrew as a living and spoken language. The Jewish presence in the land would be a launching ground for specifically Jewish endeavors in education, culture, agriculture, and social organization. Cultivating these aspects of Jewish life, Jews could extend their contribution to the broader arc of humanity. Homeland Zionism proposed an institutional infrastructure that would receive Jewish refugees from a war-torn and devastated Europe. Jewish refugees would be settled in a peaceful and welcoming land.[25]

For homeland Zionists, a communal gathering of Jews in Palestine fulfilled the ancient Jewish promise of a homeland. In the emergency years of the Holocaust, the Jewish homeland would grant sanctuary for the dislocated Jews of Europe. As with the state Zionists, by the early years of the twentieth century, homeland Zionists feared that the specific Jewish difficulties in Europe would leave the Jews of Europe in dire political, cultural, and spiritual shape. As the Nazis came to power, these fears increased.

Perhaps the most eloquent spokesperson for homeland Zionism was Martin Buber, himself a refugee from Nazism. By the time he arrived in Jerusalem in the late 1930s, however, the die was already cast. State Zionism was ascendant. Or so it seems when looking back from our vantage point.

Buber, along with others like Magnes, argued passionately that their Zionism was the only way forward for Jews and Judaism. To choose a state was to choose a final division between Jew and Arab. A state necessitated a militaristic polity toward and a displacement of Palestinian Arabs. Displacing

---

24. For one such look, see *What Does a Jew Want? On Binationalism and Other Specters*, ed. Udi Aloni (New York: Columbia University Press, 2011).

25. The positive elements of homeland Zionism are exactly what Hannah Arendt thought would be lost in the formation of a Jewish state. See her "Zionism Reconsidered," in *Jewish Writings*, 343–74.

Palestinians would, in turn, lead to constant wars. Jews would be seen as perpetual foreigners in the region. With the birth of the state of Israel in 1948, Hannah Arendt predicted that the Jewish state would become a modern Sparta.[26]

If a Jewish state was created, Arendt believed an important opportunity would be squandered. The lessons of the Holocaust and the end of World War II provided a significant moment for Jews to adopt a politics of living with and among other nations. Instead of falling back on weakness and the charges of antisemitism, Arendt envisioned Jews as a political force, participating equally in a world where power was interdependent and evolving.

Jews had the advantage of being without a colonial past. Therefore, the Jews of Palestine could be a positive and innovative bridge between the East and West. Arendt hoped that the Jews and Arabs of Palestine would become a model of East-West cooperation in a world that had just emerged from a global war and was now entering the decades of the Cold War.[27]

Arendt thought that World War II was the end of Western civilization as it had been known and inherited. Everything that was believed about Western civilization had come toppling down over our heads. What the world needed were models of a new civilization, one that could sustain rather than destroy life.

In Arendt's view, Palestine could function as a small experiential model serving a greater international need. Jews had suffered catastrophic losses in the Holocaust but now, back on their feet, Jews could become beacons of hope. Why squander a Jewish and global hope on what would be a small and embattled state?

Many of Arendt's predictions came true. The views she shared with Buber, Magnes, and Einstein have transpired. Israel turned its back on almost everything homeland Zionists valued. Rather than pacific, Israel became militarized. The normalization of Jewish life that state Zionists longed for continues to elude Jews. The institutions of the state have rendered Jewish Israelis anomalies in the Middle East.

True, Hebrew is now a modernized spoken language, whereas before it was primarily used for liturgical purposes. But that Hebrew is also used in ways unforeseen by the early Zionist thinkers. Today, Hebrew is used to displace, capture, torture and murder Palestinians. In this and other ways, Israel has continued and has perhaps exacerbated Jewish abnormality. However,

26. Arendt, "Jewish Homeland," in *Jewish Writings*, 388-401.

27. For a fascinating contemporary take on Arendt's understandings, see Judith Butler, *Parting Ways: Jewishness and the Critique of Zionism* (New York: Columbia University Press, 2012), 114-80.

the abnormality is of a different sort than Jews previously experienced. The abnormality is one of Jewish power used against others struggling for their own justice.

Whereas Arendt and other homeland Zionists foresaw a center for Jews in Palestine as a bridge between East and West, today Israeli naval forces detain others who attempt to bridge the East-West divide. The Israeli Navy's interception of the flotilla of boats carrying medical supplies and other necessities for Palestinians in Gaza is commonplace. The Gaza flotillas are similar to the bridge Arendt foresaw that Jews could be—exemplars of the need for justice and models of that very possibility in a world desperately in need of reconstruction.

Instead of welcoming the boats bound for Gaza as an opportunity to begin again, Israel deflects its injustices by asserting that the boats themselves symbolize a threat to Israel's existence. Yet if Israel looked at the Gaza flotillas from another perspective, they might see them re-presenting the idea of homeland Zionism to a triumphant state Zionism.

The Gaza flotillas are a disturbing memory of what the Jewish return to Palestine could have been. They call Jews to return to a normality characterized by justice-seeking for Jews and for others as well.

In Jewish history, turning away from justice is considered abnormal. But, then again, when the abnormal becomes the new normal, the subversive memory of suffering becomes a defense against the hopes of a dispossessed people existing on the other side of Jewish power.

Still, the dispossession of the Other is the dispossession of the one who dispossess. So much so, that the oppressors' memory of its dispossession is used as a—normal—weapon against others.

RABBIS OF CONSCIENCE SPEAKING PASSOVER TRUTH TO POWER

After decades of existence it is difficult to argue that Jewish life in Israel is "normal." Israel is constantly at war or in preparation for war. Israel has yet to have a year, let alone a decade, where Jews carry on life without its occupation of Palestinians or threat of war with its Arab neighbors. In another historical twist, Israel now turns away or deports African migrants and asylum seekers. Israel makes it increasingly difficult for international justice seekers to enter its borders.

The dream of state Zionists is unrealized. Homeland Zionists were correct when they argued that state Zionism's dream of normalization was unachievable. From another perspective, it may be that instability is at the core of Jewishness. This makes the prospect of Jewish "normalization" in any configuration illusory. Neither homeland nor state Zionists reckoned with this contingency.

State Zionism obscures homeland Zionism *and* the reality of 1948. Holocaust consciousness obscures the dream of homeland Zionism *and* the reality of 1948. The recovery of both homeland Zionism *and* the reality of 1948 are tied together as a possible future for Jews inside and outside the state of Israel. This recovery may hold the possibility for a reckoning with the Holocaust or at least the lessons we should take from this overwhelming tragedy.

The question raised by homeland Zionism and 1948 is whether Jewish empowerment after the Holocaust has liberated us. Has our newfound global assertiveness led to a healing of the trauma of the Holocaust?

Making visible the obscured in Jewish life is arduous. Alas, there are other roadblocks in the way. One such roadblock is Christian Holocaust theology, a theology that seeks forgiveness from the Jewish people for the sins of antisemitism. Christian Holocaust theology does this through an uncritical support for the state of Israel. In Christian Holocaust theology, Israel becomes the Christian vehicle for repentance. Because of this repentance, Christians are cautioned to affirm Israel without criticism. If the Palestinian issue enters the discussion, then Christians are accused of abandoning their vehicle for repentance. Hence, they have returned to their former antisemitism.[28]

Another roadblock is a politically connected Christian Zionism that views the ingathering of Jews in Israel as a sign of the end times. Christian Zionists believe that the Jewish return to Israel means that Jesus will soon return. Although there are varying end-time scenarios among Christian Zionists, the consistent pattern is ignoring the dispossession of Palestinians from their land. Or, worse, the plight of the Palestinians is part of God's providential plan. Palestinians and the Arabs nations become the devil in disguise or perhaps the devil incarnate. In Christian Zionism, Palestinians exist to thwart God's designs for Jews, Israel, and the second coming of Christ.[29]

28. For an overview of Christian Holocaust theology, see Stephen R. Haynes, *Prospects for a Post-Holocaust Christian Theology* (Oxford: Oxford University Press, 1991).

29. For an overview and critique of Christian Zionism, see Stephen Sizer, *Zion's Christian Soldiers: The Bible, Israel and the Church* (Nottingham: Inter-Varsity Press, 2008). Also see Victoria Clark, *Allies for Armageddon: The Rise of Christian Zionism* (New Haven: Yale University Press, 2007). For one Jew of Conscience take on both Christian Holocaust theology and Christian Zionism see Mark Braverman, *A Wall in Jerusalem: Hope, Healing, and the Struggle for Justice in Israel and Palestine* (New York: Jericho Books, 2013).

Other roadblocks include the Constantinian Jewish establishment, the Progressive Jewish establishment, a powerful Israel, a dependent, self-interested, and politically regressive Arab world, and a fractured, ineffective, often corrupt, Palestinian Authority. Some believe that Hamas is another roadblock in the never-ending Israeli-Palestinian saga. If and how the failure of the Arab Spring will change this dynamic remains an open question. It will take decades to know the answer. Is there that much time left on the various Middle Eastern clocks?[30]

The interfaith and political dialogue is a major obstacle to resolution of the Israeli-Palestinian crisis. The interfaith dialogue started after the Holocaust as a way of reforming Christianity in light of its historic antisemitism and Christianity's connections to the Holocaust. Jews in the dialogue correctly asserted equality and justice as the cornerstone for the future of Jewish-Christian relations.

Yet, in the end, criticism of religious traditions and communal sensibilities went only one way—toward Christians and Christianity. When Jewish culpability in the displacement and occupation of Palestine became obvious, Jews demanded their Christian partners' silence. For the interfaith-dialogue Jews, unquestioned support for Israel is part of Christian repentance for the antisemitism of the past. Any criticism of Israel's policies toward Palestinians is a revival of antisemitism. Over the years the original dialogue became a deal, with the Jewish establishment restraining their Christian counterparts who are increasingly in touch with the suffering of the Palestinian people.[31]

The interfaith deal makes a just future for Jews and Palestinians difficult to envision. It also makes it more complicated. Like the life of politics, interfaith deal making is a bargaining process. Each party seeks to preserve its own interests, even if this causes dislocation and death to others.

Deal making is often a form of triage. Decisions are made as to who is worthy and unworthy of scarce goods and power. Scarcity is defined by the powerful. There may indeed be enough to go around if decisions are viewed in a different way. This is true with religion, too. Decisions about who to align with and who to push to the edge of the table are often based on the self-interest of the communities involved and the particular historical contexts within which they live and flourish.

30. There are many books on the Arab Spring. One interesting analysis is found in Lin Noueihed and Alex Warren, *The Battle for the Arab Spring: Revolution, Counterrevolution, and the Making of a New Era* (New Haven: Yale University Press, 2012).

31. On the interfaith deal, see my *Judaism*, 116-24.

Over the years, the interfaith dialogue/deal has lost steam. More and more Christians absent themselves from it. Holocaust remembrance events suffer from a loss of energy and attendance. Increasingly, other genocides are added to remembering the Holocaust. The Holocaust itself is no longer enough to spark interest, perhaps because, along with some Jews, more and more Christians see that the Holocaust now functions to limit dissent about Israeli policies toward Palestinians.

The Holocaust as a lifeline to Israel is coming to an end. So, too, the endless discussion of antisemitism is seen as a relic rather than a contemporary challenge. Instead, in a bold breaking of the interfaith deal, Christian denominations are introducing and passing resolutions to use boycott, divestment, and sanctions (BDS) against Israeli policies toward Palestinians. The organized Jewish community strikes back, using the accusatory politics of antisemitism. This is increasingly rejected by Christians who see support for the state of Israel and actions against its unjust policies as a dual demand of their faith.

These Christian denominations are squarely against antisemitism. They are also against injustice. Though it has been a difficult struggle, more and more Christians are seeing Israel as an international political actor that must be held to international standards of justice. The special exemption for Israel is coming to an end.[32]

There are Jews, even Jewish Voice for Peace rabbis, who support BDS efforts against companies that support the occupation of Palestinians. The rabbis who wrote the Passover Haggadah, which emphasizes two people, one future, in the land of Israel-Palestine, also wrote in support of several Christian denominations and their boycott resolutions. Pointedly, they mentioned the upcoming Passover season, a season of liberation for Jews but, hopefully as well, for Palestinians.

In a jointly signed letter, the rabbis write that in the weeks and months ahead, the United Methodist Church and the Presbyterian Church-USA will make a "crucial vote" on whether to divest from companies that profit from the Israeli occupation. Although both churches are being "viciously attacked for what many of us have been saying all along," that a true foundation for

32. The discussion on the BDS deliberations of the Methodist denomination could be followed on May 2, 2012 on *Mondoweiss*, http://mondoweiss.net/2012/05/united-methodist-church-to-debate-and-vote-on-divestment-today.html. For the outcome and commentary on the vote, see "Methodists Vote Against Ending Investments Tied to Israel," *New York Times*, May 3, 2012. Also see the 2014 publication of *Zionism Unsettled: A Congregational Study Guide* published by the Israel/Palestine Mission Network (IPMN) of the Presbyterian Church, (USA).

Israeli-Palestinian peace can be found only through mutual recognition, justice, and equality, the rabbis encourage the Christian denominations to stand firm. "We believe that investing in companies that profit from the Israeli occupation furthers injustice, reduces the chances for peace, and is contrary to the Jewish values we hold dear," the rabbis write. "We take on the challenges raised by the churches' initiatives to stand up for those core values." As for Passover, the rabbis are clear: "The Jewish values we hold dear will be in evidence tomorrow, as we sit down at the Passover Seder table and recount our story of slavery and deliverance. We will remember our bondage, an experience we do not wish upon ourselves or others. We believe in freedom/*herut* for all. And we stand with others who share the same belief. We hope you do too."[33]

In their letter, and also in their Passover Haggadah, the rabbis accept the Christian denominations and their resolutions as a challenge for both Jews and Christians. By doing so, they affirm a new Jewish-Christian dialogue that features Palestinians as a joint vehicle for Jewish and Christian repentance. This repentance is symbolic—cast in the Passover season—with substantive political action. The boycotted companies include Caterpillar, Motorola, and Hewlett-Packard. Collectively, these corporations enable the Israeli occupation of Palestinians by providing the equipment to destroy Palestinian homes and orchards, developing perimeter surveillance systems for Jewish settlers, and installing biometric ID systems at Israeli checkpoints that control the movement and freedom of Palestinians entering and leaving Israel.

As the rabbis write, destroying homes, defending stolen property and discrimination are not Jewish values. Therefore, to "advocate for an end to an unjust policy" is not antisemitic. Nor is it antisemitic to invest "your own resources in corporations which pursue a vision of a just and peaceful world, and to withdraw your resources from those who contradict this vision."

At the Passover Seder the rabbis stayed true to their exhortation to the Christian denominations. Instead of the traditional Ten Plagues that are recited during Passover—blood, frogs, lice, wild beasts, blight, boils, hail, locusts, endless nights, and the slaying of the first born—the rabbis recited the plagues of occupation, poverty, restrictions on movement, water shortage, destruction of olive trees, home demolitions, settlements, political prisoners, profiteering, denial of the right of return, and erasures of histories.

In Israel-Palestine, triage is obvious. In spite of this movement on the interfaith front, we have a long way to go. The interfaith ecumenical deal is breaking down. The movement on the political front is much slower. In fact,

33. See an "Open Letter to the United Methodist Church and the Presbyterian Church (USA)," written by the Jewish Voices for Peace Rabbinical Council at http://www.rabbis-letter.org/.

there is a political deal that characterizes American politics: no criticism of Israel. In the American political arena, Israel is always different.

Although the political Israel deal looms large among the Republicans in a more obvious way, with each political figure vying to outdo the other on his or her pro-Israel stand as we saw in the 2012 presidential-election cycle, there is a broad bipartisan consensus on Israel as well. Imagine for a moment future candidates for president of the United States from either party speaking to any of the following topics: the 1948 war as an assault on Palestine; the ethnic cleansing of the Palestinians conducted by Jews; homeland Zionism as an alternative view of living in the Holy Land; Holocaust consciousness as obscuring realities on the ground in Israel-Palestine; Christian Holocaust theology as a way of Christian renewal that apologizes to Jews and enables the displacement of Palestinians. Imagine a presidential candidate attempting such analysis.[34]

Now imagine a savvy political advisor seriously proposing these views to a candidate that seeks to become president. Closer to home, introduce these ideas, with some insistence, to a local rabbi or Christian pastor. See if this can be done without those around you, including the cleric you are talking to, feeling that you are antisemitic or, at least, verging on antisemitism.

Support for Israel runs deep in American religious and political culture. So, too, the absence of Palestine and Palestinians in these discussions is notable. If Palestinians are present, often their presence is seen as negative. How dare Palestinians disturb traditional support for Israel?

For sure, there are antisemites. Any person who is active on Middle East issues has experienced this on occasion. The issue is that fine line between arguing for others—on the principle of justice—and arguing against Jews—because Jews are Jews. Where is that line? When is it crossed? If protest against Israel's abuse of Palestinians becomes a disguised antisemitism, we have traveled far without moving at all.

The folly of antisemitism is evident. Why shouldn't Jews embrace the dream come real in institutions of the state of Israel, with Star of David flags flying? Is it wrong for Jews to feel a sense of strength and place when these symbols surround them? Of course, there are those who seek to dismantle Jews of their inheritance through words that alienate, subordinate, and deride. Jews with power can seem threatening, especially to antisemites.

Even the language of human rights can be used in this way. Pleas for justice can be made as if history is uninvolved. Some act as if Jewish particularity should

34. For President Obama's struggle with this issue see Josh Ruebner, *Shattered Hopes: The Failure of Obama's Middle East Peace Process* (New York: Verso, 2013).

disappear. Few who deny Jewish particularity instruct Palestinians on the need to deny their existence as a people.

Palestinians deserve human rights and justice. They deserve to embrace and celebrate their own particularity. Palestinian particularity testifies to their struggles and suffering, as well as a destiny that has emerged on the world stage.

After the long haul of land denied and life lost, the ordinary can become so prized that almost anything is preferable to injustice. Yet fidelity to the history of struggle, sacrifice, and suffering is what gives depth to all that has gone before. It is the foundation of what might come after.

2

Are the True Colors of the Jews Empire Blue?

The state gives. The state takes away. Jewish statehood was a prize won on the battlefield, yet it soon morphed into a garrison state, just as the homeland Zionists predicted. The ethnic cleansing of Palestinians foretold the future—for both sides.

Jews thought that placing the word *Jewish* before the word *state* would make Israel a different kind of state. Even state Zionists, who hungered for normality, thought that Jews and a Jewish state were different. After all, creating a state *ex nihilo* was hardly the norm. And being such a small minority in the Middle East argued against Israel's chances to survive and flourish. Too, state Zionists bet on an ingathering of Jews settled in their native areas of the world. The odds seemed stacked against the entire project. Nonetheless, state Zionists were confident. Jewish history was on their side. As it turns out, they were—exceptionally—correct.

So within normalization, Jewish exceptionalism remained the norm. The variance between state Zionists and homeland Zionists on the issue of Jewish exceptionalism was only a matter of degree.

It took greater hubris to think exceptionalism when it came to a state functioning as state. How could a Jewish state be unlike other states? Anyone who studies history knows that, despite differences of culture and geography, the imperatives of statehood are similar. That a Jewish state could escape the demands of economics, bureaucracy, politics and a military that all nations face was folly. Israel was destined to be a state like other states.

Nonetheless, the belief that placing "Jewish" before "state" could make Israel different was emphasized. Such a notion is downplayed today—Israel's history is too scarred—but throughout most of Israel's history the exceptionalism of the Jewish state was written and spoken about boldly. This involved Israel's outsized sense of its ability to contribute to the world. It also included the boldly proclaimed stance that Israel's military, unlike other militaries around the world, was purely defensive and characterized by a "purity of arms" informed by the Jewish ethical tradition. When reading the early arguments for Israel after its birth and then again in the post-1967 rhetoric—including the early rhetoric about Israel's occupation of Jerusalem and the West Bank as temporary and benign—one is struck by the depth of Jewish exceptionalism.

Obviously, state rhetoric is a showcase, the kind of patriotic boasting that few take seriously. Yet language about Israel strikes another register. In Israel's state rhetoric, but also in Diaspora Jewish writing, the creation of Israel represents a seminal moment in Jewish and world history. After two thousand years of wandering and dispersion, the Jewish return into history is trumpeted. Since Israel is founded just years after the catastrophe of the Holocaust, the drama of the Jewish return is heightened. With such a dramatic entrance and with all of Jewish history and hope behind it, how could a Jewish state be like other states?

How naïve can Jews be? Only an imagined exceptionalism could save the state of Israel from following the imperatives of modern statehood that include bureaucratized governance, concentrations of economic power and a state monopoly on violence. Seeing through exceptionalism on that front, homeland Zionists understood the imperatives of being a state. As victims of states everywhere, and most recently the Nazi state, Jews everywhere should have understood this well.

If the Jewish homeland had taken root, would the Jewish homeland have been different from other homelands? Homeland Zionists had their own naïveté. In and of itself, the increased Jewish presence in the land would have placed pressures on ideals of self-governance in a non-state form. As well, how realistic their hope of a shared Jewish-Arab Palestine could have been is an open question. Movements toward community and equality are fraught with empire leanings and power struggles, too.

It is doubtful that homeland Zionism could have transcended the pitfalls of what already was a complicated situation. After all, most of the homeland Zionists were European in background and outlook. Hannah Arendt's great hope of Jews being a new, unsullied bridge between East and West was itself naïve. Along with Judah Magnes, Martin Buber, and Albert Einstein, Arendt tried her best and was certainly ahead of her time. But she, too, was marked by their heritage and context. In the end, Arendt, Magnes, Buber, and Einstein combined Jewish and Western exceptionalism into a fascinating dynamic of moral and civilizational uplift. Each argued that a Jewish homeland would be an important example for the world and good for their Arab neighbors. Through the establishment of a Jewish homeland, Jews would be highlighting Jewish contributions to the world. Jews would also contribute Western ethical, political, and economic values to the backward, but expectant, Arab peoples.[1]

EINSTEIN'S THEORY OF ZIONIST RELATIVITY

Whatever the similarities of state and homeland Zionism, when Israel became a state the homeland vision diminished. In its first decades, a remnant of this homeland vision remained, even as the great carriers of that vision were leaving the scene. Magnes died in 1948, Einstein in 1955. Buber carried on the vision within the state until his death in 1965. By the mid-1960s, the Jewish establishment was vilifying Arendt for her writings on the trial of the Nazi murderer, Adolf Eichmann. Feeling that nothing could be accomplished, Arendt "retired" from Jewish life. With the 1967 war, Jewish investment in Israel soared. Homeland Zionism faded in Jewish memory.

Today, most Jews in Israel or elsewhere are unaware that an alternative Zionism ever existed. Buber and Arendt are two of the most famous Jews of the twentieth century, exceeded only by Einstein whose fame is global. Yet how many Jews or, for that matter, non-Jews know of their stances regarding a Jewish state?

Albert Einstein's Zionism is the least explored among this quartet. Like Arendt and Buber, Einstein was an exile from Nazi Germany. His views about the Jewish condition were experienced close at hand. Einstein was an internationalist and, for the most part, a pacifist. What he saw in the creation of the state of Israel was a well-trod path that Jews could not escape. When in 1952, Einstein, perhaps the most distinguished scientist of the twentieth century, was offered the presidency of the state of Israel, he refused. Earlier in the massacre of Arab villagers at Deir Yassin in 1948 by Jewish right-wing forces, Einstein saw a form of Jewish fascism emerging. He appealed to Jews and the world to oppose fascism in whatever guise or uniform, including its appearance in the form of Jewish power.[2]

---

1. Like most homeland Zionists, Arendt was thoroughly Western in her understandings. Thus, among other things, she proposed that Jews should become part of a federation comprised of other small European people-groups. In her mind, the Jewish settlement in Palestine would be feasible only if it was attached to such a federation. For Arendt's thoughts on this matter, see Gabriel Piterberg, "Zion's Rebel Daughter: Hannah Arendt on Palestine and Jewish Politics," *New Left Review* 48 (November-December 2007): 39-57.

Einstein was ambivalent about Jewish power itself. Could Jews afford to be without it? Einstein believed that Jews needed to be smart about power. It could be used for good. It could lead into the darkest areas of humanity. Although Jews should have learned the lessons of the abuse of power well, Einstein was afraid that Jews had learned only the lessons of being powerless. An address Einstein delivered on the occasion of the celebration of the "Third Seder" by the National Labour Committee for Palestine, at the Commodore Hotel in New York City, on April 17, 1938, captures his sensibilities and the complexity of his emotions about Jews needing and assuming power.

Titled "Our Debt to Zionism," Einstein reflected on his understanding of what it means to be Jewish and the relation of Judaism and the state:

> I should much rather see reasonable agreement with the Arabs on the basis of living together in peace than the creation of a Jewish state. My awareness of the essential nature of Judaism resists the idea of a Jewish state with borders, an army, and a measure of temporal power, no matter how modest. I am afraid of the inner damage Judaism will sustain—especially from the development of a narrow nationalism within our own ranks, against which we have already had to fight strongly, even without a Jewish state.[3]

Einstein continued with the lesser of the options, the Jewish state: "We are no longer the Jews of the Maccabee period. A return to a nation in the political sense of the world would be equivalent to turning away from the spiritualization of our community which we owe to the genius of our prophets. If external necessity should after all compel us to assume this burden, let us bear it with tact and patience."[4]

That Einstein delivered his address during the Passover holy days is instructive. Considering as well that, in 1938, the power of the Nazis was reaching its apex, Einstein's words take on even more import. Like other homeland Zionists, and Jews in general, the situation of Europe's Jews weighed heavily upon him. Einstein knew that many Jews like himself were already

2. For Einstein's views on Zionism, see Fred Jerome, *Einstein on Israel and Zionism: His Provocative Ideas about the Middle East* (New York: St. Martin's, 2009).

3. Albert Einstein, "Our Debt to Zionism," in Adam Shatz, ed., *Prophets Outcast: A Century of Dissident Jewish Writing about Zionism and Israel* (New York: Nation Books, 2004), 63.

4. Ibid.

refugees and that many others were dying. Jews were in their most difficult situation, perhaps since the time of Titus. But, as Einstein notes, the Nazi period saw limited emigration possibilities for the Jews of Europe. Jews were trapped. Most were fated. The debt to Zionism, therefore, was even more important to bring to the fore. Zionism was meeting a crisis in Jewish life and history:

> In this hour one thing, above all, must be emphasized: Judaism owes a great debt of gratitude to Zionism. The Zionist movement has revived among Jews the sense of community. It has performed productive work surpassing all the expectation anyone could entertain. This productive work in Palestine, to which self-sacrificing Jews throughout the world have contributed, has saved a large number of our brethren from direst need. In particular, it has been possible to lead a not inconsiderable part of our youth toward a life of joyous and creative work.[5]

Einstein affirms the debt Jews owe to Zionism. But here Einstein is referring to a movement among other movements. For Einstein, Zionism was an insurgent force in Jewish life and making a significant contribution to the overall quality of Jewish life in a time of extreme crisis. Yet for Einstein the direction of Zionism was already problematic, as was its ascendancy. Praising its good works, Einstein places the broader essentials of Judaism and Jewish history as a priority.

Einstein praised aspects of Zionism because it advised Jews that there was a Jewish future. Zionism also placed concrete tasks before Jewish youth, which demonstrated that they are the future of a people destined to survive the Nazi crisis. Nonetheless, Einstein notes clear warning signs already present, not least a triumphant Zionism, especially in its state variant. If state Zionism triumphs, Jewish survival might find itself digging its way out of the same trappings it longed to escape.

Einstein's awareness of resistance to a Jewish state—"with borders, an army, and a measure of temporal power, no matter how modest"—had given way to the point where Jewishness without borders, an army, and significant power was becoming almost unimaginable for Jews. His fear of the "inner damage Judaism will sustain—especially from the development of a narrow nationalism within our own ranks" is so deeply ingrained in Jewish life today that few Jews

5. Ibid., 64.

would recognize the damage done. Most Jews would not be able to identify what Einstein was talking about. The Judaism/Jewishness they know is the only Judaism/Jewishness known. Is there any other kind?

In a tongue-in-cheek take on Einstein's famous scientific theory, one reviewer of his writings and speeches on Zionism labelled it Einstein's Theory of Zionist Relativity. Wherein after World War I, and with the rising tide of antisemitism that ultimately issued in Nazi Germany, Einstein declared himself a human being, a Jew, an opponent of nationalism, and a Zionist. For Einstein, there was no opposition between any of these specific notions. In fact, as a human being and a Jew, Einstein was an opponent of nationalism and a Zionist because he saw Zionism primarily as a form of Jewish uplift. Einstein rejected the nationalist component within Zionism. Or, rather, he recognized a non-nationalist nationalism within Jewish history, a collectivity of purpose and contribution that was part of humanity's uplift. For Einstein, real nationalism, in its non-Jewish and Jewish variant, was part of humanity's and Jewish decline. That accounts for Einstein's Theory of Zionist Relativity. The non-nationalism of Zionism could be affirmed. The nationalism of Zionism needed correction, if not condemnation.[6]

Israel took a different route than Einstein and the other homeland Zionists proposed. Because of this, since its founding Israel has devoted significant resources to its defense and has become one of the largest and most sophisticated arms merchants in the world. Like dislocated and occupied people everywhere, Palestinians want their patrimony returned. Israel's resources have also been mobilized for offense. Since its founding, Israel has consistently expanded its reach and territory. The ethnic cleansing of Palestinians has continued in war and in peace.

As Einstein predicted, Jews and Judaism have adopted a narrow nationalism at least with regard to Israel. An inner damage has taken place. As Arendt predicted, Israel has become a modern Sparta. Becoming a modern Sparta, Jews have taken on the militarized internal qualities of the citizens of Sparta. This new attachment to a narrow nationalism has taken its toll on all things Jewish, including dissent. The rabbis who wrote the Passover Haggadah and the letter of support to the Christian denominations that are entertaining proposals to boycott, divest from, and sanction (BDS) those who profit from the Israeli occupation of the Palestinians are remnant dissenters. Are their Passover narratives and letters of support updated versions of Einstein's Theory of Zionist Relativity?

---

6. Glenn C. Altschuler, "Einstein's Theory of Zionist Relativity," *Haaretz*, July 17, 2009.

1938 through 2012—these are the years covered between the two Passovers. There has been a sea change in Jewish life. Whereas Einstein pondered the possibility of a narrow nationalism and Arendt worried about Israel becoming a new Sparta, the rabbis are living their anxious predictions as facts of contemporary Jewish life. In 1938, the Ten Plagues were easily transposed in contemporary terms: the Nazis were the new pharaohs. In 2012, for the rabbis, the pharaoh is the Jewish community whose hardened heart has to be transformed.

When Salvation Knocks on Your Collective Door

Wherever Europeans travel in the world, they recreate a European reality. The European Jews who founded Israel wanted to recreate Europe in the Middle East. This small parcel of holy real estate provided that horizon. First, however, Arab culture, the decaying East, and the backwardness Westerners and European Jews ascribed to it, had to be transformed.[7]

Looked at from the "developed" West, the backwardness of the Arab world was taken for granted. Even many Jewish refugees from Nazi Europe, themselves victims of "advanced" Western civilization, accepted this notion without subjecting it to critical thought. Being Western, Jews were advanced. Arab Jews made the situation even more confusing. European Jews thought that their Arab co-religionists were wanting in education and culture. Confusing being Jewish with being Western and modern, it was difficult for many European Jews to accept the Jewishness of their Arab Jewish brethren.

For all the backwardness assumed, it seems ironic that the Jewish armies fighting for Israel's birth were filled with refugees who had barely survived the extremity of Europe's violence. Few saw the other irony that the refugees from Hitler were creating new refugees in Palestine. Whatever thoughts they had were buried in a militarism that seemed so necessary at the time.

Jewish refugees from the Holocaust could ill afford reflection on where they had come from and what they were doing to others in Palestine. The narrow confines of nationalism do this to every people. Jewish exceptionalism could not escape the inversion that the rabbis now relate during Passover.

Although barbaric, the Nazi death camps were thoroughly modern. Recycling in its modern form became the norm at Auschwitz. Death was rationalized. Experts from all scientific and industrial fields were present at the

---

7. For how the West has viewed the East, see Edward Said, *Orientalism* (New York: Vintage, 1979).

death camps, among them IG Farben and IBM. Without advanced modernity, annihilating the Jews of Europe remained an unrealizable dream.[8]

No doubt we need to expand our vision of the history of the Holocaust, but for now let us remain in the barbarism/modernity typology. In some ways we have moved little in this area of thinking since the Holocaust. We still tend to view the world in a dichotomy of development and underdevelopment as the key to understanding what is and is not civilization. Of course, the Western side of this dichotomy is assumed. We, the West, are developed. They, the East, are not.

The Jewish settlers of the early twentieth century had the sensibility of an advanced people—we—encountering a backward, peasant culture—them. Advance was primarily seen through the lens of technology, and a certain kind of technology at that. The land of Palestine seemed barren to European Jews. Absent was the climate that gave birth to lush greenery and forests. Food production was also different, again responding to the different possibilities of sustainable agriculture suited for the region. As well, the contrasts of culture and religion were notable. Instead of seeing difference, however, most Jewish settlers saw a divide between ancient and modern, civilized and uncivilized.

In the Holocaust, the very advance that European Jews hailed as the essence of civilization made their plight more difficult, if not impossible. Modern warfare raged around Jews living in many countries. The death camps were built in areas that were connected by sophisticated transportation systems. The killing process and the disposal of Jewish bodies were continually updated and made more efficient. How to kill so many and what to do with their bodies—indeed, how to keep the corpse conveyor belt moving—meant constant innovation and the use of the latest in advanced technology.

Hitler lionized Henry Ford both for his antisemitism and for his modern technological achievements. Ford's mass production of automobiles became the model for the death camps. Applied to Jews, the death camps featured the mass production of corpses. IBM, another company that Hitler lauded, was instrumental to the Nazi system of isolating, tracking, and forcing Jews into ghettos, concentration camps, and death camps. Using the Hollerith machine, a mechanical tabulator based on punched cards that rapidly tabulate statistics from millions of pieces of data, IBM was of immeasurable help in Hitler's anti-Semitic policies. The Nazi death machine was as complicated as it was brutal. In fact, the advances in technology made it easier for the Nazis to organize the death of millions of Jews and actually to commit their brutality.[9]

---

8. On IBM and its role in the Holocaust, see Edwin Black, *IBM and the Holocaust: The Strategic Alliance Between Nazi Germany and America's Most Powerful Corporation* (Washington, DC: Dialogue Press, 2001).

The advances of Western civilization provided a distance wherein the most uncivilized acts could be committed with an organizational élan that helped deflect the brutality of the Nazi mass-death machine. Did the same advances also help deflect the suffering caused to Palestinians in the creation of the state of Israel? The Western/Eastern divide may have helped in other ways as well. If the West, advanced and civilized, is the right stuff of the present, it is also the right stuff of the future. Seen from this angle, the backward are lacking. They are relics from the past, existing, to be sure, but standing in the way of a creative future. It is easy, then, to determine who is deserving of a home and who is not—who can claim the land as a home and who can more or less live anywhere regardless of where they once lived and called home.

Soon after the collapse of the Third Reich, Jews began reflecting on the future of Jewish life and humanity after the Holocaust. By the early 1960s, this reflection crystallized into a theology with a liturgical cadence. The birth of Holocaust theology was noted everywhere. Jews reflected on the most audacious and barbaric of crimes, the mass death of millions of Jews—in the heart of Europe, in center of Christian culture, in the middle of the twentieth century. How to describe the crimes against the Jewish people? What language could convey Nazi brutality? For those that had never experienced the "Other Kingdom," even the images of the Holocaust had to be sorted and explained.

Over time what was once difficult to explain and subversive of our understandings of morality and civilization was mainstreamed. The Holocaust became a popular subject. With the development and proliferation of academic courses on the Holocaust, the possibility that the once subversive Holocaust could become trivialized had to be confronted. As importantly, the political uses of the Holocaust for the support of Israel also began to trivialize the event itself.

Translating Jewish suffering in the Holocaust into a mandate for Jewish empowerment in Israel made the use of the Holocaust a necessity. The danger, though, was similar to what Einstein pointed out in relation to Zionism run amok. Narrow nationalism could be buttressed by interpretations of the Holocaust that normalized Jewish power. The inner danger to Judaism and Jewish was hard to avoid.

But then, at the beginnings, the hard work was establishing the Holocaust as an event worth considering. How far it has gone can be seen in the journey of Elie Wiesel, who barely survived Auschwitz and just decades later helped found the United States Holocaust Memorial Museum in Washington, D. C. His journey in Auschwitz is related in *Night*, which itself had a journey.[10]

9. Aspects of the collusion of IBM and Ford in Nazi Germany can be found in Edwin Black, *Nazi Nexus: America's Corporate Connections to Hitler's Holocaust* (Hilton Head Island, SC: Dialog Press, 2009).

As it exists today, *Night* is much shorter than the original manuscript. It has a different ending. The original longer manuscript ends with a group of Jews, Wiesel included, seeking revenge on a defeated Germany. The shorter *Night* ends in existential angst.

The original ending was too harsh. Or was it simply too harsh to be read by those who wanted a more reconciling ending? The pared-down *Night* is haunting enough. Still, there is room to question—if one has the courage. Isn't the desire for revenge an appropriate ending? After the Holocaust, some wonder if that desire for revenge was transposed from the Germans to the Palestinians. The founding of the state of Israel is a response to the Holocaust. For some Jews, at least, Palestinians are the new Nazis.

Reading *Night*, one thinks primarily of Jews. One thinks of their Nazi adversaries. Of course, Israel and the Palestinians are mostly absent in *Night*. But any reading of *Night* today conjures Israel as an answer to the Holocaust. With Israel, Palestinians necessarily come to mind, in a negative light, as adversaries of Israel, the answer to the Holocaust. Reading *Night* with a critical eye, however, changes the trajectory. One thinks of the Palestinians as the last victims of the Holocaust.

Night is about the Holocaust—and much more. The Holocaust highlights aspects of Jewish history. It also obscures facets of Jewish life after the Holocaust. Annihilation of the Jews in the Holocaust is followed by the birth of Israel. That is the Jewish story, one that is largely affirmed in the West. What follows is the ethnic cleansing of the Palestinians, a story that remains underground. What we see is as important as what we don't see. The millions who read *Night* and study the Holocaust in public schools and universities do so as Palestinians are expelled from their land. We study the Holocaust as the Wall is built around Palestinians in Jerusalem and the West Bank.

We are living in another contradiction. The lessons of the Holocaust, of *Night*, are "Never Again" to Jews. The same warning should apply to all peoples. That "Never Again" cannot be limited to the extremes of violence as in the Holocaust, creating a rating system for atrocity that triggers our response only when mass death is upon us. Rather, the Holocaust should be about ending the cycle of violence and atrocity wherever it is found so that never again should people suffer dislocation, domination and death. The Holocaust calls us to confront the use of unjust power and to offer compassionate assistance and

---

10. On the journey of *Night* see Naomi Seidman, "Elie Wiesel and the Scandal of Jewish Rage," *Jewish Social Studies* 3 (Fall 1996): 1-19.

hope to those who are suffering. This is exactly what was so often denied Jews during the Holocaust.

Can we study immense suffering in history and be silent as suffering happens around us in the present? The answer is decidedly yes. Then the question becomes whether the study of historical suffering moves us to address suffering in present. No doubt, the Holocaust does move some to pay attention and act to relieve suffering in the present. But the Holocaust can freeze us in the past—or provide a safe harbor for emotion and outreach to a world that no longer exists.

For Jews in general, the Holocaust, at least the way it is narrated, has inured many Jews to other contexts of violence and atrocity, including the Palestinians who suffer at Jewish hands. Too often, the Holocaust demobilizes Jews rather than mobilizes them to act justly. Instead of using the Holocaust to justify the exclusion of Palestinians, what if the Holocaust became a rallying point for Jewish confession and a movement toward justice for the Palestinian people? If the Holocaust began to primarily move Jews in that direction, one wonders if the Holocaust would be so emphasized—and popular—in the Jewish community. Is the Holocaust emphasized primarily because it has become an enabler of Jewish power?

In life, we highlight and obscure. We do not have to look far into our own lives or the lives of our communities to find this. Religion is expert at highlighting and obscuring. The chief rival of religion in this arena is the state.

Think of the image of Pope Benedict at Auschwitz, soon after he became pope. Remember that he only used German once there, that he belonged to the Nazi Youth, and that for millennia the church he headed denigrated and persecuted Jews as a matter of God's truth. Now read traditional Christian theology with the certainty that the "new" Israel replaced the "old."

Imagine the statues that represented Judaism and Christianity found in medieval cathedrals. Remember how the church and the synagogue were modeled. The woman representing the church had her crown, New Testament, and flowing robes all in place. The woman representing the synagogue had her crown falling off her head while holding a Bible turned upside down. She was blindfolded. The perfidious Jews could not see.

Each pope inherits that church and that symbolism. He leads a church that bears great responsibility for the Holocaust. When he visited Auschwitz, Pope Benedict became the chief mourner of the Holocaust. It is a strange inversion of history that is so obvious it is often overlooked. How did the representative of the church that first ghettoized Jews, the same church that signed a Concordat with Hitler—and who lived as a German during the Third Reich—become the official mourner of the Jewish dead?[11]

The image of the pope, the church, and Christianity bends history backwards away from its antisemitism. As the church admits its culpability, it forgives itself in the same gesture. By traveling to Auschwitz as a spiritual pilgrim, the pope—and Christianity—has it both ways.

Yet, if we think more expansively, another, even more somber, picture emerges. Think of the church historically in relation to Jews. Now think of the church in a parallel history of the peoples residing outside of Europe. Remember forced conversion and slavery outside of Europe, as well as mass death in the preindustrial age in the Americas and elsewhere. Christianity's globalization is achieved through commercial trade and trade in human bodies. Think Christian religious domination. Think conquistadores. Think Christianity and empire.

When Pope John Paul II went to Santo Domingo in 1992 to celebrate the five-hundredth anniversary of Christianity in the Americas, he played both ends of the historical record. The pope confessed the crimes of some Christians who came to the Americas. The pope affirmed that these same Christians brought the "message of salvation" to the continent. For the pope, the salvation the missionaries brought was the important reality to remember on the anniversary. There was exploitation on a massive scale from which the church, along with commercial enterprises, benefited. The pope admitted as such. Nonetheless, the pope admonished the faithful to remember the saving faith that was brought to the natives.[12]

By highlighting confession, John Paul II obscured the massive suffering and destruction of the Americas. As with Benedict at Auschwitz, the pope celebrated the most important advance in the history of Americas—the coming of Christianity—but also civilization as defined by Europe. As with the Holocaust and the creation of Israel, once again the interrogation of "civilization" was left aside. In this case, the pope added a transcendental salvation, a concept even more difficult to dispute from inside the Christian faith. Yet, for the native peoples, salvation is always offered by "advanced" civilizations and their religions, even if it means displacement and death.

The role of a second salvation is important here. Although Christians believe that salvation comes from Jesus the Christ, in its contemporary

11. For a take on Pope Benedict at Auschwitz, see Craig Whitlock, "At Auschwitz, Pope Invokes a 'Heartfelt Cry'," *Washington Post*, May 29, 2006.

12. Pope John Paul II's address at Santo Domingo can be found in Alfred T. Hennelly, *Santo Domingo and Beyond: Documents and Commentaries from the Fourth General Conference of Latin American Bishops* (Maryknoll, NY: Orbis, 1993), 156-60.

appearance the pope at Auschwitz "saves" Christianity. The mass graveyard of Auschwitz is the place where Christianity reached its terminus. Using Christian terminology, it awaits resurrection. The pope uses the Jewish dead to accomplish this resurrection. The question remains whether he and the church, at least the church he wants to maintain, has learned its lesson. Or does this Auschwitz salvation, like the one that arrived in the Americas, trump the reality of what occurred?

Is the state of Israel the salvation for Jews after the Holocaust? Salvation here is stretched to its limits, though it still may apply. Perhaps this is the reason why the details of Israel's history, especially the events that accompanied its birth are declared off-limits. Salvific objects are like liturgical elements; they must be dressed and honed for worship. The salvation that came to the Americas and after Auschwitz is also cleansed and represented as worthy of devotion. The details if admitted are confessed to be transcended. The foundational sins, that which put the later events into motion, are obscured.

If Israel as salvation is ritualized, would it be more honest to hold high Star of David helicopter gunships instead of pious, moralistic, words for the Holocaust dead? In the Ark of the Covenant, the Torah scrolls could be replaced by silver models of helicopter gunships. Perhaps model settlements could be included. This would avoid obscuring the reality that the Jewish community actually affirms. If this seems blasphemous so be it. At least it would occasion reflection, more or less the same reflection that the pope's "saving" appearance at Auschwitz should occasion.

In Holocaust remembrance, the survivors are cleansed of their trauma mostly by banishing them from sight. Others, usually without any immediate relation to the Holocaust recite their stories. The Holocaust survivors become holy objects that are represented only; they need not appear in person. Or a few survivors like Elie Wiesel become emblematic of the Holocaust. They are honored to the extent that they become Holocaust icons.

Is Israel, at least for Jews, especially those who live far away from its reality, an icon as well? After all, the America defenders of Israel do not live in Israel. Those who visit Israel usually do so via guided tours that highlight the achievements of Israel and leave out Palestinian history and Palestinians themselves. The truth is that a majority of American Jews have never even visited Israel. Moreover, American Jewish ignorance about the real rather than symbolic Israel is palpable. Jewish defenders of Israel are even more ignorant of the reality of Palestinian life. They, like Israel, function better as symbols, albeit negative ones.

For Palestinians, of course, the holy objects of the Holocaust and Israel are their demise. American Jewish defenders of Israel function in a similar way. In their heart of hearts, Palestinians wish to be released from their power. One wonders, if the Holocaust dead could speak, what they would say if they knew that Pope Benedict was "saving" Auschwitz for the Catholic faithful. What would the indigenous people of the Americas have to say to Pope John Paul II's proclamation that the message of salvation was more important than their lives and deaths? The same question placed before Palestinians regarding Israel as the "salvation" of the Jewish people might engender a similar response.

The dream and reality of salvation come sharply into view when we read of or meet the victims of salvation. Those who are consigned to destruction and death because they do not meet the criteria for salvation are doomed, at least when "salvation" is modernized and armed. Continents and nations are "won" usually because of superior power and military and economic tactics. Salvation is simply along for the ride.

Christianity was along for the ride in the Americas. It was along for the ride as the pope blessed the victims of Auschwitz. Is Jewishness along for the ride as Palestine is destroyed?

The reality of salvation is so difficult to contemplate we try to keep it from view. Perhaps that is because salvation, shorn of its power, is weak and vulnerable. In a weakened condition, salvation is exposed, humbled. Einstein's view of the essential nature of Judaism resists the idea of a Jewish state—let alone the reality of one. He fears an "armed" salvation—the development of a narrow nationalism—because it will assault the inner nature of Judaism. Einstein associates the inner nature of Judaism with the "spiritualization of our community which we owe to the genius of our prophets." This is all before Israel became a state.

What would Einstein have said about a Holocaust twinned to Israel as salvation? To twin the two, both have to become invulnerable to historical renderings and critical thought. In becoming militarized, they have to become spiritualized. Militarization and spiritualization go together. In turn, the Jewish prophetic has to be disciplined and weakened—and spiritualized–too.

As Einstein thought about Israel, so it is with the Holocaust. When linked with a narrow nationalism, the Holocaust becomes a salvation which functions as a blunt instrument used against all comers. The difference is that the Holocaust and Israel lack the genius of the prophets, who can only be held captive for so long. Instead of prompting Jews to think in salvific categories, the contemporary Jewish prophetic distances itself from a militarized mourning.

Violence in the name of salvation awakens the prophetic spirit. A warning sounds. Something has gone terribly askew.

As evidenced by the popes, we obscure difficult histories to forge ahead. Without such obscuring, we would be mired in the sins of omission and commission that color our lives. Individually, it may be difficult to think how obscuring makes the world go round. So think collectively. Think of American politicians who herald the United States as a light unto the nations without rehearsing the history of the ethnic cleansing of Native Americans or the history of slavery. Our politicians are mirror images of us. They forget what we, too, want to forget.

Think how America came to be How the British Empire became the Commonwealth. How France became France. Saying Britain, America, and France in the politics of statehood is more or less like saying Jew, Christian, and Muslim in the politics of religion. How did these religions come into existence? Who suffered in the name of their birth and expansion?

It is like Pope Benedict, or any pope, at Auschwitz. The sins committed in the name of the state or religion need to be washed away for us. Then we salute whatever flag is flying in the night sky. Most flags are interchangeable. Can any flag be so different from the one that flies in its stead somewhere else?

We ask whether we can live without obscuring the cycle of violence and atrocity in which every nation and religion, at least historically, has been involved. Highlighting this cycle suggests the possibility of a future beyond the cycle of violence and atrocity—that is, if we can take the heat. Because if we use the very cycle of violence and atrocity that ensnared us, like some Jews use the Holocaust, what hope is left for the future?

Obscuring the past so as not to dwell there has its benefits. As well, it serves the powerful to continue the past, if only in a somewhat different way. Institutional slavery is condemned, while present-day slavery, under another name, flourishes. Past ethnic cleansing is condemned, yet ethnic cleansing continues. Those who fought ethnic cleansing in the past are elevated as heroes. Those who oppose ethnic cleansing now are branded terrorists. Does this transformation apply to Jews and Palestinians?

One people's ethnic cleansing is another's fight for freedom. One religion's salvation is another's perdition. How do we judge which one is which? There must be a basis for judgment other than which religion we affirm. Is there anything to be affirmed about ethnic cleansing? What is to be condemned about it? It is the same with the distinction between terrorism and freedom fighters. On the freedom fighter's side or against it, do the same questions apply?

Who judges terrorists and freedom fighters? Surely, an objective standard can be found and applied.

Few are able to step out of "their" religion or ideology and see the "other" side. Once we experience the other side, it is more difficult to dismiss it. That is why the powerful seek to limit our view.

The powerful fear that those who witness the other side might cross over. There is always the possibility of joining the other side. In what circumstances is this possible and right? What does crossing over mean on a personal and communal level? Is it a betrayal of your community and who you are supposed to be?

From the Jewish "salvation" perspective, it is important to understand the dream *and* the reality of 1948. Recently, a group of Israeli architects followed the arc of Jewish settlements as they have moved with the expansion of Israel. The settlements are the moving boundaries of the still-undeclared boundaries of Israel. Now witness the Wall built around the Palestinians in the land left to them. This leads to an increasingly difficult question: Can Jews understand the dream and protest the reality of 1948 and beyond?[13]

The "other" side, the Palestinians, have been pushed into Jordan, Lebanon, and Syria, into other parts of the Middle East, indeed, all over the world. A Palestinian Diaspora has evolved. If it not yet larger than the Jewish Diaspora, it will be soon.

Yet one never knows in history. A great reversal may be in the offing. One day Jews, who spell the Jewish Diaspora with a capital "D," will realize that Palestinians refer to their communities outside the land with the same designation. Since Jews live in the Diaspora and Palestinians live in the Diaspora, one day it might be said that the Jewish Diaspora now includes the Palestinian Diaspora or the reverse. In the future, there might be only one Diaspora, *the* Diaspora, Jews and Palestinians together.

A COVENANTAL GOD ON THE EMPIRE DIVIDE

The Jewish dream has rarely included Others—consciously. It has always included Others—concretely. We know historically there have been Others within the Jewish community, Others who through voluntary and sometimes forced conversion have become Jews. At times in history, Others have been ruled by Jews. Although mostly silent and silenced in canonical texts, ancient

13. Rafi Segal and Eyal Weizman, *A Civilian Occupation: The Politics of Israeli Architecture* (New York: Verso, 2003).

Israel included Others, too. Others were with Israel in Egypt and in the liberation from slavery. Others were with Israel in the Promised Land.

Others have always been active participants in shaping the Jewish journey. It takes a lack of imagination and historical acumen to believe that Jeremiah and Isaiah, Ezekiel and Amos, spoke exclusively to ancient Israelites. No doubt there were others who heard their words, joined the crowd, egged the prophets on, and even rebelled against them. Yes, Israel was Other to Egypt—in Egypt and to the Canaanites—in Canaan. Israel was also Other to itself—with Others.[14]

Is modern Israel any different? Within Israel's 1967 borders, more than 20 percent of the population is Palestinian. They are the non-Jewish Other to Jewish Israelis. Within Israel, there are Jewish communities that are almost as Other to one another as the non-Jew is to the Jew. There are millions of Palestinians in the occupied territories ruled by Jews as well. In Jewish settlements, Jews, though dominant and set apart, are living side by side with Palestinians. This is yet another otherness division—and inclusion—that is bound to have a profound effect on the future of Jewish life.

The Orthodox/Secular-in-Israel divide continues to deepen. The divide between Jews from Europe and Jews from the Arab world is long standing. Jews from Ethiopia and the former Soviet Union are divided from each other. The Orthodox, secular, Arab, Ethiopian, and Jews from the former Soviet Union are divided among themselves. As these divided groups live and struggle together, a natural integration around similar political and economic interests takes place as well. This integration produces new divisions. However the old and new divisions play out, the otherness of Jews to one another is hardly new.[15]

In Jewish history, the question of otherness is sometimes highlighted, at other times obscured. Accentuating solidarity is necessary in times of crisis. But hiding difference is temporary. Difference has a journey of its own.

Difference within solidarity is another theme in Jewish history. It is the essence of Jewish Diaspora reality. It continues in the land. During most of Jewish history, Jews in their otherness, among and with Others, are outside the dreamed and real Promised Land. The hundreds of thousands of Jewish Israelis who live outside the state of Israel repeat this ancient pattern.

---

14. A fascinating take on Ezekiel can be found in *Ezekiel's Hierarchical World: Wrestling with a Tiered Reality*, ed. Stephen L. Cook and Corrine L. Patton (Leiden: Brill, 2004).

15. On the Orthodox-secular split see the recent debate on military service for Orthodox Jews in Israel in Allison Deger, "'Netanyahu is a Nazi': Scenes from an orthodox anti-military draft protest in Jerusalem," Mondoweiss, March 6, 2014. http://mondoweiss.net/2014/03/netanyahu-orthodox-jerusalem.html

This latter phenomenon is mostly absent from Jewish literature. The Israeli Diaspora increases yearly. Why have those who returned now left? What a strange and instructive marker for Jewish history, especially in a time of Jewish empowerment. Exploring the Israeli Diaspora and its meaning in light of Jewish history is important.

The Israeli Diaspora is wholly voluntary. No prophet has pushed them out. Nor has God, at least as we know God. After Auschwitz, it is difficult to imagine God thundering that the Jewish stay in the Promised Land is done. Or that Jews better start moving into exile before God moves them there. Or that God is punishing Jews with exile for their sins of pushing the Other out of their land.

The Israeli Diaspora is set apart from the older Jewish Diaspora in a variety ways. Israeli culture and spoken Hebrew set Israelis apart from Diaspora Jews. The military experience of Israeli Jews sets them apart as well. The lens through which both communities look at the world is different. Although many Israelis see themselves as Western and identify with Europe and America, their home has been the Middle East. American Jews have lived almost exclusively in America. They see Israeli culture through American and Jewish Diaspora symbolic representations.

The reverse is true as well for Israelis born in Israel. Most have never lived outside of Israel. Factor in the experience of Jews facing antisemitism in the West and Israelis oppressing the Palestinian people and one can see the very different encounters that both Diasporas have with their surroundings. In general, the Jewish and Israeli Diasporas are Other to each other.

There are many reasons for the Israeli and Jewish Diaspora disconnect. European Jews who survived the European night know the obscurity of dark interiors. Today, Jews are in the spotlight as never before. They are accepted almost everywhere as the bearers of the good tidings of civilization. It is therefore difficult to imagine how it is that Jews have rarely acted as uncivilized as they do today.

Definition and perspective is important. Most Jews do not see the "uncivilized" part of Jewish behavior toward Palestinians. Jews, the civilized, are innocent. The Other, the Palestinian, is uncivilized. Therefore whatever is done to the Other is to protect the civilized. Of course, Israelis have seen all of this and have participated in or witnessed aspects of this behavior.

For the most part, American Jews do not want to know what has been done in their name by relating to those who have done the deeds. By remaining ignorant, Israel can endure as a shining beacon for American Jews. Yet Israelis resent American Jews for using them as symbols, for not understanding their real situation and for choosing the soft, naïve life of the Diaspora.

Jewish Israelis' have disdain for the ignorance of American Jews. If their ignorance is real, it demonstrates how isolated American Jews are. If their ignorance is willed, it demonstrates an inability to cope with the reality they celebrate and enable. Either way, Jewish Israelis have to wonder how American Jews live with themselves in their celebration of an Israel that does not really exist. Unspoken by American Jews is the trauma Israelis have lived with and caused. This includes the trauma of what they have done to Palestinians. American Jews want to be far away from this trauma. Is this because American Jews are also traumatized by Israel's behavior and seek to distance themselves from those who embody it?

Yet being far away, seeing Israel through an American lens and being largely ignorant of Israel scarcely humbles Jews in the American political arena. Through powerful lobby groups like the American Israel Political Action Committee (AIPAC), American Jews and their allies argue for conservative policies and American foreign aid and military actions that reinforce right-wing tendencies in Israel's political life. Those Israelis who want a different direction toward Palestinians and the Arab world are often frustrated. They see their political process outsourced to Jews who form the political and economic elite of America.

As it turns out, Jews with empire are no different than Others with empire. In the land, where ever that land is, and toward the Other, empires perceive themselves to be innocent. The state of Israel has the same mindset. American Jews often do as well.

The dream of empire is never defined as a plague for the Other. Or, if it is, that plague is seen as necessary for the betterment of the empire and thus redounds for the benefit of all humanity that deserves empire's light. To be bearers of the empire's light has its burdens. That burden is carried for the Other as well. Beneficence is claimed even if that means displacement and enslavement for the deserving many. In empire's rulebook, it may be the only way forward.

In the end, empire works out the kinks of otherness as its homage to the eschatological ends of the human journey. The City on the Hill, however formulated and named in different empires throughout history, is ostensibly for everyone. Thus the "amen" the ruled are expected to proclaim. But it rarely works that way. Empire wonders why the displaced and occupied lack gratitude. Experiencing resistance firsthand, empire is bewildered. It is only a matter of time until the light shines through.

Within empire there are subjects, including those who benefit from empire, who are likewise ungrateful. Some are ungrateful immediately. There is something that triggers dissatisfaction from the beginning. Others become ungrateful over time. For some, consciousness is raised by the victims who survey the altered landscape. They note the causalities among the rhetorical beneficiaries of empire. Soldiers who fight the wars that solidify empire are among the first to see through empire's discourse. Those who survive the wars suffer physical and mental injuries that change the direction of their lives. Others convey the created and stolen goods of the empire elite. The few individuals that remain untouched by empire's waste note the waste that surrounds them. Wherever these empire beneficiaries turn their head there is ruin. They witness at close range the empire divide.

Thus it is that some Israeli soldiers have broken their silence and formed groups such as Breaking the Silence. Forced into situation where they are face to face with the Palestinians they occupy, some soldiers withdraw from service in the military. Others provide testimony of what they have been forced to do as soldiers and sometimes what they did under pressure which they now regret. In the main, they are concerned less with the outrageous behavior that some exhibit in any military occupation of another people. Instead, the soldiers are concerned with the underlying logic of the Israeli occupation of Palestinians. That logic is rational in pursuing what the state of Israel wants, more and more Palestinian land with less and less Palestinians, and harsh, in that the logic is sophisticated and unrelenting. As demonstrated in their testimonies, the Israeli soldiers are less interested in addressing every aspect of Israeli government policy than they are with that which "obliges us to look directly at Israel's actions and ask whether they reflect the values of a humane, democratic society."[16]

As in the days of old, Jews are found on both sides of the empire divide. There are these Israeli soldiers representing Jews of Conscience. They know what has been done. Their testimonies serve as confessions. There must be another kind of logic. Is there something beyond living in fear and making others fear you?

There are Constantinian Jews who, like their Christian counterparts, choose empire as their salvation. After the experience of the Jewish people at the hands of empire, it is understandable to jump at the chance to do empire's bidding. Mostly this bidding is disguised in the religious rhetoric that emphasizes innocence. If you look closely, however, empire, being its own religion, is also transported into the official religious liturgy of the dominant religion, even when that religion is Judaism. Empire takes hold among theologians even when those theologians are Jewish.

---

16. *Our Harsh Logic: Israeli Soldiers' Testimonies From the Occupied Territories, 2000-2010,* ed. Breaking the Silence, (New York: Henry Holt, 2012), 6.

Once again, Elie Wiesel is a case in point, though he is only the best known among others. Wiesel has made a fortune writing and speaking about the Holocaust. At the university level, some of the highest-status, best paid university teachers in the humanities teach in Jewish Studies programs that emphasize the Holocaust. This is yet another strange inversion of one's status being tied to remembering the mass death of Europe's Jews.

Though the Holocaust is weighty, other equally significant subjects are less lauded and less well paid. It could be that Holocaust status and salary is equal to the subject's significance. Are the sufferings of Others less important? Would a professor teaching the Rwandan genocide be feted as Jews teaching the Holocaust? Often the salaries for chairs in Holocaust Studies are paid for by well-to-do Jews. But the wealth of the Jewish community is directly connected to the success of Jews in the American empire. The Holocaust—including the Holocaust Memorial Museum as a symbol of Jewish standing in America—is linked to that same success. Connecting these dots, thinking about and symbolizing the Holocaust is thus connected to empire. Some have written of the Holocaust industry and the selling of the Holocaust. Perhaps it is time to begin to explore the links between remembering the Holocaust and American empire.[17]

Once linked to empire, liturgy and theology develop a rhetoric in waiting, if you will, a reserve that empire can call upon. Over time it becomes difficult to know whether empire or religion blessed the other first. Yet whatever part of the chicken and egg empire/religion argument you choose, it remains that religion combines with empire rapidly. Once tied to empire, it is almost impossible for religion to disentangle itself. Every empire needs religion to trumpet its arrival as more than power. For its own status, affluence, and authority, religion is happy to oblige. As much as any community or institution, religion loves to consume the spoils of empire.

When awakened to the fateful combination of religion and empire, what are we to do? Whatever side we are born into, whatever side we ultimately choose, religion and empire infuse our daily life. Whether it is education, housing, transportation or a thousand other aspects of modern life, we are always located somewhere on the fault lines of empire.

Yet the question remains for Jews after the Holocaust. If Jews are now affluent, with status and privilege, should they choose to be with those on the

17. For two views relating to the use of the Holocaust, see Norman Finkelstein, *The Holocaust Industry: Reflections on the Exploitation of Jewish Suffering* (New York: Verso, 2003); and Tim Cole, *Selling the Holocaust: From Auschwitz to Schindler: How History is Bought, Packaged and Sold* (London: Routledge, 2000).

other side of the empire divide? Knowing that the society's most Jews live within harbor reservoirs of antisemitism, what are the consequences of such a choice? Jewish history serves as a warning. Does that warning signal an eternal fate?

Jews have always existed on both sides of the empire divide. The ancient Israelites experienced this divide, big time. Moses was raised in the Pharaoh's palace. Before Moses, Joseph was elevated there. Both had journeys of arrival and departure.

There came a time when the legacy of Joseph was no longer remembered in Egypt. Perhaps this is why Joseph signaled his desire to be buried in the Promised Land. Although raised as royalty, Moses eventually saw through the empire system. After fleeing Egypt for murdering an oppressive guard, Moses discovered his vocation and his God. Moses' discovery occurred in exile from the empire within which he was raised.

Moses' return with his brother Aaron was dramatic. Their encounter with empire was fraught with danger. Moses and Aaron came to the Pharaoh's palace numerous times. It is perhaps the most famous encounter with empire in history.

One can read the Bible as an extended dialogue with whatever empire reigns supreme. The prophets rail against empire as a vocation, though this time the empire is in the Promised Land. The argument for and against empire in the Hebrew canon is within and even defining of Jewish particularity. Jewish particularity is constantly in conflict with the otherness of empire, whether it is somewhere else or in the land. For the prophets, empire in Egypt recalls empire in Israel. Biblically speaking, they are more or less the same.[18]

Again, we return to the dream and the reality. The Jewish dream is to live in a just and peaceful world. The teachings of Moses, often referred to as the Law, is a path toward individual and collective justice and just relations between individuals. This, in turn, leads to shalom, which combines the hope for peace, justice, and harmony. Moses' teaching is voluntarily chosen and, if need be, enforced. The Law has a power that overrides the individual even as it seeks voluntary consent. That is why justice and charity are so closely connected in the Hebrew canon. They are also separated. Although it is best when both are practiced, if the choice is one or the other, then justice is commanded.

Here we find the essence of the covenant. To think "essence" hardly means a one-dimensional understanding. In the canon and throughout Jewish history, however, justice resides at the heart of the covenant. If there is no justice, the

---

18. A good overview of the Hebrew prophets is found in Jack Lundborn, *The Hebrew Prophets: An Introduction* (Minneapolis: Fortress Press, 2010).

covenant is emptied of content. In a community without justice, idolatry reigns. The covenant flees.

Refusing idolatry is the demand that we place no "Other" god before us. This means no god but the God of liberation. God cannot be God without justice. Long before the contemporary emergence of liberation theology, the Jewish God is a God of liberation.[19]

Already in the Promised Land, Israel turns away from community toward empire. This turning began in the desert wanderings. So the dichotomy between empire and community exists from the beginning of Israel, as do the warnings against it. Highlighting empire necessarily obscures community. Yet community continues to exist, now within empire. Empire lurks within community, too. Rarely if ever, is there a time when only empire or community exists.

Since empire is pervasive, most often the challenge is the creation of community within empire. In this endeavor the Jewish prophetic speaks volumes. A paradox ensues. The justice-seeking covenant is always under assault by empire. Yet the covenant remains alive. It is precisely when the covenant is under empire's assault that community, disparaged and given up for dead, resurfaces. Community forms on the margins, shows its face, speaks its piece and embodies its testimony. Community once again becomes vibrant. When the material formation of community seems impossible due to severe injustice, it becomes tangible in expectation.

Even those who seek to dispatch the covenant unto death hear its clarion call. It is precisely for this reason that the living covenant and those who shape community around it is relentlessly pursued by empire. The empire pursues the covenantal community without remorse and far out of proportion to its worldly power. Is this because there resides within the covenant and the covenantal community an Other-Worldly power?

"Other" is a descriptive preface to the covenant's power. Imagine Moses and Aaron in Pharaoh's palace, a ridiculous juxtaposition in anyone's imagination, let alone in a slave people's canon. Imagine the prophets after Moses and Aaron and the vitriol that the powerful unleashed on them. The covenant they announce resonates well beyond the evident power the prophets wield. We still read their words. Their warning and hope continue to resonate beyond their evident power today.

Even the rise of kings within Israel is shadowed by the King of Kings, God. As predicted by God, no king of Israel delivers a sustainable justice. Whatever

19. For a take on the interaction of Jewish and Christian theologies of liberation, see my *Toward a Jewish Theology of Liberation*, 3d ed. (Waco: Baylor University Press, 2004), 143-200.

their initial intentions, rulers of Israel move toward empire—this is explicit in the Hebrew canon. Even God has to be argued out of God's own imperiousness.

At times, the God of Israel is an empire God. At other times, the God of Israel embraces community. Because of this duality, the covenant limits God. In the wilderness wanderings, Moses argues God out of certain actions. When God is through with a backsliding Israel and offers Moses shelter under God's domain, Moses places himself among the people. Moses's stubbornness is dramatic. God thinks again. God changes God's mind. When God listens to Moses' reasoning, God is more compassionate and more intelligent in God's decisions. When God listens to arguments against unilateral judgment, God is more just and merciful as a result.[20]

God can be a poor judge of God's own behavior. God's poor judgment is often linked to God's imperial designs. Israel's entry into the Promised Land occasions a change in God's behavior. The back and forth that Moses provided is lacking. God misses Moses. God is bereft.

There is a difference between leadership of the oppressed and leadership of the liberated. God seems to be innocent of this dynamic, or has forgotten the essence of empire. God's desire for community resurfaces in the words of the prophets. In the search for justice in Israel's society, God is reenergized.

When Conscience and Destiny Collide

Do the prophets cross the empire divide?

Becoming a promised people with a unique destiny among the nations is different than "having" a Promised Land. Like us, God has difficulty understanding the difference between dream and reality. God and humans share this challenge. Both are culpable in their pursuit of empire. It is here that conscience intervenes. Conscience is the divide. In the exercise of conscience, dream and reality are separated. As well, they are judged.

Conscience is the end of theory. Conscience is a call to action. When justice is enacted, conscience is practiced. Conscience reads empire against its grain. Conscience acts against empire. Conscience desires community. Conscience represents a struggle against empire and toward community. This is the human struggle. Is it also a struggle for God?

---

20. My point here is that in the Bible discussion and argumentation are as common as unilateral decisions by God. For a popular but interesting take on Moses, see Jonathan Kirsch, *Moses: A Life* (New York: Ballantine, 1998).

Conscience says no to aggression against others, even when that "no" works against self-interest. Aggression goes around. As it comes around, aggression breeds structures and attitudes that make for more aggression. To sustain aggression, the individual and society are mobilized and militarized.

Aggression needs an ideology that proclaims its innocence. All aggressors are innocent in their collective mind. And since the collective is informed by individuals, individuals have to internalize innocence as well. Every "innocence" project involves religion and the state. Both promise blessing and absolution. Mobilized bodies and institutions desire a known eschatology. Religion and the state are only too happy to oblige.

Mobilized innocence is the biblical code as the Israelites enter the land. Moses and Joshua warn Israel about its behavior in the land. Most of these warnings are internal. The Others in the land are given short shrift. They are the dispensable Other, the Other in the way, the Other that has to be cleansed.

As we read the biblical text, we are torn. The thrill of the entering the Promised Land is palpable. Still, we hope that Israel's conscience will awaken, that the plunder and destruction will be forestalled. Perhaps the die was already cast. Could there have been another kind of entry that concurred with Israel's destiny?

Conscience and destiny collide. Conscience is the awareness that violating the Other violates self. We know that dislocating and destroying Others is wrong. Whatever the circumstance, violating another is never an absolute good unless other factors are present. Those other factors are represented as overcoming conscience. They are argued as a greater good. Religion and state are brought in to do the heavy lifting. Nonetheless, even then or later, conscience confronts destiny.

However interpreted, when Others are violated, conscience knows the innocence project is troubled. Every innocence project has a troubled conscience.

Destiny seeks to silence conscience. How else could there be so much violence in the world? The world suffers an endless cycle of violence and atrocity. It is a cycle that the world has yet to overcome. Even with impending doom, the cycle continues. This after the Holocaust, the event so terrible that some thought it might bring this cycle to an end. Yet before the Holocaust dead were buried, the Atomic Age was upon us. Hiroshima and Nagasaki were warnings.

Genocides took place one after another. In Indonesia. In Cambodia. In Rwanda. Mass death in the Congo continues. These are some of the glaring cases of the cycle of violence and atrocity. There are many others. Today Syria is in free fall. More than a hundred thousand Syrians have been killed Millions have been displaced.

Will Syria be the last to experience the cycle of violence and atrocity? The lessons of the Holocaust have made little difference. The historian Gil Elliot named the twentieth century the century of the dead. The twenty-first century continues in its footsteps.[21]

Was the original sin of the people Israel the violation of the Other in the land? For the Canaanites, the Israelites were a disaster. Israel's Promised Land was their living home. The Canaanites knew this land as their own. According to the Bible, the Israelites crossed over in military formation with a formulated invasion plan. They carried that plan out with a terrible precision. Little was left in their wake.

Whether the crossing into Canaan actually occurred is debated. Some historians believe that Israel was already in Canaan and that the Exodus from Egypt involved only one or two Israelite tribes. There is little historical evidence of Israel's Egyptian sojourn. The real history is shrouded in mystery, and much of that mystery involves the dramatic retelling—or inventing—of Israel's memory. The original sin of Israel might be the fashioning of a narrative that, lacking historical basis, nevertheless became central to Jewish history.

What should Jews do with a narrative history that features the liberation of slaves and the displacement and destruction of indigenous peoples? Jews enter into a conundrum. If the entry into the land is doubtful historically, so, too, is the Exodus story. If Jews jettison the original sin of Israel as historical hyperbole, they cannot fall happily back on the freedom story either.

The story Jews recall at Passover each year ends with the vision of the Promised Land—the dream—rather than a detailed rendering of Israel's entry into the land—the reality. Perhaps the fashioners of the Passover narrative intended to preserve the dream by anticipating a reality without stating it.

During Passover, Jews are commanded to narrate the story as if we are there. Since the Passover story glosses over the entry into the land, we do not have to enter the land as if we are there. During Passover, Jews maintain innocence in the suffering of slavery without being tainted by the culpability of cleansing the Promised Land.

The rabbis may have deliberately obscured the entry into the land because they understood intuitively that the questions at the Passover meal—Why is this night different than all other nights?—might move in the wrong direction. It could lead to the next question, that of Israel's original sin of entering the

---

21. See Gil Elliot, *The Twentieth Century Book of the Dead* (Boston: Scribner, 1972).

land at great cost to others. If Jews contemplated the reality of entering of the land rather than the dream, conscience could point inward. Perhaps Jews would declare the Jewish entry into the land *traif,* unclean.

The entry into the land is troubling. When contemporary Israel reentered the Promised Land as a state in 1948, it also cleansed those already living there. When Jews celebrate liberation at Passover and on Israel Independence Day is it better to leave the next step (un)narrated?[22]

Other questions remain. In the biblical narratives, slavery, liberation, and the entry into the land are undivided. They are all of one piece. Can Jews today then create a division between slavery, liberation, and the entry into the land, opposing slavery and choosing liberation while challenging the entry into the land? If all of these events are in doubt historically can we divide what we remember? Or does the memory have to remain unified? Should Jews even remember what apparently did not happen, at least in the way it is recalled?

Passover is a subversive memory of slavery and liberation. It casts doubt on the empires of the world, then and now. If Jews are an Exodus people, how does this memory function when the people Israel and the state of Israel actually become attached to empire or become empire itself?

IMAGINE THERE'S NO EMPIRE

As the foundational telling of Jewish history, the division of the Passover narrative is fraught with inconsistencies. It requires historical leaps of faith. Huge gaps within the narrative are left without explanation. The telling of Israel's story changes its meaning depending on the living context of the Jews telling the story.

Real or imagined history changes with the context of the storytellers. The early followers of Jesus had a very different take on the Gospel stories than Christians living just four centuries later. When Constantine and his successors ultimately proclaimed Christianity the empire's religion, the Gospel stories were reinterpreted. The early Christians lived mostly on the margins of empire. The empire powers treated them as such. When Christianity became the religion of the empire, the marginal became the pillars of the empire. The dissident vision of Jesus and the early Christians was marginalized. Jesus became the glue of empire. He literally became the King of Kings.

---

22. For a fascinating account of Israel that relates to the possession of land and material after ethnic cleansing, see Tom Segev, *1949: The First Israelis* (New York: Free Press, 1986).

If we apply the same rigor to the Christian narrative that we apply to the Passover story, similar problems arise. There is little proof of the Gospel stories about Jesus. The Romans crucified Jews by the thousands. Evidence of Jesus' crucifixion is difficult to verify through strict historical methods. The dramatic Passion narratives may be as much literature as they are history. The resurrection stories are matters of faith. Despite this, Christians retell these stories as if they are fact.[23]

It may be coincidence that the history of the followers of Jesus and their entry into and life within the Christian Promised Land—that is, the "saved" Christian community after Jesus' death and resurrection—is also absent from the Easter narrative. The dream of Christian life includes the difficult passage from suffering with Jesus and the world in bondage, to the resurrection as redemption/liberation for Jesus and for the world. Yet this telling obscures the history of Christian discipleship as it unfolds in history. This history is deeply culpable. Christians rarely face their history squarely.

A more accurate way to render the Christian Scriptures would be to narrate Christian history as moving from the birth of Jesus to Auschwitz and beyond. Constantinian Christianity would be the Christian entry into "real" history. In this scenario, Constantinian Christianity is the original sin of Christian destiny, as opposed to the dream of Christian innocence. Then, like Jewish destiny, Christian destiny unfolds on the backs of subjugated others.

This subjugation includes Jews, but is by no means exclusive to them. The Christians of the third world that comprise most of the Christians in the world today were conquered through an imperial missionary understanding of Christian destiny. Indeed, Christians in Peru, the Philippines, and Kenya, among many others, share the ignominious designation of having been conquered by a gospel empowered by empire. In North America, Native and African Americans were also conquered by that same gospel. Thus we ask whether the original Gospel stories, like the Passover story, once entangled with empire, can be disentangled. Try it if you can: imagine Christianity without empire.[24]

When the Christian dream invades another's reality, nightmare ensues. The difference between the Jewish dream and reality as recorded in the Jewish canon and the Christian reality as lived out is that most of Christian history is

23. There are different contemporary versions of this story and its authenticity. For one important understanding, see John Dominic Crossan, *The Historical Jesus: The Life of a Jewish Mediterranean Peasant* (San Francisco: HarperSanFrancisco, 1991).

24. An attempt at this can be found in Joerg Rieger, *Christ and Empire: From Paul to Postcolonial Times* (Minneapolis: Fortress Press, 2007). See especially his conclusion, 313–21.

now documented in historical scholarship. Israel's original sin, though occluded in the Passover retelling, is preserved in the canon, even if historically the telling cannot be verified. Christian reality, though historically verifiable, is outside of the canon. Most Christians know little of that history. In the church liturgy, history is left outside. The original sin of Christianity is pretending to the dream while excluding historical reality.

Fascinating, indeed, when we also add antisemitism, the Christian dream-telling of Jewish "reality." Christians use the Hebrew canon to foretell the Christian dream of salvation. Christians identify the Jewish dream of messianic redemption as their inheritance in light of the "reality" of Israel's blindness in rejecting the Messiah foretold by Israel itself. The reality of Israel's rejection gives birth to the "new" Israel whose history, in its eschatological dimensions, ends with the death and resurrection of Jesus as the Christ.

Although the predicted imminent second coming of Jesus has yet to occur, the church triumphant, at least in its own mind, remains outside of the historical reality it creates and sustains. Christianity continues to assert its dream in real history. Jews are forced to live a nightmare within Christian salvation dream time.

Debased Judaism—and Jews—is Christianity's predicted outcome of Jewish "real" history. It becomes a self-fulfilling prophecy. The type of God of Israel Jews ultimately affirmed and their denial of the dream Christians affirm—salvation arrived—becomes the real history Jews are forced to live after the Jewish canon is closed. Is it any wonder that Jews suffered so terribly at the hands of the Christian dream? Today Jews—and many Christians ask why Christians with a conscience did not interrupt this dream with an alternative reality. If conscience had interrupted Christian reality, perhaps Christians of Conscience would have crossed over to the other side of the empire divide and embraced Jews as their brothers and sisters.

Practicing conscience, crossing over the empire divide, Christians would have found "old" Israel underneath the heel of the "new" Israel. That discovery could have initiated the disentangling of Christianity from empire. Perhaps the terminus of that entanglement, the Holocaust, would have been a nightmare forestalled. Imagining a world without Christian empire, we imagine a world without the Holocaust. Unfortunately, both were real. Altered and sometimes inverted, their trajectories continue on.

Time marches on. Now there is a tradition of Christian liberation theology. Although disparaged by recent princes of the church—though perhaps to be affirmed in Pope Francis's pontificate—liberation theology continues to flourish among the poor and the oppressed in various parts of the world. In Christian liberation theology, the power of empire is disrupted by the cries of the poor—in real history.

On the Jewish side, new narrations of the Passover story abound that infuse renewed life into a vibrant Jewish theology of liberation. As we have seen, the Jewish Voice for Peace retelling of the Passover story features the role of Israel in displacing and occupying Palestinian people and land. After the initial blessings, the middle matzah is held before those assembled at the Seder. The following is read aloud:

> We will now break the middle matzah, hiding one half to be found after as the afikomen. Once the matzah is broken, it cannot be repaired completely. Irreparable damage has been done—but the pieces can be reunited. As we break the middle matzah we acknowledge the break that occurred in Palestinian life and culture with the establishment of the State of Israel in 1948 when hundreds of villages were destroyed and hundreds of thousands of people displaced. The damage cannot be undone—but repair and return are possible.[25]

After this reading each participant at the Seder takes turns reciting the names of the Palestinian villages that were destroyed by Jewish forces on April 6 and 7 in 1948. By juxtaposing the hope for Jewish liberation in the Exodus and the birth of Israel with the unacknowledged history of what happened to Palestinians, Jews are forced to confront at an existential level the violence of Israel's birth. Since Passover represents the time of Jewish liberation, this confrontation between dream and reality forces Jews to add a fifth question to the four questions traditionally asked at the Passover table: "Why is it that on all other Passovers we have celebrated our freedom, but on this Passover we mourn our actions against Palestinians in the creation of the state of Israel?" The answer: "We mourn our actions against the Palestinians people and seek a liberation that includes Jews and Palestinians alike."

---

25. "Israelis and Palestinians: Two Peoples, One Future: Passover Haggadah 2012/5772" is found at http://www.scribd.com/doc/87713706/Hagadah-JVP-Final-2012 For Jewish theology of liberation see the 3rd edition of my *Toward a Jewish Theology of Liberation* (Waco: Baylor University Press, 2004) and the 25th anniversary edition of the Spanish edition with a new translation and commentary of *Hacia una teologia judia de la liberacion*, ed. by Maria del Mar Rosa-Rodriquez (San Juan, Puerto Rico: Editorial Isla Negra, 2014).

Is the future of Jewish and Christian life the story telling of how reality infected the dream, displaced it, and became a perversion of the origins, so that faith might once again coincide with conscience? Of course, the origins of Jewish and Christian life are themselves tainted. The question for the future is whether these religious movements of conscience will remain aberrations or whether the broader community can take on the reality of history as its own.

3

Empire Boomerang

When one community's dream telling becomes another community's reality, often a nightmare ensues. The indigenous people of Canaan experienced this when Israel arrived in the Promised Land. When Christianity became a state religion, Jews were denigrated and ultimately ghettoized. The American dream spelled doom for Native Americans. A similar fate befell the Palestinians in 1948 and beyond when the Jewish dream of return became their displacement.

There is an ironic dimension when dreams become reality. Victory and defeat are inverted. Over time, though, often winners and losers become neighbors. In retrospect, the great suffering involved seems pointless.

When awakened from the dream/nightmare, individuals and communities wonder what those in the past were thinking. Did whites really enslave Africans and bring them to the Americas? Was antisemitism really central to Christian belief and practice? Did post-Holocaust Jewry really expel, denigrate, and then ghettoize Palestinians? In the end, what goes around comes around. The reality that came to the Palestinians one day may come in a different form to the state of Israel and to Jews around the world. The better alternative is to end the cycle of violence and atrocity. Sadly, that alternative is often discovered too late. The suffering continues.

Although time frames differ and conscience often awakens slowly, the dream-reality-nightmare transposition is there from the beginning. There are those who see through the dream and experience the nightmare—on all sides. Those who experience the reality on their bodies, land, and culture understand immediately that whatever the aggressor proposes as dream is for them a nightmare.

The victors brandishing the dream see the nightmare as well—in the face of the Other who is vanquished. The dream may obliterate the face of the Other for a time. Indeed, the dream's most important function is the obliteration of the Other's face. Those who awaken from the dream see nightmare.

How to speak of the nightmare that comes within the mobilized dream? For those on the losing end, there are few outside their community who listen. Some who hear the cries of those caught up in someone else's dream are living within a nightmare themselves. They have a dream of their own that might one day become a nightmare for someone else.

For those within the empowered community, the dream mobilized is the community's destiny being fulfilled. Waking up from the dream and seeing nightmare, then finding your voice to speak out within the community, is akin to treason. Those who speak reflect the nightmare back to the community. Such speech is punishable by excommunication or worse.

The awakened speaker becomes a mirror for the dream deferred or, better, for the dream that has its boot on another's neck. The speaker's neck is liable to experience that same boot. Does this boot on the Other, and now on the speaker's neck, tell us something about the power necessary to keep the dream from unraveling? When the dream is mobilized with the power to crush dissent, how does conscience find its way?

At different times in history, the worse appellation to be applied to the dreamer was Canaanite-lover, Jew-lover, or Palestinian-lover. These are obvious takeoffs on the Nigger-lover theme so deeply woven into the texture of American life. We should not leave out Indian-lover or, the post–September 11th designation, Muslim-lover.

"Lover" designations symbolize boundary crossings. Well after the boundary is crossed, when the boundary is finally erased, such boundary crossings are considered no-brainers. What was forbidden becomes an obvious path to follow. With time, the community narratives change. The oppressed either disappear or are assimilated. When the dream is initially engaged and mobilized, however, the boundary crosser is feted with penalties large and small.

That what once was rejected one day becomes the norm is little comfort to the initial victims or the boundary crossers themselves. Even then, the victims and boundary crossers are enfolded into a history that may have new victims. As old boundaries are erased, new boundaries appear. New boundary crossers come forward. They, in turn, are punished, as the once-rejected are now accepted and feted with memorials and museums. This happens in the very halls of power that may have committed atrocities against the besieged community in the first place. As the museums are built, the once-victimized, now-empowered community may be assaulting new others.

The victim/new oppressor reversal abounds in history. This may be the unintended legacy of the United States Holocaust Memorial Museum in Washington, D. C., and of other Holocaust memorials and museums that dot the landscape of America. Courses on the Holocaust fill the junior and high school curriculums. Students take these courses before they arrive at universities that feature still other Holocaust courses. The study of the Holocaust may also be part of this victim/new oppressor reversal.

In America, Europe, and Israel, study of the Holocaust is part of the elite curriculum. When the Holocaust is honored, it becomes a status and power upgrade for Jews. Yet as Jews use their power against others, the reversal of oppressed and oppressor is already in motion. Such a reversal is the surest way to stifle the prophetic voice. It is also the occasion for the explosion of the prophetic.[1]

When we place the Holocaust in such an honored position, what are we honoring? The easy answer is that we are honoring the victims of the Holocaust. In honoring the Holocaust, we raise the rank of the victims of the Holocaust to martyrs.

Martyrdom is deep within the Jewish tradition. Martyrdom means witness. The Holocaust dead were victims. When we describe their death as martyrdom, we assert a meaning beyond victimhood. Those who lost their lives in the Holocaust did not die in vain.

It is doubtful that the most of the Holocaust dead felt their death to be meaningful. If they hoped their death might be understood as meaningful one day, we cannot discern the meaning they hoped for. If the murdered understood that their death was without meaning, but we attach a meaning to it, the issue is joined. What meaning do we ascribe to their suffering that they were unable to discern? Whose authority allows such an ascription?

When meaning is ascribed, we ask whether that meaning is coming from the Holocaust dead or from our need. If that meaning comes from our need, we must analyze how our need and how the Holocaust dead fulfil it. If our need is fulfilled when we ascribe meaning to the Holocaust dead, does the same meaning apply for others who have and will come after those who assert the original meaning? If the victims of the Holocaust are martyrs and felt meaning before their death, are the meanings we ascribe to them the same as what they understood? Does it matter if their meanings and ours are different?

If the meaning or meaninglessness the Holocaust victims felt is different from our own, what right do we have to override the victims and, if so, how do we secure that right? Whatever we say about the dead of the Holocaust has at least as much to say about us as it does about them.[2]

1. The creation of the Holocaust Memorial Museum is itself a fascinating story. See Edward Linenthal, *Preserving Memory: The Struggle to Create America's Holocaust Museum* (New York: Columbia University Press, 2001).

The meaning of the Holocaust may rest in the victim/martyr designation. Since it is our designation, we can argue about the terms endlessly. The actual victims/martyrs have no say in what we decide.

As Holocaust memory evolves, memory's time frame shifts. The last generation of Holocaust survivors is upon us. Even this is complicated. While the voices of the survivors are connecting points between their and our speech about them, they have lived for decades in very different circumstances. As the Holocaust survivors die, those who were murdered fade further into obscurity.

Although the survivors are unlikely to remember every detail of their ordeal, the outline of their experience remains with us. Yet what remains is spoken through the filter of the survivor's later experience. We who listen to the survivor's voice hear their filtered experience through the filter of our own experience. Filters multiply. Time and experience make the reality of the Holocaust increasingly distant from our lives. In America, we hear their filtered experience within American ideals and ideology, for example, America as a City upon the Hill, with church–state separation enshrined in the Constitution. Unlike Europe of the Nazi era, in America, Christianity accepts Jews. In America, Jews are ascendant.

Holocaust survivors and those Jews who listen to their stories are deeply affected by the American ethos. America today is fundamentally different in tone and emphasis than Europe in the 1930s and 1940s. These filters change the Holocaust, even as we seek to know what happened and why.[3]

The Holocaust is now viewed through the filter of an empowered state of Israel. Israel claims the Holocaust as its foundational reason for existence. Israel also claims the Holocaust as a shield against Palestinians and the Arab world. If the victims of the Holocaust were victims and martyrs, then Israel demands these categories for itself.

Like those murdered in the Holocaust, Israel is both victim and martyr. The Holocaust allows Israel to claim innocence and testify to something more than itself. Still, Israel's claim to be involved in something more than itself is hardly limited to the Holocaust.

---

2. In 1970, a fascinating discussion took place between Richard Rubenstein and Elie Wiesel on this topic. See John Roth and Michael Berenbaum, eds., *Holocaust: Religious and Philosophical Implications* (St. Paul: Paragon House, 1998), 349-70.

3. In many ways, the Holocaust has taken on the American ethos, that is, it has become Americanized. For two early discussions of the Americanization of the Holocaust, see Hilene Flanzbaum, ed., *The Americanization of the Holocaust* (Baltimore: Johns Hopkins University Press, 1999); and Alan Mintz, *Popular Culture and the Shaping of Holocaust Memory in America* (Seattle: University of Washington Press, 2001).

That "more" is Jewish history and Jewish destiny—as seen through the Holocaust—from the vantage point of an empowered Israel. Any counter-testimony to the evolving Holocaust/Israel canon is suspect. No one outside or within the Jewish community is allowed to provide a counter-testimony to the Holocaust victims/martyrs or to Israel's innocence. If a counter-testimony is spoken, it is suspect.

Counter-testimony is subversive. It might undermine the testimony of those who died and those who survived as it has become known and understood. Counter-testimony might also undermine the physical entity, Israel. Since Israel sees itself as carrying the memories of the Holocaust victims/martyrs forward, memory must be guarded and employed in the "right" way.

Counter-testimony to the Holocaust/Israel is defined as illegitimate from the outset. Only a perfidious individual or community would purposefully undermine the memory of those who died for a meaning beyond themselves, especially one that is precariously carried forward by Jews in the twenty-first century. This is Holocaust logic—as interpreted by empowered Jews in America and Israel.

If Jews who died in the Holocaust had a vote about the dream of 1948, which way would they vote? If the dead accepted their designation as martyrs, would their vote be different? Now take the reality of 1948. What would the vote of the victims of the Holocaust be? What would the martyrs of the Holocaust say about the birth of Israel? Would they care about the Palestinians?

Those who are alive control the vote of the Holocaust dead. But in 1948, just three years after the "liberation" of the camps, which way would that tally have gone? Or now, as the occupation of the East Jerusalem and the West Bank become permanent? In which way would the victims/martyrs of the Holocaust vote during the Israeli bombing of Beirut and the crushing of the Palestinian uprising in the late 1980s? What would they say about Jewish settlements in the West Bank and Jerusalem? The crushing of the second Palestinian uprising in 2000 or the 2008 invasion of Gaza? Would they say amen to the continuing construction of the Wall in occupied Palestinian territory during the first decades of the twenty-first century? What would the victims/martyrs of the Holocaust say about Israel's saber-rattling regarding Iran?[4]

If victimhood is a democracy of the dead and martyrdom a status designation by the living, what lessons do they provide to Jews and others? In truth, victimhood and martyrdom empower certain perspectives and policies as

---

4. I once invited a Palestinian to speak in the Holocaust course I teach. She started out with this question in relation to her journey as a Palestinian: "What would Anne Frank say?"

designated by the living. The dead have no vote. There are no referendums by the dead.

The murdered in the Holocaust carry a power few other victim peoples do. It is hard to imagine an international body recommending a state for other victim/martyred populations. Now imagine that recommendation being exclusive of those within the boundaries of the state. Or the proviso that heirs of the victims can rule over those they occupy.

The case of South Africa is instructive. There a change to the internal structure of the state was accomplished. Equality was struggled for and won. Although the massive internal change in South Africa severely diminished power for the former ruling ethnic population, the results of South Africa's victims/martyrs victory is a secular democratic state for all. The reality of an ethnically divided state had been dislocation, ghettoization, and death. The dream of an inclusive South Africa that contains the former victimizers as full citizens was fueled by the past exclusion of the victims/martyrs.[5]

If the dislocated and dead of South Africa could have voted their hearts, the result probably would have been mixed. Their dream may not have been inclusion. Their dream may have involved the making of a new South Africa where only black and colored South Africans lived and governed. The resisting generation overrode the dream of vengeance. Part of the decision for inclusion in the new South Africa was tactical. The international community would have been reluctant to support a free South Africa if their dream was exclusion and cleansing of the defeated. Yet the decision for inclusion was also ethical. The leadership of the resistance thought a new South Africa would only be partially achieved if the color of the victors and victims were reversed.

Those who suffered and survived in South Africa dreamt large. The reality of the new South Africa is testimony to the dream—and its limitations. The historic hope of the people of South Africa includes their victims/martyrs. It includes as well as the present mix of dream and reality that is the new South Africa. Both hold a special place of honor in the contemporary world.

Yet it is hard to argue that this honor approaches the power in the international imagination that the victims/martyrs of the Holocaust and their inheritors/spokespersons enjoy more than a half a century after the event. Is this because Jews are more important and South Africans less so? Because empowered Jews in Israel are Western and white and empowered South Africans are black and colored? Amazingly in this day and age, the memory of victims/martyrs may still follow the color line.

5. For a discussion of apartheid in South African and Israel, see Virginia Tilley, ed., *Beyond Occupation: Apartheid, Colonialism and International Law in the Occupied Palestinian Territories* (London: Pluto, 2012).

Those who carry the message of the dead of the Holocaust observe their mission as a burden. How else could the legacy of the dead of six million Jews be characterized? Those who shoulder that burden feel that the world refuses to accept this mission. Or if the world accepts it outwardly, the carriers of Holocaust memory believe inwardly that the world is only waiting to reverse course.

There are Palestinians and Arabs who refuse even an external assent to the Holocaust dead. Within the Holocaust memory framework, the Jewish sense of burden is understandable. Yet if the burden is carried with affluence and power, if it is memorialized in thought, film and museums, with medals awarded from the United States Congress and the Nobel committee, at what price does an oppressed Palestinian people assent to the oppressors' "burden"?

Reaping rewards for the burden one carries makes the burden lighter. However, being rewarded for carrying the memory of the Holocaust forward may also diminish or even trivialize the memory of the dead. In the halls of power, trivialization is laid at the feet of those who question what is being done in the name of the victims/martyrs. But the memory of suffering is more complicated. Does the memory of suffering, when carried against others, enhance the meaning of the Holocaust or diminish it?

For example, imagine a Palestinian in a West Bank refugee camp, only miles outside of Jerusalem, hearing that Elie Wiesel, the international spokesperson for victims/martyrs of the Holocaust, has been awarded the Nobel Prize for Peace. Now imagine a Palestinian refugee camp under siege today in Syria. Although such an award was impossible for Wiesel to imagine in Auschwitz, the reality of Auschwitz led to Wiesel's dream life, including the Nobel Prize, wealth and stature—for himself and other Jews, too. What once was dream became reality.

For Palestinians in refugee camps, however, Wiesel's movement from Auschwitz reality to his Nobel dream is a nightmare, because it is built on their suffering. Wiesel's Nobel Prize is a symbol of the world's solidarity with Jews and Israel, even as the Palestinian refugee population remains and grows daily. In countries around the Middle East their lack of a homeland, existing without a state of Palestine, continues to impact Palestinians negatively.

We can move further afield or closer to home. The Jewish-American dream is hugely successful. Jews often recall the Golden Age of Spain as a benchmark for Jewish flourishing. Yet Jews know that the Spanish model is double-edged. Acceptance was followed by displacement in 1492. Eras of Jewish flourishing came to a crashing end. This is how it has been in Jewish history.[6]

When the Jewish Golden Age in America is thought to be different from the one in Spain, doubts appear. In the meantime, Jews enjoy the benefits of the American empire. Do Jews believe that a nasty end to their American sojourn waits?

Perhaps the possibility of America's demise and the consequences for Jews is rhetorical. Perhaps it is offered to obscure the privileges Jews think they are entitled to enjoy forever. By complaining about the bad end few Jews believe will occur, Jews use past and projected suffering as a way of being unaccountable for today's deeds.

The American Golden Age, America as the Promised Land—for Jews. This may be the case. The American dream is complicated. Jews are aware that Native Americans and African Americans have a different view of America's promise. For African Americans, this is further complicated by their own evolving journey, as hauntingly articulated by Martin Luther King Jr.

King appealed to the American dream, which had been the African American nightmare. King hoped that the dream of America might emerge from that nightmare, though he doubted it would emerge during his lifetime. In his last years, King felt that the dream of America was more difficult to achieve. King knew that he would not reach the Promised Land of black freedom. He was even less sure that such a land would ever exist in America.[7]

In King, we see longing and frustration. The American dream of equality and justice is longed for, but out of reach. Perhaps this is part of the dream and reality of American history. King's articulation of the clash between dream and reality continues today. King may have been a dream weaver, but he did so by exposing America's rough edges. His last civil rights campaigns and speeches about the Vietnam War show a concern for the continuing divide between the American dream and American reality. When King went global on the color line, America fared little better if not worse.

For King, one bookend of American history was America's founding generation, who fought for freedom *and* owned slaves. The other bookend was the civil rights movement *and* the war in Vietnam. With these bookends, King increasingly saw the American dream/reality/nightmare scenario as a promise that might not be reached.

6. On Jews in the Golden Age of Spain and afterwards, see Zion Zohar, *Sephardic and Mitzrahi Jewry: From the Golden Age of Spain to Modern Times* (New York: New York University Press, 2007).

7. See James Cone, *Martin and Malcolm and America: Dream or Nightmare?* (Maryknoll, NY: Orbis, 1992). Also see Rufus Burrow, JR., *Extremist for Love: Martin Luther King JR., Man of Ideas and Nonviolent Social Action* (Minneapolis: Fortress Press, 2014).

Perhaps King thought that if he reached and entered the America of equality and justice, he might experience it as an exile without end. Black freedom is bound to be complicated. In one of his last speeches King entered the Moses narrative as if he was there looking out over the Promised Land he would not enter. King encountered the paradoxical situation that Jews experience in America. It is similar to the experience of Jews in the state of Israel. Jews hope for a reversal of the reality within the context of a dream. Jews know that the resolution may be unfavorable to the dream.[8]

In America, the Jewish dream of living a normal life has been achieved. Jews live as equal citizens. The pursuit of political, economic, cultural, and religious freedom within the parameters of equality and respect is assured. The "normal" for Jewish life in America is abnormal in Jewish history. This is true for reasons other than the achievement of equality.

The Jewish "normal" in America is a peculiar ascendancy. Unlike other Americans, it highlights Jewish events outside the American experience. The Holocaust and the birth of Israel are European and Middle Eastern events. Yet Jews have imported them to America with great effect. The success is so impressive that the Holocaust and Israel now seem intimately tied to America—as if the Holocaust and Israel are part of American history.[9]

The Holocaust and Israel are Americanized. We see both through the American lens. The separation of Holocaust, Israel, and America is unthinkable. In public speech in America, such separation is deemed unpatriotic.

JEWS WRITING GOD'S PART IN AMERICA THE CHOSEN

A strange American Golden Age it is for Jews in America. America is golden for Jews because of the previous difficulties of Jewish history. Jews ride high in America despite the fact that an off-shore historical event and a contemporary political entity provide their anchors.

Economic ascendancy is crucial to this ascendancy. It allows Jews to leverage success in America politically while also being rooted elsewhere. The Golden Age of American Jewry is found here. Jews are fully present in the American dream. They are connected to the Jewish dream outside America.

8. An interesting side note to King's journey was his relationship with Abraham Joshua Heschel, the great Jewish theologian. For part of their journey together relating to the Vietnam War, see Edward K. Kaplan, *Spiritual Radical: Abraham Joshua Heschel in America, 1940-1972* (New Haven: Yale University Press, 2007), 311-12, 320-22.

9. For an interesting exploration of the theme of the Holocaust in American life, see Peter Novick, *The Holocaust in American Life* (New York: Houghton Mifflin, 1999).

Thus, in time frame and in perception, Jewish identity and destiny are both American and beyond America. Americanizing what is outside America helps give Jews a leg-up.

Jewish rooting in America is the opposite of the Jewish experience in Europe. In Europe, Jews tried to sink roots that never took hold. Despite periods of acceptance, Jewish hopes of being at home were continually frustrated.

Today, Jews have roots in America and live lives oriented around Jewish history before and outside of America. Although Jews assume that this is the normal way of living personal and communal life, is there any other community in America that across the generations is able to be both distinctly American and also not? Here we need to think beyond parade nostalgia or a good-feeling romanticized travel back home, so distinctive in America. Jews live this connection in and through an engaged American foreign policy and an unending stream of American aid, arms and strategic coupling with Israel.

The charge of dual loyalty against Jews does surface from time to time, though this charge is usually a deceptive throw away rather than an engaged discernment. Such charges were briefly leveled in the national media in the wake of the September 11th terror attacks. A huge complaint of the Muslim world, including the Al Qaeda movement and others of like mind, is the American connection with Israel. Jews are cited as a dominant force in the American support for Israel. This charge was quickly dispatched by the Jewish establishment as anti-Semitic. Soon the enhanced American security state was deeply involved with training and equipment in anti-terror techniques provided by Israel.

The question of American foreign policy being tilted toward Israel is hardly reserved for the purveyors of terror. Nor is it reserved for those who call attention to America's global empire. Some Americans critical of American support for an expansionist Israel wonder whether support for Israel is good for America. This includes Jews in America and Israel who ask if uncritical support for Israel is in the best interests of Jews, Israel itself, and the wider world.

With September 11th, the hostility of some in the Muslim world rose to the level of paramilitary attacks on American soil. This posed the issue of whether their anger could be assuaged if the American alliance with Israel was broken. Such charges were related to Jewish influence in America. Is American foreign policy unduly influenced by a community whose interests lie outside of America's interests?

Establishment Jews beat this charge back. They did so by highlighting Israel's fight against terrorism with America's September 11th experience. America and Israel were targets because "we" share the same values, or so it is asserted. More than a decade after September 11th, anyone who disrupts "our" common identity is defined outside the American consensus. America is exceptional. America has a peculiar destiny. The same can be said of Jews and the state of Israel.

Although originally connected with the people Israel, the "Chosen People" idea has been expressed frequently in history. These are individuals and communities who have something special to give to the world. Those who receive the Chosen message, "our" destiny for "you," are oftentimes armed to the teeth in order to push someone else's destiny away. Thus the United States and Israel may have yet another bond—both are white settler states that displaced and cleansed the indigenous people from their land.

History without the Chosen Ones would seem much easier, less violent, just living the life we have, without pushing the limits of meaning. Yet if there is a recurring theme in history, the Chosen Ones is it.

The people Israel existed long before America. America is a latecomer in the Chosen People business. Israel's articulation of its chosenness started early. It remains. In the biblical narrative, even the world's creation is viewed as leading to Egypt, the Exodus, and Israel's entry into the Promised Land. The Bible views creation and beyond as a dramatic bridge to the real story, Israel's liberation. In the biblical narrative, this is God's understanding, too.

How bold Israel is: Israel writes both its own history and God's. For the writers of the Bible, Israel and God are intertwined. According to the Bible, at least, Israel and God are more closely connected than other peoples are. Other peoples gain significance in relation to their interaction with Israel and God. In the Bible, Israel and God are one. Neither exists without the other.

Israel draws a fascinating picture of God. The God of the entire universe is a mountain God. The God of the universe that Moses discovers on a mountain is primarily Israel's God. The God whose name is unannounced and unpronounceable is one with the history of Israel. Israel knows no other God. If God knows any other people the way God knows Israel, it is unannounced in the biblical text. We do not even know for sure that God is interested in other peoples. On this possibility, the Bible is vague.

Yes, in its early, pre–Exodus life, Israel has a number of gods. After Egypt, these gods remain. When called upon, however, these gods are found wanting. A main drama after the Israelites leave Egypt is to keep Israel's eyes focused on liberation and the one true God. Israel strays from God, yet Israel's drama is sure and defined. Why Israel continues to honor and sometimes worship other gods is a subplot. Everyone knows where the Bible is leading Israel.

Israel's other gods are like love affairs. Although they threaten the covenantal marriage, the covenantal marriage remains the central drama. Without the other gods, the real God, Israel's God, is too pat and static. Other gods are tropes that make Israel's God real and powerful. Still, God watches Israel and notes how weak and unfaithful it is. Israel's God knows the score. So does Israel.

Israel's gods are under every green tree. In the end, though, Israel's tribal gods give way to the one true God of Israel. The biblical narrative partly revolves around the gods/God contest. True, on God, Israel hesitates and vacillates. Israel vacillates on other issues, too, including the justice of the desert wanderings and the value of kingship when Israel is settled in the land.[10]

When Israel enters and settles in the land, her mission is accomplished, or so it would seem. Yet here the drama intensifies. Having yearned, struggled, and suffered to reach and hold the Promised Land, it turns out that Israel does not want to live only in that promise. The path is too rigorous. It is too straight, too narrow. As well, the penalty for failure is excessive.

The choice of an earthly king is part of Israel's freedom. It may also be the result of Israel's fear of what it means to live with God if it fails to tow the line. As an escape hatch, Israel substitutes its own line of authority.

Most scholars see Israel's God narrative as the gradual establishment of monotheism. Over time, Israel's tribal gods disappear. An alternative view is to see the God of Israel as a tribal god establishing supremacy over other tribal gods.

Here's how it goes. When the God of Israel appears on the scene, Israel is down and out. A certain God, among many others, stakes a claim on Israel. This God makes retrospective claims about God's role in creation and ties God's power and prestige to the Exodus event. From the moment God stakes a claim, the controlling force is the tribal God of Israel, who now leads the Chosen People out of bondage.

In the desert wanderings, controversy is intense. Israel falls back, hopes for something more, rebels, even against the Chosen designation. Israel brings its other gods to the fore. Perhaps these gods can free the people from their dangerous desert sojourn. The tribal God of Israel has second thoughts. The God of Israel is unsure of God's own direction, then isn't, exerts power, then seems powerless. God is in control of Israel. God cannot control Israel.

---

10. On the different gods that existed within ancient Israel, see *Under Ever Green Tree: Popular Religion in Sixth-Century Judah* (Ann Arbor: Eisenbrauns, 2001). Also see Patrick D. Miller, Paul D. Hansen, and S. Dean McBride, *Ancient Israelite Religion: Essays in Honor of Frank Moore Cross* (Minneapolis: Fortress Press, 2009).

Israel is constantly embroiled in conflict. Each conflict makes a larger point about the life of Israel, God, and the human journey. Yet the drama itself is the central theme. Chosenness binds. Chosenness costs. Destiny's path unfolds with many twists and turns. Destiny belies certainty.

The People (and Their God) Who Dwell Alone

Think Deuteronomy, the end, when Moses realizes that the Promised Land is out of his reach. The Bible leaves it to interpretation whether Moses' destiny is fulfilled by simply viewing the land or if God forbids Moses from entering the land as a penalty for disobeying God. Perhaps God saves Moses from entering the land as a final warning about Israel's troubled destiny.

Moses' last oration is full of warnings. For Moses, Israel's destiny is right there, just over the horizon. Soon it will be within the land. Moses experiences the "right there" only in anticipation. Israel experiences what Moses does not.

Moses' warnings are predictive. Though he wants Israel to succeed in the land, Moses knows that the margin for error is thin. Israel has failed many times and in the land there are no do-overs. Meanwhile, God is watching every move Israel makes. Moses' tone is ominous. The reader understands his admonishment is falling on deaf ears.

There isn't anything on the other side of the Promised Land either, at least anything or anyone, including Israel, would want to experience. Moses says it all. Failure in the land means exile. Exile means desolation and death. What exile can mean without a sense of anything beyond the Promised Land is left to our imagination. Moses describes death in the land as a primary penalty but the stakes are even higher for Israel as a collective. Failing in the Promised Land means dispersion and the result, living without a destiny, is another kind of death. The stakes are as high as they can be.

Moses' warning is framed as a lament. He sees a dark future awaiting Israel. In that future, Israel is without him, their leader and intercessor. Though Joshua is handed Moses's mantle and God promises to be with him as he was with Moses, as Moses's successor Joshua is clearly diminished. Moses is the last of Israel with the power to appeal to both God and Israel on an intimate level.

Knowing of Moses' intimacy with God, Israel experiences him as a mini-God. Without Moses and with the other gods diminished, no one of his caliber is left to intercede with God on their behalf. In slavery, Israel was alone without God. Now Israel is alone before God.[11]

Like God, Moses had a difficult time with Israel. He continually bemoans his fate as God's chosen to lead the people out of Egypt. Even so, Moses' leadership within Egypt was simple compared to the desert wanderings. In Egypt, Moses primarily deals with the Egyptian leadership. In the desert, Moses is triangulating between God and the people. The people are increasingly dubious about God and Moses' leadership. Moses, the leader of Israel's liberation, becomes a negotiator and a judge.

Once Moses finds his voice and speaks truth to Pharaoh, God does most of the work. Moses reasons with Pharaoh. With God's help, Moses gathers the people for their short journey into freedom. So Israel thought. So Moses thought. If God knew beforehand that Israel's journey was only beginning and that the rough patch was ahead, the Bible only provides hints. Nor is there commentary on whether Moses knew that the travails of slavery would be looked upon fondly as Israel confronted the harshness of the desert.

Israel's narrative is spectacular. Israel's triumph is trumpeted. The defeat of Pharaoh is definitive. But there is more, much more, to the story.

The biblical text elicits too much hope and too much despair. The rewards and punishments are out of bounds. Israel's narrative is, at times, more than human and, at other times, less than human. God mirrors Israel here, too. Israel invests too much hope in God. God makes too many claims about God's power. Israel's hope is God's hope. Israel's disappointment is God's disappointment.

Even God's creation, the backdrop of the story, is over the top. Out of nothing, our world, formed in seven days, with the last day set aside for rest. God sees it all. God breathes the world into existence. Or God shapes the world, dividing this from that, with God's hands. Since the Bible views creation as the prehistory and as a prelude to the formation of Israel, perhaps clarity is unnecessary. The universe and earth itself are only a stage for the history of Israel.

If stressing creation as the backdrop for the history of Israel seems arrogant, think Christianity. Christianity sees creation and the history of Israel as the backdrop for the coming, life, death, and resurrection of Jesus the Christ. What happened before or after is seen in relation to the Christ event, without which the world is chaos.

Islam is like this, too, except Muhammad is in the forefront. In Islam, Israel and Jesus are prelude to the final prophet. But before Muhammad, at least for Israel, Moses was the final prophet, and for Christians, Jesus was the Messiah. Is there something about Israel and its successors that demands competition for chosenness, salvation and finality?

---

11. For a popular but interesting take on Moses, see Jonathan Kirschner, *Moses: A Life* (New York: Random House, 1998).

Religious narratives of every community are seen from their vantage point. Religious narratives are written and read as such, even though the *after* of all these scriptures is indecisive, wanting, and failed. The conclusion they assert did not happen then, has not happened, and will not happen in the future. Like their Jewish counterparts, Christian and Muslim theologians spend the better part of their days parsing the promise and the reality, the difference between the two and how fulfillment can be unfulfilled and still be fulfilled.

The "thus it happened" and the "not yet" of theological discourse is fascinating. It mirrors our lives, except it is narrated with cosmic meaning attached. An example: We have an experience that seems to be the end. We doubt there could be anything more beautiful and fulfilling. Then, lo and behold, we find it is the beginning of another round. The new beginning finds accumulated experience of limited value. In many ways, we begin again—at the beginning.

After is a difficult time. Our life may be spent searching for the experience we already had, or the experience we should have had. The "not yet" is often the only experience we have. Many of us never reach "thus it happened."

Our self-involvement is overwhelming. This is true in religion, too. Could there be any movement, thought process, or theology more self-involved than Israel? The main competitors are Christianity and Islam, both of which are now global in scope. Perhaps Jews should thank God that the Jewish world has stayed local and small, even in its dispersion. The world divided into these three religions might even be worse off than the world divided into two. Perhaps a tripartite religious division would not have worked. Or perhaps the division is a reality, in a less obvious way. Israel remains the root of the monotheistic tree. Christianity and Islam are branches.

Israel's message has expanded under different names and claims. Even so, Christianity and Islam could have overwhelmed Israel if Israel had been less self-involved. Over the last two thousand years, self-involvement and the Jewish situation in the world saved Jews from a fatal entanglement with empire. Jews suffered under empires and survived them, though with great losses. Jews had a few empires of their own but have largely missed the empire parade—until now.[12]

12. The lack of empire—thus the lack of involvement in colonialism—is one of the themes that Hannah Arendt explores in her desire for a Jewish-Arab encounter in Palestine. She believes that the Jewish lack of involvement in colonialism could preface a new meeting of West and East after the destruction of World War II. For these and other views of Hannah Arendt, see Gabriel Piterberg, "Zion's Rebel Daughter: Hannah Arendt on Palestine and Jewish Politics," *New Left Review* 48 (November-December 2007): 39-57.

It seems that Israel notices its branches mostly when they bend back and assault her. Conversely, Christianity and Islam constantly notice Israel, often in a negative way. Whatever mood Christianity and Islam are in, they rarely ignore Israel—just the opposite. One way of testing the waters of Christianity and Islam is to measure their present attitudes toward Jews.

Perhaps this is why the people Israel always seeks its own place to dwell. Already in the Exodus narrative, Israel dwells alone as part of her destiny. Or, more accurately, dwelling alone is Israel's destiny. Without that aloneness, Israel ceases to exist.

The power of the Exodus story would diminish if Israel had been brought out of Egypt to construct a pluralist democracy. If the destiny of Israel was to assimilate to the broader Canaanite culture, Israel's narrative would have ceased. One wonders if the God of Israel and the people Israel itself would disappear in an integrated society where freedom, equality, and prosperity were guaranteed for all.

Perhaps this is the ultimate challenge of America for Jews. This may be why Jews in America look outside of America for theological sustenance. Embracing the European Holocaust and the Middle Eastern state of Israel as our own may be a way of sustaining Israel's distinctiveness in an increasingly pluralistic America.[13]

In the Bible, the God of Israel also dwells alone. When Moses and Aaron enter the palace, a competition between gods begin. Such a competition seems beneath the God of Israel as we come to know God later. Since Pharaoh's priests are portrayed as magicians, it seems strange that the God of Israel would stoop to compete with them. Yet in the early demonstrations of power, Egypt's priests hold their own. This makes Israel's God seem almost ridiculous. The Ten Plagues follow. They demonstrate God's power. They also show God's limitations.

Why does an all-powerful God demonstrate power over against those who, biblically speaking, represent no-God? Why does the God of Israel have to force Pharaoh's hand, if God is all-powerful? The narrative speculates that God wants Pharaoh to see God's power firsthand and then bow before God. This rationale is difficult to accept. It seems beside the point. A strike from God that frees Israel from Egypt would do the trick.

---

13. Nonetheless, it is Norman Gottwald's understanding that the charge of ancient Israel in the land was to create a socially equalitarian decentralized tribal confederacy. What that would mean for the non-Israelites in the land is unclear. See Norman Gottwald, *The Tribes of Yahweh: A Sociology of the Religion of Liberated Israel, 1250-1050 BCE* (Maryknoll, NY: Orbis, 1999).

The plagues are powerful indicators of who the real God is. They also prolong the siege. The siege deepens the suffering of ordinary Egyptians, most of whom know nothing of Israel or their slavery. God's power is aimed at Pharaoh. It is hardly a teaching moment for ordinary Egyptians. Thus God seems unjust in bringing forth the plagues. There is too much suffering. God can accomplish the task at hand in a different way.

Israel's God may be interested in Egypt's leadership getting the point. As for Egypt, though, out of sight, out of mind. Once Israel leaves Egypt, God uses Egypt only as a negative trope for what Israel might become in the future. Even in the land, the God of Israel is hardly sanguine about Israel's fate. At any moment, Israel might become Egypt.

The biblical text is quixotic. Israel is not compared to Egypt when Israel is enslaved within the Egyptian empire. Only when Israel becomes free in its own land can Israel become Egypt. Israel becoming Egypt is a bondage that Israel never experienced before. Being enslaved to empire is another kind of slavery for Israel. It is Egypt inverted.

None of us dwell alone. Israel has never dwelled alone. Does God dwell alone? If God does not dwell alone, are there other gods that dwell with God? Israel has always had other gods, even today, if we count as gods beings and loyalties worthy of our time, treasure, and devotion.

For contemporary Jews, the Holocaust might be defined as a god. Israel, the state, might also be defined as a god. Jews are counseled that both are worthy of our ultimate loyalty. Guarding the memory of the Holocaust and defending Israel as a Jewish state is defined as *the* Jewish fight unto death. If we place the Holocaust and the state of Israel into the Exodus narrative, the Holocaust is our slavery, Israel our redemption. Most Jews bow at the altar of both.

As with any unexamined faith, dangers lurk. If we critically evaluate the Exodus narrative in light of today, the state of Israel may be the Egypt of old. This would leave the suffering subjects of Israel's empire, the Palestinians, as the new Israel. If this ultimate reversal happened in the Bible, it can happen again. It may have happened already.

Recurring images of aloneness are highlighted in the Exodus narrative. Aloneness may also go back to the desert wanderings and the Ark of the Covenant that traveled with Israel. The Ark was placed within the Tent of Meeting when Israel paused in its desert sojourn. The Tent of Meeting was a no-go area. There Israel was alone in the middle of the desert. At the center of the Israelite community was the Tent of Meeting. The Tent of Meeting was an unusual stand-alone. It was packed with unbridled power.

Or this aloneness may go back to Sinai when Moses ascended the mountain to be with God. When Moses came down the mountain, Israel stayed at a distance. The God of Israel was all-powerful and unpredictable as well.

Israel witnesses God's ascendancy in their desert journey. When God's plans flounder, Israel is angry. Rebellion is in the air. When God thunders from the mountain, there is fear and trembling. God, who could not get God's way, does. The results of being in proximity to God are variable. As we know from the Bible, being alone with God can be marvelous. Being alone with God can also be devastating.

Surrounded by Others

Is it the fate of Israel and Israel's God to dwell alone? Surely, it is difficult to find another founding religious narrative that suggests aloneness so crucial to a people's mission.

Israel's aloneness is also exaggerated, one supposes, for effect. It may be that Israel dwells alone in its narrative to gain space to approach the Holy. Israel claims the Holy as its own. No one else need apply.

Israel's imagined distance from others and from God is retrieved in our time. Just as the people Israel did not dwell alone in reality, Jews do not dwell alone today. This includes Jews in the state of Israel who live side by side with Palestinians. With more and more Jews leaving Israel and with the majority of Jews never having lived there, Diaspora Jews and Jewish Israelis live among others.

As we have seen, Jews have a sense of being alone though they rarely dwell alone. This may help us understand why Jews ritualize the Holocaust and Israel as if both events are abstracted from and singular in history. This allows Jews to claim aloneness in an increasingly diverse, integrated, and globalized world.

Jews did not dwell alone historically, but they recall their history as if they did. Jews do not dwell alone today, say in America and Israel, and yet often imagine themselves alone. Is there a way to bridge the divide between the "alone" dream and "dwelling together" reality?

Do Jews actually want to live alone? Of all the places where Jews live today, Israel is the state where Jews imagine they live most distinctly alone. Even here, though, it is difficult to square this desire with the fact that more and more Israelis leave Israel for other parts of the world.

Jewish Israelis who leave Israel choose to live among others. Couple this with the historical statistics of in-migration to Israel. In the early years, Jews who came to live in Israel were committed Zionists who had lost faith in

Europe. Those who came to Israel after the Holocaust did so when Europe proved unsafe for Jews. There have been few significant in-migrations since: Prime examples are Jews who came from the Arab world, mostly in the 1950s, when after the creation of the state of Israel the Arab world proved difficult for Jews; and beginning in the 1990s, when the Soviet Union self-destructed and Jews and others who turned out not to be Jews fled to be free of anything Soviet.

American Jews have never moved to Israel in great number. A high percentage of American Jews who immigrate to Israel return to America a few years later. The dream of Israel is quite different from the reality. While there is some in-migration to Israel from Jewish communities in France, Latin America, South Africa and elsewhere, many migrating Jews seek residency in the United States, Canada, and Australia. Despite the fanfare and theology, only a small percentage of the Jewish population in the world settles in Israel as their first choice of residence.[14]

American Jews dream of living alone in Israel. Still, since most American Jews remain in America, Israel exists in their imagination. How American Jews imagine Israel is quite different from Israel's reality. In Israel, perhaps 30 percent of the population is non-Jewish. This includes Palestinian Arab citizens of Israel, Bedouins, Druze, African and Asian minorities and even a percentage of Russian "Jews," whom are not Jewish at all. The latter are counted as Jews mostly because they are white and European. In short, they are European rather than Arab. A significant percent of the Jewish population of Israel is of Jewish Arab background. The multicultural aspect of Israeli society is rarely part of the American Jewish dream of Israel, either.[15]

Although Israeli Jews know they live with others, they pretend to live alone. Israel is for Jews only. Why else would Jews live there? Rather than dwelling alone in Israel, Jews live side by side with Palestinians. This is so within Israel's internationally recognized borders, within Israel's actual borders that stretch into East Jerusalem and the West Bank, and in proximity to Israel's borders in Jordan, Lebanon and Syria.

"Surrounded" by Palestinians and other Arabs—this is how Jews in Israel often think of themselves. American Jews portray Israel in a similar way. Meanwhile, Jews in America who imagine Israel living alone do not live

14. For population figures for Soviet Jewish immigration to Israel, see Majid Al-Haj, *Immigration and Ethnic Formation in a Deeply Divided Society: The Case of the 1990s Immigrants from the Former Soviet Union in Israel* (Leiden: Brill, 2004).

15. For an overview of the history of Arab Jews, see Norman Stillman, *The Jews of Arab Lands in Modern Times* (Philadelphia: Jewish Publication Society, 2003).

alone, either. The American situation of living with others seems obvious. Yet the American Jewish situation is hardly more obvious than the situation in Israel. Israelis are not surrounded by Arabs. Jews and Arabs—including Jewish Arabs—live side by side.

That Jews in America dwell with others is perhaps less obvious to Jews who live in and think of Israel. Is this because of the different kinds of people with whom Jews in America and Jews in Israel dwell alone with? For the most part, Jews in America think of themselves as living in America with people who, like them, are of European descent. Of course, with each passing year this is less and less the truth. In the Jewish imagination, African Americans are the exception, being non-European, but also having been slaves in America and thus deserving freedom. African Americans do not threaten the Jewish sense of being with other Europeans because they are different in background and have little ability to challenge the Jewish place in America. In fact, Jewish support for the civil rights movement enhanced the status of Jews in America. Paradoxically, support for African Americans rights allowed Jews a discourse that ultimately enhanced the notion of Jewish exceptionality.[16]

Jews in America connect with the Jews of Israel within the context of European history. Since most Jews in America are of European background, Israel's European character is an extension of a shared history. By identifying with Israel as Jewish and European, Jews in America identify European history as their own.

Like all communities, the Jewish sense of history is selective. Jews in America, via Israel, feature Europe as Jews experienced it and re-vision it in the present. This experience in and re-visioning of Europe includes the following narrative: Jews as forming in Egypt, entering the Promised Land, living in Europe, suffering discrimination, being ghettoized, forming a distinctive and lively culture, surviving European Christendom, dying within the Holocaust, emerging from the death camps, and creating a strong and vibrant community in America and Israel.

Though simplified, this telling of European Jewish history is the essence of how Jews remember it. Since every community has their own understanding of history, Jews should hardly be held to a different standard of communal memory. Still, it is fascinating how this plays out. Jews see European history as revolving around Jews, with Europe beginning and ending there. In the Jewish

---

16. Years ago the African American intellectual Harold Cruse wrote about the Jewish perception of who Jews dwelled with or apart from. See his *The Crisis of the Negro Intellectual: A Historical Analysis of the Failure of Black Leadership* (New York: Morrow, 1967).

imagination, Jews dwelled alone and were murdered by surrounding hostile European Christians.

What do Jews take from European history today as Jews are now accepted and feted? What Jews remember most is the Holocaust. Paradoxically, it would be impossible to have the Holocaust as a place of honor in European history if Jews were still unaccepted and dishonored there. So in America, where Jews live (though they sometimes imagine themselves to be in Israel), and in Israel, where Jews live and are supposed to be (but don't always live and increasingly leave), Europe is remembered primarily as a Jewish graveyard.

At a time when Jews have never been safer or more empowered, Jews emphasize their displacement and destruction. Instead of seeing their displacement and destruction in the broad arc of the suffering of many peoples, Jews imagine themselves suffering alone. This is yet another replay of the biblical account of Israelite history. As we have seen, the Bible pictures Jews as if they were alone, certainly singled out, with the central drama being the Israelites and everyone else the foil.

It is fascinating how Europe has evolved over time. Europe has its own sense of timing and a renewed sense of its place and destiny in the world. Yet, for Jews, Europe is finished, except in Jewish memory, which reduces Europe to how Jews narrate their history and articulate it in the world. In this historical rendering, Europe had its day in court, which is about the Jewish sojourn there. In the Jewish court of opinion, Europe has been tried, convicted, and imprisoned.

For Jews, Europe is spoken of and summed up in Holocaust memoirs that abound and through Holocaust memorials in Europe and, more importantly, in the United States. Jews even expect Europeans to accept the Jewish conception that the history of Europe is over and exists only in Jewish articulation. Jews are often shocked when a contrary view is presented.

To a large degree, the non-Jewish population of America has its own version of the "Europe is over" sensibility that Jews share. Old Europe ended with the founding of the United States. The old light, which for centuries was mired in the darkness of religious warfare and despotic rule, has been replaced by the new beacon of American freedom. By combining religious freedom and democracy, America is the way forward in contemporary world history as Europe once was, or could have been, before losing its way. The Jewish understanding of America dovetails with aspects of this narrative.

In this view, America is a light unto the world. Yet in the main, American Jews think American history began with the influx of Eastern European Jews in the 1880s and beyond. For most Jews, the "before" of Jewish immigration is another country and history, mostly belonging to others, with little relevance today. What makes America is its modernity. Who is more associated with America's modernity than Jews?[17]

If Europe is over, America is alive in its Jewishness, more or less like the Jewishness of Israel, at least in the American Jewish imagination. Jews live in other places, for example, Canada, Argentina and France, with more than a million Jews between them. But for Jews in America and Israel, these other countries barely hold their own. When communities only hold their own, they lose ground. When there are promised lands like America and Israel, Jews begin to leave their native communities. The hemorrhaging begins. It only takes a spark to ignite another exodus.

South Africa is interesting in this regard. As a relatively small but vibrant Jewish community, for years Jews in South Africa both upheld and subverted apartheid. When the dam broke and apartheid came to an end, the Jewish exodus began. Whatever the views of the community and individual Jews were on the racial system in South Africa, the apartheid system embraced and ensured Jewish ascendancy. As a strictly European system, Jews negotiated apartheid with aplomb. When the protective walls of apartheid crumbled, Africans came into leadership. Jews began to leave. The only question was to where.[18]

Jews have little to complain about in relation to the political arrangement in America and Israel. Jews are protected and empowered as citizens in America. Israel privileges Jews. American citizenship is without concern for ethnic or religious identities. On this playing field, Jews do fine. In Israel, citizenship in its full meaning is reserved for Jews. In the context of American and Israeli citizenships, there is much for Jews to celebrate.

The complex terrain of those who (don't) dwell alone remains. On the practical side, Jews are like the Other Nations. Jews want what everyone else wants. On the theological side, Jews are not like the Other Nations. Jews do not want to be like everyone else. Jews think themselves Other to their Other. Jews think of themselves as set apart.

Becoming like others is becoming Other to Jewishness. Those Jews who want the power and accuse Jews who see being set apart as an injustice are accused of treason. It upsets the apartness that Jews with power hold to as well.

---

17. This does not mean that the modernity has been easy on Jews, far from it. See John Murray Cuddihy, *The Ordeal of Civility: Freud, Marx, Levi-Strauss, and the Jewish Struggle with Modernity* (Boston: Beacon, 1987).

18. Israel also had no problems with being enablers of apartheid. For the relationship of Israel and apartheid South Africa, see Sasha Polakow-Suransky, *The Unspoken Alliance: Israel's Secret Relationship with Apartheid South Africa* (New York: Vintage, 2011).

The divide among Jews is between those Jews who are set apart by getting what they can outside of the Jewish community to insulate Jews from others and those Jews who want liberation for themselves and for others as a prophetic justice set-aside within Jewishness. Jews seeking justice remain committed as the struggle intensifies, even as victory becomes more distant. When the revolution takes place and a new society is in the offing, Jews find another divide somewhere else.

It seems that being on both sides of the empire divide is a Jewish need. When the divide diminishes, another hunting ground is found. Where others fear to tread, Jews often show up—in their true colors.

This is empire boomerang. What Jews once feared, Jews now are. But can Jews have empire and justice, too? Can Jews live with others while envisioning their life as living alone? A corollary question can be asked of Israel's God. If God is the God of all, can the God of Israel be primarily for Jews?

4

The Search for Jewish Identity

What are the true colors of Jews? If Jews have "true" colors, they haven't always been the same. In history, Jews have worn coats of many colors, Joseph-style. Are Jews chameleons, changing colors with the season?

Is there is an essence to Jews that comes from ancient Israel and is passed down from one generation of Jews to another? Such an assertion raises a variety of questions. If there is a Jewish essence, why do individual Jews act so differently? If there is a Jewish essence, why is it that throughout history Jews can be found on both sides of the empire divide?

Since Jews exist on both sides of the empire divide, the Jewish essence may also be divided—among non-Jews and Jews themselves. Some believe that part of the Jewish essence is to be at war with non-Jews. Culling Jewish history, the argument can be made that yet another part of the Jewish essence is to participate in an endless series of civil wars with fellow Jews. Perhaps the dream and reality of the Jewish essence is at war with itself. Dwelling alone but not alone, Jews struggle to retain the essence of what it means to dwell alone—with others.

The Promised Land is filled with others. Those who survive Israel's entry into the land are viewed alternately as strangers and fellow travelers. Once identified within the gates of Israel, justice is demanded for the stranger, who ceases to be a stranger. Fellow travelers become part of Israel. Like the multitudes that left Egypt with Israel and the tribal reality of what becomes Israel itself, Israel has never been racially or religiously pure.

The experience of being Israel and being with Israel is overpowering. If you are with Israel, you become Israel. Does that mean that the Other ceases to be Other and is therefore in line to receive the Jewish "essence?" Identifying with Israel, others become Israel. Over time, tribal and religious distinctions fade. Participation in the Exodus overwhelms otherness. The loss of otherness comes through shared experience. Shared experience is deepened by adopting a common memory—the Exodus—as the foundation for community. Through memory, slavery and liberation becomes a common journey, even for those who join Israel later. Those who identify as Israel become that memory. In turn, the memory becomes part of the Jewish essence.

The memory of suffering and liberation moves in various directions. One direction is toward security for Israel. Another direction is the embrace of others. Perhaps embracing others is part of the Jewish essence that remembers Israel is also Other to itself. In addition, reaching beyond the borders of Jewish life may represent the desire to overcome the otherness central to the Jewish essence.

Historically, all Jews were Other to Israel. Forming Israel was difficult. Binding Israel was a task. Keeping Israel together has never been easy. Is that why historically there are so many boundaries created that define whether one is or outside Jewishness—because Jews are torn between being Israel and desiring to be free of their identity?

Israel is constantly being torn asunder. As soon as Israel hurries out of Egypt, factions develop. The desert wanderings feature handwringing and rebellion. In the land divisions widen. There are disputes over tribal hierarchies. There are arguments over kingship. The prophets drive a wedge within Israel.

From the beginning, Israel has these divides as part of its communal memory. Existing in the biblical text, Jews read these divides out loud. In turn, they are studied and interpreted. This lays the seeds for future Jewish civil wars.

The Jewish civil war has returned in present days. Although it is difficult to convey a concept like essence in our postmodern era, anyone who experiences the emotional level that the Jewish civil war engenders knows something deep and abiding is at stake. Put simply, the contemporary Jewish civil war is about Israel's essence—how Jews are living that essence or how they are straying from it.

Now if there is an essence, it follows that there has to be a destiny. Otherwise, what would be at stake to cause these civil wars? Essence and destiny go hand in hand. So when Jews debate what it means to be Jewish in our time, a destiny is affirmed, which in turn confirms both a future as well as a foundation in history. The Jewish civil war of the twenty-first century has its roots in the origins of Israel.

Another contentious issue is whether God plays a role in the contemporary civil war as God did in ancient Israel. In Biblical times, God is omnipresent. Still, God is intimately involved in Israel's history as if his reputation and very being depended upon it. Does the God of Israel still have a stake in the outcome of the debate over Jewish destiny? We live in a time when God seems to be silent. Is God on either side of the Jewish empire divide?

Israel's God is impossible without Jews. The God of Israel is originally known through ancient Israel. The opposite is equally true. How would we know about the people Israel without the God of Israel? After this long sojourn together, whether Israel or God would actually exist without the other is doubtful. A more codependent relationship is hard to imagine.

If Israel was once unknown and therefore the God of Israel was unknown, it seems that what we do not know would hardly matter. However, the drama involving the God of Israel and God's chosen ones is surely worth the price of admission. Of the many communal narratives in the world that involve a people and a God, this one stands out.

With so many claims and questions, the disputes within Israel's journey are understandable. In the relationship of God and Israel there are flash points to consider. To begin with, one party or the other asserts control, which then is rebelled against. Sometimes the complaint is sustained. One or the other party changes course. In dire cases, the people Israel commands, overrides, or surrenders. In dire cases, the God of Israel commands, overrides, or surrenders. When either God or Israel seems at peace or is down and out, another struggle suddenly erupts. Both are back on the scene.

When disorder reigns, Israel's drama turns tragic. Already in slave times, the struggle for liberation is convoluted. Who can believe in a God that finally appears and advises Israel that its slavery is already over—when Israel's slavery is at full tilt?

God's pronouncement of liberation is a heady mixture. God presumes that the slaves are already one people. God is obviously incorrect in this presumption; clearly, unity is far from accomplished. And since the slaves know that their liberation, if it can be secured at all, is more complex than God's thundering, it must have been hard to hear God's all-so-certain voice. Indeed, God's rescue plan makes the slave's situation more arduous.

This is only the beginning of Israel's predicament. Remember that, in reality, Israel has yet to be formed. Further, the demonstration of God's power and the hardening of Pharaoh's heart spell trouble for the slaves. Their lot is already precarious enough.

The Israelite slaves hardly need a half-remembered and mostly absent God thundering about their destiny. What proof is there that this God is powerful enough to bring them out of Egypt? Or that this reappeared deity will not disappear or discover another mission somewhere else and leave Israel stranded?

Remember that the fantastic plagues Jew recall were, at least in the beginning, ineffectual. Remember, too, that the desert wanderings seem aimless. Where in God's name are the Israelites being led? In fact, for the Israelites, at times it is unclear whether God has left the scene—and them. Has the leader of leaders left Israel to wander and die in the desert?

God is insistent and angry. As God struts and Moses and Aaron enter Pharaoh's palace, the not-yet Israel suffers. Then come the plagues that God is certain will break Pharaoh's will. Unexpectedly, with each plague, Pharaoh becomes more insistent. Israel suffers more. Not-yet Israel needs a swift blow and release from their condition. All-powerful God fails to deliver.

Then the unasked questions appear. To be liberated, why does Israel have to leave Egypt? Geographic displacement is rarely easy. If the Promised Land is so near, why does Israel have to wander in the desert for forty years? Yet another crushing delay. The Bible records that Israel's sufferings in the desert are worse than the bondage from which they were freed. Many want to return to the relative comfort of slavery.

The wandering in the desert is dreadful. God's ability to deliver on God's promises is severely challenged. The God of Israel is put to the test. What type of God would spend so much energy trying to convince Israel's enemy of the rightness of their cause, finally take God's people out of Egypt, and then seemingly place Israel's final liberation permanently on hold?

God issues the proclamation of proclamations: the great majority of the Exodus generation, the generation that toiled in Egypt and has been seasoned in the desert, will not enter the Promised Land. This includes Moses, God's invested and indefatigable leader.

With Moses, the drama is personal. God knows Israel like the back of God's hand. At the same time, God knows relatively little about God's people. In Israel's eyes, God is unpredictable, at least in the beginning. In God's eyes, Israel is thoroughly predictable, especially in their faults. If God "knows" Israel, why is it that God has so much trouble recognizing and correcting Israel's fault lines?

True, liberation from Egypt is finally accomplished, but at a snail's pace. God's reason for the desert wandering is that Israel is unprepared for the challenges ahead. An objective observer might question why Israel's liberation takes so long, why there is so much back and forth, especially with a God that claims to be all-powerful. It seems that God should be able to make Israel ready for its triumphal entry into the land.

Preparing Israel for the land seems a small task compared to taking on Egypt's empire. So why does God fail to change Israel? This failure becomes more obvious in the land. Israel mimics Egypt by creating an unjust political and economic order. This augurs one of the great reversals in history.

As with Egypt, God judges Israel a disaster in the land. God rebukes Israel by sending the prophets. When Israel turns away from the prophets, Israel is forced from the land. Being forced from the land, Israel's experience is far worse than slavery. At least, this is the biblical account of things. The sufferings of Israel are extreme.

God should have known this would happen. Israel's stiff-necked qualities are obvious in the desert wanderings. True, the land is promised to Israel. Therefore, we might expect better behavior when Israel comes into its inheritance. Yet the Bible provides little reason to believe that wandering Israel will live up to that promise. The Bible anticipates the bad end that is coming. God does as well. Then why let Israel enter the land when disaster is likely?

Moses is crucial in holding things together in the desert. He also foretells Israel's future travails. God knows Moses intimately. God is aware of his strengths and weaknesses. Moses knows God as much as any human can know God. Moses and God work as a team throughout the liberation saga and in the desert wandering. A closer working relationship is hard to imagine.

God and Moses exhibit a mutual concern for each other's well-being. In general, they are frank with one another, though sometimes they are coy. Both hide aspects of Israel's life or God's judgments as if the other won't find out. Just as often, however, God and Moses speak truth to one another.

Their frank exchanges have consequences. Sometimes God changes Moses' mind. Under God's direction, Moses acts against his better judgment. On occasion, Moses changes God's mind. Sometimes an action God was determined to announce to Moses is deterred by Moses' objection. After hearing Moses' counsel, God refrains. Though the junior partner, Moses is fully present to God. God, though often distracted, is attentive to Moses' needs.

Moses knows the Israelites better than God does. His loyalty shines through. At times, Moses communicates his displeasure with Israel. On occasion, Moses eggs God on in his own displeasure. In the final analysis, however, Moses stands fast with Israel even when God warns against it. When God threatens to disown Israel, Moses refuses to sign on God's dotted line.

God wants Moses to side against Israel. Moses steadfastly refuses. Moses declines even when he knows that God's anger is justified. At different points in the biblical narrative, both wonder whether Israel's condition is terminal. This is an ominous sign, to be sure. It may be that Israel is unable to fulfill its destiny.

Moses hangs with Israel. Even when he concludes that God cannot change what Israel is unable to change, Moses remains steadfast. God hangs with Israel, too, even when God concludes that God cannot change Israel either.

So Moses stands with Israel against God—within Israel's terminal condition. Moses and God share an intimate knowledge of the tragedy of Israel. For reasons that are undisclosed, both are reluctant to share this knowledge with Israel. There is knowledge about Israel that Moses refuses to divulge to God. God also refuses to divulge knowledge about Israel to Moses. Sharing, giving, and withholding are parts of any intimate relationship. It is no different with God and Moses.

Are the secrets that Moses and God share known to Israel? The biblical text is discrete. Nonetheless, reading between the lines traces are discerned. The particulars are less important than the overall themes of Israel's life. What is at the heart of the people Israel?

Since Israel lives its own life and has forty years to ponder its contradictions before entering the land, Israel must have intimations of what will determine its fate. This is important for Israel to know or to figure out. After all, everything is at stake. In the end, though, it is crucial for Israel to know what makes her tick for another reason. Israel's fate may be part of its essence.

At its foundation, Israel is unstable. Therefore, part of its essence is movement. However, Israel's movement is distinct. It is unnatural. Israel moves toward, then away from, what is usually defined as stable and normal. True, Israel longs for stability. Israel also resists stability. Following Israel's journey, the difficulty of balancing these two divergent sensibilities is obvious. It is hard to settle the unsettled.

Israel is unable to deal with its longing for stability. Its instability is too compelling. God is unable or unwilling to bring forth that stability. Though God commands what Israel is to achieve, in God's heart of hearts God is dubious. Perhaps this is the deepest secret Moses and God share.

At times, Israel is stable in its instability. At other times, Israel's instability is part of its stability. There is no resolution of Israel's contradictory sides. God and Israel eventually give up on the project. Resolution is not in the cards.

In the end, God and Moses recognize this pattern as central to Israel's personality. Cosmetic adjustments are made, especially when Israel's world becomes so dark that its destiny threatens to implode. God and Moses stave off Israel's disintegration. By thinking through the situation, God and Moses negotiate Israel's way out.

Israel's exit strategy is temporary. The weight of Israel's contradictions is heavy. Israel survives by the skin of its teeth. As it turns out, it is difficult for anyone, even God, to lead Israel.

EXILE, ISRAEL'S SAFE HAVEN

Israel is led out of slavery. Once in the land, it is forced into exile. Exile is horrific. It means devastation of the land and slavery for the Israelites, and death on a large scale. Those who survive in exile are restless. Exile is estrangement. No rest for the wicked.

Outside the land, Israel has an out-of-body experience. Even when Jews thrive in exile, they rarely feel at home. When they feel at home, the land beckons. Israel experiences a psychic tug of war. Israel struggles on either side of the exile/land rope. Israel longs to return to the land. In the biblical account, longing is expressed through lamentation and later, in the rabbinic system, through prayer. Yet the facts belie this sorrow. When able to return to the land, only a small portion of Israel returns.

The desire to return to the Promised Land is another memory dream that fails the reality test in an accusatory way. Jewish literature notes that some Jews enjoy the comforts of exile. The accusation is serious. Exile is described as the easy way out. When Jews prefer exile, they choose to live outside Israel's destiny. Israel's destiny is more difficult. Perhaps refusal to return reflects the fear that another exile awaits. Whatever the reason, in Jewish literature, by refusing to share Israel's burdens, Jews become foreign to themselves.

Exile is otherness. Choosing exile means choosing to be the Other to whom Jews are as a people and to whom the individual is as a Jew. Jews who choose exile turn their back on the God of Israel. As long as exile is punishment for Israel's sins, the God of Israel remains connected to the people. When exile becomes home, God flees the scene.

Already in the desert wanderings, Israel looks better in memory than it does in reality. That is true for the land as well. When remembered from a distance, the land of Israel is easier to hold dear. The Promised Land is embellished and romanticized. Memory preserves the core of the land's meaning. Reality defiles it.

Does Israel prefer to remember God from a distance? In the land, and before it, God breathes down Israel's neck. God's proximity gives life to Israel. God makes it difficult for Israel to breathe.

Whatever the tribulations of exile, God has done the deed. God punishes Israel. God throws Israel back onto itself. God leaves Israel with the dream of return but without any illusions. Israel feels guilty in exile. Israel also fears a return to the land. Israel treads water.

While Israel treads water in Babylon and other less safe places, Israel is more or less on its own. God's judgment stands. Israel also judges Israel in exile. Exile isn't easy for Israel. Should Israel make it easy for God? In Jewish history, exile is a two-way street.

The reality of exile is condemned in Jewish texts. Living in exile is different. The dream is return. Usually, the land is safely out of reach. When return becomes possible, God calls Jews back to the land. Israel hears this call through its leaders. Jews hesitate. They wonder if Israel can trust its leaders and their claim that God is calling them. There is a more substantive issue. Can Israel trust God?

In the Bible, Israel rarely reflects on God's trustworthiness. Rather, the discussion is about what God can and cannot do, in real history, as opposed to the dream of God's power. Here Jews play the Exodus story against itself. By endlessly retelling the Exodus story at the Passover table, Jews decide that Israel's liberation needs to be told. Who among Jews believes the outcome?

Wherever Israel is, their unredeemed reality remains as it was before the retelling. And, to the point, much of Israel's life is lived out among the nations. Historically, Jews are on bottom, or very near the bottom, or slated for the bottom. Simply stated, Israel's liberation is consistently discredited. Liberation exists as a hope. Israel's hope is unrequited.

Perhaps instructively, the Exodus narrative is placed in the same dream category as the Promised Land. Better to recite and remember the Promised Land than live the dream as if it was or could be in reality. Observe Passover. Get on with your lives.

Jews remember God and the formation of Israel, all the while keeping a distance. As with so much regarding Israel, little changes. Jews are in exile. They cannot slide any further down the Chosen People pole. In exile, it matters little what God wants or feels. For the most part, Israel is out of reach.

The biblical text leaves open the obvious. How can Israel be outside God's reach just by traveling miles down the road from the Promised Land? The Bible does not provide an answer. The question is rarely asked.

The narrative goes silent. Israel is vocal. Israel pours out its feelings. Heartfelt exile emotions flow. They are memorized. They are chanted. Lamentation is the order of the day and night. Meanwhile, Israel remains out of God's reach, often happily. Although Israel is vocal in its lamentations, whatever happiness it experiences it keeps mostly to itself.

Israel's mourning is real. As with life, it is more complicated. The dream Israel mourns was impossible to reach. The consequences are devastating. Israel's mourning is conflicted. The dream of being with God in the land remains. The safety and well-being that being out of God's reach affords—the reality—is chosen.

Is Israel's mourning a put-on? If so, it is significant. Israel has difficulty admitting that it wants to forgo another assignment in the land. Nor does Israel admit that its previous life in the Promised Land was a scandal. By recreating Egypt within Israel, Israel's behavior was indeed scandalous. Yet God's punishment was so far out of proportion to the sins of Israel that God, too, became a scandal.

Israel is stubborn. It has difficulty admitting its own behavior because that might justify God's. God's behavior was reprehensible. The biblical narrative cries out but refuses to condemn God. Does that make the Bible a scandal?

Although Israel's lamentations admit that God's punishment fits Israel's crimes, Israel fudges. Does Israel believe in a God that punishes so ferociously? Israel's lamentations are as disingenuous as its behavior. Israel only half-heartedly wants to restore itself in the land or be restored by God.

Considering the magnitude of being Israel, Israel may desire to be something other than it is. Even so, it is doubtful Israel can escape who she is. Perhaps Israel has a shelf-life with a stamped expiration date. Israel is unable to unilaterally pull its own plug. Can God?

After all these trials and tribulations, being Israel is so fraught with danger that anyone would want to escape this God-land identification. Whether Israel can opt out of being itself is dubious. It is an option that does not find its way to the biblical negotiating table. Although Israel's exile predicament comes precisely because it acts like the Other Nations, God is unwilling to release Israel from its destiny. Israel is bound.

If God is so disappointed with Israel and Israel wants to be free of its assigned destiny, it is a wonder that God keeps Israel bound. It might be a win-win for both parties. Israel would be free of God and God's demands. God would be free of the burden of Israel. Seems like a deal: both parties are released; it's a no-fault divorce. Once the union is dissolved, Israel and God are on their way. But where?

God and Israel are bound together. Perhaps God fears that by freeing Israel, God might disappear from the world stage. The anxiety that surrounds this all-powerful God is out of place. It seems that the God of Israel, who claims to be the God of the universe, is intimately tied to these former slaves, desert wanderers and exiled failures. The anxiety of the God of Israel is mirrored by the anxiety of Israel itself. If God disappeared would Israel suffer the same fate? For God and Israel, being too close is difficult. Enacting a definitive separation is unthinkable.

Perhaps another arrangement can be considered. God would be free to roam, remembering Israel on occasion. Israel would be free to roam, remembering God on occasion. This arrangement allows an intimate bond to remain. Though strained, it endures through distance. When the connection appears to be endangered, God and Israel can be reunited. The dream is accomplished, for a moment. Reality sets in. Another separation is agreed to.

The Heartbeat of the Prophetic

There is another restlessness that Israel's distance from God cannot resolve. It is coupled with Israel's distance from itself, another apparently irresolvable problem. Israel's restlessness precedes and is found within the land. It is found before and in exile. Paradoxically, it is also the essence of Israel's stability in the land and outside of it. This restlessness is the prophetic, the primal indigenous of the people Israel.[1]

Israel's dream and reality is challenged most directly by the prophetic. We know the prophetic is real in Israel's life. The prophetic forms the underlying structure of the Bible. In the biblical text, the geography of the prophetic is expansive. From the origins of Israel, the prophetic encircles Israel. In the Bible, Israel is continuously confronted with the prophetic. At various times, Israel confronts the prophetic. Israel seeks to leave the prophetic behind, only to be confronted by it again. The sequence is repetitive. Even so, the prophetic retains its dramatic presence. Without the prophetic, the biblical narrative collapses. Or, better, without the prophetic, the core of the Bible disappears. No destiny emerges. No depth or drama is found. No reason to open the pages of the Bible.

What is Moses if not a prophet? In the beginning, Moses, with Aaron, calls Pharaoh to account. Later, Israel in the Promised Land is under prophetic judgment. This is before the Israelites enter the land. Moses' final oration is prophetic to the core. The refusal of idolatry and justice are central. Moses outlines a litany of abuses to which Israel will almost surely succumb, as they indeed do. The result will be prophetic judgment. God judges Israel's abuses. Though the details are many, the primary charge is that Israel will turn away from its destiny. Moses defines that destiny as the formation of a community

---

1. I am indebted to Martin Buber for the insight that the prophetic is the true indigenous of the people Israel. On the prophetic, see Martin Buber, *The Prophetic Faith* (New York: Macmillan, 1949).

characterized by justice. In Israel, justice will be enshrined. Everyone will have their fair share. Justice will be achieved as a remembrance of God's call for liberation. Or else.

When injustice reigns in Israel, Israel's liberation is squandered. Messengers begin to appear. In the tradition of Moses, these messengers announce the penalty for Israel's transgressions. They also announce the possibility of repentance. Repentance is the way of return to God's favor and must be embodied. Justice is repentance embodied. That is what the prophets do: they embody repentance and justice.

The prophetic call for justice in the land is the same call Moses and Aaron announce to Pharaoh. The difference is that there is no expectation that Pharaoh will deliver on God's command. Egypt is empire full-tilt. Empire never heeds the prophetic call. Empire's DNA precludes it.

In the Promised Land, the burden is on Israel. There, Israel is free to create a just society. Indeed, God commands Israel to do this. Without justice, Israel reconstitutes Egypt—in the land. Why would Israel struggle for so long and why would God be so concerned for Israel if Egypt's empire was only moving down the road to the Promised Land?

Israel's life in the land follows the pattern Moses warns against. Specific prophets take on the themes Moses announces. The prophets bring them alive in different times and places. Still, each prophet has a distinctive voice. Unfortunately, the reaction of Israel is more or less the same. Israel's ears are closed.

Like Moses, the prophets disturb the peace. They seek fundamental change. The prophets note that the stability Israel finds in injustice is unstable. Injustice's instability is hardly ever remedied and, if it is, not for long. Moreover, injustice leads down a road from which there is no return. That road is idolatry, the most dangerous—and unstable—road that Israel can journey on. Once initiated, the prophets come one after the other. They are constant. They are insistent. They are as unrelenting as Moses' original demand to free the Israelites from bondage. Judgment is going to happen. The prophets say, "Watch out!"

Like Israel seeking distance from the land and God in exile, Jews seek distance from the prophets. No one in the world wants the prophetic, especially after experiencing its consequences. Take Israel's side. Think with her. What would it be like if you were stuck with the land *and* the prophetic? Now think, what would it be like if, when outside the land, the prophetic remained?

Think like Israel. In the land, you attempt to reduce the land's significance. The Promised Land is a land like any other. Outside of the land, you capitalize on the hope of returning. You make the land a thousand times larger in your imagination. You do this precisely because you know you would not go back even if you were offered everything. Make the land you will not return to monumental. Then freeze the prophets in the land. You are out of harm's way—you hope.

Think of the positives Jews might reap with the prophetic but also think about the down-side. Justice is hard, especially for those benefitting from injustice. Even for those on the bottom of the socio-economic ladder overturning injustice is a risk. If they are successful a new system has to be built, often from scratch. If they fail, the bottom drops out. They are worse off than they were before.

Regardless, the prophets refuse paralysis. They have little interest in weighing the pros and cons. Even if they do so initially—in their own lives when they are chosen for a life that will consume them—God has little interest in the back and forth or whether the prophetic will work or fail. Inside and outside of the land, the prophetic destabilizes Israel's life.

The prophetic refuses to reduce the value of the land within the land. When outside the land, the prophetic refuses to allow the dream of (not) returning overwhelm the demands of justice where Jews are living. The prophetic is the ultimate double bind. It is the glue of Israel. It unglues Israel. Whether Jews like it or not, they are stuck with the prophetic.

If this was not difficult enough, the demands of justice are only part of the prophetic. While justice may be difficult to achieve, the struggle for justice is reasonably demanded. Justice is a goal which both the individual and the community can struggle for. Yet the prophetic is that and more. From the beginning of Israel, that "more" is the sticking point. "More" is about the covenant and the law revealed at Sinai. "More" is the vehicle for Israel's destiny. For Israel, too, that "more" is intrinsic, inherent, and indigenous. No matter how hard it tries, Israel cannot get away from "more."

What is Israel's "more?" It is the prophetic. The prophetic is a profound wrestling with the complexities of creation, God, and the human. The prophetic wants justice but the prophetic probes a deeper level than justice itself. The prophetic explores the very heartbeat of the cosmic journey as we experience it on earth. Paradoxically, that heartbeat is supremely earthy. Prophetic hands are dirty. The outcast and the marginal are at the center. They are the ones who experience injustice's cycle of destruction and death. The prophetic is never a theoretical construct.

The heartbeat of the prophetic is that "more." At times "more" may even be against those who want justice as something good and right. The prophetic views the stakes as higher than a justice of needs and wants. That is why the prophetic sometimes disturbs the prophetic itself. Especially when the prophetic is intoned too easily or is taken on a superficial plane, the prophet demurs. The prophet's suspicion—of the prophetic—is in order. The prophet displaces the prophetic so the prophetic can regain its depth.

That disturbing note—"more"—disturbs the prophetic. "More" is embodied in the prophet who lives the prophetic at ground level. This, as the biblical prophets remain involved with the God of Israel. The prophets are God's representatives on earth. In biblical times, God communicated directly with the prophets. The prophets spoke for God.

In our time, the prophets speak for God without hearing God directly, at least as God was heard in ancient days. Sometimes contemporary prophets speak against God. Where was God in the Holocaust? Where is God today as the cycle of violence and atrocity continues? Still, the ancient and modern phases of the prophetic are linked at least with the question of God. After all, if life is without ultimate meaning, why travel the perilous prophetic road? If life is without ultimate meaning, why live your life as if something besides self-interest is at stake?

The prophets were a *novum* in world history, then. The prophets remain a *novum*, now. Today the prophets challenge the achievement of human progress, and they stand with the victims of that progress.[2]

For the prophet, the justice that will arrive, hasn't. For the prophet, the justice that arrives, arrives too late. "More" justice is delayed, even as the "most" enlightened societies benefit from structures that divide the affluent and poor. Meanwhile, the prophet experiences the smooth talk of liberal sensibilities disconnected from the rumblings of history. Surface interpretations of progress further distort the memory of enslaved ancestors. It hardly matters what community the enslaved ancestors come from. They speak for those who suffer in the present.[3]

Like empire, progress sees the future in its own image. Those who fall by the wayside as progress is achieved are viewed as regrettable victims, aberrations on the way to the supreme goal. For those involved in progress, everything comes out in the wash. So it is for the captains of industry, political figures, and elites of all kinds. But the prophet is fundamentally disturbed by the

2. On the reemergence of the prophetic voice in the twentieth century, see my *Peter Maurin: Prophet in the Twentieth Century* (Washington, DC: Rose Hill Books, 2003), 7-20.

3. This reflects Walter Benjamin's take on the prophetic. See his "On the Concept of History," in *Walter Benjamin: Selected Writings*, Volume 3: 1935-1938, ed. Howard Eiland and Michael Jennings (Cambridge: Harvard University Press, 2006), 389-400.

squandering of human beings and hope. No justice-in-the-future-speak will do.

The prophet is suspicious of Israel. The prophet is suspicious of the world. The prophet is suspicious of God. The prophet is also connected to Israel, the world, and to God. The prophet is in solidarity with Israel, the world, and God. The prophet is frequently disappointed by all three. At times, the prophet is embraced by Israel, the world, and God. At times, the prophet is banished by one or the others. Rescue when needed is likewise problematic. Alternately, the prophet is saved or abandoned by all three.

The prophet has suspicions about the mission he has been sent on. Does any part of this triumvirate, including God who commands the biblical prophet, believe that the prophet's mission can or will be realized? In this sense, the prophet's calling, though laudable, is laughable. More, the prophet's intensity makes him look ridiculous. Is there any person more pathetic than the prophet proclaiming what everybody knows will never happen?

For the prophet, cynicism is too obvious an option. Though the world's disappointments and corruption breeds cynicism, the prophet avoids cynicism. Cynicism is too easy.

The prophet discerns a divergence between motives and possibilities, between hiding from destiny and being unable to step up to the challenge. The prophet applies this to Israel, the world, and God. Only a steeled commitment will suffice. The prophet's ability to avoid cynicism is sometimes difficult to identify with. The prophet is the most impatient of individuals. Yet it is the prophet's patience or, perhaps, her endurance that forecloses cynicism. The prophet continually fails. She is in constant danger. Yet failure and danger are precisely the prophet's testing grounds.

The prophet is constantly on trial. Her ability to endure even her lamentations is part of the trial. But of Israel, the world, and God, the prophet is the most dependable. The prophet is the most faithful. Perhaps because the prophet is close to the ground, of the three the prophet shows the most compassion. Though riddled with doubt and fear, the prophet is the most certain and courageous. Is this because part of the prophet's task is to simultaneously hold Israel, the world, and God together?

In the prophet's mind, that triumvirate is always on the brink of dissolving. If and when it occurs, the universe as we experience it is thrown into chaos. In the biblical world, the prophet holds things together. When the prophet fails, that is one matter. If the prophet is unable to endure, that is a more serious matter.

The prophet is surrounded by failure. The prophet embodies failure. The paradox is that the prophet's endurance twists his failure and the failure of Israel, the world, and God into a hope that is earthy and transcendent. Prophetic hope is hope against the odds. Through endurance, the prophet becomes the central drama of humanity. The prophet tells us that the human drama is less about civilization or progress than it is about a wounded fortitude, a traumatized survival, and an indignant patience that, despite the apparent evidence, signals conscience remains on the horizon.

On God, the prophet is split. Without God, the prophet makes little sense. With God, the prophet is launched into the world. Once launched, however, the prophet is alone. Contact with God is episodic at best. In the biblical world, sometimes God swoops down and rescues the prophet right when he is about to be done in. Other times, the prophet escapes by a hair through his own devices.

God commissions the prophet to speak to the people Israel. Yet God knows that the prophet's mission is fated. Israel is not turning around. Why doesn't God let Israel suffer its fate without involving God's servant?

Why God exposes the prophet to such danger is a mystery. Perhaps God, though confident that Israel will not turn around, is conflicted about that certainty. On occasion, Israel surprises God. There is an odd chance this might happen again.

Warnings are a test that God knows will go unheeded, but God has a need to speak God's piece. Nonetheless, the prophet is placed in a no-win situation. While the prophet is a beacon of hope, no-hope is almost guaranteed. So the prophet, suspicious of hope, even as she desperately holds out a last-chance possibility, is once again caught in between. The prophet is the tragic bearer of a hope that dwindles by the moment. The prophet's endurance keeps hope alive, though everyone knows hope lessens each time the prophet appears.

If hope fades, does the possibility of meaning in history disappear? In the biblical vision, justice, hope and meaning are intertwined and linked with the destiny of Israel. Unjust Israel is an Israel that has lost its way. It is an Israel without hope. How, then, can Israel struggle toward its destiny? How can Israel struggle with its destiny if it is both unjust and without hope? Without a destiny, the meaning of Israel collapses.

The issue of meaning ranges wider than Israel. Without the prophetic, there is no meaning in history. There in fact may be no meaning in history. The prophet embodies the possibility of meaning in history.

ETHNIC CLEANSING AND JEWISH IDENTITY

How does the prophetic function decades after the founding of the state of Israel and the Palestinian catastrophe? What does the prophetic mean after a history of suffering and struggle for Jews and now after a history of suffering and struggle for Palestinians? Both peoples have dreams and realities. If justice-in-the-future-speak will not do for Jews because of the prophetic, and will not do for Palestinians because of their concrete situation, what is the way forward?

History is humanity's rearview mirror. History effects the present without determining the future. Though the future is indebted to the past and present, the future is open. The future can unfold in various directions. While human agency is rarely the sole determining factor in creating a future, the future always involves human agency. One aspect of human agency is ethical values. History is neither free nor out of reach. The present has been created. We create our future.

The future, then, is the combination of past and present with another dose of human choice involved. Up to a point, the future can be framed within logical reasoning. Through reflection, suppositions, and trends, outcomes can be predicted. Outcomes extrapolated from the present are important to chart. It tells us where we are going, as far as we can discern. However, with the best-laid plans and analysis, and when the obvious and hidden trajectories are surfaced, the future remains an open book. As each page of history and the present turns, the plot thickens.

We know narrative clues of changeable trajectories have been missed or misinterpreted. Other elements within diverse histories arrive unexpectedly. What seemed inevitable may or may not come to be. Even if the main outline becomes as predicted, other themes arise that may affect history's course. Once a trajectory changes, other trajectories are come into play. What comes to be is rarely what appears to be on the way.

On the Jewish side, the continual expansion of the state of Israel is clear for all to see. It was there in the years following 1948 with the establishment of the state beyond the borders defined by the United Nations Partition Plan. It was clear in the military expulsion of the Palestinians during those years in great numbers and in the years after in smaller numbers through social, economic, and budgetary policies of the Israeli government. Expelling populations can be hard and soft. Expulsion makes life difficult, if not impossible, for Palestinians who remain. Palestinian children have a difficult future ahead of them.

The 1967 Arab-Israeli war was a watershed moment for Israeli expansion. When looked at from the longer historical arc, the war allowed a continuation of Israel's expansion that stretched back to the origins of the state. The aftermath of the 1967 war featured the acquisition of new territories in East Jerusalem, the West Bank, and the Gaza Strip. In pre-state days, Jews were settled primarily in the coastal areas of Palestine. With the creation of Israel, Israelis moved into the vacated interior. After the 1967 war, Jews moved into parts of the newly conquered territories.[4]

The post-1967 settler movement created new Jewish populations within and around Palestinian population centers. This had the further effect of isolating and diminishing Palestinian life. The post-1967 Jewish settlement movement accomplished in East Jerusalem and the West Bank what the post-1948 settlement movement had previously accomplished in the interior of Israel within the postwar armistice lines. Over the years Israel moved eastward, leaping, then creeping, then leaping again. Israel expanded exponentially, then incrementally and in 1967 exponentially again.

The latest post-1967 war settlements were controversial from the beginning, even within Israel itself. The controversy was overridden. Whatever "peace process" is underway, Israeli expansionism continues apace. Some believe that Israel has used these various peace processes as a stalling tactic, working under the radar to continue taking more land. Israel has manipulated the world's hope for peace. Under its guise settlement expansion continues and helps Israel keep afloat during difficult times. It leverages the possibility of a just settlement to maintain its dwindling international legitimacy. All the while, it accomplishes what it wants to.

The world has changed considerably since the heady days of Israel's lightning victory in the 1967 war. For the first time more Jewish groups are speaking openly of the complexity of the 1948 war. It seems that a main barrier toward a deeper analysis of Israel's history and future—speaking openly about the original sin of Israel's birth—might be breaking down. The issue at hand is where that breaking barrier would lead, if anywhere, or how that barrier breaking could be placed back into the Israel-analysis bottle.[5]

This is the first time in the history of Jewish dissent that the ethnic cleansing of Palestinians in 1948 has been openly discussed and promulgated by dissenting Jewish groups. Some Progressive Jews who vigorously fought the inclusion of Israel's birth and the ethnic cleansing of Palestinians are crossing into the fledgling community of Jews of Conscience. If this attrition continues

4. For an overview of the Israeli-Palestinian conflict, see Mark Tessler, *A History of the Israeli-Palestinian Conflict* (Bloomington: Indiana University Press, 1994).

5. See Peter Beinart's essay, "The Failure of the American Jewish Establishment," *New York Review of Books,* June 10, 2010. Also see Alan Wolfe, "Israel's Moral Peril," *The Chronicle of Higher Education,* March 25, 2012.

and broadens, what does this mean for dissent and dissenters within the Jewish community? If this expanding group is beaten back by Constantinian Jews, will this precipitate a definitive break within the Jewish community over Israel?

In the not-too-distant future, those who speak openly about the ethnic cleansing of Palestinians may break with the state of Israel completely. Some already have. The pressing issue then will be whether they cease to be in dialogue with the Jewish world as it is known today. Progressive Jews who begin to speak of 1948 may well be exiled from the Jewish world as others before them have been. In exile, what they sought to foreclose may become their teachable moment for normative Jewish life.[6]

The exile of dissenting Jews grows daily. Whether this will engender a broader debate of Jews and non-Jews about what it means to be Jewish is as yet unknown. Constantinian Jews could hold the key to Jewishness for the foreseeable future, with anything outside of their definition considered inauthentic. Or the Constantinian definition of Jewishness may collapse in the coming years, over the decades, or tomorrow.

Identity definitions that remain solid for decades may shift suddenly. With the 1967 war, everything changed in the Jewish community seemingly overnight. One year before and one year after the war signified a distinctly different in the way Jews saw themselves and affirmed their identity. Another event of great magnitude might suddenly come upon us. Whether that event is destructive or constructive, the weight of history might move decidedly toward a new definition of Jewish identity. What Jews of Conscience believe could become its core.

Previously, Progressive Jews purposefully stayed on the right side of the established Jewish identity boundary by discussing only the after-shocks of the 1967 war. For years they maintained that it was only after 1967, especially with the Jewish settlements in the West Bank and Gaza, that things had gone wrong with Israel. Concentrating on the aftermath of the 1967 war left intact their strategic vision of two states, Israel and Palestine, living side by side in peace and harmony. 1948 was dangerous to their identity paradigm. It raised doubts as to whether the entire enterprise of Israel was irretrievably wrong; or, alternately, whether a two-state solution was just; or, with the settlement expansion continuing, still possible.

However, even with the creation of the state of Israel now on the table, Progressive Jews continue their traditional understandings that Israel is a right and proper response to the Holocaust. In their view, the wrong that befell

---

6. This loss of Jews, especially young Jews, to the cause of Israel is a major fear of Peter Beinart's *The Crisis of Zionism* (New York: Times Books, 2012).

the Palestinians is a regrettable byproduct of the need for a Jewish state. This was compounded by the Palestinian rejection of state Zionism and Israel. Progressive Jews continue to see the formation of Israel as a Jewish need after the Holocaust. In their view, though wrongs were committed, Israel means no harm to Palestinians. The formation of the state of Israel is redress for Jewish homelessness. Palestinians must affirm this need. In turn, Jews want the best for Palestinians.

Progressive Jews continue to believe that the negativity of the Arab world toward Israel is part of their backwardness. Although the clash of Jewish and Palestinian needs is a problem that warrants intense attention, the Progressive Jewish perspective is that the application of Jewish ethics can solve the conundrum. However, Jewish ethics can take root only if there is an upgrade of Palestinian and Arab abilities in the ethical, political, economic, and educational realms.[7]

Although Progressive Jews acknowledge the imperfections of Israel, they believe the roadblock to peace is having a "true partner for peace." The Palestinians could become that partner through self-reform. Israel should be its ally in this reform. Progressive Jews suggest Jewish know-how as a bridge for Palestinians into modernity and security.

The unspoken colonial sensibility of Progressive Jews is critical here though frequently unevaluated. After all, for many Jews it takes an imaginative leap to think that Jews might have a colonial mentality. Progressive Jews wonder why the Palestinians continually turn East, toward the Arab world, when Israel, Jews, and the West await them with open arms. Few Progressive Jews wonder if Palestinians, of their own accord, see Israel, Jews and the West as their beacon. From the Palestinian perspective these entities and conceptual categories are part of their predicament. Why should Palestinians believe that what has oppressed them will suddenly be their ticket to freedom?

Progressive Jews, like the mainline Jewish establishment, see proof of Palestinian backwardness in their rejection of Israel's "generous" offers of peace. Their mantra is confirmed: "The Palestinians never miss an opportunity to miss an opportunity." With a little less liberal optimism and critique of Jewish reticence to extend a helping hand to Palestinians, the Jewish establishment can live with this analysis. In fact, it is a bridge between the two sides. At times and with fierce arguments notwithstanding, Jews continue to stand as one on Israel. After all, if Progressive Jews do not stand with the Jewish establishment on Israel

---

7. Michael Lerner's *Tikkun* is fascinating in this regard. As interesting is his ability to expand the borders of his critique while still maintaining his central bias. For his updated views, see his *Embracing Israel/Palestine: A Strategy to Heal and Transform the Middle East* (Berkeley: North Atlantic Books, 2012).

and the Palestinians, how can they establish their credentials as the hoped-for next generation of Jewish leadership?

To be the next Jewish establishment in America, certain sensibilities must be affirmed. To begin, the implicit affirmation of the superiority of Western and Jewish culture is crucial. To hold that view, even with criticism, Western and Jewish innocence must be maintained. Therefore, the clash between Jews and Palestinians is considered tragic rather than intentional. Harm done to Palestinians is considered aberrational.

We return to the post-1967 years of occupation and settlement. Although chastened and contested, Progressive Jewish discourse still views Israel as the place where residues of Jewish innocence and redemption remain. Holding onto Israel is important for more than the state itself. For if Israel can no longer fulfill its symbolic significance of Jewish innocence and righteousness, the fear is that there may be little if anything left of the core of Jewish identity. With Israel tottering, the symbolic significance of the Holocaust may likewise diminish. Then what?

The unease around the discussion of 1948 and the formation of the state of Israel is palpable. The underlying anxiety is that this might be the tipping point in Jewish identity from which return is impossible. The ethnic cleansing of Palestinians may prove too heavy a burden for Jewish identity to survive. For Progressive Jews, Jews as ethnic cleansers is unthinkable.

Since the unthinkable has already been thought—and done—how is it possible to keep Jewish identity together? Like the Jewish establishment, for Progressive Jews ignorance might be the glue of contemporary Jewish identity. If return to Jews as innocent and righteous is no longer possible, Jewish identity has to change. Jewish life is an extended conversation and the Jewish ethical tradition, including the prophetic, flows through Jewish history like a river. After acknowledging 1948, where does the Jewish river run to?

For those who acknowledge 1948, Jewish identity could remain, at least in some minds, separate and apart from non-Jews, but only as it becomes separate and apart from Jews who refuse to acknowledge 1948. Or, in its dual separateness, the Jewish river could run to the sea, running against the currents of contemporary Jewish history and into other community rivers. Fears surface. Does Jewish identity become polluted by mixing with other community identities? Jewish identity might ultimately disappear by becoming one with elements that were once foreign to Jews, at least as Jews previously dreamed of Jewishness.

In Jewish history, what is deemed foreign often presages the surfacing of other, forgotten elements of Jewish identity. Such designation of "foreign" is hardly restricted to Jews. For the most part, foreignness is a state of mind for community identity formation around the world. The separateness and exclusivity that communities claimed in earlier eras at a later date seems outmoded or even silly.

With the passage of time, even earlier calls for sacrifice and martyrdom become time-worn, an argument to the death over what is ultimately considered trivial. Later generations hardly comprehend what was at stake or, if they do, reject it as outside of any identity they want to carry forward into the future. At some point, community-identity assertions cease to make sense.

Identities change. On the Jewish side, the claim of continuity is often made without thinking in modern historical terms, or perhaps identity has its own historical method. For Jews, the memory of formative events, like the Exodus, is immediately de- and re-contextualized. For Christians, the liturgical reenactments of Jesus' life similarly construe history in a distinctive, continuous way.

Memory that infuses identity formation is substantially different than modern renderings of history. This is especially true when identity memory upholds the social and political order. It is true, too, when identity memory subverts oppressive power. There can be an amalgamation of identity memory and modern critical history. Jews have played a pioneering role in this endeavor. Sometimes Jews are able to keep identity memory and critical history in tension as a part of the ongoing Jewish conversation. It is difficult to imagine contemporary Jewish intellectual life without it.

Yet that tension may be yet another casualty of the Jewish civil war over Israel. Increasingly, emotion rather than considered reflection is the order of the day. Either as a Jew you are "for" Israel or you are "against" Israel. If you are "for" Israel, you are for the oppression of Palestinians. If you are "against" Israel you are for the destruction of the state of Israel. However, the middle ground of applying the thrust of Jewish history and critical thought may yield a middle position that honors Jewish history and calls Israel to account—on behalf of Jewish history and suffering Palestinians. But in civil wars the first casualty is reasoned thought. Thus it is Jew against Jew—with Jewish history on the line.

This tension is crucial to contemporary Christian theologies of liberation. Liberation theologians establish a Christian identity in dialogue with the world. The merging of Jesus' teaching in the context of the prophets with the sociopolitical theories of Marx and other social and political commentators represents the genius of liberation theology. This is what makes liberation theology so dangerous to established power structures. This is also what is found in the Jewish Voice for Peace Haggadah. The ancient Passover narrative becomes the way for Jews to interrupt and transform their views of contemporary Israel-Palestine.[8]

Christian liberation theologies have been part of the Christian civil war over the last decades. Both the Constantinian Christian establishment and liberation theologians have been adamant—either as a Christian you are "for" Christianity in its empire formation or you are "against" the church as it is and for deep social and political critiques of the status quo. The way out of this civil war may be surprising to both Jews and Christians. Could the way out be the gathering of those on either side of the empire divide with their counterparts, Jewish and Christian? On the conscience side, this would mean the joining of Jews and Christians of Conscience in a solidarity that is new to both Jewish and Christian history.

THE COMMANDING VOICE OF PALESTINE

Identity formation is a delicate balancing act. Jewish thinkers are critical of modern historical movements when they abuse power. A minority of Jewish thinkers have trained a similar spotlight on Jewish history. For the most part, however, contemporary Jews focus their critical spotlight outwardly rather than on Jewish identity. Unfortunately, this is a trait that many communities embrace. How much easier it is to think of "them" and "their" history. Religions and ideologies of all stripes declare their own history off-limits to analysis. The innocence and redemption of each community is affirmed. Other communities are found lacking.

Because of the prophetic, Jews have an especially difficult time keeping the spotlight shining outward. After all, the biblical prophetic is internal, intensely focused on the sins of the people Israel. Therefore, tremendous energy and resources are expended to direct the prophetic focus outward. But, then, the Jewish prophetic keeps bending back into internal Jewish space. Soon the discipline the Jewish establishment imposes on the prophetic breaks down.

The Holocaust and Israel are two events off-limits to critical Jewish thought. This barrier has religious connotations as well. Some Jews have written of the formation of a Holocaust/Israel Judaism that begins and ends with both events. Within this sacred arena only certain kinds of thought are allowed if one's Jewishness is to be considered authentic.[9]

---

8. For a history and development of liberation theology, see David Tombs, *Latin American Liberation Theology* (Leiden: Brill, 2002).

Only a chosen few are allowed in the sacred arena of Holocaust/Israel. Thought barriers hold possible entrants back. Is this barrier similar to the one at Sinai? The lightning and thunder emanating from Mount Sinai were so fierce the Israelites backed off and stood at the mountain's perimeter. Today, Jews back off from the rumblings of the mountain that is the Holocaust and Israel.

Years ago, the late Jewish philosopher, Emil Fackenheim, wrote that because God was silent in the Holocaust the orienting vision of Jewish life shifted from the Commanding Voice of Sinai to the Commanding Voice of Auschwitz. Where God is silent, the martyrs of the Holocaust speak. For Fackenheim that call is to action—on behalf of Israel as a response to the Holocaust. Today, it would be more accurate to say the Commanding Voice of Auschwitz and Jerusalem. Now there is another competing voice heard by a minority of Jews—the Commanding Voice of Palestine.[10]

Of all of Israel's leaders, only Moses ascended and returned from his mountain sojourns with God. The people saw and listened in awe. Even Israel's grievances quieted when the Sinai events were experienced in full measure. Critical sensibilities existing before Sinai were suspended, declared off-limits. This was because of the overwhelming power in the air. Fear and hope co-mingled. A sacred event was occurring, and what it might portend for the future was unknown.

Whether Israel could live with Sinai in its daily life became the immediate question. Mountains are as mountains are. They are imposing, bringing life but also death. Mount Sinai was infused with God's presence. Imagine living with that knowledge, especially when the God of Israel is unpredictable. The sacred event of Sinai was defining. The issue was what to do with such an overpowering event after it occurred. For the people Israel, what was possible and impossible after Sinai?

The prophetic was already engraved in Israel. Although it was destined to take another more radical turn in the land, the prophetic contained the same riddle. The prophetic is defining. Fulfilling the prophetic is impossible. Millennia later the Holocaust and Israel stand in continuity with Sinai and the prophetic. They redefine what is possible and impossible.

Have Palestinians and Palestine intruded here, redefining the assumed trajectory of the Holocaust and Israel? If so, what does this mean in the world and in Jewish identity formation? Whatever the result, the Jewish prophetic is

9. Adi Ophir explores Holocaust/Israel religion in his *The Order of Evils: Toward an Ontology of Morals* (New York: Zone, 2005), 527-56.

10. Emil Fackenheim writes about the Commanding Voice of Auschwitz in *God's Presence in History: Jewish Affirmations and Philosophical Perspectives* (New York: New York University Press, 1969).

defining of this further question: How should the prophet proceed here? What guidance does the prophet have when the internal sin of the Jewish people is oppressing an Other to Jewish history?

For most contemporary Jews, the Holocaust and Israel are stand-alones. All approach these momentous events with trepidation. But even here the question is crucial: What is at stake in the Holocaust and Israel? What about these events is defining? Is there something sacred in mass death *and* a Jewish state?

The Holocaust and Israel are sacred only if we refuse to look at either from the vantage point of history. However overpowering and even frightening it can be, the sacred is often a gloss on history, a mystical take on the actual that highlights and distorts reality. The sacred takes on the visage of a dream or a nightmare. Why has the Holocaust become transcendent and untouchable? It may be that the reality of the Holocaust, mass death with a name, is too disturbing.

The very name "Holocaust," and its derivations *Shoah* and *Churban*, dress the wounds of the suffering and make them presentable. By using these Hebrew/Yiddish designations, Jews attempt to rescue the use of the Holocaust from others who now use the term to address their own suffering. Changing the name of the Holocaust is an attempt to retain its Jewish exclusivity. Does it once again make the Holocaust portable, like the biblical Ark of the Covenant?[11]

At first glance, it is blasphemous to suggest such a transposition. The God who travels with Israel in the desert wanderings is counterpoised to mass death that travels in memorials, monuments, theology, and liturgies which invoke the Holocaust. Perhaps the transposition is incomplete. It could be that the difference between God and mass death has collapsed in Jewish life.

Heightening and ordering the mass death of Europe's Jews by naming it Holocaust/*Shoah*/*Churban* may be the only contact that contemporary Jews have with God. Conceivably, the Holocaust has become a substitute God or God's substitute. Is the real God close at hand when Jews invoke the Holocaust? Or are the lamentations around the Holocaust a Jewish cry for an absent God?

Ancient Israel had a strict prohibition against naming God. The distance created by refusing to name God was countermanded by the presence of God's power in the traveling Ark and in the Tent of Meeting. We do not know whether the ancient Israelites experienced these manifestations of God as God or as conduits for God's presence. Nonetheless, Israel's God was quite distant and startling close at hand. The Holocaust may function as a way of

11. Years ago, Lucy Davidowitz charted (and complained about) how others interpreted the Holocaust. See her *The Holocaust and the Historians* (Cambridge: Harvard University Press, 1983).

manifesting death close-up while keeping death at a distance. If this is the case, the Holocaust, like God, is called upon when suffering is too near and when Jews need to distance themselves from it.

The Holocaust, like God, also has a power in its very naming. Through it, Jews order their understanding of Jewish history. Does this naming and ordering also obscure what happened to the Jews of Europe? All names are a summing-up, highlighting aspects of reality and obscuring others. The naming of the Holocaust orders a reality that lacks order. Naming the Holocaust bestows meaning on an event that can be experienced as meaningless.[12]

In the Jewish tradition, the Holocaust as a name for the destruction of European Jewry may be like the traditional letters for God, a way of approaching God while maintaining a distance. In traditional Jewish prayers, *Adonai* ("Lord") is substituted for the unpronounceable name for God. "Holocaust" could be akin to applying a name to God without touching God's essence.

The new terminology that tries to erase "Holocaust" as the name-face on the destruction of the European Jews is instructive. The God of Israel is a unique God. Although religions like Christianity and Islam claim to worship the God of Israel, Jews nod to this assumption without conviction. The usurpation of the God of Israel by other religions is seen as temporary and unimportant. It is filed under "Expropriation of Things Jewish."

Jews have little concern here. The Jewish God has moved on. While Christians and Muslims worship the God of Israel as they perceive that God to be, Jews are involved with a different God or the same God with another name. Jews continue with their sacred reality—the Holocaust and Israel. This God is unapproachable by others.

Is making the Holocaust Jewish-only parallel to making the state of Israel Jewish-only? Or reaffirming the God of Israel as for the people Israel-only? The Holocaust, as it is called today by most Jews and non-Jews alike, claimed millions of non-Jewish victims as well. Jews place non-Jewish victims in the "death for death's sake" category. If we widen the death watch, millions more died as direct and collateral casualties in World War II. As terrible as it was, the Holocaust and its evolving terminology limit the horror of what occurred.[13]

Holocaust consciousness is partly responsible for this narrowing. It is understandable and correct that Jews are singled out in the memory of this

12. Lawrence Langer discusses the futility of ordering the Holocaust experience in *Holocaust Testimonies: The Ruins of Memory* (New Haven: Yale University Press, 1993).

13. I return to this issue later in the book. It is suggested powerfully by Timothy Snyder, *Bloodlands: Europe Between Hitler and Stalin* (New York: Basic Books, 2010).

time period. Jews have a right to remember their own dead in the way they see fit. However, when a communal memory moves into the broader public consciousness with public policy consequences, say billions of dollars annually provided to Israel by the United States government, the particularity of memory carries a caveat.

In the broader arena, a community can share their communal memory. In the best of all worlds, they cannot impose one. While there might be internal penalties for violating a communal memory, such penalties cannot be applied outside the particular community's boundary. Imposing one communal memory on another community usually means penalizing that community for having and highlighting its own memory. A substitution takes place. This betrays an agenda of memory as a form of power over others.

The power of memory should respect communal boundaries. If a community wants to affirm another community's memory alongside its own, that is all for the better. Remembering another community's memory as being as important as your own is a sign of the community's vibrancy and confidence. Still, such affirmation is optional. If acceptance is demanded, then one community's memory becomes another community's diminished memory of itself.

This is especially true with the memory of suffering. Such memories can be hoarded by one community and imposed on another. However, in the end the memory of suffering is used as a tool of power rather than a path of solidarity toward others who are suffering. Usually the imposition of the memory of suffering means that the community's suffering is in the past. It is now empowered. Further, the community has been mobilized and militarized in the name of that suffering. In a strange twist of logic, often the memory of a community that suffered in the past is used to stifle the just grievances of a community suffering in the present.

In many ways, this has happened with the Holocaust. Tremendous suffering has been mobilized and then militarized by the Jewish community in support of Israel. Events of suffering experienced by other communities are seen as lesser or derivative of the Holocaust. The Holocaust becomes a bully, overpowering the suffering of others as somehow less important.

There can be little quarrel with Holocaust memory per se. How could there be? The issue is how Holocaust memory is used and where it takes Jews in the world. Does Holocaust memory cross community boundaries with power over others or as a plea for solidarity with all peoples who are suffering? In Holocaust discourse, the option is stark, whether the Holocaust means never again to the Jewish people only or never again to *any* people.[14]

Only through solidarity can Holocaust memory be thought through critically and then, in light of critical analysis, thought again. Otherwise, it becomes a blunt instrument of power to be used at will against others without accountability. The Holocaust symbolizes so much in the contemporary world but more and more the Holocaust has become paradigmatic for a formerly suffering people who in their new-found power stand on the almighty side of the empire divide.

Can the memory of suffering, once established and empowered, cross back over the boundary it has recently crossed? Can the memory of suffering retrace its steps, assuming the shape it had before it was empowered? Or does the memory of suffering, once it assumes power, cease to be memory in any meaningful sense?

Once having crossed the boundary, the memory of suffering may fall back into silence. What is left is power and empty rhetoric that defines how those who suffered are to be memorialized. When suffering is used to empower one community over others, a later generation may never know that the memory of suffering was once articulated as a form of solidarity. Another possibility is that a particular community's memory of suffering, when shared, might be transposed into other memories of suffering, finding its place and another life there. Involved with other memories of suffering, the initial memory of suffering, distorted through power, may be renewed for the community that lived and then bequeathed it.

This may already be the case with the Holocaust. With its memory abused by the Jewish establishment and to some extent by Progressive Jews, the Holocaust needs to find a home somewhere else. When and where that might be, though, remains an open question. Jews of Conscience carry the memory of the Holocaust forward. With what other communities might the Holocaust be shared as it retraces itself back to its original subversive quality?

While naming their memories of suffering and retrieving them as well, communities that share memories of suffering become memory carriers. Here one community's memory of suffering becomes one memory among others, even in its internal life. On the one hand, the outstanding quality of suffering, the particularity of a memory of suffering, is downplayed in the broader community. On the other hand, the memory of suffering attains a mutual respect in the broader community. Since, with this type of sharing, the broader community expands its view of humanity, there is a greater likelihood that particular memories of suffering will survive.

14. This understanding of the subversive memory of suffering is found in Johannes Metz, *Faith and History and Society: Toward a Practical Fundamental Theology* (New York: Seabury, 1980).

Not in Our Name

The broader community's memory of suffering is greater than any one particular community. And since the standards of speaking these memories vary, with cross-communal listeners, shapers, and critics involved, any one community's memory of suffering will constantly be vetted within the community's present context.

The memory of suffering is placed in motion. In one context, the memory of suffering might be subversive of unjust power in the present. In another context, the memory of suffering might be used to buttress unjust power. When the latter happens, the challenge is to reawaken that memory so it can be brought to bear on that power. Challenging and making power accountable, especially when it uses the memory of suffering to commit injustice, is far from simple. To use it to reverse the injustice is even more difficult.

Memories of suffering serve agendas. Since memories of suffering are always used, then they, like power, should be held accountable. With the thought of accountability in mind, as well as memory's role in the formation of identity, one way of disciplining the memory of suffering is the disciplining of identity. Disciplining identity means that while identity can be formed within a particular community, the identity-claims made on the larger identity-diverse public must be limited.

One way of disciplining identity is by placing those who use the memory of suffering in their political, religious, and social discourse in motion with other geographies of suffering. This compels those who have a particular experience of suffering into relation with the experience of another's suffering. In turn, this raises the immediacy of suffering—as suffering was once immediate for the articulator of the memory of suffering.

One difficulty in confronting the memory of suffering is that it can become strategically frozen in time. This keeps memory alive *and* off-limits to criticism. Keeping the memory of suffering alive and immediate as it recedes into the past necessarily means an ordering to preserve that memory. Often this means militarizing memory as well.

In this transposition, the victims of suffering become martyrs, who in turn become symbols. Finally, the victims/martyrs/symbols become mobilized. The transposition from victims to martyrs to symbols is a journey the victims never experienced themselves. It can only be experienced in their name—for them. Action is taken because of them—in their name.

Yet as soon as the victims become martyrs and action is taken in their name, "Not in Our Name" groups surface. "Not in Our Name" means not in the identity that has formed around the Holocaust dead, where the victims have become martyrs and violence is justified in their names. When the Holocaust and Jewish identity become conflated, unity is demanded even when ethical questions are urgent." When "their" and "our" become so conflated that "their" is "ours" and "our" is "theirs," the unity demanded is also defied.

A civil war breaks out within the community that seeks to separate "their" and "our." In the Jewish case, if "their" and "our" is left without a struggle—for example, the desire to build a fortress Israel over against the Palestinians or the desire for Jews and Palestinians to live in mutual equality—both sides could be seen as coming from the same "their" and the same "our." Looking at Jewish history from either perspective would suffice. If both are seen as ways of being faithful to the memory of suffering, then the Jewish community could applaud both. No negative judgment is rendered. Indeed, only an affirmation of authenticity is issued.[15]

How such diametrically opposed directions can be faithful to the memory of suffering in the Holocaust is hard to reconcile. Although an impasse seems to have been reached—either you are for fortress Israel or for the sharing of Israel-Palestine—in the Jewish community, both directions are seen by their bearers as *the* form of fidelity to the victims/martyrs/symbols of the Holocaust. The memory of suffering is mobilized within each group as the essence of what it means to be Jewish in our time.

At stake is present-day fidelity as a Jew. Still, though this contemporary understanding of fidelity is bitterly contested and fraught, it remains limited. What makes the memory of suffering of such import is that Jewish identity outlives the lives of individual Jews. The mobilization of memory is seen from the vantage point of an ancient history that reaches far into the future.

Because the Holocaust is becoming more distant in time, some Jews fear a cascading effect of the loss of Holocaust memory. If Jews—and non-Jews—lose the memory of the Holocaust, support for the state of Israel might wane. If the Holocaust and Israel are lost, the meaning of that suffering and the need for Jewish empowerment could vanish. Judaism, Jewishness, and Jewish history would be adrift or even lose it reasons for being. The end result—erasure from history. The particular journey of the Jewish people might cease.

The Holocaust functions to preserve Jewish identity in the world. The Holocaust becomes like the Exodus, seemingly in reverse, though perhaps as

15. On the Jewish civil war, see my essay "On the Jewish Civil War and the New Prophetic," *Tikkun* 16 (July/August 2001): 24-27.

the prelude to another (re)creation story of the Jewish people. If we see the Holocaust as slavery in Egypt and the state of Israel as reprising the Promised-Land role in the Bible, then the need for the Holocaust as the center of Jewish identity is understandable.

There are additional aspects to consider. When we think of the inevitable question raised by the Holocaust—Why remain Jewish or raise Jewish children after such suffering?—a thoughtful person might propose bracketing it. Let the Holocaust be. Get on with Jewish life. But since Jews have often been singled out for denigration and abuse, simply forgetting the Holocaust might invite another round of suffering somewhere down the road. While past, the Holocaust could be part of the Jewish future. Are Jews who hold onto the Holocaust as a protective shield wrong about this?

Modernity has likewise taken a toll on Jewish identity. Jews were drawn to modernity as a way out of the religious domination of Christianity and Jewish authority structures. Yet modernity also disdained particularity, especially Jewish particularity. The Holocaust mobilized modern Jews to strengthen their sense of Jewish identity within modern life.

An added advantage of the Holocaust is that it did not demand an allegiance to God, who modern Jews, under the sway of an Enlightenment worldview, had difficulty believing in anyway. Jews could have it both ways. They could retain their Jewish identity within modern culture while adhering to the Enlightenment's secular principle. Jews could be thoroughly modern and maintain their difference.

Here, the function of Holocaust memory becomes clear and urgent. In a situation where the Jewish people and their identity are under assault from the Holocaust and modernity, the desire and ability to carry Jewish identity into the future is at stake. An event of such horrific magnitude becomes the identifying characteristic of Jews for Jews and for others.[16]

Is Holocaust consciousness like the decision to go forth from Egypt as a people against great odds? In both cases, the memory of suffering is essential. In both cases, a future beyond suffering is hope. This may be why the Promised Land and the present-day state of Israel are seen primarily as dreams rather than as practical realities to be encountered. This may also be why the reality of the Promised Land is less remembered than the dream, even though the reality was and is defining in the Jewish journey.

---

16. The Holocaust and then Israel gave Jewish identity a new lease on life. The question now is whether that lease is coming to an end and, if so, what might replace it. The fear is that there might be nothing left of Jewish identity when the current identity formation comes to an end. Thus the oppressive force used to retain the present identity configuration.

Adding together the difficulty of maintaining and mobilizing the Jewish community to continue as a community after the Holocaust is a major reason that Israel remains a dream for most Jews. But since Jews know quite well that dream and nightmare are closely related, the anxiety surrounding Israel is heightened. In Jewish history, the transposition of dream into nightmare is obvious, even primal. If Israel has become a disaster, where is the Jewish safe haven?

With all that is at stake those who speak and write critically about the reality of Israel on the ground take their chances. Are they simply breaking with the normative pattern of Jewishness that surrounds them? Or, by invoking the prophetic, are they also replicating another "essence" pattern of Jewish history? The prophetic pattern seizes the reality of the Promised Land and throws it into the face of a sinful Israel. Today sinful Israel means Jews who, having escaped from Egypt/Holocaust, reconstitute Egypt/ethnic cleansing.

Colonialism within Jewish Identity

Most Jews see the Holocaust and Israel as primarily involving a struggle for Jewish history and identity. The Palestinians, the surrounding Arab states, Europe, and even the United States are considered ancillary players in a Jewish drama. What is highlighted or downplayed by Jews depends on the Jewish need for character interaction, movement, and resolution.

These players in the Jewish drama are Other. Whether they are spoken for or their voice is heard in Jewish circles, it is heard through a Jewish prism. On the one hand, the less the Other speaks, the easier it is for their silence to be manipulated. On the other hand, the more the Other speaks, the easier it is for the Jewishness of the drama to be emphasized.

In the Jewish drama, for example, Palestinians are often portrayed as simple peasants led by uncivilized ruffians. They can also be portrayed as articulately insistent on their rights over against Jewish rights. The simple Palestinian peasants are used to recall a medieval scenario where the overlords own the estate. The serfs are unhappy about their plight in life. The more sophisticated who articulate Palestinian rights are used to sound another, more ominous alarm. They are portrayed as inheritors of Hitler's mantle.[17]

---

17. Indeed, the latest addition to Holocaust literature is exploration—with political purposes in mind—of the Arab-Nazi alliance during World War II. See Edwin Black, *The Farhud: Roots of the Arab-Nazi Alliance in the Holocaust* (Washington, DC: Dialog Books, 2010).

One way of breaking through the impasse in Jewish life is to mediate between those who believe that the Holocaust mandates power for Jews over against others and those who believe the Holocaust mandates solidarity with suffering others. This raises a series of complex issues. The most obvious issue is whether Jews can only be empowered by themselves or whether Jews can achieve an interdependent empowerment with others. Another issue is whether it is possible for Jews to be empowered and to be in solidarity at the same time. Interestingly enough, the opportunity to combine empowerment *and* solidarity is jointly affirmed by the Jewish establishment and Jewish dissenters on every issue except Palestinians. Or perhaps it is the same for both and depends on how Jewish power is exercised and the situation of the Palestinians is viewed.

In public discourse, at least, few if any Jewish spokespersons plot openly against the Palestinians simply because they are Palestinians. Destructive policies against Palestinians are most often couched in a defensive posture, as in "Israel is reluctant to employ force and does so only when Israel's territorial integrity is challenged." This implies that the wars that Israel is "forced" to engage in would stop if the Palestinian and Arab world would end their refusal to recognize Israel as a Jewish state. The most recent example of Israel being "forced" into war was the 2008 invasion of Gaza. After the war, the question of force was played out in the highly contentious United Nations-authorized Goldstone Report. The war talk over Iran carries many of the same signifiers.[18]

Although it is easy to find agreement in theory on the "Israel-being-forced" scenario, the fact is that the Arab world as a whole has been unable to challenge Israel militarily in decades. The most recent challenge came by way of Hezbollah in Lebanon in 2006. Depending on one's analysis, the Arab world has been incapable of significantly challenging Israel militarily since the 1973 war or even earlier.

The greater challenge is the legitimacy of a Jewish state constructed on what was Palestine. Although significantly modified in the last decades, the lack of Palestinian and Arab recognition of Israel as a Jewish state has been strong. Yet everyone knows this is almost exclusively symbolic. When Palestinians and Arab states recognize the state of Israel, as the Palestinians have done, it never seems enough. Their recognition is treated as a ruse if not an outright lie. The reverse, Israel's recognition of the Palestinians as a people and a state, is rarely discussed.

The space the state of Israel carved out for itself is recognized within the international nation-state system. If anything, Israel has lost much of its

---

18. For a take on the Goldstone report, see *The Goldstone Report: The Legacy of the Landmark Investigation of the Gaza Conflict*, ed. Adam Horowitz (New York: Nation Books, 2011).

international status precisely because of its policies toward the Palestinians. Israel's continuing expansion into Palestinian territory, coupled with the building of the Wall within the West Bank, has raised further questions about Israel's intentions. Israel refuses either to grant Palestinians a real state or absorb and integrate Palestinians into the fabric of Israeli life as full and equal citizens. Because of these actions, Israel has become an international pariah including during the 2013-2014 American-brokered peace process.[19]

Israel and the world have been moving in different directions. Since Israel's founding, the world has moved toward an understanding of citizenship without regard to ethnic, racial, or religious backgrounds. To a great degree, the world has adopted the Enlightenment understanding of equal rights and responsibilities within recognized national bodies. This is coupled with international agreements that restrict the rights of powerful nations and the monitoring of these agreements by international bodies established to enforce international law.

The state of Israel is the home for an ingathered Jewish population. Yet its policies of occupying the Palestinian people are at odds with global public opinion and international law. Israel is unfazed. Often Israel caricatures international law as a conspiracy against the state of Israel and, by logical extension, against the Jewish people. This places those who trumpet international law in the category of antisemitism.

Israel is increasingly seen as an international outlaw and as a colonial outpost in the third world. While colonialism in terms of physical settlement on the land of others has been repudiated by the global community, economic and cultural neocolonialism is alive and well. Thus Israel's physical occupation of the Palestinians is passé. World War II saw the final death knell for geographic colonial empires. This is precisely when Israel came into being.[20]

From the beginning of the state of Israel, Jews fought against the idea that Israel was the last gasp of Western colonialism. Because of the situation of Jews after the Holocaust and because of the long sojourn within an antisemitic Europe, Jews were granted a Jewish state as recompense for that suffering. Most Jews saw Israel in these terms as well. Rather than the biblical understanding of return, Jewish travails in Europe were most often cited for the creation of a

19. Topics involving Israel as a pariah nation can be found in Virginia Tilley, ed., *Beyond Occupation: Apartheid, Colonialism and International Law in the Occupied Palestinian Territories* (London: Pluto, 2012). On the challenge to integrate Jews and Palestinians see Ali Abunimah, *The Battle for Justice in Palestine* (Chicago: Haymarkey Books, 2014).

20. On Israel's colonial mentality from a Palestinian perspective, see Nur Masalha, *The Palestine Nakba: Decolonising History, Narrating the Subaltern, Reclaiming Memory* (London: Zed, 2012).

Jewish state in the Middle East. Since the state of Israel was settled by European Jews and its political discourse and politicians came from Europe, this appeal to European history was understandable.

Outside the European sphere, the founding of Israel looked different, especially after Israel's expansion after the 1967 war. From a non-European perspective, Jews that were settling, developing and expanding a state were first and foremost Europeans. Moreover, they had the backing of the European powers and the United States. A clash was inevitable. Coming from their suffering in Europe, Jews saw themselves as entitled to their own state. Much of the third world came to see Israel as the latest European colonial adventure. The third world could hardly accept this new colonialism when they were struggling and overturning the last vestiges of colonialism in their own countries.

From the perspective of the third world, colonialism is written all over the state of Israel. If Israel is, among other things, a colonial state, is colonialism within Jewish identity itself? From the perspective of the Palestinians and the surrounding Arab nations, Israel is clearly a form of colonialism. Does that mean that what looks to others like a colonial project is a colonial project-only?

Few Jews see it this way and even Jews of Conscience have diverse views on Israel as a colonial state-only. Yet it might be important to think through these ideas that come from outside. Whatever the Jewish community ultimately does with ideas that come from outside, another perspective can be instructive. It may illumine the ideas that others have, or at a minimum, force Jews to look more deeply within and find alternative explanations.

Here the question deepens. It might be that the colonialism charged from outside is also found within the state of Israel and Jewish identity itself. If colonialism or, as well, a colonial mentality, is within the state of Israel and Jewish identity, it could be a modern post-Holocaust phenomenon. Or the colonial mentality may have been there from the beginning of the people Israel. Is a colonial mentality, hence a colonial identity, part of the essence of what it means to be Jewish?

There are colonial identities in communities throughout the world. If Jews find an ancient or modern colonialism within Jewish life, how is it to be rooted out? On the one hand, if Jews are deeply tied to a colonial mentality as Jews and in their projects like the state of Israel, then Jews have to wrestle with the possibility that rejecting that mentality necessitates a distancing from and perhaps even the abandonment of the state of Israel, Judaism, and even Jewishness itself. On the other hand, if a colonial mentality or colonialism is essential to the survival of the state of Israel, Judaism, and Jewishness, should

Jews be expected to give up their identity, sense of community, and state for the greater good of Palestinians or humanity in general?

If Jewish identity is marked by a colonial mentality, this hardly means that other identities, religions, and states are free of colonial markers. If other identities are found to harbor these same elements, should they voluntarily undertake or be forced to cease what helps make them who they are?

In its own worldview, modernity and thus secularism is free of colonialism and the identity formations that come with it. Unfortunately, the reality is more complicated. In terms of power and reach, modernity may be the most powerful and expansionist, thus colonial, ideological formation in the history of the world. In this view, modernity functions as a politics with its own eschatology. Perhaps modernity is the colonial religion *par excellence.*

Every entity and identity endowed with power has a colonial sensibility lurking within it. Any entity and identity that exists over time has a variety of elements within it. Being on the winning and losing sides of different struggles and societies, as all long standing entities and identities have been, means incorporating, assimilating, and rejecting elements of diverse cultures, politics, and religions. For example, Christianity and Islam are latecomers to monotheism. As global enterprises, both are obvious examples of religious communities that carry elements of religions and cultures they have come into contact with. Could it be any different for Jews and Judaism?

5

Thinking Israel's (and Palestine's) Anniversary

During the sixtieth anniversary of the birth of the state of Israel in 2008, 1948 was in the air in ways that it had rarely been before. Rather than celebration, soul searching was the order of the day. Looking back was a way of looking ahead. What was the future of a land where, after sixty years of struggle, violence, and injustice, Jews and Palestinians still live side by side?

Only five years later, for Israel's sixty-fifth anniversary, the voices on both sides were muted. Little had moved. Doom was on the horizon. As we move toward Israel's seventieth anniversary, less and less is expected. The latest peace process notwithstanding, few believe a just alternative to the present impasse will be come to be. If anything rhetorical movement disguises what is on the Israeli-Palestinian negotiating table. A truncated and humiliating autonomy is proposed for Palestinians. Even so, Israel demands more and more.

Nonetheless, recalling and analyzing the sixtieth anniversary, where arguments were loud and insistent from all sides, is important. Sometimes, Jews were far apart from each other; sometimes they stood as one. Sometimes Jews and Palestinians were divided; other times they joined together. Jews and Palestinians were on opposing teams. They were also in the same camp. What does this bode for the future?

The sixtieth anniversary of Israel was also the sixtieth anniversary of the Palestinian Nakba, their catastrophe. There was more writing about the Palestinian catastrophe in the European and American press than ever before. The Holocaust/Israel sensibility, so deep within the West, was publically challenged. More of the public began to see the formative events of Holocaust and Israel related to the Palestinian Nakba.

Anniversaries are important. They are a time to take stock. Israel and Palestine's sixtieth anniversaries showed movement but were also contentious. The Holocaust/Israel fault line became more inclusive of Palestinians, even as the oppression of Palestinians continued apace. For Palestinians, as well as for some Jews, the issue was the needed movement beyond rhetorical acknowledgment of mutual anniversaries. Unfortunately, when the celebration and lamentations were over, the movement on the ground was backward. It set the stage for the decade to follow. Will Israel/Palestine look better or worse on their seventieth anniversaries?

Israel's sixtieth. The Palestinians' sixtieth. A contentious time. Boundaries were marked. Boundaries were crossed. Jews and Palestinians stood on both sides of the empire divide. Separated. Together.

Obviously, Jews and Palestinians are separated in their full identity. But when Jews and Palestinians come together, who are they? What and who do they represent? In solidarity they remain Jewish and Palestinian. Or perhaps a new identity is forming, albeit for now without a proper name.

If a new identity is formed, what happens to their background histories? Coming together, Jewish and Palestinian history may fade from view, or each history may become accentuated. Coming together could serve as a launching pad for future boundary crossing or hinder further movement toward a joint identity. Do Jews and Palestinians bonding together become remnants of their own communities or simply become a new remnant community? In the crossing of boundaries, is either community enhanced or are both communities abandoned?

THE STATE OF ISRAEL AND THE NAKBA: TWO VIEWS

Two takes on the state of Israel and the Palestinian catastrophe during the sixtieth anniversary provide a snapshot of the discussion Jews and Palestinians had as their crisis crystallized sixty years earlier. In many ways, what happened then remains today. The first snapshot of Israel at sixty is from Akiva Eldar, a dovish Israeli Jew who was then the chief political columnist for *Haaretz*, a leading liberal newspaper in Israel. The other is from Souad Dajani, an American of Palestinian descent who holds a PhD in Sociology from the University of Toronto and has researched and written extensively on the Israeli-Palestinian conflict. When exploring part of her Arab roots in Lebanon in the early 1980s, Dajani had to flee the Israeli bombardment of Beirut. Since that moment, she has been an activist for the Palestinian cause.

The catalyzing event for Eldar and Dajani's dialogue was President Bush's meeting with Palestinian President Mahmoud Abbas. Here we have a Jewish critique of President Bush from the perspective of justice for Jews and

Palestinians met with a harsh rebuke from a Palestinian who has heard the "peace" argument form Jews too many times.

Akiva Eldar writes:

> If Bush cared about Israel remaining a Jewish country, he would not have let Abbas leave the White House last month bruised and battered. The Palestinian president told him that when the Palestinian delegates to the talks saw the Israeli positions, they thought Ehud Olmert and Tzipi Livni were playing a joke on them. In addition to all of the "settlement clusters," including, of course, the territorial "fingers" of Ariel, Ma'aleh Adumin and Givat Ze'ev, the Israelis demanded to remain in control of the entire Jordan Valley, almost to the outskirts of Nablus, while leaving intact all of the Jewish settlements in that area—all in all, some 600 square kilometers, amounting to about 10 percent of the territories. Israel also demanded that all of Jerusalem, including the Holy Basin surrounding the Old City and the Old City itself, would remain under Israeli sovereignty; Palestine would be given control only over the Temple Mount, which is held by the Muslim Waqf authorities in any case; not a single refugee would be allowed back under a Palestinian right of return, and Israel would not acknowledge any responsibility for the fate of the 1948 refugees.[1]

Souad Dajani responds:

> On the surface this sounds interesting and thought-provoking, and not likely an opinion you'd read about in the mainstream US media. But we've been so thoroughly indoctrinated in this country to champion the "right of Israel to exist" as a racist entitled Jewish state on the backs of those it deliberately dispossessed, that most people are not likely to challenge the premises of the piece below. . .
>
> The piece is misleading at other levels as well—as disastrous as Bush and Olmert may be as individuals, the situation is institutionalized to the point that all US presidents and Israeli leaders essentially subscribe to the same policy: The US will never impose any peace agreement

1. Akiva Eldar, "Bush Should Stay Home," *Haaretz*, May 13, 2008.

on Israel that the latter doesn't favor, and—if I recall correctly the words of former Israel PM Sharon, "We control America."[2]

Eldar demands the end of the Israeli occupation of East Jerusalem and the West Bank, and insists that Gaza should be freed from the state of siege under which it lives. In both cases, Israel is the transgressor and must act to reverse its own policies. He counters most Jewish perceptions that Israel is ready to trade territory for peace. Rather, he realizes that the Israeli offer and American inaction amount to acquiescence in a permanent occupation of all Palestine. This means Israeli control from Tel Aviv to the Jordan River with millions of Palestinians remaining in between.

The liberal minority in Israel lauds Eldar for his strong and well-intentioned rebukes, as he argues a political point from an ethical perspective. Other, more conservative Israelis criticize him for mimicking the arguments that Israel's adversaries put forth. Within the Israeli political landscape, Eldar's public stands against Israel's policies toward the Palestinians are controversial and often unpopular.

Nonetheless, Dajani dismisses Eldar's mission to save the Jewish soul, saying the time for that is long past. Instead, she finds him misguided, perhaps even purposefully deceiving his audience, and questions his intentions. She asks indignantly whether anywhere else in the world besides Israel would he or other Jews make the same arguments about a similar political situation.

Even more boldly, Dajani claims that Eldar's argument is racist, since he remains committed to a separation of Jews and Palestinians, even as he argues for a certain level of justice. Moreover, her charge that Israel is a "racist entitled Jewish state" is limited neither to its occupation of parts of Jerusalem and the West Bank nor to its treatment of Palestinians in Gaza. She argues that Israel within its 1967 borders is racist, as is Eldar's presumption that Israel's withdrawal from part of what is left of Palestine would absolve Israel of further decisions. As long as Israel dominates Palestine in historic Palestine, Israel remains what she believes Israel to be: racist—and racism is racism, no matter who suffers from it and who presides over it. Dajani asks how long Eldar and other Jews can maintain this racist position.

Eldar refuses to go there. Although he mentions the Palestinian refugees, he does so without a political nomenclature. Eldar believes that the Palestinian refugees need a place of their own to live. Part of saving the Jewish soul demands that Israel must recognize its responsibility for the origin of their

---

2. Souad Dajani, e-mail commentary on "Bush Should Stay Home," May 13, 2008.

plight in 1948. For Eldar, however, the solution for the entire Palestinian plight is bound up in the birth of a truncated Palestinian state in East Jerusalem, Gaza, and the West Bank. The refugees who live outside of Palestine should be free to "return" there, even if they were originally from inside what today is Israel. Eldar argues that only Israel's partner, America, has the power to force Israel to another vision of justice.

For Dajani, Eldar's offer is too little, too late. Moreover, Dajani believes that the United States has little interest in pursuing what Palestinians need and deserve. For Dajani, international law demands a Palestinian state and the return of the 1948 refugees to their home within Israel. What's more, she argues that Israel's origins and life since its birth are riddled with apartheid. Whatever the borders and rhetoric of the state of Israel, Israeli "apartheid" is the order of the day, and this apartheid state is run by Jews. Only through the dismantling of the Jewish character of Israel can the Jewish soul be saved.

In *Lords of the Land*, published a year before Israel's sixtieth anniversary, Eldar and his co-author, Idith Zertal, confirmed Dajani's understandings of the limitations of his analysis:

Four decades have passed since the 1967 war, after which Jewish citizens of Israel began to settle beyond the border of their state in contravention of International Law, which prohibits an occupying state from transferring population into occupied territory. For approximately two-thirds of its history, Israel has been an occupying state. The State of Israel has been free of the malignancy of occupation for only nineteen of the first fifty-nine years of its existence. The vast majority of Israel's inhabitants do not know any other reality. The vast majority of the four million Palestinians who live under occupation do not know any other reality. The prolonged military occupation and the Jewish settlements that are perpetuating it have toppled Israeli governments and brought Israel's democracy to the brink of an abyss. They have transformed the very foundations of Israeli society, economy, army, history, language, moral profile, and international standing. A state that emerged out of the catastrophe of European Jewry, and from it drew the legitimacy for the means of its establishment and for the very fact of its existence, is being crushed from within and is increasingly the subject of bitter controversy abroad because of the settlements.[3]

Eldar and Zertal paint their picture of Israel with broad but insistent strokes, surfacing Israel's fundamental challenges without embellishment. They believe as well that these challenges have been with Israel since its founding, but now have reached a breaking point. Looking beyond Israel's sixtieth anniversary, they are pessimistic. "On the brink of an abyss," "Being crushed within"—this is hardly celebratory prose.

Depending on one's perspective, Dajani is either far ahead of Eldar or far behind him. Calling Israel an inherently racist state is a heady charge. Calling for the dismantling of Israel as a Jewish state raises fears of another Holocaust. To some, denying a special home for Jews in their own state is itself a form of racism.

Dajani is unimpressed by such arguments. She has heard enough about Jews, the Jewish soul, and the Jewish ethical tradition. For many years, Jews on the left have been calling for Israel's withdrawal from parts of Jerusalem and the West Bank. They have also been musing about the Jewish soul and how the occupation of Palestinians first and foremost damages Jews. The damage is twofold. First, there is the damage done to Jews who actually carry out the policies of occupation. Occupying another people encourages even worse behavior in the occupier, which is then brought home. Then there is the damage that occupying another people does to the Jewish ethical tradition. How can Jews claim to be different from other nations when, like other nations, they control subject populations for their material benefit?

Dajani finds the Jewish argument circuitous and one-sided. Because of the Holocaust, Jews need to be secure in their own state. Palestinians have to be removed from their land to satisfy this Jewish need. Palestinians cannot bemoan their removal as a catastrophe. Instead, Palestinians have to accept their dislocation as warranted by Jewish history and then provide guarantees for Israel's security. Palestinians must argue their own needs within the already tilted Jewish argument. Once inside the Jewish line of reasoning, there is little leeway for others.

Dajani starts from another, Palestinian place, which she recognizes as self-sufficient. Within the Palestinian frame, the Jewish argument looks weak and self-justifying. The security guarantees that Palestinians provide Jews never prove enough for Israel, anyway. Meanwhile, Israel continues to expand. Palestine continues to contract. Well-meaning Jews lament the loss of the Jewish ethical tradition, even as almost all Israeli intellectuals, including Eldar, serve in the Israeli army. Therefore, those who lament the loss of the Jewish

---

3. Idith Zental and Akiva Eldar, *Lords of the Land: The War Over Israel's Settlements in the Occupied Territories, 1967-2007* (New York: Nation Books, 2009).

ethical character are involved in acts that further diminish Palestine. The ultimate irony is to hear Jewish pleas for security and recognition as Palestinians continue to suffer. In the end, who has and who is need of security? Dajani wonders whether Israel has made Jews safer or placed them in greater danger.

For Dajani, the dispossession of Palestinians is a crime. It matters little who committed the crime, Jews or others. Racism is racism, a crime is a crime. Israel has created an abyss for Palestinians that they have been forced to live within. For Palestinians, Israel has never been a democracy. Remaining a Jewish state highlights Israel as an ethnocracy.

Dajani affirms that the Holocaust occurred. It also gave birth to the Nakba. In Dajani's view, the Jewish catastrophe does not justify the establishment of Israel on Palestinian land. If Israel's soul is being crushed from within, it has less to do with the latest post-1967 settlements than with the settlement project that gave birth to Israel itself.

Dajani minces few words. She turns a deaf ear to the notion of a biblical Promised Land, a Jewish return to Zion, or even the Holocaust as mandating Jewish empowerment. Holocaust musings do not impress her. Israel is a racist ethnocracy and a settler state, pure and simple. No matter how sophisticated his arguments, Eldar cannot argue his way out of Israel's contradictions. The contradictions were there from the beginning. They will remain until the state of Israel as a Jewish state ceases to exist.

What are Jews to do with this discussion? Clearly, there is a need to hear both sides of the argument. Since both sides seek what is good and right from their own perspective, listening to these differing views without pejorative judgments is important.

Those who do listen hope for common ground to emerge, if only so some kind of ordinary life can resume, or be established, for Jews and Palestinians. Yet in the West, Jews and non-Jews find Dajani's ideas difficult to listen to without hearing them as antisemitic. For Dajani, this difficulty testifies to the colonialism and racism of the West and of Jews who live there. They are so accustomed to hearing their voice as the only voice that the maligned Other, the Palestinians, is perceived as a menace, threatening everything good and right in the world.

Both Eldar and Dajani seek justice. Despite their differences, they are on the same side. Or are they? Considering that some others in the arena, right-wing settlers and Land-of-Israel politicians on the Israeli side, and on the other side ideologues and politicians who want to recreate a Palestine free of Jews on all of the land that once comprised Palestine, Eldar's and Dajani's differences are less stark than they might think. Is that the case?

For many Jews on the "same side," Dajani's right stuff forces Jews to a place that is forbidden. For many Palestinians like Dajani, Eldar is just marking time and believe that his unstated intention is to make their initial dispossession permanent. Thus, she argues for a reversal of the Israel that came into being. Eldar cautions against this, asserting that any questioning of Israel as a legitimate, Jewish state is beyond the pale. Jews in their anguish and hope may even recognize these questions as legitimate, but to accept them as politically achievable goals is to envision the end of the Jewish state and its culture. Carried to an extreme, it might mean the end of Jews in historic Palestine.

Dajani thinks the continuation of Israel as a Jewish state is unthinkable. There is no room in the international system for ethnocracies. Ethnocracies are inherently racist. They dispossess and oppress as a matter of right.

For Eldar, the end of the Jewish state is unthinkable. Where would Jewish Israelis exist if not within the state of Israel? For Eldar, Israel as a Jewish state, at least within its internationally recognized borders, is a democracy. It is the extension of that democracy into East Jerusalem, the West Bank, and Gaza that is the threat to the flourishing of a Jewish Israel.

ZOCHROT: JEWS REMEMBERING THE NAKBA WITH COMPASSION

Another reflection on Israel's sixtieth comes from Alice Rothchild, a physician, and co-chairwoman of Jewish Voice for Peace in Boston. In her previous writings, Rothchild focused on the trauma and resilience of both Israelis and Palestinians as they struggle for freedom and justice. In an op-ed published in the *Baltimore Sun*, Rothchild reflects on what she calls "the other side of Israel's birth."[4]

Rothchild begins her essay by citing a series of anniversaries with which America was "obsessed" during 2008: the fifth year of the Iraq war, the fortieth anniversary of the King assassination, and the sixtieth anniversary of the birth of Israel. Rothchild believes that anniversaries are important as markers since "each such marker shapes our understanding of history, framing how a story is to be told and how it is to be remembered." Nonetheless, she is struck by an anniversary that is not as much in the news: the other side of Israeli independence, the Palestinian catastrophe.

4. Alice Rothchild's reflection, "The Other Side of Israel's Birth," was published in the Baltimore *Sun*, May 14, 2008. She is the author of *Broken Promises, Broken Dreams: Stories of Jewish and Palestinian Trauma and Resilience* (London: Pluto, 2007) and the director of the 2013 documentary "Voices Across the Divide."

Rothchild continues by describing a recent tour with Eitan Bronstein, an Israeli who directs the Israeli organization Zochrot, and Mohammad Jaradat, a Palestinian and co-founder of a Palestinian advocacy group, Badil. *Zochrot* is the Hebrew word for "remembering." The group's mission it is to help educate Israelis about the more than 700,000 Palestinians who were expelled during Israel's birth. Zochrot documents the locations of more than 450 destroyed Palestinian villages by interviewing and photographing Palestinians living in Israel and surrounding refugee camps. In doing so, Zochrot "creates a living human memory that encompasses the other side of history."[5]

Badil, which in Arabic means "alternative," researches and advocates for Palestinian residency and refugee rights. Badil is part of a Palestinian movement for civil society, a movement that Rothchild believes is largely unknown in America. They also advocate for the Palestinian refugees' right of return to Palestine, which includes areas that are now part of Israel. Badil is quite insistent and detailed about this right and the possibility of carrying out a real return of the refugees. For Badil, the Palestinian right of return is far from a theoretical construct. Palestinians can and will return to the homes from which they were displaced. It is only a matter of time.[6]

Listening to Bronstein and Jaradat, Rothchild is struck by how memory shapes our understanding of history and how "dangerous it is to blind ourselves to the realities of the past." Noting the importance of memory, Jews have shaped the memory of the Holocaust. Through their shaping of Holocaust memory, Jews honor the victims of the Holocaust and justify the behavior of its survivors. Jewish remembering has created a "story in which we Jews are all at some level survivors, claiming Israel's victories as our own."

Holocaust memory has also shaped the narrative of indigenous Arab resistance to a Jewish state so that "acknowledgment of the human suffering that was a consequence of Israeli military victory and political policy" is seen by Palestinians as a "personal as well as a political threat." Bronstein asserts that the way Jews remember Israel's birth reinforces Israel's failure to recognize its responsibility for Palestinian dispossession. The result is that this important part of Israeli history is rendered "invisible," at least to Jews.

Bronstein believes that embracing this "invisible" history is the first step toward acknowledging Palestinians as fellow human beings. It is the only way to begin a process that leads to a permanent reconciliation between the two peoples. Unfortunately, the decision in the first years of Israel's existence to prevent Palestinians from returning to their ancestral homes—a policy that

5. Information on Zochrot can be found on its website, http://www.zochrot.org/en.
6. Information on Badil can be found on its website, http://www.badil.org.

continues today—was a political decision that promotes a constant state of friction and war between Israel and its neighbors.

As Jews and Palestinians express little hope for a just and peaceful future, Rothchild thinks that Bronstein "offers us a path where Israelis acknowledge the price of their victory and take responsibility for their share of the Palestinian catastrophe." At the same time, she believes that Jaradat is working for the "kinds of civil rights that are enshrined in international and human rights law, reminding us that Palestinians deserve nothing less than we would expect for ourselves." To Rothchild, both share the understanding that "acknowledging the Palestinian refugees' internationally recognized right to return and developing creative solutions—from resettlement to financial compensation—is the foundation of a lasting resolution of the conflict."

Rothchild wonders what would happen if the Palestinian tragedy were to be recognized alongside the Israeli victory. "Perhaps taking the risk of acknowledging the pain of the 'other' and seeing 'the enemy' as a real person is how peace is ultimately made," Rothchild writes. "The dispossession of two-thirds of the Palestinian population in 1948, and the consequences borne by generations of families living in Israel, the occupied territories, refugee camps and the Diaspora, can no longer be hidden." For Rothchild, it is time to "acknowledge that other anniversary and to move forward with eyes and hearts open to the suffering of all the children of Abraham."

"A memory grounded in compassion." For Rothchild, this is a different way from how Holocaust memory has been used of late. Using Bronstein as an example, Rothchild suggests that he is reviving the other side of history as a memory Jews can carry forward. The question is whether that openness, surely an advance, or better, a recovery, is enough. Indeed, given the cycle of violence and atrocity that is in place and continuing, what, in fact, is enough? If it is a question of redress for those who died in the Nakba during Israel's birth and after, whether of actual violence, natural causes, or heartbreak, how does memory address their lives? For the heirs of the Nakba, more than remembrance is needed.

With Bronstein, Rothchild posits recognizing the tragedy—with compassion—as a beginning. She does not envision beginning again from scratch, the impossibility of that being obvious. However, Rothchild suggests that the memory of violence and atrocity can be healed through recognizing the violations and, at least, offering "creative" solutions to the history which occasions this memory. But when Rothschild wonders what would happen "if this tragedy, *Al Nakba*, were to be publicly recognized alongside the Israeli victory," does she suggest that Israel's birth and the dispossession of Palestinians be seen as equally compelling events?

Rothchild believes that both sides deserve recognition: Israel is to be affirmed and the plight of the Palestinians is to be redressed. However, that redress can only come within the affirmation of Israel as it is, at least within its pre-1967 borders, precisely the borders that occasioned the Palestinian refugee crisis in the first place. By accepting Israel's "victory," it seems that Palestinians, but also Jews and others, also accept the fact of Palestinian dislocation. Some creative adjustments for resettling some refugees and providing financial and other compensations for the majority of refugees are to be offered. In Rothchild's mutual recognition does Dajani's "racist entitled" Jewish state remains intact?

Rothchild writes that Jews have shaped the memory of the Holocaust. In doing this, Jews honor the Holocaust dead and justify the behavior of its survivors. Jews see themselves as heirs to the Holocaust and claim Israel's victories as their own. However, this memory identity forces indigenous Arab resistance to a Jewish state on the defensive, making it more difficult to acknowledge the human suffering of the Palestinians as anything other than an existential threat.

Rothchild is correct. Jews do see themselves as survivors of the Holocaust and, through Holocaust education in Europe and the United States, many non-Jews see Jews in the same light. As much as Israel's victory needs to be analyzed through a different spectrum, it seems that the "survivor" claim of living Jews also requires a fresh analysis. The great majority of Jews alive today were born well after the end of World War II. This demands that the Jewish claim to be Holocaust survivors or heirs to the Holocaust be challenged as well.

The same can be said of claiming Israel's victory "as our own." The great majority of Jews living in Israel today either were living outside the land during the 1948 war or were born well after, and thus share that victory only through a constructed national consciousness. Rothchild leaves unaddressed how American Jews, again with the great majority being born after 1948 and most never having visited Israel, let alone fought in any of Israel's wars, claim Israel's victory "as our own." Leaving aside Jewish Israeli citizens born after 1948 for a moment, if Jews outside of Israel do make such a claim, what does it mean theoretically and practically? "Sharing" Israel's victory but living in nation-states that do not legally discriminate according to ethnic or religious backgrounds or affiliations seems disingenuous.

When it comes to the Holocaust and Israel, "our" is in danger of becoming so theoretical that the event and the state become imaginative constructs.

Meanwhile, real Israelis and Palestinians are forced to the sidelines, becoming bit players in a larger historical drama. The question, then, is whether Rothchild is reinforcing "our" identification by questioning it in soft tones. Palestinians might want her simply to drop her compassionate listening and decide whether "our" applies, or doesn't. Some Jews of Conscience might demand the same. Rothchild could respond with the question as to who in America would listen to her plea if her tone were more forceful.

Like any community, in the main Jews want it both ways. On the one hand, Jews outside of Israel want to live one way—with others in a pluralist state—and have Israelis live another way—as separate and privileged. On the other hand, Jews want to carve out separateness and privilege in places that Jews live, say in America and Israel, and now, for the first time in two thousand years, Jews have accomplished this and demand its retention in the West and Israel. So, by having the Jewish empire cake and eating it, too, it is possible to remember the original sin of Israel's birth without pursuing its political implications. This might be the original sin of Progressive Jews: in acknowledging the Palestinian demand to remember, Jews may hold on to their victory and feel better about it.

Journeying together and recognizing the Other sounds good. It certainly beats the denial of the tragedy that befalls the Other when the Other is not recognized. Still, there are many more sides to the compassion Rothchild suggests. Rather than compassion, displaced peoples need justice. Often as not, that justice means denying or overriding the victory that the victors continue to enjoy.

In many cases, the victory of the victor overrides the generations and beyond, even if the victory is no longer claimed. Sometimes a victory ends without anyone wanting to claim it. The victory is too fraught with dislocation and death to be championed any longer. Or those who continue to champion the victory are confined to the fringes of a society that has been transformed. By that time, even those who benefited from the original victory disown the victory as a place for celebration.

The original defeat of the Other becomes the locus of historical analysis, curiosity, and sometimes pride. Although the victor and the defeated live side by side in an integrated and increasingly more equal way, the original victory becomes a place of shame where only irredentist movements tread.

On the sixtieth anniversary of the creation of the state of Israel, this moment was reached by increasing numbers of Jews and non-Jews alike. From the literature that poured out during the anniversary, the dispossession of the Palestinians gained great play, certainly much more than before.

At Israel's fiftieth anniversary in 1998, for example, the celebrations were muted. The political situation was bleak, with the collapse of the 1993 Oslo Accords. Just three years earlier, Prime Minister Rabin had been assassinated by an Orthodox Jewish Israeli. Rather than diminishing, settlement activity in Jerusalem and the West Bank increased. The second Palestinian uprising was on the horizon, beginning just two years later.

Clearly, the political situation was on everyone's mind during Israel's fiftieth anniversary. Even then, mnay Jews could no longer celebrate Israel without affirming the need for some kind of political accommodation with the Palestinians. 1948 appeared in Jewish commentary but, in the main, it was still in the deep background of political and moral discourse. Few commentators spoke of the need for Jews and others to recognize the origins of the political impasse in 1948. That awaited the sixtieth anniversary.

What accounts for this shift from a call for a strictly political accommodation between Israeli and the Palestinians to a call for a reconsideration of the anniversary structure itself? Why the new emphasis on Israel's responsibility for the dispossession of the Palestinians? What accounts for the burgeoning sense that dealing with the 1948 dispossession at its core might bring about a more sane approach to a dysfunctional political solution?

Part of this shift was occasioned by revisionist Israeli historians who documented Israel's culpability in the Palestinian's dispossession in 1948. Another part of this shift was the continuing expansion of Israeli settlements in Jerusalem and the West Bank. The persistent expansion raised the issue of whether Israel would ever to return to its pre-1967 war boundaries. Though still several years away, the construction of the Wall around Palestinians was in its political genesis. The history, violence, and permanence of Israel's expansion also undermined mainstream Jewish discourse regarding Israel and the Palestinians. The discourse of Progressive Jews was on the defensive. It increasingly seemed out of touch with the realities on the ground. On Israel's fiftieth, everything seemed up for grabs.[7]

The passage of time and the seeming intractability of "solving" the Israeli-Palestinian conflict may have forced a deeper reckoning with the origins and history of the conflict. Other issues, like the increasingly distant claim of twenty-first-century Jews to be "survivors" of the Holocaust, may have been at

7. One of those revisionist historians is Benny Morris, whose political trajectory has shifted far to the right. For his early work on revising Israel's history, see his *The Birth of the Palestinian Refugee Problem, 1947-1948* (Cambridge: Cambridge University Press, 1989). Another revisionist historian, Ilan Pappe, continues to extend his critique in *The Idea of Israel: A History of Power and Knowledge* (London: Verso, 2014).

play as well. The passage of time makes the changing perspectives regarding the Holocaust and Israel inevitable.

On Israel's fiftieth, the inherent tension of maintaining a specific Jewish identity in tandem with renderings of the Holocaust and a Jewish state became more urgent and more difficult. In an increasingly interconnected global system of power relations and public opinion, the Jewish claim to innocence was on the ropes.

What was brewing on Israel's fiftieth anniversary became more obvious a decade later. Without a fundamental shift in Jewish sensibilities, the next decades are likely to see further erosions in the ability to make certain Jewish identity claims. That is why the sixty-fifth anniversary was muted. Looking ahead, it is difficult to imagine the fundamental shift Dajani demands.

While Rothchild correctly argues that recognizing the claims of the Other on the victor is a step forward, it is unclear how this step will be realized. Will such recognition be a defensive measure to ensure that Israel's initial victory remains intact? As Rothchild's interlocutor, Dajani suggests that only with a further reckoning may justice one day appear. Stopgaps will hardly do. A further unraveling is needed. One day it will come. For Dajani, that day has already arrived.

Mohamed Jadarat plays a secondary role in Rothchild's analysis. Perhaps this was predictable, considering the audience to whom Rothchild is appealing, or because Jews continue to have the upper hand in describing the options Jews and Israel face. More telling is that even as Rothchild seeks to raise awareness of the Nakba, it is a Jew rather than a Palestinian that narrates the story.

Nonetheless, Jadarat's appearance on tour with Bronstein is instructive. Emphasizing "indigenous resistance to a Jewish state," Jadarat is a radical voice in an American newspaper. That a Palestinian is, as Rothchild puts it, "working for the kinds of civil rights that are enshrined in international and human rights law, reminding us that Palestinians deserve nothing less than we would expect for ourselves," is also to step outside of the usual Israel-and-Palestinians-dialogue framework.

Rothchild accomplishes a great deal in a condensed space. While achieving a two-state solution of the Israeli-Palestinian conflict might delay or end the questioning of Israel's birth, it can also work the other way. To an American audience, the challenge of wanting for Palestinians what we want for ourselves has to do with citizenship and equal rights under the law, without regard to ethnic or religious background. The critical reader applauds Jadarat's sentiments but wonders if he is working fertile ground with the Jewish audience Rothchild is addressing.

Although indigenous Palestinian resistance to a Jewish state could, at least in theory, be restricted to a Palestinian state alongside Israel, Israel's Palestinian population comes into play here. So does the original displacement of Palestinians who reside outside of Israel's borders. Palestinian indigenous resistance to a Jewish state thus ups the ante. It was the very desire for a Jewish state that prompted the ethnic cleansing of Palestine. It is the maintenance of that Jewish state structure that denies Palestinians from having what we would expect for ourselves.

Whatever the agreed-upon framework of their discussion of 1948, Bronstein and Jadarat chart important and subversive terrain. Yet their terrain seems coded. Is this so as not to disclose the full intent of their intended subversion?

Rothchild's framing of the Nakba is important. In Iraq, for example, she clearly views the United States acting like an imperial and colonial power. Absent power and a certain outlook on the world—that is, the U. S. desire to assure its access to Iraq's oil, thus protecting "our" resource in another part of the world—why else would the United States invade Iraq?

Talk of America's misguided imperialism is acceptable discourse to the liberal Jewish American audience Rothchild addresses. So, too, is her reference to Martin Luther King Jr. In most minds, King is associated with the cause of civil rights as a justice and reconciliation movement. King inspires people from diverse ethnic and religious groups to tackle the nightmare of oppression and separation. Thus King counters the nightmare of segregation and injustice with the dream of equality and mutual acceptance.

Yet King was much more than his dream. Before his assassination, King spoke out against the Vietnam War. Over time, King increased his understanding of the communities of color across nation-state boundaries. King's dream of America became more troubled as he began to speak of America as a purveyor of violence, arms dealings, and military interventionism on a global scale.[8]

The catch is whether King's dream and his later, more radical, years would resonate to Rothchild's audience if translated in terms similar to Dajani's. Maybe it is best that Rothchild, like Eldar, trims her sails when it comes to the main issue she addresses. But the question of trimming sails is the cost to those on the other side of power. For Palestinians, Rothchild's trimming her sails may help seal their fate.

8. On the more radical side of King, see Thomas Jackson, *From Civil Rights to Human Rights: Martin Luther King Jr., and the Struggle for Economic Justice* (Philadelphia: University of Pennsylvania Press, 2006).

JEFF HALPER: RETHINKING ISRAELI APARTHEID

Jeff Halper is an American-born Israeli who came to live in Israel in 1973. For many years Halper was a lecturer in anthropology at the University of Haifa and Ben Gurion University as well as director of the Friends World College Middle East Center in Jerusalem. He is now the coordinator of the Israeli Committee Against House Demolitions (ICAHD), an Israeli and international organization that rebuilds homes on the West Bank that have been demolished by Israel. On the occasion of Israel's sixtieth anniversary, Halper wrote an essay that sought to rethink Israel's future. Though somewhat dense at times, Halper's thinking is provocative.[9]

Halper begins with the anniversary itself as the "rise of the Jewish State on the ruins of Palestinian society." Noting this, Halper asks Israelis and Jews everywhere to pause for "sober reflection and reevaluation," rather than celebration. Halper does cite reasons for Israelis to celebrate but his reasons are delivered tongue in cheek. Israel's economy is strong and has some powerful friends from the past and the present, he writes. Yet both are suspect. Though the shekel has become one of the strongest currencies in the world, Israel's economy is "fueled by diamonds, arms, high-tech, security services and tourism."

So why not celebrate Israel's economic and diplomatic success? Although Halper believes there are many reasons not to celebrate the anniversary, most of them exist "beyond the bubble that insulates the Israeli public from its wider reality." Halper continues:

After sixty years, however, several fundamental developments have materialized which were not anticipated by the Zionist movement nor Israel's founding, but which must be squarely acknowledged and addressed. First, the vast majority of Jews did not and will not come to Israel. Israeli Jews represent, if emigrants are factored in, less than a third of the world Jewish community. Only 1% of American Jews ever came, and most of them are religious, even ultra-orthodox Jews, or the elderly, who live there only part-time. The reservoir of potential Jewish immigrants has been exhausted. Second, some 30% of Israel's population—almost 50% if we include the Palestinians of the Occupied Territories who, it seems, will stay permanently

9. Jeff Halper, "Rethinking Israel After Sixty Years," Counterpunch, May 15, 2008. For a further exploration and extension of these ideas see his *War Against the People: Israel, the Palestinians and Global Pacification* (London: Pluto Press, 2014).

under Israeli rule—are not Jews. This is the Demographic Bomb, made even more threatening to a "Jewish state" by the fact that the Palestinians are a people whose national rights can no longer be denied. Israel/Palestine is a bi-national country which somehow must either be partitioned or shared. And finally, the greatest irony of all, it is Israel, by its own hand, through its massive settlement project, that has foreclosed partition and created a thoroughly bi-national entity which can only lead to a one state or apartheid.

Halper alludes to the paradox that Israel's "success" may be part of its demise. Israel is accepted as a successful nation-state, yet, as he details, this success belies Israel's overall failure to create a Jewish state for Jews only. Despite Israel's existence, most Jews choose to remain in the Diaspora, and Israel's non-Jewish Palestinian population, is growing. For all practical purposes, there is already a one-state reality. Since Israel rules this expanded territory with millions of Palestinians within it, Halper claims Israel has become an apartheid state.

Halper believes any celebration of Israel is shadowed by pessimism about the future. Everyone knows that the Israeli-Palestinians situation is, for the most part, unresolved. What has been resolved is quite explosive. Nonetheless, few are thinking of the negative consequences of Israel's victory.

Halper believes Israel's "victory" is already its undoing. "These realities are irrefutable, Halper writes. "They have been exhaustively documented and are plain to anyone with the eyes (and open-mind) to just look. What remains for anyone sincerely looking for justice, peace, security and the well-being of Israel (dare I say of both peoples?) is to unflinchingly face this political equation and rethink the viability and justice of Israel as a Jewish state." For Halper, only then will Israel find a way—"based on reality and the best interests of these two inextricably linked peoples rather than on wishful ideological preferences"—to deal with the facts on the ground as well as the rights, claims, and needs of all who live in Israel/Palestine.

For Halper, this task requires a "fundamental re-conceptualization" of the two-state solution and, with it, the "very possibility of preserving Israel as a Jewish state." However, rethinking demands a political program that can resolvethe Israeli-Palestinian conflict. Halper believes that such a political program is essential to "redeeming Israel," either as a state or as a "national entity" within a wider binational state or regional confederation. Otherwise, the most dramatic development over the last decades, the "disappearance" of the two-state solution, is ignored. Halper is insistent: "Anyone familiar with Israel's massive settlements blocs, its fragmentation of the Palestinian territories and their irreversible incorporation into Israel proper through a maze of Israeli-only highways and other 'facts on the ground,' anyone who has spent an hour in the West Bank, can plainly see that this is true."

Halper writes of the expansion of Israel's "matrix of control" throughout the West Bank. This, coupled with an "absolute" American refusal to place international pressures on Israel to withdraw from Palestinian territory, has, in Halper's opinion, rendered a viable Palestinian state unattainable. Unless this is changed, Halper believes that Israeli and Diaspora Jews will become the "world's new Afrikaners ruling permanently over an impoverished Palestinian mini-state." Halper calls this evolving future a "chilling thought."

In Halper's view, Israel's statesmen think of the future as staying the course. More settlements and increased use of power is the only vision they have. Contravening this understanding, Halper believes that Jews and Palestinians have to think seriously of an alternative future. The two-state solution is foreclosed. A binational apartheid future has already arrived. This future is unjust and, to Halper's mind, unsustainable.

Rethinking begins by recognizing the facts on the ground. This leads Halper to the shocking conclusion that the end of the Jewish state has arrived. Continuing to discuss Israel as a Jewish state is fantasy. Such a state no longer exists. Rethinking likewise means that Jews have to argue for the end of the binational apartheid system. Further, Halper believes that Israel's matrix of control in the West Bank belies the rhetoric of the "peace" process. In Halper's view, Israel's hold on the West Bank is firm and unmovable.[10]

For Halper, rethinking Israel-Palestine is essential. The problem is that most Jewish commentators' "rethinking" has not gone far enough. Like many Israeli politicians, they believe Israel has the mechanism for delaying a political solution and avoiding the predicament of apartheid by maintaining a *de facto* apartheid. As well, a majority of Israelis think it enough simply to assert a two-state solution and support it as a general idea. By doing so, they can then be considered in favor of peace. To the contrary, Halper thinks that most Jewish Israelis, like most Diaspora Jews, "*require* a Palestinian state as a condition for the existence of a Jewish one, the alternative being a bi-national state which is anathema to a Jewish one."

---

10. For Halper's understanding of the matrix of control, see his "The Matrix of Control," *Perspectives*, Media Monitors Network (http://www.mediamonitors.net), January 29, 2001. For a full-length discussion of this subject, see his *Obstacles to Peace: A Reframing of the Palestinian-Israeli Conflict*, 3d ed. (Jerusalem: Palestine Mapping Center, 2005).

Halper believes that is why many Jews, including such "searching and otherwise radical figures" as Noam Chomsky and Uri Avnery, along with the Peace Now, Brit Tzedek, Rabbis Michael Lerner and Arthur Waskow, and members of Rabbis for Human Rights, "cling tenaciously" to the two-state solution and refuse to admit that it is no longer viable as a solution. However, Halper cites a growing number of Jewish organizations that are unable to reconcile Israel's facts on the ground and America's unconditional support for its occupation policies with the possibility of a genuine two-state solution. Although most do not yet embrace a one-state solution, these groups "advocate a kind of holding pattern" until a viable solution emerges.

For Halper, Jewish activists and intellectuals enable Israel's holding pattern to continue. Asserting a peace process, holding out the Zionist dream, having the power and continuing to refer to that dream, Israel continues as if the bottom has yet to fall out. The result is that even Israel's Jewish critics fail to recognize how far Israel has gone to foreclose the two-state solution.

Although Progressive Jews are often labeled by the Jewish establishment in Israel and America as self-hating and treasonous for their "radical" criticism, they have failed to analyze Israel's new reality correctly. Halper believes that even these maligned critics lag far behind the realities on the ground. Israel uses its power to keep the dream alive, all the while pursuing the practical realities that undermine that dream. Progressive Jews keep their dream alive while ignoring the realities which make that dream impossible. The dream and realities with regard to Israel are irreconcilable. Misunderstanding this represents a tragic failure of the Jewish imagination.

Halper suggests this failure comes from an ingrained fear. On the one hand, Israeli power cannot resolve the issues confronting the Jewish future. On the other hand, Jewish critics refuse to acknowledge how deep the problem is. On both sides, Jews have a deep-seated fear of imagining a truly binational reality—a democracy for Jews and Palestinians without regard to ethnic or religious background. Without a Palestinian state, at least in the Jewish imagination, the dream of a Jewish state fails.

Halper is silent about the need for a Jewish state. Nonetheless, he suggests that it is more important for Jews to hold on to the illusion of a Jewish state than to admit it has ceased to exist. Israeli and American Jews can hold on to this false dream only because Israel's power precludes a declaration of the one-state reality. To recognize that Israel controls all of Palestine crosses a line that the Jewish power elite and its critics refuse to cross. Halper sees this as the Jewish red line. Halper interrogates those who hew to this boundary with a series of difficult questions:

Did the Palestinians really flee or did we, the Israeli Jews, drive them out? If almost half the inhabitants of that part of Palestine apportioned by the UN to the Jews in 1947 were Arabs, how could we have turned even that small bit of land into a "Jewish state"? Is Zionism then, truly free of war crimes or did we in fact conduct a deliberate and cruel campaign of ethnic cleansing that went far beyond the borders of partition? In that context, was the occupation of the entire land of Palestine the result of Jordanian miscalculation or, from a perspective of forty years later, was it actually an inevitable "completion" of 1948, as Rabin and many others have said? Can we reconcile a genuine desire for peace with a steady annexation of the Occupied Territories, including almost 250 settlements? Do we prefer a false peace—insulation from attacks even as Palestinian resistance to occupation grows—to territorial concession leading to a *viable* Palestinian state? Can we really expect to "win," to frustrate Palestinian aspirations for freedom in their homeland forever, and if we do, what kind of society will we have, what will our children inherit? Do we have a responsibility towards the Palestinians as the people who dispossessed them of their land, first and foremost the refugees of 1948 and 1967 and the tens of thousands of families whose homes we wantonly demolished?

For Halper, the time is already very late. The red line is increasingly indefensible. On the part of Israeli Jews who claim to speak in the name of world Jewry, Halper asks whether they can expect the Jewish Diaspora to support "an ongoing crime against the Palestinian people that implicates them and, in turn, undermines the moral basis of their community, convictions and faith." The hardest question for Halper is the moral basis of Zionism:

Are we truly the victims, or have we perpetrated a terrible crime for which redemption means coming to terms with what we have done—a task far harder than simply making peace? If Palestinians are understandably preoccupied with throwing of the oppressive Occupation and reclaiming a least a part of their country, their identity and their freedom, shouldn't we Israelis be equally preoccupied with cleansing ourselves of the transgressions that require us to suppress our guilt, shirk our responsibilities and, in the end, fail to reconcile with the Palestinians with whom we are so entangled despite a hundred "generous offers"?

Halper's thought moves in several directions. First, he acknowledges Israel's history of ethnic cleansing in its birth and the decades that followed. If the 1948 war and after is a time of ethnic cleansing, so, too, is the 1967 war and after. Although Israeli Jews ostensibly speak in the name of world Jewry, Halper believes that it is unrealistic and unethical to saddle Diaspora Jewry with this "crime."

In the meantime, Israel cannot win the battle with Palestinians without so distorting the moral basis of Zionism that it becomes a farce. Zionism is now open to ridicule by Jews and non-Jews alike. When Halper raises the question as to whether Israelis are truly the victims or the perpetrators of a terrible crime, he places Israel's political situation in moral and ethical categories.

Halper asks Jews to reflect on the reason the Zionist movement emerged in the first place. Why the desire for a Jewish state? In the dream of Zionism and the state of Israel, why were Palestinians left out? Rendering Palestinians invisible undermined the very moral and ethical thrust of Zionism and Israel from the beginning.

The issues here are important. If there was a moral and ethical thrust, but that is no longer recoverable, is there a way forward? If morality and ethics were lacking from the beginning, and since the situation is as it is now anyway, what can be done?

Pushing Halper's analysis, one wonders if a new moral and ethical base for Israel can be established if morality was absent in the beginning. Or, if there was morality but it was too limited, how can an expanded moral and ethical base be established now?

Halper hopes to chart a way out of the Jewish conundrum. To begin with, Jews can no longer claim the status of victims. That claim functions as a way of shirking Israeli and Jewish responsibilities to Palestinians. It also obscures the fact that Jewish and Palestinian life is "entangled" as Jews live side by side with Palestinians.

The holding pattern has to end. To break out of the holding pattern, Halper believes that Jews need to affirm that the Zionist and Israeli dream is entangled with the ethnic cleansing and contemporary suffering of Palestinians. Only then will Jews decide in practical terms how a moral and ethical base can be established for the future. As Halper views it, "Nothing remains, if we want to salvage a national Jewish/Israeli presence in Palestine/Israel, but to courageously confront what we did in both 1948 and 1967, so as to transform the 60 years into the turning point whereby we finally deal with the presence in our country of another people with equal claims and rights." Halper continues with a hope that is both political and ethical: "And if, in the end, *because of our policies*, a bi-national polity emerges in Israel/Palestine, well, if done in a spirit of mutual recognition and reconciliation, it may in fact represent the original and ultimate aspiration of Zionism: a genuine homecoming of the Jewish nation to the hearth of its civilization." Halper believes that would be a cause for "genuine, unfettered celebration."

Halper charts a Jewish way out. He also fudges. He falls into the same trap as the other Jewish critics of Israel he analyzed. Halper believes that Jews in Israel and the Diaspora must confront the crimes of the state of Israel. If they do, at the end of the day, Israel and its Jewish critics may reclaim the original vision of a Jewish state. This original vision may then be offered in a "spirit of mutual recognition and reconciliation."

By invoking the original vision of a Jewish state, Halper reverts back to a simplistic understanding of the original aspiration of Zionism, as a "genuine homecoming of the Jewish nation to the hearth of its civilization." This, according to Halper, continues to be worth struggling for and winning. Then the celebration—now "unfettered"—can begin.

"Unfettered"—this is out of place, given how Halper's essay unfolds. Followed to the logical conclusion, Halper's thought precludes that kind of celebration. The issue Halper avoids in his conclusion, one that he discussed earlier, makes such a celebration impossible. Halper knows—and writes—that the original vision of Zionism and the Jewish state was complicated and flawed. While it did see the Jewish return as a homecoming, a place for Palestinians in that homecoming was never contemplated. In state Zionism, it was rarely thought about. The place Palestinians did not find in Israel's history was not intended to be found.

What Halper suggests, but is unable to hold to, is that an unfettered celebration is impossible unless Israel's entire enterprise from beginning until the present is abandoned. This is where Halper's logic leads him. This is why his conclusion seems hackneyed. Is Halper reduced to clichés because, in truth, Jews cannot trust themselves finally and irrevocably to cross the red line that he and other dissident Jews invoke?

Halper moves far beyond Rothchild. He names ethnic cleansing and cites 1948 and 1967 as defining moments within Israel's conscious program of removing Palestinians from the land. In the end, though, Halper abandons the political language of reality and reverts to the Zionist dream. Although Halper moves away from this sense of innocence throughout his essay, he retains the desire to reclaim that innocence. Then the "original and ultimate aspiration" of Zionism might reassert itself—which Halper knows is unable to address the situation.

It is difficult to imagine how a Jewish state could have been created without the expulsion of the non-Jewish population living in the land. Whatever Jews imagined when they thought from afar about a recovered Israel, once arrived they knew that a "genuine homecoming" within a state demanded ethnic cleansing in one form or another.

Halper may be strategically throwing "dream" crumbs. They represent a rhetorical flourish for the end of the essay. But the result is that Jews may see the reality of the situation without thinking that the original Zionism dream was malevolent. Or is this Halper's attempt to reclaim what he thought was there in the first place? After all, if Halper didn't believe in the Zionist dream, why did he immigrate to Israel in the first place?[11]

Perhaps because of his personal journey, Halper cannot quite reach the point that his analysis seems to lead him. It may be that there is neither a way back nor a way forward without jettisoning the dream that even Halper cannot dispense with—at least on Israel's sixtieth anniversary. On Israel's anniversary, Halper is restrained. Like many Jewish dissidents, he is incapable of reaching the conclusion his thinking leads to.

Mazin Qumsiyeh: Israel's War Crimes, Nonviolent Resistance

Mazin Qumsiyeh is more like Dajani than Halper. Qumsiyeh was born to a Palestinian Christian family in Shepherds' Field, Bethlehem. For many years, he split his time between the United States and Palestine. In the last years, he returned to Palestine to live where he is active in justice work on behalf of his people. Before returning, Qumsiyeh taught biology at Duke University and Yale University.

Qumsiyeh's writings over the years on sharing the "land of Canaan" are thought-provoking. So, too, are his "Wheels of Justice" tours around the United States, which feature peace activists from diverse backgrounds who travel and live on a bus. During the tours, the participants speak at events and meet with those interested in the Israel-Palestine issue.[12]

11. Halper provides the outlines of his biography in his book, *An Israeli in Palestine: Resisting Dispossession, Redeeming Israel*, 2d ed. (London: Pluto Press, 2010).

For Qumsiyeh, like Dajani, the Nakba is ongoing—and getting worse. There is no solution in sight. The question for Palestinians is what to do in light of this situation. How can Palestinians organize to overcome their worsening plight? What will it take to reverse the horrible situation?

As with Eldar, Qumsiyeh begins with the arrival of President Bush to celebrate Israel's sixtieth anniversary. Obviously, for Qumsiyeh, this is a time to organize against such a celebration and visit. Qumsiyeh lists twenty options for Palestinians in the face of "Zionist Israeli oppression." As he lists these options, one wonders which of these options Jewish Israelis like Jeff Halper can sign on to. From the perspective of the Jewish establishment, most, if not all of these options are antisemitic in tone and character. Is this a fair assessment?

Qumsiyeh's suggests nonviolent uprisings in the post-1967 areas where Israel controls Palestinian territory and in the areas Israel occupied in 1948. His suggestion to wait for the collapse of the "US/Israel empire"—indeed, to hasten it—is provocative. Others of his proposals are whimsical. For example, Qumsiyeh's suggests Palestinians intermarry with Jews as a way of infiltrating Israel by way of citizenship. Below is his checklist of possibilities:

> 1. Collaborate or succumb to the power structures, play along and obey the people in power (e.g. Palestinian police be trained by the CIA and operate to quell Palestinian violent and nonviolent resistance) and hope for whatever handouts the chiefs decide.
> 2. Revive the Palestine Liberation Organization with the original charter to liberate all of Palestine from Zionist colonial rule (democratized PLO).
> 3. Engage in massive nonviolent resistance in the areas occupied in 1967 (3.6 million Palestinians form a base).
> 4. Engage in massive nonviolent resistance in the areas occupied since 1948 (1.5 million Palestinians who are Israeli citizens form a base).
> 5. Start an Intifada/uprising in the areas occupied since 1948 (violent and nonviolent resistance, nonviolent resistance ongoing now can be intensified).
> 6. Start an Intifada/uprising in the areas occupied since 1967 (violent and nonviolent resistance, nonviolent resistance ongoing now can be intensified).

12. Qumsiyeh provides information on this and other of his activities on his website http://qumsiyeh.org.

7. Engage in nonviolent resistance in areas outside of Palestine (300,000 Palestinians in the US, 350,000 in Lebanon, 2 million in Jordan).

8. Engage in resistance outside of Palestine that involves targeting Israeli Zionist companies and interests worldwide by economic sabotage.

9. Engage in targeting individuals that support war crimes and support Zionist control (e.g. Richard Perle, Alan Dershowitz, Israeli leaders etc) with the logic that this creates a cost for engaging in or supporting war crimes and crimes against humanity.

10. Engage in educational campaigns and media campaigns. Lobbying, writing, speaking out etc with the logic of capturing hearts and minds by telling the truth of what colonial Zionism has done.

11. Build alliances with powerful states that could provide protection or support.

12. Wait for the US/Israel empire to collapse of its own weight and idiocies (Israel pushed the US to go to war on Iraq and are now pushing for a conflict with Iran, these are bankrupting the US).

13. Convert to Judaism and claim the right of return as a Jew.

14. Engage in boycotts, divestments, and sanctions which are helpful also in raising awareness about the apartheid nature of Israel.

15. Depend on God's will and His designs for the future.

16. Attack fellow Palestinians you disagree with.

17. Live for the moment, build for your family, forget the collective interest.

18. Intermarry with Israeli Jews and move back to Palestine to live with your spouse and produce lots of children.

19. Convince enough Israeli Jews to abandon Zionism and vote for a post-Zionist state for all its people.

20. Write poems, do music, perform plays and other resistance arts.[13]

Qumsiyeh's strong side is politics and nonviolent struggle. Still, the Palestinian situation requires large doses of satire. Qumsiyeh points to the absurdity of the Palestinian plight as a way of disarming hopelessness. He makes the option of Palestinians assimilating to whatever cultures in which they

13. Mazin Qumsiyeh, "Palestinian Options as the Nakba Turns 60," http://qumsiyeh.org/articlesbyqumsiyeh. Also see his book, *Sharing the Land of Canaan: Human Rights and the Israeli-Palestinian Struggle* (London: Pluto Press, 2007) and *Popular Resistance in Palestine: A History of Hope and Empowerment* (London: Pluto, 2011).

abide seem silly. But he is dead serious when he balances his first point about collaboration with his ninth point about war crimes. Qumsiyeh concludes that his list is suggestive, that there are many options for action, and that the worse sin for Palestinians is to accept their fate as a given:

> Actions will speak louder than words and will shape our destinies in the next 60 years. As Palestinians, now the sacrificial lambs for a supine world community, we can shape our future with choices we make. Silence and collaboration are both complicity in this epic injustice that best epitomizes the 21st century, the injustice of continuing ethnic cleansing/continuing Nakba. Just like Palestinians, those who show backbone and support this noble struggle also have equally varied and contradictory choices. But that is the subject of another discussion. For now, the choice that remains relevant is the one posed by Martin Luther King, Jr.: "Cowardice asks the question—is it safe? Expediency asks the question—is it politic? Vanity asks the question—is it popular? But conscience asks the question—is it right? And there comes a time when one must take a position that is neither safe, nor politic, nor popular; but one must take it because it is right."

Qumsiyeh suggests that the entire American imperial structure has to be challenged. Imbedded in the imperial structure is the America-Israel alliance. He might, and sometimes does, stretch this further by including the leadership of various Arab countries like Saudi Arabia and Egypt. Only a massive and intelligent campaign of nonviolence can break the death-hold of empire. Then the economic and political international system will begin to work for the benefit of the world's population.

Like Rothchild, Qumsiyeh cites Martin Luther King Jr., and the later King at that. But he takes Rothchild's analysis one step further. Qumsiyeh believes that one injustice leads to another. The opposite is true as well. One justice might lead to another justice. Qumsiyeh makes a link beyond Dajani when he writes that the Palestinian cause against Israel is just the beginning of justice movements around the world.

Yet, as it is true on the Jewish side with regard to a positive assessment of Israel, Qumsiyeh believes that Palestinians should regard their movement as real and symbolic. If Palestinians can make inroads against the Israeli empire, it is just a matter of time before others will rise up against their oppressors. So the

Palestinian cause is real. However, the loss of Palestine is symbolic as well. For Qumsiyeh, diminishing Palestine mirrors a global problematic.

Qumsiyeh is unbowed—but the situation would soon become more urgent with Israel's invasion of Gaza just months after the sixtieth anniversary. The colonization process once again erupted in war. The causalities of occupation increased. For Qumisyeh, the Israeli invasion of Gaza, as well as the entire Zionist enterprise, is a war crime. Israelis should be treated as war criminals. To combat war crimes, international courts of justice should be appealed to. But, as well, citizen initiatives, especially boycotts, divestment, and sanctions (BDS), should be pursued. Qumsiyeh is against empire wherever it is. Perhaps this is why he describes himself as a "Bedouin in Cyberspace, a Villager at Home."

Joseph Massad: Uprooting the Palestinian *Judenräte*

Finally, we turn to Joseph Massad, a Jordanian-born Palestinian who teaches modern Arab politics and intellectual history at Columbia University in New York City. Writing on the sixtieth anniversary of the Palestinian catastrophe in the Egyptian newspaper *Al-Ahram*, Massad argues against commemoration of the Nakba. Rather, Palestinians must resist the very notion of the Nakba as a historical event. This is especially important because, for Massad, the Nakba continues today. Palestinians continue to be displaced and cleansed from their land. Thus the historical nature of the Palestinian catastrophe must be resisted. By "resisting" the Nakba, Massad seeks to redefine the Palestinian struggle itself.

For Massad, one of the most difficult issues to understand in the history of Palestine and the Palestinians is the meaning of the Nakba. The Nakba is often portrayed as a discrete event, one that took place and ended in 1948. Massad asks what the political stakes are in classifying the Nakba as a past event, by commemorating it annually, by "bowing before its awesome symbolism," as if it was past. What are the results of making the Nakba a "finite historical episode" that one remembers but must ultimately accept as a given in history? Massad wants to invert and transcend the understanding of the Nakba as a finite historical event.

Although some suggest that Israel should acknowledge and apologize for the dispossession of the Palestinians in 1948, Massad demurs. In this confession scenario, Israel could be forgiven and thus be able to forget its crime, a crime that is ongoing. Instead, Massad suggests that the Nakba as a historical event be left behind. Otherwise, Palestinians will become stuck in historical commemorations. Meanwhile, the situation on the ground continues to deteriorate.

For Massad, the Palestinian catastrophe is much older than sixty years. Thus Massad thinks that making this year the sixtieth anniversary of the Nakba's "life and death is a grave error." The Nakba is "pulsating with life and coursing through history by piling up more calamities upon the Palestinian people." Moreover, the Nakba is a historical epoch that is more than 120 years old and counting.

Massad's narrative of the state of Israel begins much earlier than most. He views the Jewish colonization of Palestine as having started in 1881 when pogroms in Russia reached a peak and Jewish emigration to the United States and Palestine commenced. It has never ended. By back-dating the European Jewish history that gives rise to the Zionist movement, Israel becomes more than a state. Instead, Israel becomes the embodiment of the larger Zionist movement, which is more than twice the age of the state itself.

By extending the origins of the state of Israel back in time, Massad does the same for the beginning of the Palestinian catastrophe. Although much of the world would like to present Palestinians as living in a post-Nakba period, Massad insists that "we live thoroughly in *Nakba* times." For Massad, what Palestinians are doing on Israel's sixtieth anniversary is less an act of commemorating ethnic cleansing than it is an act of witnessing to the ongoing dispossession that continues to destroy Palestine and the Palestinians. "I submit, therefore, that this year is not the 60th anniversary of the *Nakba* at all, but rather one more year of enduring its brutality; that the history of the *Nakba* has never been a history of the past but decidedly a history of the present."[14] Yet Massad futures the Nakba by asserting a continuity of Palestinian suffering from 1881 to the present. That is why Massad feels that commemoration of the Nakba is misplaced. The Nakba did not begin in 1948 nor did it end there.

The extended range and continuity of the Nakba is important. Massad alleges that those who want Israel, Jews, and others to recognize the Nakba as a historical occurrence prepare Palestinians for further disaster. They want Palestinians to accept their dispossession as a permanent reality. Massad warns Palestinians that even well-meaning Jews who see the Nakba as a historical occurrence to be acknowledged are a danger. They position the Palestinians to accept a permanently diminished Palestine. Unfortunately, according to

14. Joseph Massad, "Resisting the Nakba," *Al-Ahram*, May 15, 2008. Also see his *The Persistence of the Palestinian Question: Essays on Zionism and the Palestinians* (London: Routledge, 2004). For his recent understanding of Zionism framed in the spirit of Marx's famous thesis on Feuerbach see "Thesis on Zionism," published in the *Electronic Intifada*, December 9, 2013 http://electronicintifada.net/content/theses-zionism/12982

Massad, this includes much of political leadership in the Palestinian Authority as well.

Massad seeks to extend the historical understanding of the Nakba as an abiding reality for Jews and Palestinians. Consequently, Palestinians should refuse to accept recognition and apology for the Nakba without a commitment to end the ongoing catastrophe the Palestinians face. Otherwise, no matter how confessional, the power remains in the court of those who would conquer Palestine and leave a Palestinian remnant behind. Massad continues with a linguistic exploration:

> THE MEANING OF *NAKBA*: While the *Nakba* has been translated into English as "catastrophe", "disaster", or "calamity", these translations do not fully grasp the active ramifications of its Arabic meanings. The *Nakba* as an act committed by Zionism and its adherents against Palestine and the Palestinians has rendered the Palestinians "*mankubin*". English does not help much in translating *mankubin*, unless we can stretch the language a bit and call Palestinians a catastrophe-d or disaster-ed people. Unlike the Greek catastrophe, which means overturning, or the Latin disaster, which means a calamitous event occurring when the stars are not in the right alignment, the *Nakba* is an act of deliberate destruction, of visiting calamities upon a people, of a well-planned ruining of a country and its inhabitants. The word was coined by the eminent Arab intellectual Constantine Zureik in his August 1948 short book on *The Meaning of the Nakba* that was ongoing as he wrote it, just like it is as I write these lines.

Here Massad enters more deeply into the definitional aspect of the Palestinian catastrophe. By extension, he confronts the importance of naming such a formative event. Interestingly, but certainly not coincidentally, the term *Nakba* as applied to the Palestinian plight is developed in the shadow of the formation of the state of Israel and the Holocaust. During those years, Jews searched for the meaning of the destruction of European Jewry. The issue facing Jews was how to name an event without parallel in history out of which contemporary Jewish life would now be lived. The issue is different for Palestinians. For Massad, naming the Palestinian catastrophe as Nakba is too static. It implies that a disaster has been visited upon the Palestinians without

Israel's active desire and power to keep the disaster in force. As well, the Holocaust is over. The Nakba continues.

The dispossession of Palestinians is hardly a matter of fate. Massad writes that the Nakba is an "act of deliberate destruction, of visiting calamities upon a people, of a well-planned ruining of a country and its inhabitants." Massad's understanding of the history of Israel-Palestine comports with much of the new understandings that Israel historians have developed about 1948. Still, he argues that their grasp should extend the period of destruction backward in time. And forward.

For Massad, the time extension before and after the 1948 period requires a structural extension so that pre- and post-1948 can be viewed as continuous. In doing so, the terminology of the Nakba has to be changed. The Nakba has rendered the Palestinians "*mankubin*"—a catastrophed and disastered people. Palestinian resistance to Zionism, of which the state of Israel is its structured and empowered heir, seeks redress rather than commemoration. Massad believes that since the beginning, Palestinians have resisted the "racist and colonial logic of the Nakba." If Palestinian resistance failed to prevent the expulsion of Palestinians and the "outright theft of their entire country," nonetheless it has succeeded in "overthrowing Zionist official memory."

Massad sees memory as a key component of Palestinian resistance. "When Palestinians insist on naming their country, their cities, and their villages with their original names," Massad writes, "they are not only resisting the vulgar names that Zionism has bestowed on the land, they are also insisting on a geographic memory that Israel has all but succeeded to erase physically." Israel insisted for decades in denying that the Palestinians exist as a people, or as a name. "Zionist cruelty" insisted that the "very name 'Palestinians' should not even be uttered."

Massad judges that, for Israel, "Palestinian" functions as some "magical incantation that could obliterate them at the existential level." Are they wrong in feeling that way? Massad considers "Palestinian" is itself the "strongest form of resistance against their official memory." After all, "'Palestinian' has also been generative of continuities in Palestinian culture, identity, and nationality. Israel had hoped to obliterate all of these completely. Their survival threatens its "mnemonic operation of inventing a fictional memory of non-Palestine, of non-Palestinians."

Palestinian counter-memory directly confronts Israel's achievement of obliterating Palestine as a geographic designation. For Massad, this counter-memory is an affront to Israel's continuing efforts to degrade Palestinians national identity and leave it with a pre-Nakba history. "The survival of the

Palestinians after the Nakba started, and despite its assiduous efforts to efface them, has made the *Nakba* a less than successful Zionist victory," Massad writes, "It is in this context that Israel's insistence on calling Palestinian citizens in Israel 'Israeli Arabs' is designed to silence their Palestinian-ness. Israel's insistence that Palestinian refugees be settled and given the nationality of their host countries is aimed also to erase their name."

These are strong words. Like Dajani and Qumsiyeh, Massad judges Israel and its racist and colonial logic. The fact that the Nakba is ongoing rather than a one-off historical event is testimony to this logic. Zionism's underlying rationale allows Jews to displace Palestinians and rename Palestine in an ongoing and permanent way. By cleansing Palestinians from their land and changing the names of Palestinian towns and villages, Israel desires to erase Palestine's existence. In fact, though catastrophed and disastered, Palestinians retain the memory of Palestine. By retaining the memory of Palestine, Palestinians deny Israel her final and most important victory.

Massad returns to his foundational understanding of Israel's colonial thrust and Palestinian resistance. Israel wants to eliminate Palestine because it is Palestine that haunts Israel at an existential level. "Palestinian" resists this erasure by generating "continuities in Palestinian culture and life, in Palestinian identity and nationality," in and outside Palestine.

Massad sees Palestinian resistance as key. Because of Palestinian resistance, Israel fails in its goal of obliterating the memory of Palestine. Because Palestinians keep the memory of Palestine alive, they are able to maintain their identity. Without that identity, the Palestinian struggle would be lost completely. Massad believes that Palestinian survival, even if outside the land and confined to asserted memory, threatens Israel's "fictional memory."

Massad refers to Zionism and the state of Israel only in its racist and colonial quest to dismember Palestine and disembody Palestinian identity. Massad is mostly silent about Diaspora Jews who may or may not claim to be Zionists but who enable the disembodiment of Palestine and Palestinian memory through uncritical support of Israel. He is likewise silent on those Jews who simply sit on the sidelines hoping for the Palestinians to go away. Nor does he write much about Jews who resist Israeli policies toward Palestinians.

Massad's relative silence about Jews is fascinating. In fact, the memory of Palestine or its disappearance is crucial to Jewish identity, creating an identity parallel of sorts between Jews and Palestinians in and outside of nation-state parameters. Although Israel is a state, Massad sees Palestinians as a community within Palestine and outside of it. Jews see themselves in this way as well, so that today Palestinian identity and Jewish identity are, to some extent, codependent.

After all, the dismemberment or empowerment of Palestine and Palestinian identity deeply affects the future of Jewish identity.

This is beyond the scope of Massad's writing and perhaps his concern. For the most part, Jews are absent from Massad's analysis. When they are mentioned, it is as if Zionists and Israelis purposely embarked on a racist and colonial mission. Fair enough, since Palestinians experience Jews as Zionists and Israelis. However, Massad's sensibility suggests the prospect of a fascinating reversal.

Could it be that Jews, in the essential sense of that term, can only exist when the Nakba ceases and is reversed? Massad may see Jews who take on a colonial and imperial identity as outside Jewishness or having departed the authentic Jewish scene. The Jewish refusal to recognize Palestine and Palestinians may function as a mirror for Massad's refusal to recognize Zionists as Jews. In this sense, only the shedding of the colonial and imperial aspects of Jewish identity will be the homecoming Halper writes about. Is the resurrection of Palestine the only way forward for Jews?

There is another important silence about Jews in Massad's essay. Jews may cease being authentic Jews if colonialism and imperialism is at the core of their identity. Nonetheless, their identity as real people is intact. What will happen to the Jews who live in Israel-Palestine once the racist and colonial structure of Israel is dismantled? Will the state of Israel be destroyed, along with Jews who seek to retain its Jewish character? Or, if Jews and Israel remain in a transformed state, what function will that state serve and will anything Jewish about Israel be preserved?

In reversing the normative expectations of Palestinians in Western discourse, Massad's silence about Jews is an important commentary in and of itself. As part of his politics, Massad silences the Jewish voice. This is because Massad feels that Jews have dominated the land and the discourse about it.

Massad's primary concern is Palestinians. This makes sense, since that is his community. Yet Massad strikes a different note in Middle East discourse, at least in the West. That discourse privileges Jews even when the focus is ostensibly on Palestinians. Massad wants nothing to do with this privilege. He reverses it. Palestinians speak and are spoken about. On the sixtieth anniversary of the birth of Israel, only Palestinians narrate. Jews are silenced.

Should Massad have a concern about Jews? By deemphasizing Jews , Massad signals a sea change from the typical Jewish and Palestinian discourses found in Europe and America. Foremost in the minds of most Jewish writers on Israel is concern for Jews and their security. Often Palestinian writers do as well.

Some of the concern expressed by Palestinians is well meaning; some is simply strategic argumentation.

In current discussions, though displaced and almost destroyed, Palestinians are cautioned to begin their analysis by assuring Jews of their desire to accommodate them in the land. This strange inversion of who is insecure and who must be reassured of their security lies deep in Western history. It surfaces even in Palestinian expressions of dissent from the mainstream Western understandings of Jews and Palestinians. Although assertive and defiant, Mazin Qumsiyeh may be affected by this when he constantly calls for nonviolent action and for a Jewish-Palestinian sharing of the land.

Massad's essay appears in an Egyptian newspaper. His Arab audience has none of these qualifiers. The struggle is for Palestinian survival rather than salvaging the Jewish soul. In turn, though, Massad refuses to romanticize Palestinian leadership. To ensure Palestinian survival, Israel must be turned back and transformed. Palestinian survival correspondingly demands an unequivocal "no" to its own "collaborationist" leadership.

Massad believes that Israel's recognition of Palestinian peoplehood in the 1993 Oslo Accords came at too high a price. In exchange, the Oslo agreements limited the Palestinian future. According to Massad, Oslo did this by reducing the Palestinians to one-third of their total number. This was done by excluding the right of the Palestinian refugees to return to their homeland. In signing Oslo, therefore, Israel worked with a "collaborationist" Palestinian leadership. The price the Palestinian Authority paid for Israel's agreeing to recognize the Palestinian people was the "de-Palestinization" of the rest of the Palestinian people.

What did Palestinians receive in return? Massad is right to the point: "The Palestinian collaborating leadership, under the guise of the Oslo Accords, has agreed to multiply Israel's Jewish population by a factor of three, wherein Israel would be recognized as the state of all Jews worldwide and not of the Jews who live inside it, let alone the Palestinian citizens over whom it rules." Still, this arrangement failed. Israel wanted more than it received with Oslo Accords. The Palestinians have less than they had when they signed them.

Despite this failure, the Palestinian Authority continues to "collaborate" with Israel. This collaboration takes on a more sinister color than one could anticipate. Clearly a student of history, Massad strikes a startling comparison: Palestinians should view the Palestinian Authority as Jews remember the Jewish

Councils that presided over the Jewish ghettos in Nazi-occupied Europe.[15] The terrain Massad enters is fraught:

> Hard as it tried to legitimize itself, the Palestinian Authority could not but be seen for what it is: the creation of the Israeli occupation, an authority which in its structure and logic is not unlike all colonial puppet regimes in Asia and Africa serving their masters, not excluding the *Judenräte* (Jewish Councils) that the Nazis set up in occupied Poland's ghettos to run Jewish life, collect taxes, and run the post offices, *inter alia*; or the Bantustans that apartheid South Africa set up as alternative homelands. The Palestinian Authority's attempt to acquire the power of naming the Palestinian and Jewish peoples failed as much as Israel's attempts before it. Palestinians continue to insist on their name and on their inclusion in a Palestinian nation, while non-Israeli Jews insist on not joining Israeli nationality, no matter how much they may support Israel. The politics of naming is the politics of power and resistance. The power to name creates fictional histories against material realities. While Israel has succeeded in imposing physical and geographic realties, its attempt to obliterate historical memory has failed. Palestinians are always standing in the way of its falsification of their history and its own.

Though generally refraining from Jewish issues, here Massad appeals to the Jewish question in a wider framework. Surprisingly, the Jewish question runs parallel to his comment on the Palestinian people's refusal to accept the "de-Palestinianization" of the rest of the Palestinian people. De-Palestinianization is achieved when Palestinian leadership limits Palestine to the West Bank and Gaza, thereby eliminating Palestinians within Israel and the refugees outside of Israel/Palestine from final settlement considerations.

For Massad, non-Israeli Jews "insist on not joining Israeli nationality, no matter how much they might support Israel." This might be the opposite or, indeed, the same resistance that Palestinians have toward their leaders "naming" political and identity realities for them. Interestingly, the Palestinians resist denationalization, as defined by their leaders, while Jews outside of Israel resist

15. His play on the Jewish Councils in Europe is telling. For a portrait of those councils, see Isaiah Trunk, *Judenrat: The Jewish Councils of Europe* (Lincoln: University of Nebraska Press, 1996).

nationalization, as defined by their leaders. Is this a fruitful coincidence between Jews and Palestinians?

Still, Massad's greatest provocation may be his virtual silence about Jews. This is a reversal Jews are not used to. Dominating the discourse on Israel/Palestine, Jews expect to be highlighted. Massad acts as if Palestine is void of Jews. The absence of Jews, even Jewish arguments for and against Zionism, is jarring. When Massad does mention Jews, he is nuanced. This occasions another provocation, at least to contemporary signifiers involving Jewish identity. For Massad, Palestinian nationalism must recover and repopulate their native land to undergird Palestinian identity. Jewish nationalism, however, is a false identity of racism and colonialism. Jews, like other communities, are obliged to reject false identity.

If in fact Palestinian nationalism is positive and essential to survive the continuing Nakba, and Jewish nationalism, at least as it involves a state, is false, does the Jewish state survive only because of its power? Massad indicates the need for a power reversal. Jewish nationalism is not essential to Jews and Judaism. If Israel's power ends, Jewish nationalism ends. In Massad's view, the land is far from decisive for Jews. Perhaps this is why Jews outside of Israel resist Israeli nationality.

Massad identifies Jews as Diaspora-centered. Jews are Jews when they are without a state. Even with a state, Jews outside Israel resist state nationality. It appears that Massad thinks that if Israel ceases to be a Jewish state, all will be fine for Jews and Judaism. Perhaps it will be better for Jews. Geographic nationality is a political and ethical burden for Jews. It also distorts Judaism. Are Jews coerced into a false state-identified identity by establishment Jews in Israel and America? Will the Palestinian Nakba end because of Palestinian resistance and Jewish state-identity withdrawal?

Although this is outside of Massad's reflection on the sixtieth anniversary of the continuing Nakba, there is a hint in his assertion of the nonterritoriality of Judaism—that Jews may ultimately reject the permanent mobilization the state of Israel demands. If Palestinians remain steadfast, perhaps Jewish nationalism will simply fold and leave the scene. Certainly, the overdetermined focus of the Jewish establishment reveals an anxiety about Jews and territorial nationality. The pressure on Jews, even the railing against Palestinians as interlopers and as the new Nazis, possibly reveals more about the fear of Jewish attrition than fear of the fear of the Palestinian struggle for justice. Is the Jewish establishment trying to beat territorial Jewish nationality into a mobilized but reluctant Jewry?

Massad enters the terrain of the Holocaust with a twist. Obviously, he is not about to retreat and offer the Holocaust as a justification for Jewish fears.

Just the opposite, Massad continues the theme of the Jewish Diaspora, this time as a community under assault in Nazified Europe. Rather than appealing to Jews by recognizing the suffering Jews endured because of their lack of power, Massad instead focuses on collaborators that the Jewish community endured in the ghettos of Europe and how they dealt with traitors in their midst. This included ostracizing, imprisoning, and even murdering them. Massad's message is clear: Palestinian collaborators should be dealt with in the same way.

Far from denying the Holocaust or assuaging Jews about their fears of another Holocaust, or in a predictable way addressing the usual "security" needs that Israeli and Jews in general demand, Massad turns the Holocaust image inward. As with the *Judenräte*, he uses the Holocaust to taunt the Palestinian Authority.

Massad urges Palestinians to overthrow their collaborationist leadership. Massad uses the *Judenräte* as a Holocaust image of collaboration that presages a final solution of the Palestinian question. Rather than Israel, the Palestinian Authority will be held responsible. Since the state of Israel can be seen as a response to the Jewish Councils that ruled over the Jewish ghettos, Massad implies that a Palestinian remnant can survive its leadership and mass dislocation like the Jewish remnant survived the Holocaust.

Massad does not linger on the Jewish experience of mass death. Extending his analogy makes one wonder where Massad is leading us. If the Palestinian situation is this extreme and may one day be taken to the final level of mass death, how and where will Palestinian life be rescued? For some Jews, remnant Jewish life after the Holocaust was saved in Israel, the very state that assaults Palestinians. Massad leaves any such conclusion to the reader's imagination.

Massad stays far away from "final solution" rhetoric. With over a hundred years of Palestinian dispossession, Palestinians remain on the world map. Rather than disappearing, Massad believes that Palestinians will triumph in their own land. Massad makes no reference to mass death while discussing similarity in leadership patterns.

Massad steers clear of the complex situation in which the *Judenräte* found themselves. For a defeated people, the options for survival are complex. Nor does he address the limited power and information the Jewish leadership had with regard to the Nazis' plans or the paths they followed. At least at first, the *Judenräte* were in truly unchartered territory. By the time they realized what would happen to the ghettoized Jews they led, it was already too late.

Is Massad being too harsh? On the one hand, Massad could cut the Palestinian leadership some slack in staying away from the Jewish-leadership-in-the-Holocaust analogy. He could retain his already devastating "colonial puppet" analogy. On the other hand, Massad is being strategic here. By employing rhetoric that exposes Palestinian leadership, he proposes a Palestinian future beyond the continuing Nakba.

Massad is compelling when he writes that the "politics of naming is the politics of power and resistance. The power to name creates fictional histories against material realities." True, Israel has succeeded in imposing physical and geographic realties. Nonetheless, its attempt to "obliterate historical memory has failed." For Massad, Palestinians stand in the way of the falsification of Israel's history. In doing so, Palestinians refuse Israel's definition of Palestinian history as well. Again, Massad addresses Palestinians primarily. His is a plea for maintaining Palestinian identity within the continuing catastrophe. A secondary audience is the larger Arab world. Palestinians need the Arab world to hold fast. The third audience is Israeli Jews in their abuse of power, and non-Israeli Jews, in their refusal to adopt Israeli nationality.

Massad's hope is that by Palestinians standing fast, Jews might come to understand the crime that is being committed by them and in their name. Palestinians stand in the way of the falsification of history in a way that buoys their identity and challenges Israeli and Jewish identity as well. Palestinian resistance thus prohibits Israel and Jews from falsifying their own history.

Historically, the way Palestinians stand in relation to Jews, Israel, and Judaism may be similar to the way Jews stood in relation to Christianity. Jews held Christians to account by maintaining Jewish integrity and history as a critique of the racist and colonial history that Christianity sought to hide from itself. The state of Israel seeks to hide its own racism and colonialism by imposing it on Palestinians. Palestinians live for themselves. They hold Jews accountable.

Perhaps Massad's most devastating indictment is of Palestinian leadership. They have accepted the Nakba as an unfortunate consequence of, in their view, a relatively benign and innocent Israel. If carried to its logical conclusion, collaboration with a false naming of history spells the end of Palestine and the Palestinians. Palestinian leadership would accomplish the goal that eludes Israel's power.

Massad stays away from Jewish internal politics. His notable exceptions are his occasional references to the refusal of Israeli nationality and the *Judenräte*. Nor does Massad comment on how Palestinian resistance to false naming encourages Jews to resist the false naming of Israel's history perpetrated by Jewish leadership. Following Massad's analysis, however, the attempted destruction of Palestine may be an internal racist and colonial imposition within the Jewish community on ordinary Jews by Jewish leadership in and outside of Israel. This raises the possibility that the refusal of Palestinians to accept false naming may lead to Jews to refuse that false naming as well.

For Massad, this explains why the Palestinian Authority is accepted in a positive manner in some sectors of the Jewish world. Jewish leadership needs a collaborator in the falsification of Israeli and Jewish history. If Palestinian leadership signs on the dotted line of a permanently diminished Palestine, Jews will be relieved. This would allow Jews to accept Israel's presentation of Jewish history. Is this what the slogan "a partner for peace" really means?

For Massad, the Nakba is ever present. "Ever since the *Nakba* came to describe the tumultuous actions of 1948, an ongoing struggle has raged to define it as a past and finished event rather than an unfinished action," Massad writes. "This is not an epistemological struggle but a lively political one."

Here Massad brings the ongoing Nakba within Israel itself through the plight of Palestinians with Israeli citizenship. According to Israel's narrative, the struggle of Palestinian citizens of Israel today is less a normal anticolonial struggle, or one that demands national or ethnic or civil rights, but, rather, an "abnormal" struggle to reverse the Nakba.

Massad recites the facts of Israel's specific laws that institutionalize Jewish religious and racial privilege over non-Jewish citizens. Israel presents this as a normal condition for Palestinians, a condition they refuse to accept. Even some liberal Israeli leaders suggest that Palestinian citizens of Israel should leave for countries that would grant them national rights. For Massad, the question is different: Why should Palestinians leave Israel rather than stay and demand equal rights?

In an inverted lesson from Jewish history, Palestinians are often reminded that "'much greater' peoples than they opted for self-displacement from countries that denied them rights to a country that granted them rights." For Massad, this reminder is telling. It is a strange twist when Jewish Israelis, many of them previously displaced in Europe, lecture Palestinians about the acceptance of displacement as they perpetrate the Nakba upon the Palestinians. Massad continues:

If Palestinians in Israel want to remain in Israel, they must accept the normalcy of the *Nakba* and must acquiesce in their new status as *mankubin* who cannot and will never have equal rights with Jews. Their refusal of the effects of the *Nakba* is what makes Palestinian citizens of Israel want to reverse its effects by calling on Israel to repeal its racist laws and become an Israeli, rather than a Jewish state.

Israel and now President Bush insist that the effects of the *Nakba* must be accepted by all Palestinians. That the *Nakba* transformed Palestine into "the Jewish State," Palestinians are told, is not reversible and no amount of civil rights activism or national struggle will undo this major achievement. Palestinian citizens of Israel, however, seem unconvinced and continue to resist this irreversibility. Their plight, according to Israel, however, is not caused by the *Nakba* but by their insistence on resisting it.

Israel's blame game continues by constantly asserting that Palestinian refugees are like most other refugee populations, that is, victims of war. Massad refuses this assertion as a politically motivated attempt to avoid responsibility for Israel's continuing Nakba. So Israel insists that the problem does not lie with the "Zionist actions of 1947-1948 that expelled Palestinians from their homeland." Instead, Israel places the blame on the refusal of Palestinians and Arab countries to "accept the *Nakba* as irreversible and settle these poor refugees" in their host countries. Israel and its supporters insists that Palestinian refugees continue to suffer not because of their dispossession but because they "refuse to accept the *Nakba* and to accept themselves as *mankubin*."

Israel has the same explanation for Palestinians in the West Bank, Gaza, and East Jerusalem. Their problems are "certainly not a result of the *Nakba*" but of the Arab refusal to accept Israel as a Jewish state. According to Massad, Israel's logic runs like this: the problems for the Palestinians are "born of an international war in 1967 that resulted from the Arab refusal of the *Nakba* as a permanent fact. If Palestinians and their allies would just accept the *Nakba* as a past and finished event, the calamities that they still claim befall them would cease immediately."

Massad's concise rendering of the Palestinian situation is ground breaking. He insists that the Nakba be accepted as a fact, at the same time insisting that *the* Nakba does not exist. The Nakba as a one-off 1948 event may be a bad dream perpetrated by Palestinians and other Arabs—without realizing its essential and much more devastating character. In any case, Massad views the Palestinian situation as it stands as seemingly irreversible except outside of Israel. Depending on circumstances—say, the refusal to acquiesce to Israeli power under a collaborationist Palestinian leadership—the West Bank and Gaza could help resolve the historical matter. Other Arab countries have to be part of solving the Palestinian situation.

The key for Massad is that, according to the Zionist narrative, the struggle of Palestinian citizens of Israel today is not an anticolonial struggle that demands national or ethnic or civil rights. Rather, Israel sees it as an "abnormal" struggle to reverse the Nakba. Having taken the anticolonial struggle away—at least in Israeli, Jewish, and parts of global discourse, as well as the normal desire to reverse their dispossession—what is left for Palestinians other than to accept the Israeli definition of their situation?

Massad does open up the possibility of Palestinians demanding national, ethnic, or civil rights as part of their anticolonial struggle. This is the only time he alludes to a possible way of reversing the Nakba. In fact, according to Massad, Israel prefers the "reversal" rhetoric because that legitimizes its concerns about its security. Although Israel portrays a reversal as abnormal, Massad believes that desire for reversal is the normal state of affairs for a dispossessed people. Only Israeli power limits this reversal.

Although Massad lays these and other criticisms specifically on Zionism and Israel, he believes that the Palestinian and Arab refusal of repatriation outside of Palestine is foundational to the success of post-Holocaust Jewish life. When 1948 enters the discussion, and the Palestinian and Arab refusal to recognize Israel as a Jewish state, the dispossession of European Jews is cited. When the plight of the Palestinian refugees is referred to, the Palestinian and Arab refusal issue becomes front and center.

Only rarely in Jewish discourse are the 1948 war, Palestinian dispossession, and the life of Palestinian refugees after their dispossession connected—and that connection is often disjointed. On the one hand, Jews are incredulous that the Arab world did not accept the state of Israel as a good and important fact from the beginning. On the other hand, Jews speak disparagingly about how Arab governments and Palestinians themselves refuse simply to become part of the broader Arab landscape. According to this view, if Palestinians and the surrounding Arab countries had just accepted Israel and assimilated the refugees, the subsequent history of dispossession could have been avoided altogether.

In the Jewish outlook, Massad believes there are nefarious reasons for such rejections. Many Jews believe that such rejections have nothing to do with the normal desires of a displaced people to return to their former lives. Rather, they form the same wall of denial that others have previously formed around Jews. Dismissed is the idea that Palestinians find their identity and land distinctive. Therefore, the Palestinian refusal to disappear is not viewed as a positive statement about Palestinian attachment to their homeland.

Once again, we hear the Jewish call to reprieve Israel of its culpability in the displacement of the Palestinian people. In Israel's eyes, Jerusalem, the West

Bank, and Gaza are as they are because of the Arabs' "abnormal" intransigence. This, rather than the 1967 war, or because Israel had designs on East Jerusalem and the West Bank, or because once they had conquered the Palestinian territories Israel decided to settle as much of the territory with the least amount of Palestinians. Unmentioned by Israel with regard to the Palestinians is 1948.

Whatever is wrong in the Middle East, whatever complaints Palestinians have, are due to their unwillingness to accept their fate in light of what is best for Jews. Once again, the idea of Jewish and Israeli innocence is at play.

As Massad's article was published, a flap arose about the United Nations using the word *Nakba* in a call to the president of the Palestinian Authority. This occasioned Israeli Foreign Affairs Minister, Tzipi Livni, to declare that with the establishment of a Palestinian state, the end of the conflict would be at hand. At the same time, the Palestinians would then have to strike "Nakba" from the Palestinian lexicon, at least as it applied to Israel.[16]

Livni's rhetoric simply confirms Massad's main point, which, because it is so ingrained in Israeli leadership and among Zionists in general, bears repeating. For Massad, to insist that the Nakba is a present continuous act of destruction which remains unfinished is to "resist acknowledging that its work has been completed." It is Palestinian resistance that accounts for the "unfinished work of the *Nakba* and for its ongoing brutality."

Israel and its international supporters keep insisting that had the Palestinians "accepted defeat and recognized the *Nakba*, had they accepted their expulsion, their third-class citizenship within Israel, and the conquest of 1967, their calamities would have ended." For Massad, the opposite is the case. The reason that Palestinians continue to experience hardship is that they have never stopped fighting their dispossession. The Nakba continues because Palestinians refuse to accept dispossession as their final act:

Palestinians resisted the *Nakba* in the 1880s, when European Jewish colonists kicked them off land they purchased from absentee landlords and denied them labor on land they had tilled for centuries. Palestinian resistance took the form of a major three-year revolt in the 1930s against British support for Zionists to bring about the *Nakba*. Palestinians also resisted after the actions of 1947/1948 when most of their land was conquered and confiscated by the racist laws

16. This is taken from Livni's address at the Annapolis Conference, November 27, 2007. The full text can be found at http://www.mfa.gov.il/mfa/presentation/2007/pages/addressbyfmlivnito the annapolis conference27-nov-2007.aspx.

of the Jewish state. Their ongoing resistance to the *Nakba* in the West Bank and in Gaza, we are still told by Israel and the *New York Times*, is in fact what invites more *Nakbas*. If Palestinians would allow Israel to lay siege to them in the largest open air prison in the world called Gaza without resisting it, Israel would not be forced to bomb them and kill their children and destroy their homes, it would only starve them and keep them inside the apartheid wall. If Palestinians would simply accept their status as *mankubin*, the *Nakba*, as an unfinished process, would be finally completed. This logic of conquest is not exceptional at all, nor is it limited to the Israelis. Has not the resistance in Iraq more recently stood in the way of the final completion of the mission of the American invasion, which President Bush declared "accomplished" five years ago? It is Iraqi resistance to the destruction that the Americans visit on Iraq that forces the process of American destruction to continue and the American mission to remain unaccomplished. . . .

Massad goes back and forth on Palestinian resistance. In Israeli and Western discourse, this resistance is seen as a weak barbarism. From the vantage point of the West, Palestinians and Arabs in general are corrupt and backward. Their civilization, whatever it once was, is in steep decline. What appears to be resistance isn't, especially since the unwashed cannot really have a cause. The unwashed *can* have anger and resentment.

Like the September 11th hijackers and those behind the plot, Palestinians are thought to have only complaints and destruction to offer, which, of course, simply compounds the problems of their own making. Yet Massad shows that Palestinian resistance has been continuous. By reciting the various phases of that resistance over the years, he establishes this resistance as grievance-related and substantive. Continual and real resistance forces the Palestinian people to be defeated over and over again on the ground and through rhetoric. By relating Palestinian resistance to other anticolonial resistance including in Iraq, Israel's mission remains unaccomplished and, according to Massad, destined to fail.

The comparison with Iraq is problematic since, with most American troops now withdrawn, the likely long-term situation on the ground is disquieting. Massad does not address the question of what Palestinian resistance would look like if the Nakba was reversed or if Israel, at least its racist and colonial structure, ended. One possibility is that the resistance against occupation, which Massad defines as inclusive of the Israeli state within its 1967 borders, might establish a just and democratic Palestine. However, it is as likely that a scramble for power would ensue among Palestinian forces and with other Arab players in the region. What Israel would do if it was really threatened is predictable. Israel's extensive nuclear arsenal makes any military attempt to destroy Israel a potential nuclear catastrophe.

Unmentioned here is what would happen to Jews within the borders of the defunct Israeli state in the aftermath of Nakba reversal. Nor does Massad speculate as to what might happen to diverse Palestinian constituencies in the power struggle for control of Palestine with the highly symbolic Jerusalem as it center. However, the situation being what it is, Massad hardly needs to ask these questions. Should Jews in the Warsaw Ghetto have been polled about what they might do with their freedom in order to discern if their situation should be remedied? Thinking about what Jews have done with their post–Holocaust freedom, especially in Israel, might have given rescuers pause—if, indeed, there had been any in sight.

Massad concludes his argument on the need for Palestinians to continue to resist:

RESISTANCE IS NOW: Palestinian resistance today is active on many fronts. One of the key campaigns that Palestinians in Israel have mounted recently is to force Israel to repeal its many racist laws. A number of proposals and documents have been issued by Palestinian organizations in Israel to that effect. This campaign must be internationalized. The United Nations and other world forums must be enlisted in the task of forcing Israel to repeal its racist laws. This is not the demagogic attempt to call Zionism racism as the UN had done in 1975 in a sloganeering resolution, but rather to demonstrate how Israel is institutionally racist and that it rules through racist laws that must be repealed.

Palestinians and their allies have also mounted an international campaign of divestment and boycott of Israel until it ceases to be in violation of international law through its continued occupation of the West Bank and Gaza and stops its ongoing war crimes against them. This is another key campaign that has already scored a number of impressive victories.

This is not to say that Palestinians do not continue to suffer everywhere. The suffering of Gazans has been the greatest in recent years, as Israel punishes them for their refusal of the rule of the

Palöstinenserrat Israel and its Palestinian collaborators imposed on the West Bank, and tried to impose on Gaza in their attempt to overthrow the democratically elected Palestinian government. Israel's war crimes against Gazans continue apace but Gazans have had no choice but to remain steadfast and to resist.

But in resisting the *Nakba*, the Palestinians have struck at the heart of the Zionist project that insists that the *Nakba* be seen as a past event. In resisting Israel, Palestinians have forced the world to witness the *Nakba* as present action; one that, contrary to Zionist wisdom, is indeed reversible. This is precisely what galls Israel and the Zionist movement. Israel's inability to complete its mission of thoroughly colonizing Palestine, of expelling all Palestinians, of "gathering" all Jews in the world in its colony, keeps it uneasy and keeps its project always in the present continuous.

In Massad's view, Israel continues to project itself as a victim because the victims of their power refuse to grant it legitimacy to victimize them. Yet this only reinforces Massad's view that Israel understands in its unconscious but also consciously that its project will remain reversible as long as Palestinians resist. Thus Israel's occupation and narrative overkill.

As Massad sees it, the cruelty Israel continues to visit upon the Palestinian people is "directly proportional to its belief in their ability to overthrow its achievements and reverse its colonial project." The problem for Israel is not in "believing and knowing that there is not one single place in its colonial settlement that did not have a former Arab population, but in its realization that there is no place today in its imaginary 'Jewish State' that does not still have an Arab population who claims it."

Massad concludes that the Nakba remains unfinished because Palestinians refuse to let their situation transform them into *mankubin*. So, for Massad, what the world is witnessing at the commemorations of the ongoing Nakba is not only one more year of the Nakba but one more year of resisting it. "Those who counsel the Palestinians to accept the Nakba know that to accept the Nakba is to allow it to continue unfettered." Massad concludes that Palestinians know that the only way to end the Nakba is to continue to resist.

6

Tunnel Vision

Listen to Uri Avnery, the veteran Israel peace activist, commenting, as Akiva Eldar did, on the flood of visitors celebrating Israel's sixtieth anniversary. "With friends like these," indeed—Avnery doesn't mince words about these people he labels as "Has-Beens":

> Lately we are flooded with friends. The Great of the Earth, past and present, come here to flatter us, to fawn on us, to grovel at our feet. "God, save me from my friends, my enemies I can deal with myself!" says an old prayer. They disgust me.
>
> Let's take for example the German Chancellor, Angela Merkel, who made the pilgrimage to Jerusalem. Her pandering was free of any criticism and she reached new heights of obsequiousness in her speech to the Knesset. I was invited to attend. I relinquished the privilege.
>
> I shall also pass the pleasure when I am invited to the session with the hyper-active Nicholas Sarkozy, who will try to break the flattery record of his German rival.
>
> Before that we were visited by John McCain's mentor, the evangelical pastor John Hagee, the one who described the Catholic Church as a monster. Oozing sanctimonious flattery from every pore, he forbade us, in the name of (his) God, to give up even one inch of the Holy Land and commanded us to fight to the last drop of (our) blood.
>
> However, not one of them has come close to George Bush. Approaching the end of the most disastrous presidency in the annals of the Republic, he really forced a lighted match into the hand of our government, encouraging it to ignite the barrel of gunpowder between our feet.[1]

So it goes sometimes: those who want to help do the most grievous harm. But as Avnery, chair of the Israeli peace group Gush Shalom, reminds us, we have to be wary of others who, while ostensibly pushing our agenda, are really pushing theirs.

This is especially true when lives are at stake and when past guilt, like antisemitism and the Holocaust, are in play. When religious zeal, like evangelical and Armageddon Christianity, roams freely or when the ideological spokesmen of contemporary empire and American exceptionalism arrive, then the issue is joined. When these understandings combine, the "barrel of gunpowder" can ignite.

Avnery wants everyone to know that it is between "our" feet that the barrel of gunpowder is placed. By "our," Avnery means Israelis and Palestinians as well. After the dignitaries leave, if the gunpowder explodes, it explodes on those left behind.

So it has been and remains. Interested parties come and go to broker peace between Israel and the Palestinians. But in whose interest do they negotiate? Who is left when the negotiators leave and what do they leave behind?

In some ways, that is how many Israelis and Palestinians feel, as those left behind, fighting the battle that is theirs and yet not theirs. Although Israelis and Palestinians had much on their respective plates on their sixtieth anniversary, others in the vicinity and far away likewise had their plates full. Left to their own devices, Israelis and Palestinians had more than enough to digest.

The difficulty for Israelis and Palestinians is compounded by the interest of the great and not-so-great nation-state powers in their future. The claims of three great monotheistic religions on Israel, Jerusalem, the Palestinians, and the Holy Land also stalk the land. Placing so much importance on a small and contentious area of the world only makes the situation worse. What both Israelis and Palestinians want above all is some justice, some peace, and some taste of ordinary life. It is not theirs to have.

As the Israel-Palestine impasse continues, the ordinary is very far away. Visiting dignitaries come for their own political, rhetorical, and religious reasons. This only makes a bad situation worse. Who will be arriving—and departing—on Israel-Palestine's seventieth anniversary?

As scolding as he is regarding the leaders of Germany, France, and America, Avnery aims a special barb at the evangelical Christian ministers who invest their eschatological future in Israel's colonial sensibilities. Of course, that

---

1. Uri Avnery, 'With Friends Like These," *Counterpunch*, May 20, 2008.

is hardly the way evangelical leaders see it. They call it the "last days." Jews and Palestinians are only bit players in that Christian drama.

Avnery has other particular targets in line as well. His litany of "Has-Beens" is especially telling. Among them is Simon Peres, who in "all the 84 years of his life has never won an election, and who was finally handed, out of sheer compassion, the largely meaningless title of President of Israel." Another special "Has-Been" is Tony Blair, former prime minister of the United Kingdom, who was "pushed from power in his own country, but is not content to enjoy his pension and raise roses." His consolation prize is being "granted the pleasure of playing around with our conflict." Every few weeks or so he holds a press conference and trumpets his "phenomenal success in ameliorating the lot of the Palestinians." This, as the actual situation on the ground deteriorates. Avnery is caustic: "Our security establishment treats him like a bore that has to be thrown a crumb from time to time to keep him happy."

Has-Beens, indeed, but also people who know better. Avnery asks why these Has-Beens heap "mountains of fawning adulation on Israel." If congratulations are the order of the day, why are they bereft of criticism? "No occupation. No settlements. No Gaza blockade. No daily killings. Just a wonderful, peace-loving state that the bad, bad terrorists want to throw into the sea." Not one proclaims what Avnery considers the truth, that the continuation of the present policies might lead Israel to disaster. "He who has friends like these has no need for enemies," Avnery writes. "A person who sees his friend playing Russian roulette and offers him bullets—is he a real friend? One who sees his friend standing on the brink of an abyss and tells him 'go ahead'—is he a friend?"

Still, Avnery saves his most venomous attacks for the Jewish billionaires who poison what is left of the ethical possibilities within Israel.

They are all Israeli patriots. They are all philanthropists. All contribute millions to Israeli politicians. And almost all of them support our extreme Right. What makes them run? What induces these billionaires to do what they are doing? A research in depth discovers that a great many of them made their money in dark corners. Some are gambling barons, casino-owners with all the inevitable connections with violence, crime and exploitation. One at least made his fortunes from brothels. Another was involved in a scandal involving old people's homes. Yet another is a scion of a family who made their money bootlegging during prohibition days. Some are arms merchants of the most despicable kind, selling weapons to the political gangs which sow death and destruction in Africa. But money, as is well known, does not smell.

Avnery concludes once again on a caustic note by speaking about *chutzpa*, a Yiddish word for audacity, good or bad. It common usage is for comedic effect. But the situation is too serious, so Avnery avoids the metaphorical. The *chutzpa* he refers to is real and dangerous: "The *chutzpa* of billionaires in New York and Geneva and all the other places who interfere in our elections and determine the fate of our nation. The *chutzpa* of donating for a war in which not their sons, but ours, are killed. The *chutzpa* of sending billions for the establishment of settlements in the occupied Palestinian territories, and especially in Jerusalem, which are put there for the express purpose of preventing peace and imposing on us a permanent war, a war that threatens our future—not theirs." Implicit in Avnery's analysis is that these billionaires are playing games in their spare time. Meanwhile, Jews and Palestinians suffer.

Avnery knows Jewish billionaires are the tip of the iceberg. They are the flowering—or the poison—of a form of Jewish consciousness emerging over the years. Jewish billionaires are the fruit of Jewish success, though, for Avnery, that success comes through dubious enterprises under the protection of various state entities. Like the success of individuals from all ethnic and religious groups, Jewish success is often dressed up and piled high with honors it rarely deserves. On Israel's anniversaries, this, too, is left without discussion. How many of the political leaders and billionaires are profiting from injustice? The links to empire are noticeable, if unannounced. Is Jewish success itself bound up with an unjust economic global order?

This is true on the political level as well. One of the political dignitaries present at Israel's sixtieth was Henry Kissinger, the former American secretary of state. For his role in Vietnam and Cambodia, Avnery regards Kissinger as a war criminal. Avnery asks, "Where else can he and other dubious political figures come but to Israel to claim their honors and spread their influence?"—especially as their business practices and policy initiatives are more and more questioned in the United States and around the world.

ELIE WIESEL: SPEAKING TRUTH TO DARKNESS

Also present at the celebrations was Elie Wiesel. On the American nightly news broadcasts he was highlighted in the audience as President Bush spoke in the Knesset. Earlier he had written a short piece for the May 8 issue of *Time* magazine, called "Israel at 60."[2]

> Israel in sixty years? When it comes to Jewish history, it is dangerous to indulge in prophecy. Who would have predicted Abraham leaving the grandiose home of his father and his idols to discover that God alone ruled the world? And Moses, the man with a speech defect, an inspired spokesman for his people? And David the young shepherd, a warrior and king? Had anyone predicted Hitler's crimes? Only three years after the saddest and cruelest chapter in Jewish history, a sovereign Jewish State was proclaimed. Was it predictable? Was its military victory over five well-armed Arab armies predictable? And the Six-Day war? And the Yom Kippur war? And the influx of a million Jews from the Soviet Union? And the assassination, by a Jewish fanatic, of the legendary Prime Minister Yitzhak Rabin?

Wiesel thinks that predicting the future is dangerous. Nonetheless, anniversaries are as much about the future as they are about the past. On the "urgent question of tomorrow," Wiesel is an optimist. He believes that Israelis and Palestinians will live together. "Yes, there will be two states—a Jewish one for Jews, and a Palestinian one for Palestinians. Historically unavoidable, this is bound to happen. But how and at what price? That I cannot figure out. All I know is that suicide terrorism must be eliminated."

Wiesel's themes are predictable. For decades his writing and lectures have echoed similar themes in almost identical language. Once again, he writes of the "miracle" of Israel. Biblical images abound. Wiesel associates the unpredictability of the biblical drama with the unpredictability of evil in history. He highlights Hitler and the triumph of Israel in war against enormous odds.

Wiesel cites the symbolic markers of Jewish life without elaboration. Wiesel is confident that his Jewish and non-Jewish audiences alike identify with the biblical and historical events he mentions. Who would be against Abraham, Moses, and David, for Hitler, or against Israel?

On the Jewish side, the only negative that Wiesel cites is the assassination of Yitzhak Rabin, by a Jewish "fanatic." But this, too, is rescued by the public's understanding of Rabin as a warrior against the perfidious Palestinians, at least

2. Elie Wiesel, "Israel at 60," *Time*, May 8, 2008.

when armed against Israel in war or "suicide terrorism." Rabin's last years as a peacemaker are cited as if this defined his military and political career. Wiesel counts on ordinary Jews celebrating Rabin's strength, tenacity, and ethical fiber. He believes sensible Palestinians should also celebrate Rabin's life.

In Wiesel's view, only a fanatic would seek to kill Rabin's vision of a strong and peaceful Israel. That Rabin was an admitted ethnic cleanser of Palestinians during the 1948 war and was the leader of Israel's armed forces during and after the 1967 war—a period of ethnic cleansing and settlement projects not unlike the 1948 period—is left for historians to sort out. Similarly, Rabin's role as the architect of the policy of might and beatings that brutally repressed the first Palestinian uprising beginning in 1987 is absent from Wiesel's lament for the loss of the assassinated prime minister.

While Wiesel thinks that predictions about the future are "ill-advised," the facts on the ground go unmentioned. The establishment of a Jewish state is trumpeted as an against-the-odds miracle. Wiesel is silent on the issues of Palestinian refugees. He is silent on Israel's carving up of the West Bank and the "unification" of Jerusalem. Talk about the Wall surrounding Palestinian population centers in the West Bank is avoided. Wiesel is silent on the situation in Gaza.

As we have seen, Wiesel first came into the public's view as a radical Holocaust thinker. He was determined to keep the suffering of Europe's Jews from fading into oblivion. That is the known story line. But the lesser-known and more surprising detail is that the Jewish community *wanted* the Holocaust to fade from view. Before Wiesel became a Holocaust icon, he was understandably angry about the suffering he and other Jews had undergone. More, he was bitter about the way American Jews treated the Holocaust survivors.

Wiesel's essays in the 1970s bear this out. Then, Wiesel outlined his anger about American Jews who did not suffer in the Holocaust but after avoiding the issues for years, now claimed the Holocaust as their own. After many years of silence and repression of the memory of the Holocaust, American Jews wanted to emphasize the Holocaust for their own advancement. In Wiesel's understanding, the Jewish community basked in the reflected glory of Holocaust martyrdom without proximity to the actual survivors of the Holocaust. Wiesel's accusation that American Jews want distance from European Jewry was stinging. The accents, poverty, and weakness of the survivors bothered them.

Wiesel's accusation that American Jews usurped the Holocaust for their own advancement is the same accusation that Avnery makes regarding

American—and Wiesel's—use of Israel. On the Holocaust and Israel, there is voyeurism at play. Wiesel's commentary on Israel hardly escapes the same scrutiny. After all, Wiesel briefly visited Israel after the Holocaust, only to leave for France and America. On his choice to leave Israel, he is mostly silent, speaking of this only as having to do with his "cosmopolitan" vision of the world. Is Israel's nationalism too narrow for Wiesel and, if it is, do other Jews live that nationalism as a symbolic contribution to the Jewish future which Wiesel's lauds while choosing not to live?[3]

The contradiction seems obvious—American Jews accenting the Holocaust symbol and speaking for the survivors while Wiesel was distancing himself from them by assuming an iconic image, thus effectively silencing the survivors in another way. Wiesel's life journey surfaces the painful contradictions that plague Jews in America and perhaps in Israel as well: both want to claim the Holocaust by distancing themselves from it. But, again, inverted, this might ring true of dissident Israelis like Avnery. Does Wiesel's speech about Israel serve to silence Israelis—and Palestinians—who have to endure those who pronounce on their future?[4]

What accounts for Wiesel's transposition from prophetic anger against those who sought to use *and* bury the memory of suffering, to one who buries the suffering of Palestinians in the name of the Holocaust suffering he sought to rescue from oblivion? Wiesel emerged as the voice of the suffering, indeed, became the icon of that suffering. He uses that iconic image to foreclose the suffering of others.

If Wiesel sees himself as a cosmopolitan person, he frames Jewish suffering in a narrow way. For Wiesel, there is a straight line from the origins of the people Israel to the formation of the state of Israel. In doing so, he silences the suffering of Palestinians who experience the Jewish/Israel drama as a form of oppression. The very cadence of Wiesel's words and structure of his argument place the Jewish journey first and foremost. Only the echoes of others are heard, if they are heard at all. In Wiesel's framing Palestinians are menacing. They threaten to drown out the Jewish narrative.

For Wiesel, everything that happens to the Jewish people and the Israeli state is unpredictable. This includes both God's choosing the speech-challenged Moses as well as Hitler's ascent to power. It also includes the state of Israel being born, then fending off its foes. Wiesel's outline shows that in Jewish history, something more than the ordinary is at stake.

3. For Wiesel's own account of his movements and decisions in the early years after the Holocaust, see his *All Rivers Run to the Sea: Memoirs* (New York: Knopf, 1995).

4. For an angry Elie Wiesel, see his *A Jew Today* (New York: Vintage, 1975).

When the people Israel take up the challenge or when they are assaulted, the unpredictable saving arrives just in the nick of time. For Wiesel, this proves that something significant is behind the state of Israel. Being part, but also catalyzing aspects, of the world beyond the ordinary, Israel is a loved and wounded beacon that continues against the odds to survive and shine. If the survival of Israel is not an occasion for celebration, what is?

Wiesel's early prophetic anger within the Jewish community wanes as he and the Holocaust are accepted. Once accepted, his struggle changes. For the rest of his life, Wiesel's mission is to secure the Holocaust from those who seek to use it for their own agenda. The Holocaust must remain an internal Jewish drama. Anything outside of Jews, Judaism, and the state of Israel is ancillary to and a foil for the Jewish drama. That is why Palestinians are mentioned only three times in Wiesel's message. Their mention is in relation to Israel's future security and final separation of the two peoples.

To the question of how Jews and Palestinians will solve their impasse, Wiesel is unclear. Solving the impasse is "unavoidable." However, "unavoidable" has a different character than Wiesel's "unpredictable." The unpredictable is part of furthering Jewish destiny. The unavoidable lacks any direct impact on Jewish destiny.

For Wiesel, the Palestinians simply exist. Like other peoples, they deserve their due, but this is different from having a destiny. Nowhere does Wiesel perceive the Palestinians as a people with an independent destiny, much less that Jews and Palestinians have a common destiny. Moreover, in Wiesel's thought, there is little sense that Jews and Palestinians live in proximity to one another or that, in suffering and struggle, they share a complex history. Wiesel does not broach the possibility that the division of Jews and Palestinians can be overcome. The Palestinians are outside the Jewish ambit. They are one of those "unavoidables" rather than "unpredictables" that define the internal character of Jews and Judaism.

The unavoidable exists on the unpredictable's terms. Israel's destiny eliminates any grievance that Palestinians might have. If there is a grievance, it must be subordinated to Jewish destiny. Since, for Wiesel, no symmetry exists between Jews and Palestinians, the relative importance of Jewish and Palestinian history is defined in this light.

Wiesel's Jewish claims are within history. Although Wiesel is silent on the possibility of God's sanction of the Jewish journey outright, he certainly implies it. It is difficult to understand how the unpredictable keeps happening in Jewish history without a transcendent force interested in and working on behalf of the Jewish people.

With Wiesel, Palestinians are on their own. Wiesel is silent on their Islamic and Christian religious affiliations as a possible guiding light—or destiny—for them. Palestinians may or not have a nationality. Wiesel is frugal in allowing political and national rights to Israel's adversaries. That Palestinians might have a national or religious destiny on their ancestral land is occluded.

Wiesel's implicit assumption is that Palestinians have to make do with what is left over from Israel's needs. For Palestinians, their sacrifice is inevitable. Jews have finally landed back where they belong. Jews need only be aware of securing their own destiny. Otherwise, the unavoidable might detour the unpredictable in another Hitlerian scenario from which the state of Israel and the Jewish people would not recover. Wiesel notes that the "suicide terrorism" of Palestinians cannot be justified. Palestinians are without claim regarding the state of Israel.

Because the Palestinian struggle is without legitimate claims, Wiesel believes that Palestinian terror should be viewed as a contemporary form of antisemitism striking at the very heart of Jewish destiny. That this must be thwarted goes without saying. For Wiesel, Palestinian resistance is without merit—at least over against Jewish need and destiny. "Suicide terrorism" is clearly defined by the parameters Wiesel assigns Palestinians. The right of just resistance is denied them.

Wiesel rejects the charge that Israel is a Western colonial outpost. Proof positive of the ridiculousness of the colonial charge is that former imperial powers like Britain, France, and Germany, who now rebuke that part of their history, are guests of honor at Israel's celebration. The United States, who others might see as the latest Western colonial power, has taken Israel under its wing. America is part of Israel's destiny.

The reverse also seems true for Wiesel. Israel is part of America's destiny. If America refuses to protect Israel, what can America claim to be? Of course, Wiesel views America as a paragon of virtue in the world and an honest broker in the Israel-Palestine conflict. That Palestinians see America as a wielder of imperial power and as a dishonest broker simply confirm Wiesel's view of Palestinian irredentist sensibilities.

Wiesel cautions Jews with regard to criticism of America. It is futile and backward to take issue with American foreign policy because some on the right see an uneven support for Israel over the Palestinians or some on the left oppose America's invasion of Iraq. America and Israel are light unto the nations. Together they spread democracy and uphold modern civilization. Together they root out corrupt dictatorial regimes and sponsor uplift for backward areas of the world.

"But how and at what price?" Wiesel asks. How much will be the "unavoidable" cost of Israel's survival? For Wiesel, the wars that the state of Israel fights are strictly defensive. Therefore, Israel's costs are unavoidable. They are caused by others. Like the victims of the Holocaust, Israel's fallen are martyrs. They die for a cause beyond ethnic nationalism. Jewish losses are unavoidable as long as the irrational opposition to the state of Israel remains. Israel has to stay the course.

Does Wiesel's optimism about the future rest on the Palestinian acceptance of Israel's destiny as part of its own fate? Unpredictability might work here. Perhaps Palestinians and the surrounding Arabs countries will do an about-face. One day they may accept the need for and destiny of a Jewish state. Joseph Massad doesn't think so, nor does he think such acceptance would be good for Jews. But, through his analysis, Wiesel could only see Massad as an antisemite bent on Israel's destruction, and that anyone listening to him would have to be seen, at the very least, as a fellow traveler with antisemites.

In Wiesel's rhetoric, there is little to suggest that unpredictability might work in other ways. Nowhere does Wiesel contemplate the possibility that Jews and the state of Israel might realize that the Jewish state was born with tremendous violence that it directed against Palestinians and has been an unmitigated disaster for them. Such a view would admit Jewish and Israeli culpability. A turnaround of this kind would portend a type of analysis that allows Palestine and Palestinians to claim a destiny independent of Jewish history. What others think to be an unavoidable conclusion—that something has gone terribly wrong in Israel—is unthinkable for Wiesel.

Is what Wiesel thinks is impossible for Palestinians also unthinkable for Jews? If Wiesel conceded that the impossible thought of Israel as a burden was possible for Palestinians, even if Wiesel still affirms the destiny of Israel as an overriding concern, is there any room in Wiesel's message for Jews to touch upon this other unavoidable conclusion? In other words, can Jews understand both that Israel exists and will continue to exist and that, for Palestinians, Israel has been and continues to be a disaster?

In Wiesel's message, there is little room for this evolving understanding. Those Jews who carry both sensibilities in their minds and hearts are on the outside. This is why these Jews refused to celebrate Israel's anniversary. They were paying more attention to the Palestinian commemoration of their ongoing Nakba.

High-Speed Rail and the Messianic

Given the parameters of what Wiesel understands is thinkable for Jews, Jews who conclude that Israel is culpable for the plight of the Palestinians are misguided. They may believe Palestinian propaganda. Worse, they may be willfully treasonous.

If Jews grant the possibility that Palestinians have a destiny of their own, we enter a dangerous terrain. For Wiesel and other Jewish spokespersons, granting Palestinians an equal playing field with Jews is a slippery slope. If Jews recognize the displacement of Palestinians as a crime, then a remedy has to be contemplated. One potential remedy is the displacement of the Jewish state.

For Wiesel, no Jew should criticize or, God forbid, abandon Israel. Dovetailing with Wiesel, Mortimer Zuckerman, owner and publisher of the *New York Daily News* and *U. S. News and World Report*, wrote this tribute to Israel in *Time*:

> If there is an absence of war, Israeli society will continue to develop and become more integrated, mitigating divisions between its orthodox and non-orthodox, and Arab and Jewish populations, and between rich and poor. Over time, there will be a de facto and maybe even a de jure if not an emotional acceptance of a two-state solution—if not by agreement, which will be very difficult for any Palestinian leader given the radicalism and incitement of hatred within that community, then some *modus vivendi* of live-and-let-live in which people begin to focus on building their own lives rather than destroying Israel.
>
> I believe there is a special moral leadership role that Israel must provide for the Jewish communities around the world, inspiring them to continue to value the fact that they are members of the Jewish community in whatever country they are, and still honor their Jewish traditions—not necessarily in orthodoxy of religious practices, but in the recognition of thousands of years of a very unique history that has in times of peace and prosperity, enabled the Jewish community to make a huge contribution to the welfare of the world.[5]

5. Mortimer Zuckerman, "Israel at 60," *Time*, May 8, 2008.

Like Wiesel, Zuckerman emphasizes the leadership role of Israel in inspiring Diaspora Jews to embrace the values of the Jewish tradition. Although having little to do with religion, this recognition acknowledges the "very unique history" that allow Jews to make a "huge contribution to the welfare of the world." Zuckerman hopes as well that in the future Israel will "continue to develop its internal life by overcoming the divisions within Israel itself."

Overcoming the fractures between the Orthodox and secular elements of Israeli life, as well as integrating Israeli "Arabs" into the mainstream of Israel's life, is on Zuckerman's Israel agenda. What this would mean with regard to the official Jewishness of Israel is left without comment. Over time Zuckerman believes that Palestinians in the West Bank and Gaza will be rewarded with a state alongside Israel but only if their "radicalism and incitement of hatred" of Israel is mitigated. Unfortunately, Zuckerman feels that some of the more enlightened Palestinian leadership is handcuffed by an overwhelming resentment of Israel. The mass of Palestinians and Arabs still focus on destroying Israel rather than "building their own lives."

Zuckerman mentions Palestinians reluctantly, reducing them to those Palestinians who live outside Israel's recognized borders. Israel's occupation of and settlements in parts of Jerusalem and the West Bank goes without mention. Perhaps Zuckerman does not perceive the occupation of Palestinian lands as an occupation or the settlements there as illegal under international law. Does Wiesel? Since they are not discussed, it is difficult to know. Their silence on the occupation and settlements is telling.

Again, as with Wiesel, Zuckerman views Israel as innocent. Although Israel needs some internal adjustments, these will come to pass when the Palestinians extricate themselves from their thoroughly unjustified and unproductive resentment toward Israel. At the same time, the Jewish Diaspora continues to look toward Israel as an example for their lives. Although the example Zuckerman provides is that "very unique history," nowhere does he detail what that uniqueness is. Nor does he explain the impact Israel has had on Jewish history.

Like Wiesel, Zuckerman thinks that Israel is a culmination of an extended Jewish journey through time. The state of Israel and the Jewish Diaspora in America form a dual and harmonious Jewish sensibility in the world. Solving the internal problems within Israel and extending that bond between Israeli and American Jews bodes well for Jews in general. It is also important for the global community. This could include the Palestinians and Arabs, but only if their regressive culture and majority religion turn away from what Zuckerman considers their futile and senseless hate.

Two other entries in *Time* on the sixtieth anniversary are interesting—the first from Ronald Lauder, billionaire businessman, philanthropist and president of the World Jewish Congress, the second from Rabbi Adin Steinsaltz, one of the leading Talmudic scholars in the world.

Lauder writes:

> At 60, Israel is a strong and thriving democracy, flourishing in a tough neighborhood. Yet, Israel remains threatened by the Iranian proxies of Hamas and Hezbollah. Peace, security and stability in the region seem remote. But one can dream?
>
> Ten years from now, Israel will live side-by-side with its neighbors in peace and security. The Negev and adjacent deserts will blossom—an example to every developing nation.
>
> Twenty years from now, a highway and high-speed rail link will connect Cairo with Jerusalem and Damascus. Gigantic desalination plants will provide plenty of fresh water to all.
>
> Thirty years from now, Israel will be respected in the family of nations, no longer singled out for discrimination in the international community.
>
> Forty years from now, the borders between all Middle Eastern countries will be open to travel, trade, education and culture. A common market, based on the European model, will raise the standard of living for all, and the region will become a major high-tech hub.
>
> Fifty years from now, the countries of the Middle East will jointly host the Olympic Games, and the Iranian women's soccer team will win the final.
>
> Sixty years from now, history students will look back at 2008 and wonder why it took so long.[6]

Lauder's vision of where Israel is and where it will be in the next sixty years is interesting for a variety of reasons. In the first place, Lauder does not mention Palestinians at all. An ostensible Palestinian reference, Hamas, is linked with Hezbollah as being Iranian puppets. Iran is part of Israel's "tough neighborhood" where, despite the backwardness of the surrounding countries,

---

6. Ronald Lauder, "Israel at 60," *Time*, May 8, 2008.

Israel's democracy flourishes. If the Middle East as a whole is to flourish in the future it will be through Israel's integration in the Middle East.

Lauder's vision of the future is specific and eclectic. Especially important is Israel's advanced technology. Israel's modernity can push the backwardness of the Arab world forward. Echoing Wiesel and Zuckerman, Lauder believes that for progress to take place the regressive Islamic sensibility of Iran and elsewhere in the Middle East will have to be defeated.

Notice that when Israel is one hundred and twenty, Palestinians are absent in Lauder's vision. The tough neighborhood without modernity on Israel's sixtieth is modernized sixty years later. Everyone is happy. Lauder's future vision minimizes nationalism. As the European model triumphs, Lauder describes modernizing major cities like Cairo and Damascus without national designations. Israel, however, remains Israel. In Lauder's future, will Israel also forfeit aspects of its sovereignty for the greater good of the Middle East's Common Market? After all, the European model, beginning with the Common Market, leads eventually to the European Union where a shared citizenship is envisioned. A common currency is embraced. Unrestricted travel and employment permits are the norm.

Lauder envisions this commonality for the Arab states only. Israel remains defined by nationality, ethnicity, and religion. Yet, even as Israel is the engine to transform the backward Middle East into modernity, there is there something about Israel that avoids the unfolding of modernity's transnationality. Turned around, in this modern future, Israel is backward. It retains identities and borders that Lauder's modern vision of the Middle East erases.

In Lauder's future vision, Israel is accepted in the international community. Lauder writes that one day Israel "will no longer be singled out for discrimination by the family of nations." He provides few details. However, several scenarios suggest themselves, not least that Israel could lose its singled-out status if it ceases to exist as a distinctive nation-state and becomes a true democracy for all its citizens, Jews and Palestinians. This is far from Lauder's perspective. Closer to Lauder's vision is that the international community will accept Israel if Palestinians cease to exist within Israel-controlled geography. Better still is if Palestinians assimilate into major cities like Cairo and Damascus. Another possibility is that Israel will be embraced because it is a beacon of democracy and modernity in the Middle East and Israel's original and ongoing cleansing of Palestinians is submerged in the region's modern affluence. This last possibility seems closest to Lauder's sensibilities. Is this Wiesel and Zuckerman's vision of the future, too?

Despite the Middle East's Israel-centered movement into a glorious future, Lauder's envisions Israel's need to remain a Jewish state. If Lauder believed in Israel's discontinuance, it is doubtful his meditation would have been included in *Time's* tapestry. Instead, like Wiesel and Zuckerman, Lauder pictures Israel as an advanced European state in a backward Arab Middle East.

Is there room for modernity's logic to unfold in another direction? Arab states can disappear. Israel cannot. Israel's forever status may simply respond to a political need for the protection of Jews that even a glorious Middle East future fails to dispel. Or is Israel a religious entity in Jewish consciousness that survives the demise of retrograde Islam?

Lauder's argument runs this way. Europe is the vehicle through which the Middle East overcomes its Arab backwardness. Israel as Europe in the Middle East is the specific way forward for the Arab world. As important, for Lauder the disappearance of Middle East backwardness will be the ultimate demonstration that the Palestinian and Arab struggle against Israel was a relatively short-lived, misplaced, and retrograde affair. Ostensibly a political grievance, and presented as such, history will record Palestinian and Arab resistance to Israel as a function of its underdevelopment.

As development becomes the main focus, Israel is secured. "Arabness" declines. Soon rail links and desalinization are achieved. Peace is at hand. The time comes when all is forgotten. Rather than a pariah state, Israel is singled out as the engine of change and development in what was formerly the most irredentist regions of the world.

Meanwhile, from yet another perspective, Adin Steinsaltz comments:

> The continuation of the State of Israel depends on the ability of the state, or better still its people, to solve the problem of its identity. As an entity, the state is in the stage of adolescence, asking: Who am I? From its inception, it has had two very different answers: Israel is a Jewish state, or Israel is a state of Jews. This reflects the basic ambivalence of Zionism, which is, on the one hand the desire for complete assimilation, to become a normal nation to the point of annihilation. But at the same time, Zionism was a Messianic movement (even when not always religious), craving for definition and difference. This problem is expressed in every facet of life—law and education, economy and defense. So far the answers are mixed and confused, erratic like any adolescent.

As a general collection of Jews (by any definition), Israel may continue to exist by inertia, although the constant outside pressure, internal friction and the ability to immigrate and disappear will eventually disrupt the state. The only way to ensure the state is, strangely enough, spiritual—by deciding that Israel is a Jewish State that has to find its strength in reconnecting to its past, to a feeling of a mission. Army and economy may help but the state can exist only when it is built on a dream.[7]

Steinsaltz's anniversary reflections are closer to Wiesel's in the search for Jewish identity. Nonetheless, Steinsaltz goes off the beaten track. How Jews are to live and be accepted in the Middle East is absent here. In Steinsaltz's vision, only Jews appear. Everything non-Jewish, including Palestinians and other Arabs, is gathered under the rubric "constant outside pressure."

For Steinsaltz—himself born and living in Israel—Jewish identity within Israel is questionable. After decades of Israel's existence, Jews still search for their true identity. Steinsaltz sees the Israeli army as one of the mainstays for the integration of Jews in Israel. It is one of few markers that make Israel, Israel. The army is a strong internal marker because of external Palestinian and Arab pressure. The economy, perhaps the advance of modern technology itself, which is a key to Lauder's sense of the future of Israel as Europe in the Middle East, is another Israel identity marker.

Yet, for Steinsaltz, these are only part of Zionist dream, the part that has an assimilationist bent. An assimilationist view seeks to normalize the Jewish condition and make Israel a normal nation—a Jewish state rather than a state of the Jews.

Steinsaltz opts for the second definition, Israel as a state of the Jews. He is against normalization and for a set-apart Jewishness of the state. This is true with regard to the Jewishness of Jews who live in Israel like himself. Steinsaltz labels this Jewish "craving for definition and difference" messianic. In Israel, however, the messianic within Jewish life is far from accepted. Jews are confused about Israel and what it means for Jews and Judaism. Jewish identity questions are unresolved. Israel is "erratic, like any adolescent."

For Steinsaltz, the options are clear. If Israel chooses to be a state like any other state, inertia will triumph. Over time assimilation, internal friction, and emigration will dominate. Israel as a state will be disrupted. Its disappearance will be assured. Without stating it directly, Steinsaltz believes that the "constant

7. Adin Steinsaltz, "Israel at 60," *Time*, May 8, 2008.

outside pressure" is part of this scenario. If Israel wants normalization and the surrounding countries refuse it, Steinsaltz asks why Jews should remain in Israel. Safer parts of the world beckon them. Without a strong messianic Jewish identity, Israel makes little sense.

Although inertia is possible elsewhere, Steinsaltz fears inertia will lead Israel to collapse. Without the messianic, Israel will lose the loyalty of its Jewish citizens. Using Wiesel's language, the unpredictable aspect of Jewish history that has led Jews to the state of Israel cannot be maintained simply because of the unavoidable realities around Israel. There must be an internal reason for Jews to have a state. For Steinsaltz, this means an identity related to Jewish destiny.

What is the dream that Steinsaltz cites at the end of his essay? Reconnecting to the past and to a feeling of mission seems amorphous. Obviously Steinsaltz's mission is very different than Lauder's. Integration of the state within the people Israel's Jewishness is Steinsaltz's view. Lauder's emerging Europeanization of the Middle East is not enough for Steinsaltz. Jewishly speaking, it is a nonstarter, and thus utterly irrelevant.

Steinsaltz's sense of the past is akin to Wiesel's. The Jewish past is found in the Bible and after, but certainly not the Jewish past as it relates to the founding of the state of Israel or what happened and is happening to Palestinians. Like Wiesel, Steinsaltz's view of history is Judeocentric; others are excluded. More, the Palestinian Other is silenced. The only Other that exists is the "Other" within Jewish life. Steinsaltz finds this in the struggle between assimilationist Jews and Jews who want to deepen their Jewish religious identity.

INSTRUMENTALIZING TORAH-TRUE JUDAISM

As might be expected, *Time's* spectrum was narrow. Only mainstream Jewish voices were featured. Absent were Progressive Jews and Jews of Conscience. Similarly absent were anti-Zionist Jews. In the presentation of mainstream Jewish understandings, this was understandable. Nonetheless, by excluding other views, alternative futures were excluded. Considering the controversy surrounding Israel, it was irresponsible of *Time* to bar other Jewish viewpoints.

Obviously—considering the narrowness of the discussion—Palestinian voices were excluded as well. I doubt that the inclusion of Palestinians was even considered. Lacking, too, was a *Time* counterpart—"The Palestinian Catastrophe at 60." Think of the missed possibilities for opposing views to be shared. Dialogue, even if contentious, provides opportunity for forward movement.

A unique feature—"Israel and Palestine at 60"—could have explored the future in a way the Jewish mainstream had never imagined. What if Jews and Palestinians together were the agents for a contextual Middle Eastern modernization? What if, through Jewish and Palestinian integration, Israel-Palestine modeled a shared future for the Middle East? Such voices would have added to the conversation.

Would these additions have shown Wiesel, Zuckerman, Lauder, and Steinsaltz to be relevant, directly addressing the present and future? Perhaps the editors feared that in a more diverse discussion they would have been found wanting, deflecting the issues, or simply one-sided.

Time's choice of commentators was limited in other significant ways. Another important aspect of the Israeli-Palestinian discussion, the broader Arab world, was also left on the sidelines. They, too, have experienced Israel for many years. Would it benefit the readers of *Time* to hear their viewpoints? Think if *Time* had included the voices of Uri Avnery, Jeff Halper, Mazin Qumsiyeh, and Joseph Massad. *Time* readers could then contemplate an unexpected future of Israel. The future of the Middle East would look different as well.

Now think of the public's response to this expanded discussion. No doubt some would have accused *Time* of being antisemitic. Would others have breathed a sigh of relief, thanking *Time* for breaking the log-jam of thinkable thought?

Take the views of the Orthodox anti-Zionist Yakov Rabkin, whose writing on Zionism is explosive. Views like his were excluded as well. Rabkin claims that, from the beginning of modern Zionism, most Jews have been bystanders to the Zionist movement. At least in the early years, a good percentage of Jews were opponents. Although Steinsaltz is a religious proponent living within the Jewish state, Rabkin analyzes the different strands of religious opposition to Israel. Historically, opposition to a Jewish state was characteristic of traditional Judaism. In turn, Zionism represented a profound change in Diaspora Judaism. In Rabkin's view, state Zionism is guided by a secularized ethic antithetical to the religious grounding of traditional Judaism.[8]

Rabkin argues that Zionism emerged from a minority of Jewish thinkers influenced by Europe's nineteenth- and twentieth-century involvement with nationalism and secularization. These thinkers saw the Jewish future as being connected to both sensibilities. With the rise of Hitler and the Nazis, other Jewish nationalist and secular elites helped further this transformation. Zionist

8. Yakov Rabkin, *A Threat from Within: A Century of Jewish Opposition to Zionism* (London: Zed, 2006).

thought and historical events came together in a way that deeply affected the internal life of the Jewish people.

In relation to the external world, Zionists emphasized the need for Jews to transform their socioeconomic, political, and national positions. According to Rabkin, through Zionism, Diaspora Jewish sensibilities adopted worldly devices and strategies. This included the desire to wield power and establish a Jewish state.

Through this process, Judaism's Diaspora religious foundations were transformed and politicized. In a short span of decades, Judaism's covenantal testimony and its dependence on God became reoriented to power and the state. With the Orthodox Jews of that time, Rabkin sees that transformation exemplified in state Zionism. Rabkin stresses that state Zionism is more than a new kind of Jewish politics. It is an assault on two thousand years of Rabbinic Judaism.

Today, most of the Jewish religious establishment is constructively involved with the state of Israel. This includes various forms of Orthodox Judaism that initially opposed Zionism. For Rabkin, this testifies to Zionism's sweeping victory. Zionism has become normative in the Jewish world. It is so deeply entrenched within Judaism that when Rabkin writes of a religiosity before political and secular Zionism, his views are often met with incredulity and suspicion. Can such an anti-Zionist presentation be Jewish? Can an anti-Zionist be an Orthodox Jew?

Contravening the contemporary assumptions, Rabkin offers a sweeping condemnation of secular and political Zionism. Even more provocatively, he considers state Zionism a form of anti-Judaism. Ironically, many of his Orthodox religious colleagues have adopted Zionism wholesale.

For Rabkin, Zionism is contrary to traditional Orthodox Judaism's messianism. Judaism's messianism depended on the faithfulness of Jews to the covenantal life with God. Zionism transformed this dependence into a human-oriented movement of self-help. Being focused on the human, God is excluded. Ultimately, the covenant is excluded as well.

Orthodoxy's Zionist transformation represents a paradox. What was Judaism is no longer. What was defined as outside of Judaism is now seen as the only way to be Jewish. Rabkin goes a step further. He defines the Judaism that has come into being as against Judaism itself. Rabkin asks how you can have a Judaism that believes primarily or even exclusively in human agency without God.

To buttress his points, Rabkin analyses Reform Judaism and its long history of anti-Zionism. By the 1940s and beyond, Reform Judaism entered the Zionist fold. In doing so, Reform Judaism was transformed. In its nineteenth-century origins, Reform Judaism was the polar opposite of Orthodox Judaism. Reform Jews understood their mission to be a light unto the nations wherever Jews lived. If Orthodox Judaism's destiny in the world was linked with God and faithfulness to God's law as found in the Torah, Reform Judaism's understood itself as the vanguard of the prophetic voice in the world.

In order to become a beacon of light in the modern world, Reform Judaism sought to purify the ancient Jewish codes into its essence. Thus released, Jews would be free to spearhead justice in the world. Reform Judaism modernized Judaism while retaining its Jewish core. As part of modernization, Reform Judaism jettisoned the idea of Jews as a nationality. Before the Holocaust, Reform Judaism opposed Zionism. It saw Zionism as a retrogressive Jewish nationalism rooted in ancient myth.[9]

Although Orthodox and Reform Judaism were traveling in opposite directions on religious issues, both came to the same conclusion regarding state Zionism. Orthodox Jews were historically against Zionism because they awaited the Messiah for the Jewish return to the land. Rather than the land, Reform Jews saw fulfillment of its mission in progress, democratization, and the justice-seeking movements of the modern age. For their respective reasons, Orthodox and Reform Judaism initially opposed Zionism in the internal life of their communities and in the public stands of their respective denominations.

In response to the Holocaust, both movements underwent profound changes. Their opposition to Zionism transformed into a positive and sometimes militant support of the state of Israel. Both movements underwent a Zionization in outlook. Zionization became so entrenched that the movements and its members soon forgot they ever had negative views on a Jewish state.

Rabkin is critical of this transformation. For Rabkin, political Zionism distorts the Torah and God-centered foundations of Judaism. He refers to Zionism as the "nationalist instrumentalization" of Judaism as well as a "negation of traditional Judaism." As for the use of the Torah and Jewish tradition by Zionism to justify its claims to the Land of Israel, Rabkin is unsparing: "Some go as far as to compare the frequency of references to Jerusalem in the Torah and the Koran. Others invoke Judaic ritual, the daily prayers and grace said after meals in an attempt to demonstrate that for centuries the Jews have dreamed of the return to Jerusalem. But the critics of Zionism detect a deliberately falsified reading of tradition: every reference to return is

9. For an analysis of Reform Judaism and its relation to Zionism, see Michael A. Meyer, *Response to Modernity: A History of the Reform Movement in Judaism* (New York: Oxford University Press, 1988), 293-95).

an appeal to God to bring back the exiles, rather than a call to Jews to willfully appropriate the land."[10]

Rabkin comments further on this misrepresentation. For Rabkin, adding up the number of times Jerusalem is mentioned in the Bible is a crass attempt to legitimize Israeli control over the city that Orthodox Jews consider holy. Instead of political control, Rabkin notes that the "followers of the Jewish tradition see in these words an expression of messianic hope, the abdication of all pretenses to terrestrial power and an appeal for compassionate mercy. Salvation is only to be expected from God, and never from 'flesh-and-blood' human beings. To interpret these texts as a call for a war of national liberation would seem to do violence to their explicit content." Rabkin charges a wholesale distortion of texts, prayers, and even God's will. What Rabkin leaves unaddressed is whether this distortion is conscious or at times forced.[11]

For Rabkin, it is clear that Zionism and the state of Israel represent a fundamental and negative break with Jewish history. Instead of a politicized, state-Zionized Judaism, God- and Torah-centered Judaism represents the Jewish mission in the world. Rabkin understands the Jewish mission to be completely different than one of birthing and maintaining a state. Relying on God and fulfilling God's commandments is the essence of Judaism. At the same time, Judaism presents a different vision of life than the ideologies necessary for loyalty to a state.

In forming a Jewish state, Jews pursue normalization. Yet Rabkin believes that the mission of Jews is the opposite of the Other Nations. Jews are called to reject the kind of nationality that represents assimilation to the world. Rabkin views assimilation as an attempt to flee Jewish destiny. Jews were chosen and set apart as a people to model a different way of living in the world. Instead of becoming like the Other Nations, traditional Judaism sees Jews set apart as a holy nation and as a witness within the world. If Jews take on the attributes of statehood and all that is necessary to be a state, how can Jews do anything but assimilate to the world?

Still more challenging is Rabkin's traditional understanding of Jewish suffering as an affirmative response by God to the waywardness of the Jewish people. In essence, God as a loving parent punishes God's wayward children for their sins as a way of bringing them to repentance. Through repentance, Jews come closer to one another and to God. As difficult as it is to hear in our post-Holocaust world, Rabkin believes that the Holocaust was simply one more tragedy that has befallen the Jewish people. Like the other tragedies in Jewish

10. Rabkin, *A Threat from Within*, 80-81.
11. Ibid.

history, the Holocaust occurred because of the sins of the Jewish people. After the Holocaust, the Jewish response should be repentance. Instead, Jews chose a state.

Rabkin believes that Zionism is a movement that distances itself from tradition. It distorts it as well. Many Jews see Israel as the positive response to the Holocaust. Rabkin thinks that it simply compounds the sin. Through the use of power, Zionists attempt to take repentance out of Jewish life. This takes God out of Jewish life as well.

With God gone from Jewish life, Rabkin believes the lessons that tragedies like the Holocaust teach the Jewish people fall by the wayside. Instead of learning from the Holocaust, Zionism takes Jews farther afield. Thus Zionism exacerbates the suffering and should not be seen as positive response to the Holocaust. Therefore, more suffering is on its way. Rabkin is direct in his conclusion: the state of Israel is a disaster for the Jewish people.

Rabkin argues that the Holocaust should be seen as part of a "succession of tragedies that Jewish tradition has placed within the moral framework of reward and punishment, of merit and transgression, of humility and arrogance toward God." This succession includes the biblical stories of the Golden Calf, the revolt of Korah against Moses and Aaron, and the destruction of the Jerusalem Temples. Rabkin includes Zionism as a similar revolt against God. Some religious thinkers that Rabkin cites venture further afield. They see Zionism as the release of "final forces of evil as a prelude to redemption."[12]

For certain strands of Orthodox Jewry, the further away from God we stray, the closer we are to repenting. Hope is drawn from what seems to be unmitigated tragedy. The challenge is to bring the forces of evil to repentance. Rabkin wants to call Jews out of their waywardness. To do this, he identifies the real lessons of the Holocaust and warns Jews away from the state of Israel because it represents a form of empowerment without God.

Once again, Rabkin is stark in his critique. By misunderstanding the lessons of the Holocaust and believing that Israel is the proper response to this suffering, Jews engage in the idolatry defined as rebellion against God. The Bible is clear on the consequences for the sin of idolatry. For Rabkin, the consequences are the same today.

Rabkin considers Jewish waywardness within the context of being true and untrue to God's will and power. By taking the Holocaust as destruction and Israel as reconstruction, Jews attempt to limit God's power. By limiting God's power, Jews limit God's ability to judge Jews individually and collectively. If Jews are no longer under God's power and judgment, then Jews can take on the

---

12. Ibid., 190-91.

world in the way they want. To create space for a Jewish state, for example, the land of others can be stolen. Although this is possible in the Torah under God's orders, Rabkin believes that Rabbinic Judaism strictly forbids such behavior except as a response to God's will.

Rabkin cites traditional Orthodox belief that, after being exiled from the land, return to land is forbidden without God's instructions. Therefore, occupying Palestinian land because of the Holocaust compounds the sin that Jews were exiled for in the first place. Besides, if Jews take the land without God's leadership, who then is to judge their behavior in the land? Without that judgment, Jews are liable, as they have been in the past, to adopt strange gods. When Jews adopt strange gods, they participate in economic and political practices that God likewise judges as idolatrous.

Once Jews declare their independence from God and God's commandments, the state of Israel is on its own. So, too, are Jews who live within the state and Diaspora Jews who enable the state with political advocacy and financial donations. They set themselves up as God. For Rabkin, this is worse than the biblical admonition against placing an earthly king on the throne of Israel. In contemporary Jewish life, the state of Israel has become the King of Kings. The Holocaust is the king's servant. From where, then, will the prophets come to advise Jews that they have strayed from the true God's rule?

Rabkin sees a calamity on the horizon. The calamity emanates from Zionism and the state of Israel. Rabkin believes that the calamity will come without warning.

A small minority of Jews hold Rabkin's religious view of Zionism and the state of Israel. Most Jews are unaware of these views or the possibility that authentic Jews could hold such views. Few Orthodox or Reform Jews today think that active Jewish nationalism is either ungodly or regressive. For the most part, they are unaware that Zionism and the state of Israel were once understood to be an abdication of tradition to a secular nationalistic modernity.

That Rabkin publishes and promulgates his views is astonishing. Nonetheless, questions linger. Are these pre-Holocaust understandings acceptable as viable options for post-Holocaust Orthodox and Reform Jews—or for Jews in general? It could be that the Holocaust changed everything in Jewish life.

Rabkin spends less time exploring another strand of Jewish opposition to Zionism, the secular internationalist sensibility in Jewish life that flourished in the early decades of the twentieth century. Many of these justice-oriented Jews were attracted to communism and various forms of state and utopian socialism.

Historically, this is broadly referred to as the Jewish Left. The Jewish Left felt called to work with other nationalities and economic classes for the empowerment and equality of all. They saw national, ethnic, and religious boundaries as artificial and oppressive. This included explicit Jewish causes and identity.

In a just future, the Jewish Left felt that these regressive boundaries would be transcended. Loosed from the repressive and superstitious aspects of religion, capitalism, and nationality, Jews and others would establish an integrated and just international political and economic order. Since concentrating on ethnic and religious bonds was passé and negative, the Jewish Left saw the creation of Israel as the creation of another artificial nation-state boundary in the Middle East. Too, Jewish internationalists saw Israel as the latest and perhaps last creation of a Western colonial state in the oil-rich Middle East. They viewed Israel as a Western colonial misadventure as the era of colonialism was coming to an end.

The Holocaust changed the trajectory of Orthodox, Reform, and internationalist understandings of Jewish commitment and life. By the time Israel was established as a Jewish state, all three movements were changing direction. The change became definitive in the ensuing years. Orthodox Jews adopted the Holocaust as a unique catastrophe in Jewish history, though, as Rabkin notes, a minority of Orthodox remain opposed to the changes. Reform Judaism engaged in a complex and tumultuous soul-searching. In the end, the movement embraced modern Jewish nationality as a positive endeavor. The Jewish Left split over this issue. Some continued on their internationalist communist and socialist paths. Others left the Left, seeing its anti-Zionism as an ideology that denied Jewish particularity. In their view, the Jewish Left was in danger of becoming a form of antisemitism.

A New Orthodoxy

By the end of the 1967 war, the tumult ceased—at least for a time. Holocaust consciousness became predominant. Dissidents of all stripes were marginalized. While some veteran leadership within these movements struggled with the changes, the younger generation forced discussions to closure.

The authentic Jew of today was redefined as committed to the memory of the Holocaust as unique and formative of Jewish commitment and belief and to the state of Israel as it was formed and continued. By the early 1970s, the Holocaust and Israel were twinned. One could no longer be discussed without the other. The Holocaust and Israel became the essential nonnegotiable element of Jewish identity. Without commitment to the memory of the Holocaust and support for the state of Israel, one's Judaism—indeed, Jewishness—was questioned.

The authentic Jew of post-1967 life carried commitment to Holocaust memory and the state of Israel almost as a faith statement. This, as the question of God was very much disputed. In the main, and in the post-1967-war era, even the disputed question of God was resolved—as irresolvable. Thus the God question, seemingly essential to Orthodox and Reform Judaism, was bracketed. Orthodox and Reform Jews continued their belief in God, at least in their liturgical settings. In and around worship, however, other theological discussions occurred. As we have seen, Holocaust consciousness gave rise to a distinctive Holocaust theology that placed Jewish suffering and empowerment at the heart of Jewish identity.

Rabkin is again interesting here. The very title of his book—*The Threat from Within*—is instructive. Although Holocaust consciousness and support for the state of Israel are overwhelmingly dominant in Jewish life, aspects of previous theological and political Jewish understandings remain. Pre-Holocaust and pre-Israel perspectives survive on the margins in altered, perhaps preconscious forms. When the centrality of the Holocaust and Israel is challenged, the new Orthodox, Reform, and internationalist orthodoxies are vulnerable. Past Jewish perspectives continue even when submerged.

When the subversive message of new movements overcomes old orthodoxies, they seek to become the new orthodoxy. Another round of subversive movements waits in the background to challenge the new. What appears to be the ultimate triumph of a particular orthodoxy is usually short-lived. New questions confront the same movement that confronted the old orthodoxy with their new questions. What is understood as the eternal definition of faith or culture or politics is upstaged. The eternal becomes temporal. Old orthodoxies are supplanted.

Part of the movement from one orthodoxy to another, and then another, are historical events that challenge present systems of world ordering. The Holocaust as an event of overriding magnitude had to be dealt with. Almost from the beginning, it was clear that no previous Jewish system of understanding history or religion could suffice. Regarding Orthodox Judaism, it was clear that the Holocaust challenged the idea of a loving God punishing God's chosen people for their waywardness. With millions murdered, no religious system could escape a reckoning.

As Rabkin points out, however, previous catastrophes in Jewish life challenged understandings of a punishing God. Still, the mass killing of Jews as it took place under the Nazis was singular in Jewish history, perhaps in world history. It also took place in a secularizing, scientific, and technological age. The combination of the overwhelming scope of the catastrophe within the context of the understandings of the modern age delivered the *coup de grace* to traditional Jewish responses to catastrophe.

Reform Judaism had an *avant-garde* understanding of human progress. The idea of progress suffered the same fate as the loving/punishing God of Orthodox Judaism. That the Holocaust could befall Jews in the middle of the twentieth century and in Europe, the very epitome of advanced Western culture, shook the movement's supreme confidence in progress. The Reform conception of Diaspora Jews as a light unto the nations begged the question of Jewish survival. Many Reform Jews began to see the Holocaust as an assault on the entirety of their worldview.

Reform Judaism ultimately agreed with those Jews who affirmed Jewish nationality as a response to this unparalleled assault. Jewish nationality rather than the Jewish prophetic became the essence of Reform Judaism. Or, rather, Reform Judaism adopted the state of Israel as their new prophetic outreach. Could the state of Israel become a light unto the nations?

Rabkin's "threat from within" became one of the organizing motifs of Orthodox and Reform Judaism. A reversal took place when Holocaust consciousness became the norm. What had been the norm, a religious system that prohibited defining and disruptive events like the Holocaust and the state of Israel from being decisive, became marginal. Still, underneath and around the new system remained fragments of the old.

As Orthodox Jews signed on to Zionism and Israel, they did so in their own way. Some continued to believe in aspects of divine punishment for Jewish sins. Others continued to believe that the messianic ingathering in the Land of Israel came from God rather than human initiative. They also questioned how God could mandate such suffering and turned toward the state of Israel as a protector. Orthodox Jews began to see the state of Israel as complex sign of the ingathering of Jews promised to herald the messianic era.

After the initial shock of the Holocaust wore off, Reform Jews held fast to an essential optimism about human progress. The problematic of human progress and mass death remained unresolved. Today Reform Jews continue on as if their tradition is intact, even as they also know that it has lost its inner certainty. They continue to argue the mission of the Jews as a light unto the nations while affirming the state of Israel as a carrier of that light. When some Reform Jews realize that Israel-the-dream is more complex in reality, another series of contradictions comes to the fore.

In religious traditions, orthodox thought claims a status above history. Nonetheless, it arrives within history and departs in history as well. Instead, orthodoxy has more to do with the reorganization of what was before, downplaying certain elements of the tradition and highlighting others. In the end, what comes to be known as tradition contains elements that appear, disappear and reappear. Deemphasized elements of the tradition wait for another day. Nothing in tradition is lost to the extent that it is impossible to recover. What once was central now exists in the shadows; when it returns, it does so in a different configuration. Nothing in tradition is lost. Nothing in tradition returns as it was.

When Jews refuse to ascribe the Holocaust to God's punishment for waywardness, are they simply rebelling against God and God's power? When Jews pursue power religiously in post-Holocaust Jewish life, is their use of power an exaggerated case of hubris instead of the humility and repentance God calls for? Or is this refusal and pursuit a realistic adjustment of the relationship between the human and the divine?

Is Jewish reliance on God or human progress warranted after the Holocaust? Either relying on God or on human progress is a faith statement. The Holocaust certainly challenges God *and* human progress. However, investing Jewish identity heavily in the Holocaust and the state of Israel is a gamble.

If God and progress may be considered in the Jewish equation, the overwhelming nature of post-Holocaust life negates both as defining. In the post-Holocaust world, if God or progress is affirmed, a parallel argument and affirmation has to be made. At some level, and with differing perspectives, that parallel argument involves the Holocaust and Israel.

Against tradition, the mainstream of contemporary Jewish life doubts God and progress. As well, the mainstream of Jewish life abstains from questioning the meaning of the Holocaust and Israel. Insofar as Jewish tradition has reservations about the meaning of the Holocaust and the cost of Jewish empowerment, contemporary Jews limit the evolution of the Jewish tradition. Still, the formative events of Holocaust and Israel have overwhelmed the Jewish tradition. Criticism that comes from tradition has been marginalized. When the criticism from the past dressed in new clothing returns, most Jews define it as outside of Judaism and Jewish life.

When elements of the Jewish tradition return as unknown, as outside, and as treason, it begs the question of what authentic Judaism is or can be in the future. Who can claim to be an authentic Jew is up for grabs. Rabkin's sense of traditional Orthodox and Reform Judaism is accurately presented. But if his presentation is so different from what ordinary and informed Jews in their diverse manifestations think is possible or even permissible, then it can be argued that the tradition he argues has become unreal.

If the definition of what it means to be an authentic Jew is so distant from parts of the tradition, the issue then is whether the tradition has purposely been changed or whether something quite separate from the tradition has developed. It could be that a considered or forced evolution of Jewish thought and practice is taking place. Perhaps a certain claim to being Jewish is being established as another form of Jewishness is abandoned.

Rabkin questions whether those Jews who orient their life around the Holocaust and Israel are in fact Jewish. Thus he enters the question of whether there is something essential to being Jewish or whether there can be a twisting and manufacturing of Jewishness that incorrectly, indeed falsely, claims a Jewish identity. Behind the scenes of Rabkin's analysis is whether the Holocaust memorials and the state-of-Israel-anniversary celebrations have anything to do with Judaism and Jewishness. Clearly, Rabkin believes that these bold assertions of Jewish sensibilities involve a false claim.

7

Unraveling God

As we traverse the Jewish world, Palestine casts an ominous shadow over everything Jewish. Indeed, at each anniversary of Israel's birth, Palestine looms larger. During Israel's sixtieth anniversary, Palestine's presence was larger than on Israel's fiftieth, and it was still larger on Israel's sixty-fifth. Meanwhile, the celebration of Israel's existence continues to diminish.

Already events have intervened since the sixtieth anniversary. Just months after the sixtieth anniversary, Israel invaded Gaza. The settlements continue to grow in East Jerusalem and the West Bank. The Wall dividing and encircling Palestinians is now almost complete. The Arab Spring has come and gone. In the United Nations and beyond, Palestinian statehood has been acknowledged.

The pace of boycott, divestment and sanctions (BDS) continues to pick up steam. Some have called BDS the third Palestinian uprising, this uprising being conducted by the international community. Israel's isolation deepens.

The Palestinians are defining of contemporary Jewish life. They reside at the very heart of Jewish history. Perhaps it is time for Jews to see Palestinians as within an expanded covenantal framework or as fellow travelers. Or perhaps the covenant has fled the Jewish people and now resides among Palestinians. Jews in search of the fleeing covenant have to journey with Palestinians in order to embrace the essence of what it means to be Jewish.

If the covenant resides with Palestinians, Jewish life has undergone a transformation far greater than the controversial Yakov Rabkin ever imagined. If the covenant resides with Palestinians, any attempt to embrace the covenant and Jewish life today necessitates an embrace of the Palestinian people. This means that the Holocaust/Israel axis of Jewish identity has expanded outward toward Palestinians. As well, there has been an expansion inward to recover the essence of what it means to be Jewish.

The Jewish indigenous, the prophetic, comes alive in the embrace of the land through Palestinians, who are indigenous to the land. Rather than

God's will—if that can be discerned after the Holocaust—Palestinians become a conduit for a prophetic critique of the people Israel.

The Palestinians therefore embody the prophetic calling for Jews today. In this sense, the Palestinians re-present the prophetic challenge to Jews. Jews of Conscience are up for the challenge. This is another aspect of an evolving joint history, where Jews and Palestinians jointly embody the prophetic critique of unjust power, while at the same time embodying the possibility of a joint future beyond violence and injustice.

We began our exploration in search of a Jewish homeland. It is ironic that this very search may end by following the covenant into exile with Palestinians. The conditions of exile vary. The forcible exile of those who once resided in the land, or those who still live on part of the land but now under Israel's domination, is different from a Jewish exile freely chosen as solidarity with those who are suffering. Still, once embarked upon, exile is defining and unrelenting. Today Jews are called into exile with the Palestinian people.

In Israel-Palestine, the voluntary exile of Jews of Conscience and the forcible exclusion of Palestinians converge. Jews and Palestinians meet in the middle of two histories that are now irrevocably intertwined. This is no romantic idyll. When Jews throw in their lot with Palestinians, they should avoid idealizing the journey. Palestinians with no choice and Jews with many choices are poles apart in their life circumstances. Nonetheless, once a decision is made, exile is certain. Such an exile is burdensome even for the secure and affluent.

Exile is fraught with complexities. These extend from fractious politics to issues relating to Jewish identity. While Jewish exiles witness to a collective Jewish journey, profoundly personal sensibilities are at stake. Exile is a public matter. Exile is also intensely private. The aloneness and violence exiles confront in embodying the truth is demanding.[1]

Think of Jews who believe BDS should be applied to Israel like it was in South Africa. Now read the paid statement in the *New York Times* in April 2012 that compares the boycott movement of today with the Nazi boycott of Jewish businesses in 1933. Referring also to the murder of a rabbi and three children in Toulouse, France, some weeks earlier, the ad begins: "The Holocaust began with boycotts of Jewish stores and end with death camps. The calls for a new Holocaust can be heard throughout the Middle East and in Europe as well. In the wake of the murders of a rabbi and three Jewish children in Toulouse, it is time for the supporters of the Boycott, Divest and Sanction Israel movement

---

1. I wrote about this in *Practicing Exile: The Journey of an American Jew* (Minneapolis: Fortress Press, 2009).

(BDS) to ask themselves what they did to contribute to the atmosphere of hate that spawned these and other murder of Jews." The paid statement lists the names of those who should be "publicly shamed" and "condemned for the crimes their hatred incites." The statement is accompanied by the picture of a Nazi standing outside a Jewish store with a Star of David painted on the entrance. The statement also provides a translation of the sign outside the store warning shoppers away: "Germans! Defend yourselves! Do not buy from Jews!"[2]

All exiles are isolated and vulnerable. Exposure invades the person as well. All exiles experience dislocation and pain. With Jews the stakes are more than ceding territory, more than a feeling of being at odds with the community. The accusation that connects the destruction that occurred in the Holocaust with principled dissent around Israeli policies—as if dissent itself will precipitate another Holocaust—is impossible to deal with solely through rational discussion. Communally and, yes, personally, the stakes are felt. Accusations of encouraging mass murder of Jews cannot be dismissed lightly.

Jewish history is up for grabs. The stakes are more than theoretical. Distance in time from the Holocaust has increased Jewish fears rather than diminished them. High-speed rail and messianic modernity are glosses on the Jewish future. They are utopian thoughts, no matter how colonial in their sensibilities. More and more Jews think that the future of Israel is shrouded in darkness.

The Jewish community is partly responsible for the Jewish individual. The Jewish individual is partly responsible to the Jewish community. The community can be faithful or unfaithful, the individual likewise. Israel, Judaism, and Jewishness are negotiated and intertwined between the Jewish community and the individual Jew. At times, the Jewish community calls the Jewish individual to account. At other times, individual Jews call the Jewish community to account. Jews as a community have a responsibility and a conscience. Individual Jews have both as well.

How the community or the individual discerns the authenticity of its/her calling is the rub. Throughout Jewish history, both the Jewish people and individual Jews have made their claims and seen them acclaimed or defeated. Both have bowed before the other or been sent on their way. So it goes in Jewish history.

The mark of an inscribed covenant and prophetic engagement orients Jews toward fidelity. Because of that fidelity, at certain times in Jewish history

2. Published by the David Horowitz Freedom Center in the New York *Times*, April 24, 2012.

exile is unavoidable. Both fidelity and exile are ingrained in the communal and individual Jewish psyche. Is it this combination that helps explain why the people Israel, Judaism, and Jewishness survive, flourish, decline, and flourish again? Fidelity and exile may explain why Jews undergo assault, annihilation, and revive, refuse to change course, then change course—and why Jews remain constant enough to recognize themselves in memory and continue on.

Fidelity and exile are two sides of the same coin. If fidelity is the watchword, exile is always on the horizon. Exile is fidelity's witness. Exile is the witness that makes the Jewish prophetic viable and enduring. For if the prophetic were not up for exile when the need arises, it would cease to be the prophetic in any meaningful sense. Justice seeking would be relegated to a symbolic interface, a false encounter with the oppressed Other rather than an embodied prophetic presence that suffers for an authenticity larger than itself.

Since Jewishness is often defined as a practice rather than as a speculative possibility, what is the reason for Jews to think seriously along these seemingly theoretical lines? Indeed, the scenarios played out in Jewish history are most often practical responses to formative events within a framework already bequeathed in Jewish history. It is through this framework that Jews respond to particular events. Each particular event is honored in its particularity, even as the response is outlined in its general terms.

Covenant, election, liberation, land, the prophetic, exile and return—all run through Jewish history like a river. The banks expand and contract over time. The current ebbs and flows, depending on circumstance and reflection. If the river is big and strong enough, the river remains or returns to a constancy that is palpable.

Analogies help and give way. The people Israel are hardly a natural occurrence. Like any other communal journey, Jews build and continually rebuild the Jewish "world." The Jewish narrative has a constancy that is clear only when we think in canonical terms. We know that the particular narratives within the Jewish canon were shaped and reshaped, edited and redacted. These disparate parts make sense only within the broader Jewish narrative.

The broader Jewish narrative is also made up of particular narratives that are shaped and reshaped. The canon provides a broad arc within which each narrative element adds up to something more than its separateness. Such a world building is common in relation to any cultural, national, or political identity assumed, changed, or converted to. Yet in Jewish identity, there stands a distinctive that is, if not eternal, at least for humankind, incredibly longstanding.

For Jews, something important is at stake when the questions of fidelity and continuity of Jewish history are raised. Formative events raise anxiety around those stakes but it is, finally, the stakes themselves that are at issue. These stakes are enormous and hardly possible to live up to. Moreover, it takes a leap of faith to believe that in the human journey this effort can be called upon over and over again.

What's more, it takes a strong imagination to think that Jewish fidelity is somehow important to the world and the universe. Could the world really place so much reliance on any one community? Can Jewish fidelity be so important to humanity that even God is called upon to judge the matter?

The answers here are less than clear. The people Israel are called upon from the beginning to wrestle with these questions. Perhaps for a time an answer appears. Yet this answer is found within an ongoing history that has a center outside of the people and God—an existence in the covenant. Although they are differentiated at first, over time God and the covenant become one. Either can go on its way and often does. Still, the Jewish narrative envisions both traveling without either losing sight of the other. God and the covenant are outside of and within history. Thus history is important. History is also more than it appears. Is this one more negotiation to make sense of a historical journey that is "more" than ordinary history?

Such a negotiation makes it possible for a people to journey in time while transcending time. This is accomplished without making transcendence a false encounter projected onto the universe. It avoids lapsing into the contention that our journey on earth is an illusion. In the Jewish journey, meaning is asserted—within history. Yet it is far from certain or obvious how that meaning fares when tested. The test is dynamic. The test is often inconclusive. In the Jewish journey, conclusions vie with inconclusiveness. Neither overwhelms the other.

How the journey continues is the problem. The journey, though frayed, assaulted, and demeaned, somehow helps pull humanity from the quagmire it creates. The quagmire is the human cycle of violence and atrocity that marks the human journey. Jews have something unique to say about this cycle, especially since it claims to be outside and within history at the same time. At least Jews think so.

The Jewish claim is remarkable and, it would seem, unsustainable. However unlikely it may be, sustainability has been achieved. Where the Amorites and Hittites have gone is unknown. Jews still appear in the world. The survival of Jews may rest with the instability of their demonstrated sustainability, placing Jews in a continuity that has a razor's edge.

True, Jewish communities and individuals have assimilated, left the scene, disappeared from history, and fallen dead. The Jewish witness in the world remains alive. It is exploding in our time.

Despite the attrition of history, Jews continue on, make their mark, suffer casualties, rebound, and, as importantly, weave and reweave their narrative in oral and written form. The importance of this survival is rarely lost on Jews themselves. Even when others ignore or actively degrade what Jews claim about themselves, Jews continue on. When the world turns a deaf or negative ear, Jews take the occasion to ramp up their voice and claim.

When Israel and God Are Out of Sync

Jews are, indeed, incorrigible. In the Bible, God notes this time and time again. Jews have also been noted—and pursued—by peoples who have interacted with them throughout history. This has brought Israel great glory and great pain. The pursuit of Jews is yet another aspect of Jewish history that is profoundly unsettling. Paradoxically, it is also part of the stability of the Jewish people.

Can the word *incorrigible* be applied to Israel's God? History is unsettling in and of itself. It is more so when meaning is asserted and when a hard-fought fidelity is found within and through history. When God appears and is known only in history, tension heightens. When promises made by God can only be judged within the context of history, the unsettling of history, known to all, reaches beyond natural reason. If there is a purpose to history, it is unclear. Lack of clarity becomes a challenge when that very lack becomes a driving force to resolve the impasse. Since history is constantly unraveling, one expects the Bible—and God—to take that unraveling and put it right once and for all.[3]

Yet in the formative event of Israel's founding, the unraveling is constant. Moses and Aaron are busy going to and from Pharaoh's palace. God is busy sending plague after plague. Each plague involves the promise that by striking Egypt, Israel will be freed from bondage. After each plague, Egypt recovers. Liberation is delayed. If we were ignorant of the ending—when reading the Bible, we can only pretend we are ignorant—it would seem that Israel's liberation is indefinitely delayed.

Once liberation from Egypt occurs, it unravels. Israel wanders the desert. In the desert wandering, God goes back and forth with Israel. Israel goes back

---

3. The Hebrew Bible does and doesn't put it right. Or, put another way, what is resolved is quickly unresolved again. The resolution that Christianity offers later is rejected by Jews as too facile. Indeed, even for Christianity, their resolution soon unraveled.

and forth with God. God sets Israel aright or Israel rights itself. At times, Israel and God work together. Then a falling out occurs. Disenchantment reappears. A course correction becomes necessary. In the land that is promised and delivered, Moses predicts a further unraveling. As if on cue, the predicted unraveling happens as Israel enters and settles the land. Israel then gets back on track and God does as well. Both fall off again, sometimes at the same time.

Israel and God can be in sync. They can be out of sync. Sometimes, they are at ease together. Other times, they are unsettled together. Either one or the other is settled and unsettled at the same time. For a people, being unsettled is unsustainable. Yet this forces God and Israel to take more responsibility for their continuing relationship. When Israel is out of step, God takes the lead. When God is out of step, Israel takes the lead. At times, both take the lead or vie for it. Once in a while neither leads the other.

A lull in the biblical narrative is rare. When the story goes quiet, the reader takes notice. The pause is disquieting, as if tranquility means either God or Israel is absent. Usually, either Israel or God calls out to the other. Losing contact is impossible to contemplate. Once in a while, God wanders away and disappears from the narrative. Once in a while, Israel wanders away. The Bible loses track of Israel. But this is only on occasion. Absence is a prelude. There is always another encounter.

God and Israel anticipate their rendezvous. Why else call out in the night if either God or Israel actually thought the other had permanently absconded? When the people Israel and God are out of step, the atmosphere is ominous. If Israel's covenantal center and God's presence are in abeyance, what is there to think and do?

In our time, the Holocaust and the state of Israel, seemingly in sync and responding to one another, are bereft. The Jewish ethical core is damaged, perhaps beyond repair. In post-Holocaust Jewish theology, God is nowhere to be found. Where was God in Auschwitz? Where are ethics in Israel?

There is a God to be found always. The powerful assert ethics as their domain. Like everyone else, Jews stress their innocence and search for redemption. Over the last decades, Jews have declared their innocence in suffering and in empowerment. Although there is a reluctance to speak of redemption in a post-Holocaust world, Jewish discourse posits Israel, if not as redemption per se, as a redemptive response to the suffering of the Holocaust.

While specific discussion of Jewish ethics in empowerment is mostly left for the imagination today, it was spoken about boldly in the post-1967-war time period. Then the occupation immediately following was spoken of as short-lived and benign. Such rhetoric is no longer employed. It ceased to make sense decades ago and has not been replaced.

The same is true with the question of God. God was raised specifically, and defiantly, in the aftermath of the 1967 war. Instead, the Holocaust and Israel were named as central to Jewish identity. Today there is silence about God. Even the defiance is spent. Jews inside and outside of Israel exist without a narrative that makes sense of itself. Everyone knows that Jews are living on borrowed narrative time.

After the 1967 war, it was argued that the state of Israel was ancient Israel reborn. A crucial connection among ancient Israel, historic Judaism, and contemporary Jewishness was asserted, with the Holocaust and Israel serving as the connecting links. But this connection made sense only as long as the more traditional, ethical, and religious discourses remained alive and close to Jews and the Jewish experience. Partly through the passage of time and the ruinous state of Jewish ethics, pre-Holocaust and pre-Israel identity is more distant today.

This distance, combined with the collapse of a sense of innocence and redemption in the empowerment of a Jewish state, leaves Jews adrift. Those who argue for the Holocaust and Israel today do so only in terms of political and military power. Survival and security are the mantra. Those who argue Jewish ethics are seen as renegades, purveyors of decline and treason. They are regarded as portents of a second, final Holocaust. The only God-talk left is among those Orthodox Jews who see the final pangs of the messiah in the continuing expansion of Israel, or among those who seek a return to the pre-Holocaust, pre-state understandings of God's will and Jewish disobedience. Within the broader Jewish world, these understandings are quite rightly rejected.

Who in their right mind would countenance such understandings? Jews are not innocent in empowerment. Jews were innocent in their suffering. As the anti-Zionist Orthodox do in a wholly negative way, Holocaust theology twins the Holocaust and Israel in a positive way. Where anti-Zionist Orthodox Jews see both the Holocaust and Israel as a sign of God's punishment, Holocaust theologians see Israel as a response to God's abandonment in the Holocaust.

Between God's punishment and God's abandonment, it seems the only way forward is to choose the latter. However, such a choice entails the possibility of excusing the Palestinian catastrophe as a sidelight to the necessity of a Jewish state after the Holocaust. As well, it seems difficult if not impossible to excuse the necessary damage done in the emergency situation after the Holocaust.

Does the assertion that Israel was necessary, whatever the costs to the Palestinians, demand a continuing justification of Israeli policies long after the emergency years are over? On the one hand, connecting the Holocaust and Israel as God's judgment gives over Jewish innocence to an avenging God. On the other hand, connecting Holocaust and Israel because of God's abandonment frees Jews from any critique of Israeli power.

Once more we encounter Rabkin's "threat from within," though in a different way than he intended. The threat from within might have less to do with recovering ancient theodicy, thus solving the "why" of the Holocaust, and more to do with the recovery of the Jewish ethical tradition as the Jewish context changes radically. Although the question of why God's chosen suffer throughout history continues to perplex Jews, the more immediate question is how an oppressed Jewish people have become the oppressor. The corollary is obvious. What is to be done about it?

The God question remains, but shifts from theodicy to judgment. If the Holocaust and Israel do not represent God's judgment on the people Israel, can God's judgment be anticipated on Israel's misbehavior in the land?

Now if God is out of the theodicy and judgment picture and if the state of Israel is a response to the post-Holocaust emergency years at the same time that it is devastating the Palestinian people, then Jews can exclude fear of divine justice and the ethical command for justice and reconciliation. With God on the sideline, what judgment can be made on the state of Israel and who is entitled to make it? Even if the judgment and the authority to judge are sorted out, minus God's power and ethical commands, where will the power to employ ethics to guide judgment come from?

The Israeli–Palestinian situation is connected to many strands of political, economic, and religious claims and counterclaims. The conundrums multiply. Meanwhile, as the various claims are endlessly disputed, the situation deteriorates. At times, the way forward is returning backward. Yet backward presents another set of challenges that birth few, if any, answers. Although clearly there is no return to the past, the future, at least one different from the past, continues to elude us.

What better time to explore that future? After sixty-five years and counting or, according to Joseph Massad, more than a 130 years, the situation spirals downward. A new bottom for Israel-Palestine continually appears, with or without God. Theodicy is applied and rejected. If the twinning of the Holocaust and Israel is anything, it is a theodicy that begs the question of ethical behavior. Yet it is difficult to envision how a Jewish state in the Middle East, whose foundation is based on the death of millions in Europe, can be sustained forever by the Holocaust/Israel theodicy. The last important text on Holocaust theology was written in the 1980s. Time moves on. People's consciousness does as well.

State power can carry theodicy only so far until it is unmasked by those who are suffering because of its policies. With Palestinians, Jews of Conscience are writing and acting against the politics of oppression. Without them knowing or wanting to be involved with religious issues—often blanching at the very mention of Judaism and God—Jews of Conscience might be the great demystifiers of the last attempt at Jewish theodicy. As with all types of power, the power used to assuage the evil that has befallen a people must be disarmed. If power is left to its own devices, past hurt is expanded and deepened. Power promises deliverance. However, when power causes others to suffer, it furthers the cycle of violence and atrocity. The promise of deliverance is interrupted. As power is used against others in the name of past suffering, talk about past suffering becomes cheap. In time, the invocation of suffering becomes a communal and individual enabler of power. It becomes a mantra repeated so often that it seems triggered by remote control.

Over time, those who use suffering as a lever of power over others are less and less aware of how the listener receives their invocation. They also lose contact with their main constituency—the community for whom they ostensibly speak. A chasm opens. The distance between the sufferings invoked, the power used, and the gulf between the two portends a new round of suffering—and dissent. In the end, will even Jews listen or will Jews simply react to Holocaust imagery that becomes less believable each time it is invoked?

When the powerful seek to heal past suffering by dominating others, their wound only deepens. Indeed, despite their power, the future remains an open wound. Power achieved is never enough to forestall history's wounds. In the Jewish case, to justify power a second Holocaust is projected as imminent. Yet, secure in the world, Jews more and more doubt this prediction. Jews seem stuck. They are traumatized in memory while enjoying the fruits of their liberation. They are pulled in both directions. Yet the unasked question is subconsciously troubling: even if a second Holocaust was imminent could Israel save world Jewry?

For the post-Holocaust Jewish world, there are few ways to hold together a power-enabled theodicy without dire predictions about the future of Israel and thus for Jews everywhere. A definitive logic unfolds. Predicted suffering can be delayed as long as Jewish power remains in place. However, the force to hold off future suffering is never enough. Israel's military supremacy must remain dominant. Every threat to Israel and any potential threat must be eliminated. Israel's ascendancy must be guaranteed eternally.

Holding back future calamity inevitably demands authority on the military battlefield. Discourse becomes a battlefield as well. The possibility of losing the discourse war becomes an obsession. If that war is lost and dissent unmasks the need for military dominance, then where will the community be? Will the community become like Sampson, with his hair shorn, stripped of power?

So the Holocaust, which in traditional Orthodoxy is viewed as a punishment for Jewish sins, becomes with the state of Israel a punishment for others. Punishment moves toward the Palestinians in the first place and toward Jewish dissenters in the second. Jewish dissenters ask whether replacing Orthodox theodicy with a state-power theodicy is the way to deal with Jewish trauma. Is this more or less the same question Palestinians embody?

When power over others is viewed as a prerequisite for survival, achieving protection from a similar trauma becomes a way of life. Potential trauma becomes a justification for power aggrandizements. Though counterintuitive, acquiring power increases the anxiety surrounding power itself. With survival at stake, power becomes a shield against accountability. Power also feeds the delusion that power is innocent and redemptive.

The need for power in the name of past suffering becomes corrupting. The new sufferers are endlessly disparaged as real and potential threats even, and especially after, their defeat. The oppressed others become important actors in the theodicy mythos.

A mechanical repetition is established. Each player has an assigned role, preferably for eternity, if the new power structure has its way. Any threat to the power structure, any changing of roles or words, becomes a threat to the newly empowered and, at least in their mind, to the memory of suffering. Threats to the new order can unravel everything, including the wound that has not healed. Now, for ideological reasons, it becomes a wound that cannot heal.

When theodicy is coupled with power, the specificity of the community's wound is lost. Dissent against the unjust use of power threatens exposure of the wound that has yet to be dealt with adequately. Therefore, theodicy coupled with power is a projection of suffering that has never been and cannot heal. And because that power begins to function in the normal way of creating privilege and status, with the inevitable corruption this entails, probing the original suffering is declared off-limits.

Instead of admitting that probing how power is used is different from questioning the original suffering, the criticism is deflected and inverted.

Critiquing power becomes a matter of denial. So it is with the critics of Israeli policies toward Palestinians, who are routinely labeled Holocaust deniers.[4]

There are few answers to the mass suffering of any people, including Jews. Some believe it is better to project a power that keeps the festering wound distant. Over time, though, the wound remains unhealed until a healing is no longer sought. Since the wound becomes a mark of one's status and reason for being in the world, the removal of the wound becomes unthinkable.

Without the trauma, the community's reason for existence becomes more difficult to explain to others, let alone to itself. The community comes to know itself only within that trauma. This, even when the outside world sees the community as now defined by power. A disjunction arises. Trauma is used to justify the community's existence in the world. Yet more and more people see the community using its trauma as way of projecting power.

The Jewish community's Holocaust trauma has become just that. The use of the Holocaust becomes less and less understandable once the internal identity of an eternally suffering people is no longer accepted as a matter of faith.

After the Holocaust Empire Collapse

What happens when the community's identity is so out of touch with the reality that those outside, and increasingly those inside the community, experience? Those who experience this disjunction begin to reject the community's discussion of its history. What was previously accepted as a matter of faith is doubted. Eventually, it is discarded altogether.

When the Holocaust is analyzed, the community insists that it must fit into certain already internally defined parameters. Otherwise, the discussion is deemed heretical. The same is true with the state of Israel. Only prescribed ways of approaching a political or moral assessment of the Jewish state are allowed. Outside those parameters, the charge is that something other than history is being presented.

In a strange transposition, the rendering of the Holocaust and Israel in purely historical terms is seen as unhistorical. The community narrative—in fact, a community faith narrative—is seen as actual history. History and theology change places. Soon the terrain is so convoluted that the boundaries of both are erased.

---

4. This happens to Norman Finkelstein, even though his parents were survivors of the Holocaust; it also happens to me. See David Horowitz, *The Professors: The 101 Most Dangerous Academics in America* (Washington, DC: Regnery, 2007).

When the boundaries of history and theology are erased, history and speculations about God and humanity enter the realm of sacred myth. Once developed and in place, myth becomes untouchable. Thought about the direction of a community's history is interrupted. Meaning asserted or, in the Holocaust, a kind of meaninglessness that can only be overcome through power, proceeds without challenge. This is so in the realm of thought but also in concrete action. A military strategy, say among Palestinians, is ruled out in advance as a possible solution for a displaced people. Indeed, any military strategy to reclaim land taken by the state of Israel is viewed as an assault on Israel via the entirety of Jewish history. Instead of just war, self-defense is defined as terrorism.

Through a telling inversion, Palestinian resistance becomes proof of the need for a Jewish state. If Israel's occupation of Palestinian land is militarily challenged and overwhelmed, then all of Jewish history is destroyed. This in turn makes the entire history of the Jewish journey null and void. If the state of Israel as it is defined today is transformed, the struggles in Jewish history that went before it vanishes. Like the Jewish Diaspora, which Zionists view as a sign of weakness, and the Holocaust, which Zionists see as the Diaspora's tragic and inevitable destination, Israel must defend its existence by any means necessary.

The state of Israel lives or dies by its military prowess. If, indeed, death is the final call, this time, unlike the Holocaust, Jews will not die alone. If Israel goes down, its enemies will go down with her.

Another impasse appears. When the possibility of survival is counterbalanced by the real or imagined threat of annihilation, the choices are narrowed so that a person or a community either follows the party line or is exiled as a traitor. Lacking a middle ground, the attempt to establish one is fraught with so much anxiety that the middle ground gives way beneath the weight of suffering and power. Even the search for a broken middle, as a way of subverting the radical poles and hoping for an initial landing somewhere between oppressing and being oppressed, becomes treason.

Think of Jerusalem as the broken middle of Israel/Palestine. Jerusalem is certainly the middle of Israel, a city deeply rooted within Jewish history. It is hard to imagine the state of Israel without Jerusalem. On the Palestinian side, there is the longstanding Muslim and Christian attachment to Jerusalem, as well as it being Palestine's intellectual and cultural center. Without Jerusalem, there is no Palestine.

Here we speak of the real Jerusalem not the fictional Israeli-annexed and expanded "unified" Jerusalem that privileges Jews and displaces Palestinians. Nor are we speaking of the United States brokered peace processes where the

Palestinians presence in Jerusalem is symbolic and relating only to religious shrines. The broken middle of Jerusalem is where two broken people meet—and live—in full equality and justice.

The brokenness of Jewish history is obvious. The recent empowerment of Jews has done little if anything to change this condition. Brokenness is now coupled with an insecurity that appears endless. If anything, Israel's bravado functions as a cover for the trauma power cannot overcome. Living on the edge, the state of Israel and Jews worldwide are only a hair's breadth from a renewed, perhaps permanent, catastrophe.

The brokenness of Palestinian history is likewise obvious. Their situation has reached a nadir that seems without limit. While brokenness is historical for Jews but close at hand, brokenness for Palestinians is a lived and future reality. While not healing for Jews as yet, power, correctly and ethically employed, does open the possibility of permanently transforming brokenness. The abuse of that power has shattered the Palestinian world.

Brokenness and the promise of living beyond brokenness are interconnected. Jerusalem as the shared broken middle of Israel/Palestine is obvious. Indeed, it is a compelling hope. One searches in vain for a rational reason that Israel refuses to embrace this hope. Although the domestic and international politics of nations are defined by self-interest, self-interest is variously defined. Rationality in national matters rests on a variety of foundations and perspectives. Nations have their own brand of rationality. Rationality as involved only in self-interest is a perception from the eyes of the national beholder. What seems rational to one nation might seem irrational to another.

Israel and the Palestinians' rationality is clouded by history and the prospects for the future as seen by each party to the conflict. Seeing Jerusalem as the broken middle of Israel-Palestine provides a middle ground for two understandings of history and the future, compromising aspects of each while honoring both. At the outset, the dual movement of compromising and honoring seems to be the rational solution within a situation that holds little promise for a resolution without compromise. Without compromise, honor seems distant and evasive.

Since compromise has been rejected at various times by both sides, and Israel continues to press its advantage without restraint, the issue remains as to why the international community has not enforced a compromise that either side, again depending on circumstances, has asked for. Asking for outside help has been one of the foundations of both the Israeli and Palestinian quest for security and stability. Powers like the Arab world, Europe, the former Soviet

Union, now Russia, and the United States have been intimate players in a drama that is in its seventh decade.

Why these powers have played their specific roles has to do with whether their "rational" national interests have coincided with or opposed the interests of Israel and the Palestinians. While the historical question is of great interest, the more pressing question is about the immediate future. Have the various players in the region been ready for a solution based on the broken middle of Jerusalem? If they are, why is it so difficult to translate into reality?

In the end, Israel, the Palestinians, and these outside powers need to coalesce on the same page of historical compromise. If not, the political game may play to its natural conclusion. But since in politics there is no "nature," then the natural conclusion is one based upon power. Whatever the power equation is at a specific time is the "natural" situation.

Power works as power does. If the parties agree to power sharing, that is one way forward. If the parties do not agree to power sharing, then power exerted is the law of the land. How power works at a specific time always seems to be how power will work for the foreseeable future. However, power interrupted can be power reversed. When power is reversed, the "natural" situation is reversed. What was victory one day is defeat the next. Any conqueror of Jerusalem, especially Jews and the state of Israel, should be particularly aware of this historical fact.

With Israel, the power has been one-sided. While there have been moments of indecision and anxiety—the early days of the 1973 Arab-Israeli War and the 2006 conflict with Hezbollah in Lebanon are examples—the outcome has ultimately been assured. As Egypt invaded Israel and Hezbollah launched missiles into Israel, Israel expended troops and munitions into what became a stand-off. The threat of military retaliation kept other Arab nations on the sidelines. Israel also held nuclear weapons in reserve.

The point here is less Israel's past dominance in the region than its need to maintain that dominance in the future. Israel is also dependent on international players, especially the United States, lest the power situation be somehow reversed. This dominance allows the usual periodic flair-ups of low-intensity conflicts to remain contained. The danger is that conflict will escalate to the point where retreat is impossible.

With the advances in modern technology in military warfare, the margin for error is small. If Israel had days to receive shipments of arms from the United States during the 1973 war—according to some sources, using the threat of nuclear war to secure immediate assistance—days of negotiating are a luxury today. A few missiles into Tel Aviv, even without them being nuclear, could ignite devastation. Israel's response would make earlier Arab-Israeli wars look minor in comparison.

Have we come to that moment when the compromise broken-middle solutions have left the scene? Although the past and current peace processes are talked about endlessly, few believe in the diplomatic missions that carry the two-state banner. More believe it is a matter of power that defines the political and territorial realities on the ground. The facts on the ground are now what they have been more or less for decades, only worse, a one-state reality controlled by Israel. Even the so-called two-state options recognize that the only option open for Palestinians is a truncated autonomy surrounded by Israeli power.

As the facts on the ground become more defining, the ideologies that drive and oppose power are exposed as hypocrisies that prevent the realities on the ground from being called what they are. On both the Israeli and Palestinian sides, flag waving and peace appeals mystify what is obvious. Israel has extended its power and control over historic Palestine, with millions of Palestinians within Israel's control. The possibility of this being reversed is remote. Though Israel does not want those Palestinians it controls, Israel has little or no prospect of moving the Palestinians out of the territory it occupies. Simply put, there are millions of Palestinians within Israel's rule that are superfluous to the functioning of Israeli society. Indeed, they are considered a burden to Israel. While suffering terribly and having little left to lose, Palestinians have the security of numbers. Although fragmented and ghettoized, for Israel, Palestinians form a huge block to its ultimate normalization of power.

Israel is stuck. It seems that there is no way out for Israel without its enterprise unraveling further. Yet Israel as empire, like any empire, thinks the future is theirs. This includes the economic benefits that come with domination of an occupied people. Still as Jews know well, occupied—and ghettoized—peoples are unstable. One day they are docile consumers of the occupiers products, the next day they are revolting. Meanwhile, the international community watches closely. Though in the main the international community has enabled Israel and its occupation, those days may be coming to an end. Though it sees itself as alone in the world, without close cooperation and trade with the international community, Israel's margins are thin.[5]

Once again, we return to the biblical witness, but we can also think of modern empires as well. The biblical prophets warned that, like the British Empire in the twentieth century, one day the sun would set on its far-flung

---

5. As in all occupations, the profits that derive from Israel's occupation are disbursed within Israel and beyond. See "Who Profits: The Israeli Occupation Industry" at http://www.whoprofits.org/

ideology. Indeed, it did. With that prospect ahead for Israel, the question remains. What then?

When the broken middle is rejected, collapse, though perhaps delayed, is predictable. Collapsing empire throws the empire world into a tailspin. Empire elites suffer. Everyone who is dependent on empire suffers. This turns out to be the entire society. And in the Jewish case, Israel's empire collapse, as inevitable as the sun that set on the British Empire, would reverberate throughout the Jewish world.

Perhaps this is the reason why Israel's narrative, though chastened and almost silent, is still pursued. Although Israel is infrequently spoken of in positive public speech anymore, it continues to be used as a blunt instrument to pursue dissenters to its policies. If Israel is no longer defensible in public, unmasking it can still be punished. Yet the question is how long an upper-class pretense can be maintained. Are Jews like the landed gentry of the nineteenth century, determined to hold on to privilege as it slips away?

Think of the state of Israel and the Holocaust as land that is destined to be developed by others in the ever-expanding bourgeois classes. With their newfound economic power, these others demand their right to narrate their own story. Should it surprise Jews that their narration will hardly feature the Jewish narrative as their own, if it features it all, since these others, too, who will have the peculiar hubris to think that they are the center of creation? This raises the haunting question as to whether the Holocaust and Israel are already self-narrating, with Jews being only bit players in a drama out of their control.

Jews have experienced being outside the central narrative of Europe and America. Most of Jewish history has been life lived on the margins. An ethically diminished Israel suggests a return to that marginal situation. Even the comparative silence on Israel places more and more pressure on the Holocaust as the fortress that keeps Jews front and center. The anxiety within the Jewish world is that the Holocaust center will not hold. With the passage of time, the power of the Holocaust will erode. It is eroding now.

Even among Jewish youth born in the last decades, there is a distance from Holocaust and Israel consciousness. Holocaust consciousness is becoming a burden to Jewish youth precisely because it is not their generation's question. Their fidelity will be found in other issues, if it is found at all.[6]

The Holocaust and Israel have had an impact on more than Jewish lives. It may have saved Jewish identity for the future. The broken middle of Israel-Palestine—indeed, the broken middle of the Holocaust—is crucial to embrace

---

6. See Peter Beinart, *The Crisis of Zionism* (New York: Henry Holt, 2012).

as a saving remnant of Jewish identity. Yet a minimalist saving is fraught with anxiety. Perhaps Jews worry that a negotiated settlement in Israel-Palestine will deplete the will to be Jewish. Without Jewish empire, what reason will Jews have to remain Jews? If Israel is no longer embattled, will Jews see Israel as a cause worthy of their concern and effort? If Israel enters a normal life with itself and its neighbors will the Holocaust cease to be at the forefront of Jewish consciousness?

As with art, minimalism strips the world bare. Minimalism evinces a stark beauty. It can also occasion a deep anxiety about the next stage of art/narrative. Starkness might become nothingness. The way back to the human/Jewish might become too difficult. The deep anxiety is that Jews will only embrace Jewishness if the symbolic field is simple, emotive, us against them, with everything at stake. Are Jewish authorities worried that Jews will not identify as Jews if they lose their fear that their lives will once again be consumed by gas and fire?

Anxiety tells us important truths. The rescue of Jewishness through the Holocaust and Israel has an expiration date. That expiration comes without a back-up plan. What happens when the expiration date passes is anyone's guess.

The fear is that when the expiration date arrives, the Holocaust and Israel will be tossed away as useless and negative baggage. What will be available to restock the Jewish narrative store, at least for the majority who are unwilling to travel the Orthodox route? The majority of Jews may embrace the secular world without preserving their Jewishness. If the Holocaust/Israel becomes inaccessible, what will Jews choose as their identifier?

Barring another catastrophe involving Jews, there are few other Jewish identifiers left. Except for outward pieties among a small minority—this encouraged by the Holocaust/Israel axis as well—the overt religious route is already foreclosed for most Jews. Long ago, the majority of Jews embraced the core of modernity and its own religious focus on achievement and affluence. This includes the Jewish elite who count Jewishness and sporadic, highly symbolic attendance at Jewish religious services as an affirmation of their elite status. Using a religious cloak to thinly disguise one's service to empire is as secular as they come. In fact today there is a Washington, D. C., Jewish elite who count among their numbers more than a few fellow travelers and converts to Judaism—at least in its Constantinian formation.

A minority of Jews continue in the prophetic tradition of questioning authority and injustice. They, too, are thoroughly modern, thus secular, albeit with a distinctly Jewish disdain for empire. Especially in their newfound energy relating to the issues of Israel-Palestine, prophetic Jews have become involved in the Holocaust/Israel narrative. Their involvement in a dissident Jewishness may be an unconscious, last-gasp fling with the Jewish identity. Although most of these Jews left the established Jewish community a long time ago, their dormant Jewishness has been reawakened with a ferocity that betrays their own anxiety about the Jewish future.

Reversing the picture, imagine a chastened Jewish world where the broken middle is embraced. Here Jews live normal lives without physical and narrative empire. Jews flourish or not, as other communities, religious groups, and nations do, moving up and down the social and economic order without moving anywhere special and without making a huge splash. Imagine a smaller Israel, at peace with its Palestinian neighbor. Then imagine the remnant Palestinians inside of Israel and in broader Palestine living with empire-remnant Jewish Israelis. Think of Jews and Palestinians simply going about their business together, sharing education, security, and commerce in this altered reality.

Think of Israel-Palestine becoming normal, Jews and Palestinians living like people all over the world. When the worst has happened and that phase of history is left behind, over time the memory of that history becomes distant. Eventually the history of division and strife seems archaic. Youth who one day become the elders think of that time as a distant historical fog. In this imagined future, how does Jewishness cast itself? How do Jews narrate their existence?

Remember that Jews have already jettisoned their traditional religious narrative, only to be revived by the Holocaust/Israel nexus. Since there is no going back except in fantasy and rear-guard actions, the normalization of Jewish life might just be life worth living, with or without a Jewish surname.

Imagine further that the Holocaust memorials/museums that dot Europe and America lose their clientele, their public outreach, their funding, and their periodic gala opening nights. This may happen through a chastened Jewish narrative, through normalization of Jewish life and through the passage of time. Think of the Holocaust as an industry, as a material reality that produces goods and services, employs workers and scholars, funds projects and is funded, needs to pay its bill and update its products so that consumers continue to consume the products it produces. If Jewish life is normal for a period of time and the new normal seems secure for the future—after all, that is what Jews and Jewish leadership should want and work toward—why continue to reproduce the Holocaust? Will people in large numbers continue to consume the horrors of the Holocaust forever?[7]

---

7. See Tim Cole, *Selling the Holocaust: From Auschwitz to Schindler—How History is Bought, Packaged, and Sold* (New York: Routledge, 2000).

What if the United States Holocaust Memorial Museum in Washington, D. C., had lacked the material and narrative resources to be built? What if the product that the museum produces is no longer consumed? Clearly, the resources were there to build the museum and visitors come by the millions—over thirty million people have toured the museum since its founding. Obviously, the production of the Holocaust is a success. In the future, what if interest in the Holocaust declines and the numbers of museum visitors at the major memorials shrink?

Other smaller Holocaust venues might suffer the same fate. Soon writing about the decline would become front-and-center news. What begins with a bang often ends with a whimper. The Holocaust Memorial Museum opened in 1993. So far, so good. Still, historical time has a way of catching industries up short. What was a huge consumer sensation often becomes a faded memory. Other products come on line and garner the public's attention. The moment becomes theirs. Many abandoned stores and factories dot the American landscape. Included among them are monuments and museums that once drew their share of the various remembrance markets. Some of the outdated museums go out of business. Others update their collection, culling, augmenting, and modernizing.

Holocaust museums around the nation exist within a museum market industry. They are always seeking enhanced funding. The struggle for consumers of the Holocaust narrative has, up to now, been fairly easy. But already some Jewish officials discuss the issue of "Holocaust fatigue." The fear is that the Holocaust market may become saturated. One day it may become less and less obvious that one should know about an event whose publicity drowned out its deeper message.

STILL/FORMER JEWISH/ISRAELIS

Without resolution, (un)saved, no rescue, prophetic practice in the everyday, signs and symbols coming from the past—that is how it has been for Jews time immemorial. Jews have lived for millennia without the comfort—or the confrontation—of God's speech.

There have been various substitutes for Jewish God-talk, the rabbis first among them. The rabbis filled the void through their own interpretations of the disjunction of what had been promised in the land and what remained in the Diaspora. The rabbis' task was immense. Think of the Exodus and the Promised Land. Now think of European Jewish communities surrounded by a Christianity that claims to be the true Israel. Now expand that story through tribulations, ghettoization and death. How to explain the distance traveled, the expectations dashed, and the needs of life in the present?

There are some who argue that the continuity of Jewish life, even in the disjunction between expectation and reality, is false. If this is the case, the rabbis were dream weavers, patching up what cannot be held together. For Jews who embrace this critique, the rabbinic curiosity about Jewish life ends there.

Perhaps continuity is a fantasy gloss on a tradition that becomes real only through fabrication. There may be no such thing as Jewish life or a Jewish tradition. It could be that all is made up, fragments pieced together for some larger frame, which itself is an illusion.[8]

Yet seeing Jews, Jewish, Judaism as a fabricated patchwork ultimately makes little historical sense. Surely one Jewish group was cut off from another at certain times. Mass conversions and defections took place. Leaps of theological history have difficulty passing the modern analytical historical test. Regardless, Jewish life continues to be projected on the large screen of history. Now it features the Holocaust and Israel.

The state of Israel looms large here. Israel fabricated a retrograde attempt at an ethnic state, laughably enough formed in the middle of the twentieth century, when ethnic states, especially with a colonial basis, were on their way out. Now that there is a resurgence of such attempts at ethnic/religious states, it is difficult to believe that thoroughly modern Jews would sign up for this kind of endeavor.

Except in state of Israel—that most peculiar aspect of Jews and Jewish history in the modern era—every major trend in Jewish life is aligned against this possibility. In the main, even after the Holocaust, Jews want an open political, economic and social world. Democracy and freedom is the watchword. Nor do a majority of Jews seek to be governed by Jewish religious or political authorities. Perhaps this is why Israel has such a raucous political climate. Perhaps this is why Israel is discussed in mainstream Jewish circles without referring it as an ethnic religious state. Jews rarely see themselves in the ethnic religious mirror. Jews in America and Israel reserve such retrograde designations for Islam.

As we have seen, Joseph Massad is not quite sure that Jews in the main have actually signed on the ethnic/religious-state dotted line. As well, most Jews do not recognize Israel in such a description. Is this once again the Jewish sense of innocence, believing that Jews are incapable of producing what they find reprehensible in others? Nonetheless, no matter the fabrication and the

---

8. This is the theme of Sholmo Sand, *The Invention of the Jewish People* (New York: Verso, 2009).

innocence, the history of the Holocaust is real. Israel exists. Israel privileges Jews, according Jews rights that are denied non-Jews, mostly Palestinian but other minorities as well. Because of this privileging, Palestinians and others, including African migrants, are seen as demographic threats. Jewish privilege, enshrined by law, is at stake.

This analysis of privileging Jews is complimented by the Palestinian narrative of Israel's creation and existence. Because of their circumstances as second-class citizens within Israel and as an occupied population in Jerusalem and the West Bank, one could expect this kind of analysis from Palestinians. After all, they have been on the receiving end of what can only be for them a Western colonial and imperial adventure that privileges European Jews who claim a historical and divine right to their land.[9]

Palestinians quite rightly argue international law and appeal to an enlightened universal sensibility of citizenship and equal rights in a land they call their own. How could a collective, however defined or historically authenticated, claim a right from ancient and modern history to displace another people and settle their land? The insult is deepened when the conquest of their Palestine is argued as if Palestinians hardly existed or, perhaps even worse, simply existed on the land as inefficient caretakers until the rightful—and ancient—owners of the land returned.[10]

This "fabrication" charge, however, comes from the Jewish side, too, and increasingly in writing about the discontinuity of Jewish life and identity. Bottom-line questioning is the Jewishness of Jews. As well, on the political front, dissident Jews note with alarm the unholy alliance of American power as the ultimate enabler of Israel's belligerent existence in the Middle East. At first surprisingly, the most articulate of these viewpoints are held by Israeli Jews, those who, in an ironic inversion, have become the vanguard of dissent among the Jewish people.[11]

The significance of these critiques should not be underestimated, especially those that come from Jewish Israelis themselves. There are two levels of such

9. Nur Masalha, *The Palestine Nakba: Decolonising History, Narrating the Subaltern, Reclaiming Memory* (London, Pluto, 2012).

10. This concept, articulated by Joan Peters, kick-started Norman Finkelstein's career. For his overall take on the Middle East conflict, see his *Image and Reality of the Israel-Palestine Conflict*, 3d ed. (New York: Verso, 2008) and *Knowing Too Much: Why the American Jewish Romance with Israel is Coming to an End* (New York: Or Books, 2012).

11. One of the more interesting of these Israelis is Oren Ben-Dor, now living in the United Kingdom. See his essay, "Occupied Minds: Philosophical Reflections on Zionism, Anti-Zionism and the Jewish Prison," *Holy Land Studies: A Multidisciplinary Journal* 11 (2012): 33-62. Also see my response, "A Response: The Jewish (Prophetic) Prison" in ibid., 63-69.

critiques, those coming from Israelis who remain in Israel and those coming from Israelis who have departed Israel. Understanding the new vision of Jewishness of those Jews who are in exile within Israel, as well as the new vision of Jewishness of those Jews who now live in exile outside of Israel, expands our view of an alternative Jewish future.

Jewish Israelis of Conscience are on the cutting edge of Jewishness. After all, they are the ones who have lived the Holocaust/Israel axis. Jewish Israelis of Conscience embody the conundrum of Jews today. At issue is whether they embody the way out of this conundrum.

Those Israelis who remain and those who leave Israel are the vanguard of Jewishness in the world. If they embody the Holocaust/Israel narrative, they also embody its unraveling. Jewish Israelis are not afforded the luxury of a distant embrace of Jewishness seen through the American lens of Holocaust and Israel. They experience the unraveling existentially. For Jewish Israelis of Conscience, the unraveling is hardly theoretical. Nor are the consequences of living that unraveling.

Most Jewish Israelis of Conscience were born in Israel and serve in its occupation and wars. Twentieth- and twenty-first-century Jewishness is their embodied experience. They have lived the dream and experienced the nightmare. They are the products of Jewish history. They have been consumed by Jewish history. They have exported it. They are traumatized by it.[12]

There is little written about these exilic Jews. Nor is there much verbal discussion about them. The little discussion there is usually cites statistics about how many American Jews come to Israel to live and how many leave. On the leave-taking of Jewish Israelis, the analysis typically revolves around economics and the periodic lean times that prompt Israelis to leave Israel.

Even the phenomenon of the "lost years" of Israelis who, after their mandatory service in the military, travel the world for years on end, is often passed off as a rite of passage rather than analyzed for its meaning. There are longstanding communities in different parts of the world that cater to these former soldiers. As well, there are long-standing receiving communities for Jewish Israelis who leave Israel for good. There are places of exile within Israel for Jews who have not left Israel—yet.

What do these Jewish Israelis have to say to Jews in general, to the conception of Jewishness, even about the Jewish relationship to God? Culling some of their reflections, they begin with a startling fact. Some of these Jews no longer think of themselves as Jews at all. First and foremost, they think

12. See Raz Joseph, *The Politics of Loss and Trauma in Israeli Cinema* (London: Routledge, 2011).

of themselves as Israelis, as a nationality, but even that identity is increasingly questioned. Most of these Jewish Israelis have long ago deconstructed their Jewishness. Now they are deconstructing their Israeliness. All of this begs the obvious question: If these Jews are not Jews or Israelis, who are they?

Obviously, they know their past designations as both Jewish and Israeli. It is not a case of historical amnesia. Rather, in their eyes both designations have been discredited or have become transient, way stations on the path to other, more constructive forms of identification. The exile identity(s) these former Jewish/Israelis have is indeterminate. What identity they do claim is mostly formed as an over-against proposition, as in "I used to be Jewish/Israeli" or "I was born Jewish/Israeli."

Jewish/Israeli identity formations no longer make sense to them. They are identities from which to distance oneself. As well, they seem either irrelevant or irrevocably tainted. "Jewish" as a historical assignation has been used as a lever of power over against Palestinians. "Israeli" as a national identity has been used as a lever of power against Palestinians. Along the way, Jewish and Israeli have similarly been used against these Jewish Israelis as levers of power. Who wants to embrace such an identity?

These former Jewish/Israelis embody—and live—the post-Holocaust construction of Jewish identity. Some have experienced this construction as a prison. They feel like an object that is used as a symbolic construction. Yet they are also a subject, one that is mobilized and militarized to displace and occupy another people. In being so used, they, as subjects, they feel displaced and occupied as well. As subjects, these former Jewish/Israelis are objectified.

Because of this objectification, there arises an internal exile within these former Jewish/Israelis that complements their external exile. They represent the concrete manifestation of the symbolic marker of post-Holocaust Jewish identity. They are a referendum on the failure of that construction.

Like any vanguard, these former Jewish/Israelis experience a more dissonant connection to their identities than most people do. They also represent what most people are rarely conscious of. They are like the early feminists who embodied what some women thought they did not need or were afraid of. Later on, they are recognized as the norm to be affirmed.

Another way of looking at former Jewish/Israelis is that they are not former at all. They are what all Jews have become to some extent, subjects that are displaced and occupied by the post-Holocaust construction of Jewish and Israeli identity. Former Jewish/Israelis may think they are—former. But Jewish Israelis are distinctively Jewish and Israeli to anyone who experiences them. They are the cutting edge of what one day might become the reality for Jews around the world. The exile of Jews from the Holocaust/Israel identity construction that these "formers" embody may one day define the Jewish future.

That Jewish future has already arrived. Still, the delay in the understanding of that arrival is palpable, so much so that analysis of the meaning of these formers is absent from contemporary Jewish life. When it appears, the analysis is lazy. Though Jewish and Israeli, they are often categorized as self-hating or antisemitic by the Jewish establishments in Israel and America. But that only represents the power of those who think the future is theirs.

Constantinian Jews—with their Progressive Jewish comrades-in-arms—seek to deflect this understanding or redefine it, as if the ultimate Holocaust/Israel identity unraveling is not occurring. Or has not occurred and cannot occur because what cannot be, cannot be. The discussion is cut off at the pass. It is disrupted, blocked. It does not exist, is the refrain, despite evidence to the contrary.

Yet the vehemence with which the reality is met by the Jewish establishments belies an underlying anxiety that what cannot be, is happening. What is not happening, is. Therefore, the supposedly nonexistent threat must be confronted even as it supposedly does not exist. Hence, the rear-guard battle configuration that uses anti-Israel hostility and, the ultimate trump cards, antisemitism and Holocaust denial, as the tools to fight this internal (un)admitted insurgency.

The Jewish establishments in Israel and America seek to suppress from Jews and others the fact that a wholesale revolt against external and internal displacement and occupation is taking place in the Jewish world. Although apparently under control, the unraveling of the establishment's occupation of Jewish life is occurring.

This revolt/unraveling can only be understood within the context of the persistence of the prophetic in Jewish history. Predictably, the Jewish establishment seeks to discipline, if not destroy, the prophetic. As predictably, what I shall call the Still/Former Jewish/Israelis, discipline, if not interrogate, the Jewishness/Israeliness of their witness against injustice to others and themselves. Neither have a place for the prophetic in their scheme of things, at least named as such. Nonetheless, through both groups we witness once again the perennial theme of Jews on both sides of the empire divide.

THE NO-BRAINER PROPHETS GATHERING LIGHT

There are at least two conceptual movements in exploring Jewish identity. The first is accepting that Jewish identity is constructed. Therefore, Jewish identity can be analyzed with its peculiar twists and turns, diversions, ends, and unsuspected new beginnings. The second is becoming conscious that there is also something about Jewish identity that is persistent, unreconstructed, and reaches beyond specific contexts.

These two movements are in tension. Jewish identity is within and, somehow, outside of history. Or, Jewish identity is lodged in a deep layer of history that changes and continues on within time. Therefore, Jewish history is bound to and independent of time and place. In the end, we realize that critical analysis illumines aspects of Jewish identity yet fails to explain all of it.

Against the grain, the deconstruction of contemporary Jewish identity is in full force. Still/Former Jewish/Israelis embody this deconstruction in thought and action. They place their very being where their thought is. Or they think their thoughts where their body is. Of course, their deconstruction of Jewish and Israeli identity is already an identity construction. Identity transformations are like that. The naming of the new identity comes after the deconstruction of the old.

What is unnamed is what is as yet unnamable, by definition. Since the already-named identity is dislocating and occupying a previously named identity that is no longer viable, the context for identity formation is shifting precipitously. What the insurgent naming rarely realizes is that their naming, once it becomes established, is already fated. It unravels in the same way that it once unraveled a previous identity.

Such is the to and fro of life that we recognize in biological patterns of life, death, and new life. But just as we seek to freeze the cyclical movement toward death in our own biology, we seek to keep a once-embraced identity from that cycle as well. Although identity is not biology, history demonstrates that identity has its own cycles of birth, decay, death, and rebirth. The rabbinic formulation that came into being, then was found wanting, and was replaced by the Holocaust/Israel paradigm, is an example of this identity cycle.

The persistence of the prophetic has its own cycles but with a caveat. Grounding the primordial establishment of ancient Israel's identity formation, so that the prophetic is the indigenous reality of the people Israel, the prophetic has a changeable outer shell while maintaining an inner consistency. The prophetic is the indigenous reality that accompanies Jewish identity through its various permeations.

Does this identity deconstruction/reconstruction have anything to do with God or the lack thereof? Our Still/Former Jewish/Israelis—the vanguard of Jewish history—are overwhelmingly secular, as are most Jews of Conscience, with this caveat: they are secular in a distinctly Jewish way. Again, the prophetic pattern applies, this time without God. Yet a haunting question remains: Since the biblical prophets are so deeply associated with God, could the persistence of the prophetic be stripped of this apparent necessity and continue to persist?

In biblical times, God is the originator of the prophetic. God calls the prophets into being. More, God instructs the prophets as to their mission. Yet at the moment of the prophet's inception, a dialogue ensues or, if you will, a call and response occurs. Although the relationship between God and the prophet is unequal, the prophet speaks. Most often the prophet initially demurs, deflecting the call from God because of his unworthiness or the pain involved in carrying out such a call. Often it is a combination of the two.

In the Bible, after the initial call, the communication between God and the prophets is limited. God calls the prophet. The prophet, then, invokes God as the author of his mission. Almost immediately, God recedes into the background. God is off-stage, as it were, prodding the prophet, but God rarely reappears. When the prophet is on the run, behind bars, or at the bottom of a well, the prophet calls out to God, wondering where God is. After all, God has called the prophet into being. The prophet is on God's mission. Where is God? The prophet often experiences a resounding silence.[13]

Perhaps the most famous prophet plea came from Jesus on the cross, whose last words betray a sense of abandonment. Later, Jesus' abandonment is mitigated by Christianity's claim of God's messianic plan. Yet if we see Jesus within the context of the Jewish prophetic tradition, his words ring true. Likely Jesus had another end in mind. Did God as well?

But there are others before Jesus. Think Ezekiel. Think Jeremiah. Think Isaiah. Receiving their commission from God, they are in and out of contact with the divine. In times of great need, when the going gets rough and the end seems near, God sometimes hears the prophet's pleas. Other times, God seems unaware of the prophet's predicament. Moreover, the prophet's commission is sealed before the prophet's mission commences. God knows that Israel is unlikely to turn away from injustice. Why, then, send the prophet in the first place?

The prophet dwells in darkness. Her fate is deep and unremitting exile. The prophet is hidden in the public glare, even as she is still involved in dangerous public disputations. Or the prophet comes and goes, disappears for long stretches of time, then reappears. The prophet reads Israel the riot act, is pursued, caught, freed, and caught again. With all of this drama, it is amazing how little we know, if anything, about the prophet's internal life.

---

13. For a traditional rendition of the God-intoxicated prophets, though with a series of fascinating twists, see Abraham Joshua Heschel, *The Prophets* (New York: Harper & Row, 1962).

Does the prophet have a private life, an inner realm beyond the darkness that surrounds him? The Bible is quite general about the prophet's inner life, noting despair and fear, outrage and hope. Beyond that, the inner life of the prophet is shrouded. Interestingly, the inner workings of God are described in general terms, too, left mostly to the reader's imagination.

Reading the prophets, there are glimpses of light. The prophet is a gatherer of light in dark times. As a light gatherer, does the prophet share the gathered light with a small coterie of friends and loved ones? On this the biblical text is largely silent. The light gathered by the prophet is mostly shared in public, with Israel and with God, who started it all and now is somewhere far away, inaccessible. Other than for short intervals, the prophet is on her own. Her bed has been made for her by God. Now she sleeps uncomfortably in that bed, if at all. Being on the run, the prophet is conscious of her surroundings. They are the venue for prophetic action. As well, they are the danger point where the forces of empire-darkness gather. The empire has one goal—to extinguish the light the prophet gathers.

The prophet's world is already dark, much darker than the rulers or the people realize. At least for the rulers, empire stretches out forever. The people are caught in between, feeling the undertow of empire, but also thinking that their security is bound up with it. Although destructive for the ordinary person, empire is the only life they know. After empire is the great unknown. What was the unknown in the Exodus? At least in slavery there was food to eat and a bed to sleep in, a landscape that was also theirs, and a long shot of possible change. Yes, a place to be buried. In the desert, that stretched out forever; only the forbidding landscape was home.

What was the unknown in the land? At least in empire there was work and minimal security, a landscape that was theirs and familiar. With the critique of empire, the known could unravel and become even worse than slavery already was. What did the unraveling of empire bode for the future? Again, the great unknown.

The prophet is against nature and the natural flow of things, even the state of oppression, which can take on the appearance of the natural. The prophets rail against the empire promise of lifting everyone's boat if only the work continues. Against nature and the natural flow, who wouldn't despise the prophet, ultimately, even if first embraced?[14]

The prophet is uprooted by God's call. The prophet uproots those who hear the prophet's words. Those who have yet to experience the prophet's

---

14. For Martin Buber on the prophets, see his *The Prophetic Faith* (New York: Macmillan, 1949).

words know God's name through ritual incantations. Thus the boldness of the prophet who dares assert that the message delivered comes from God. The message is a judgment upon society, the rulers, and those who, through the use of slave labor or some variation, enable injustice. The prophet dares to speak for them, all the while claiming that in fact God is speaking through the prophet.

If there is no rescue for the prophet, the prophet is essentially on her own. When we picture the prophet in worn and tattered clothes—or naked—it is our image of a prophetic calling worn thin. The prophet's God-moment is becoming distant. Soon it is far away. We long to hear even a faint echo of God's presence, if only for the sake of the prophet. It might be for our sake as well. The aloneness of the prophet is too much to bear—for all of us.

In Jewish life, the prophetic call remains through the millennia, surfacing here and there, sometimes claiming God but, especially in the modern period, assuming that the prophetic call simply *is*, without even naming it—and certainly without entertaining the idea that God is involved, on or off stage. The stage is ours.

Thinking of taking direction from outside or being directed—as if there is an ultimate director—is out of bounds in the modern world. Contemporary prophets, disdaining the term itself, refuse even the thought of a Director entering the auditorium. Off limits![15]

Perhaps the stage is ours because the God-filled biblical stories are so bleak and unresolved, with so much violence and abandonment. And with what known result? The unresolved story of ancient Israel is as advertised. It remains in doubt.

True, the prophets only interrupt the empire strain of the Jewish journey. They are unable to transform it permanently. Even today, Jews remain on both sides of the empire divide. Little has changed. So why bring ancient history or the God-called prophets into the discussion? That only obfuscates the picture. What is, is. Deal with it. The struggle is now. Darkness is all around us. We need to gather light before the light is extinguished.

These points are obvious to the contemporary prophet: that no theory will save us; history is without rescue; justice has no recourse other than its own struggle. For the prophet, the unsaved reality within history is more important than theology. How does the prophet parse unsaved reality? Absent a theological gloss, the prophet refuses to transcend the reality he faces. We are alone without rescue in the struggle for justice. Jews are locked in a quandary

15. This brings to mind the trials of God conducted in some of the death camps by inmates. They conducted both sides of the case. God was represented but not allowed to speak. For a novelistic rendition of these trials, see Elie Wiesel, *The Gates of the Forest* (New York: Schocken, 1995).

of survival and advancement, while oppressing others, trumpeting the ethical core of Jewishness and being exposed for the hypocrisy that is obvious. Jews are back on their feet at the expense of others. The oppression of Palestinians will continue. It has to be stopped, but how?

For the present-date prophet, there is little reason to talk about the origins of this call, if there are origins. Or to speak of the Jewish background in relation to the prophet, as if what Jews are about in the world is a call, rather than simple ordinary life. Besides, who within the Jewish community or outside of it will continue to listen to the thoroughly compromised ethical benchmarks of Jewish history? The possibility of a Jewish particular distinctive being called on in today's world has passed, especially with so much Jewish talk of the Holocaust and the mandate to defend a thoroughly compromised Israel.

If Jewish identity in the world is torn asunder, so, too, it is torn within the Jewish prophetic community. The traditional foundations for prophetic speech are collapsing. Or, worse, they have collapsed. Is that why the Jewish prophetic in our day makes no claim other than that injustice needs to be righted?

The prophet knows a need when she sees it. The need has to be addressed. Jettisoning Jewish identity and history as a resource, we might then ask why prophetic Jews think life depends on responding to injustice. For the prophet, this is like theology, idle thought, yet another non-question.

True, what is obvious to one is not necessarily obvious to another. So much of life is perception and context. Like the prophets of old, however, today's prophet acknowledges a special vision and interpreted context. Then the prophet moves against the accepted empire grain. The prophet embraces the Jewish journey writ large, though with the knowledge that many Jews gravitate toward the grain as well. At least in the contemporary world, no Jewish question need be asked by the interlocutor or the prophet herself. It is counterproductive. It goes nowhere.

This is another reason why Jewish life is characterized by instability. Even the prophet dodges the most obvious of questions of inheritance and tradition as though her prophetic vocation depends on it.

As we have seen, first and foremost the instability comes from covenanting with the God of liberation. Then Israel embraces God's call to embody that liberation and leave Egypt. The instability of the desert wanderings is followed by the instability of life in the land. For Israel, the only stability is found in instability.

For the people Israel, God is like a hurricane. There are moments of rest in the eye of the hurricane. The eye also promises high winds and torrential rains ahead. The prophets are hurricanes on the horizon, hurricanes right up front, close and personal, hurricanes that disappear with the threat of reappearing. Like hurricanes, the prophets are impersonal, as if they are hurled at you without concern for who is in the way, and then quite personal, as in the prophet is right here, in front of you. What are we to do with such persons who we experience like a force of nature?

Are the Still/Former Jewish/Israelis prophetic hurricanes? They upset the ideals of a suffering people that are intent on building empire stability. What could be more disturbing than raining on the empire parade?

Think again of the journey of those who think their point is obvious. For the most part, these Still/Former Jewish/Israelis were born of parents or grandparents who fled the Holocaust. They were born in the state of Israel, a state that functions in the Jewish symbolic and material universe as the return of returns, the biblically promised miraculous deliverance out of the greatest suffering known in history—at least from the Jewish perspective. They grow up in embattled Israel, one that needs to be fought for and defended against the surrounding countries and a world that secretly and often overtly has few places for Jews on their horizon. The thought that Israel is surrounded by the antisemitism of the Arab countries and a generalized and eternal antisemitism of the world, conspiring against Israel and Jews is asserted and deeply felt. Now the flowering of the returning generation leaves the Promised Land. Then they argue that the framework of the Jewish state should be dismantled, spirited away, and perhaps even devoured by Israel's enemies. A more troubling desertion is hardly thinkable.

The ramifications of the Holocaust, the end of all ends, are endless. So many Jewish thinkers thought that, in the Holocaust, Jewish history had come full circle. The Holocaust also raised, in an almost insurmountable way, the question of God. The Still/Former Jewish/Israelis—as would most Jews of Conscience—concluded what is obvious to them: only a simpleton speaks about God *after*.

But then, surprise, surprise, the state of Israel came into being and no matter what one's position was on the fledgling state, it initially or eventually seemed a viable response to the Holocaust's end. Israel represented the possibility of a new beginning. A resurrection?

As we have seen, even homeland Zionists, like Hannah Arendt, though opposed to the creation of a Jewish state, saw worthiness in the homeland experiment. In fact, she was intensely involved in arguing for it, though with a caveat. If the Jewish homeland went the state route, the state would bring disaster far and wide. The failure of a Jewish homeland would be a further disaster as well. Arendt spells out the ramifications of such failures in an essay in 1948, aptly titled "To Save the Jewish Homeland: There Is Still Time":

> Palestine and the building of a Jewish homeland constitute the great hope and the great pride of Jews all over the world. What would happen to Jews, individually and collectively, if this hope and pride were to be extinguished in another catastrophe is almost beyond imagining. But it is certain that this would become the central fact of Jewish history and it is possible that it might become the beginning of the self-dissolution of the Jewish people. There is no Jew in the world whose whole outlook on life and the world would not be radically changed by such a tragedy . . .
> The loss of the kibbutzim, the ruin of the new type of man they have produced, the destruction of their institutions and the oblivion that would swallow the fruit of their experiences—this would be one of the severest blows to the hopes of all those, Jewish and non-Jewish, who have not and never will make their peace with present-day society and its standards.[16]

So much was at stake, including Arendt's sense of a new configuration of Jewish and international politics. In the homeland, the Jewish people, untainted by colonialism and imperialism, would meet and interact with a colonized people. For Arendt, this represented the way forward after the collapse of Western civilization. Now in their intellect and bodies, the vanguard of the Jewish people, the Still/Former Jewish/Israelis are leaving the idea of the Jewish rebirth and sometimes the land itself behind, declaring them a dead end. Leaving Israel in spirit and geographically, like leaving home in general, is hard to do. The stakes were high for Arendt and are for the Still/Former Jewish/ Israelis, unbelievably high.

These conceptual and physical leave-takers raise the possibility of the dissolution of the Jewish people, in that if the Holocaust is the end of all ends and Israel is the beginning from that end, declaring Israel to be another end raises the stakes to an existential breaking point. Will there be another Jewish beginning? If so, where or how will that take place? Or does the double end, the Holocaust and Israel, mean that the end will come without another round?

16. Hannah Arendt, "To Save the Jewish Homeland: There is Still Time," in *Hannah Arendt: The Jewish Writings*, ed. Jerome Kohn and Ron Feldman (New York: Schocken, 2007), 595.

Even more, many of these Still/Former Jewish/Israelis are living in the Jewish Diaspora among other non-Jewish cultures. They have ceded Jewish Israeli culture to Palestinian Arabs, but without the traditional Diaspora religious Orthodox theology. In their religious anti-Zionism, at least the Orthodox once gave the hope to a vibrant Jewish life before and after the dead end of the Holocaust and Israel. Obviously, the Still/Former Jewish/Israelis could hardly be further apart from this Orthodox sensibility. If the truth be known, they hold the Orthodox in disdain.

These leave takers do not associate much with the non-Orthodox Jewish Diaspora either. Indeed, more or less, they thumb their noses at Diaspora Jews as wannabe and vicarious Israelis. After all, Jewish American Israel enablers hardly place their lives in danger when they support a militarized Israel from afar. Again, the language is far from benign. Many Israelis think Diaspora Jews are peephole Jews, living in affluence and egging on their distant brethren to fight until the end.

What of the millions of Jews who remain in Israel, some embracing its state ideology but many who simply live as people all over the world do in the place where they were born? Except for the affluent or those with connections outside of Israel, most Israelis have nowhere else to go. Are the Still/Former Jewish/Israelis abandoning a burning building when they should be right there, rescuing Jews on the brink of disaster?

Most Diaspora Jews on the left spend their time attempting to rescue Jewishness, which covers a long list of concepts and items: Judaism, Jewish innocence, Israel, Jewish self-respect, Jewish ascendancy, Holocaust memory, and the like. But these Still/Former Jewish/Israelis want little to do with any rescue package. Or, if once interested, they have abandoned all hope of rescue. Instead, they have thrown in their lot with the "enemies" of Jews, first off being the Palestinians, but as well those in the wider world, including Christians and Muslims and anti-colonialists of every stripe, some of whom caricature Jews, demean them, call into question the veracity of the Holocaust, and spread the word that Israel is a only a colonial and imperial venture. Are these Hebrew-speaking Israeli citizens confirming the worse thoughts about Jewish history and life—as if all of Jewish history is tangled up in a conspiratorial empire blue?

Yet these Still/Former Jewish/Israelis, who do not want the label "Jewish" and who refuse to hide in the Diaspora even for the sake of upward mobility, stick out like sore thumbs wherever they live. They walk around as if they decide upon—judge—Jewish history and Jews themselves. Their indictment is sometimes extreme. They pronounce judgment on Israel, Jews, Judaism, and Jewishness as vacuous and violent.

This judgment on all things Jewish is too harsh. There are good things to be found in Jewish history in America and Israel. Not everything is so bad on the Jewish front that they should want to take leave of all that is Jewish, then act on their views and even write about them, as if the whole world is oblivious to Jews, or perhaps as if the whole world is indeed watching Jews.

In essence, these Still/Former Jewish/Israelis are delightfully still Jewish. They represent the full flowering of Jewishness, especially in their prophetic denunciation of all things Jewish. Exposing the dirty Jewish laundry on the global scene is a specialty of the prophets. The biblical prophets did this in graphic images. Some charge that with the internet's global reach, ridiculing Jewish power makes the world become more dangerous for Jews. Yet again, the biblical prophets were unconcerned with how the world, Jewish or otherwise, heard their words. They were unconcerned about the safety of Jews. After all, in their mind the condemnation they spoke was the condemnation the people Israel deserved. Why care what others think or the consequences of prophetic chastisement?

Stereotypes about Jews abound. Stereotypes continue even when certain epochs in history end. Combining the myth of Jewish perfidy with the reality of oppressing another people is explosive. These Still/Former Jewish/Israelis have lived in the intense cocoon that Israel can be. They are strangers to the West as it is lived historically and in the present. Though they identify with its history, they do so from a distance, as if they hail from a European and American frontier outpost. Therefore, they are oblivious to the nooks and crannies that Diaspora Jews know and have experienced intimately.

Leave takers from Israel are often deaf to the knowing tone of voice, the gesture, and coded language of antisemites. Indeed, some who gather around them follow their every thought for other, quite different reasons. It is as if these Still/Former Jewish/Israelis believe that antisemitism has vanished, is inconsequential, and certainly none of their concern.

Over the last decades, there has been much talk about the new and improved Jew, the tough masculine Jew who refuses to be pushed around, the Jew who will speak her mind. Diaspora Jews have embraced this mindset as central to post-Holocaust Jewish identity. Then the Jewish vanguard who fought against the odds and won, and was celebrated for their prowess, unleash themselves against the projection of Diaspora Jewish power. The new and improved Jew is unmasked by the Jews who are supposed to embody that very authority.

As it turns out, the Jewish vanguard is acting within its own type, though with a different trajectory. The Still/Former Jewish/Israelis act boldly, without concern for attitudes or feelings or even nuances, just as they were brought up to do. They rail against every constructed Jewish and Israeli image imaginable. They remain warriors—only now for justice—within Israel and as they leave to live in exile.

The biblical prophets cared less what others felt about their fellow Israelites. They hung out Israel's dirty laundry for Jew and non-Jew to see. They prophesied an emptying of the land, exile from it, and utter desolation of famine and slaughter. Such dire imagery casts shadows on the historical record. They reverberate in the Jewish present.

Scorched earth—the biblical prophets predicted and sometimes lived it. They embraced their enemies as the hand of God swooping down on Israel. In our present climate, the biblical prophets would be judged antisemitic, self-hating, and every other epithet that comes to mind. Most Jews and those in solidarity with Jews would be horrified if they heard the prophet's language leap off the Biblical page into their living room or in the public realm. Yet ironically, or fittingly, the ancient prophets are preserved as part of Jewish canonical literature. Only time will tell if these Still/Former Jewish/Israelis will be preserved in Jewish history as the closest contemporary replica of the biblical prophets. And this without even thinking, let alone mouthing, the word "God."

Perhaps these Still/Former Jewish/Israelis represent the ultimate unraveling of God. Or maybe they are the post-Holocaust/post-Israel substitute for God's voice. Subconsciously, they may represent God's voice in an era where the Jewish community has cleverly constructed a framework that allows empire without judgment by banishing God as absent and unworthy.

Banishing the absent God makes sense in the post-Holocaust world. It is also quite convenient. Since in the Jewish tradition it is God through the prophets who critiques empowerment without ethics, eliminating God from the empire playing field means the end of ethical accountability.

Through these Still/Former Jewish/Israelis, God's judgment may be returning—without God. But, then, how can we be sure that God was actually present to the biblical prophets? It could be that the vivid presence of God in the Bible is itself a vast and creative construction. Or perhaps ancient Israel simply affirmed God's presence as the only way to explain the epic history they sought to communicate.

Contemporary Jewish prophets speak justice in fiery tones without God. In our time, falling back on God seems too easy, a crutch, somehow unreal, childlike. It would cheapen Jewish history as it unfolds. If the Holocaust/Israel axis is the contemporary Jewish understanding of God, conceivably the Still/Former Jewish/Israelis are addressing God by refusing an idolatrous rendition of God. Perhaps these leave takers are too respecting of God, as in the ancient Jewish tradition, by refusing to name God.

In ancient times, real or not, God was used as wedge. God was seen as a power source that confounded every authority tainted by injustice. Israel could not feast at the table of injustice without being reminded of the terrible fate that awaited her. The first part of that fate was to be cut off from God. Our Still/Former Jewish/Israelis employ that same threat—with a twist. The coming punishment will see Jews in Israel and elsewhere cut off from empire, the Jewish post-Holocaust God par excellence.

So without naming God, the Still/Former Jewish/Israelis name the idolatry of modern Jews, the false gods of empire that Jews worship. Worse, as in biblical times, modern Jews worship the false gods of injustice in the land. In the Bible and for the Still/Former Jewish/Israelis, this is the ultimate sin.

8

Martryological Imperialism

Soon after the sixtieth anniversary of birth of the state of Israel, the Contemporary Jewish Museum in San Francisco had a gala opening in its new location. In a *New York Times* review, Edward Rothstein billed the museum, designed by the noted architect Daniel Libeskind, as the "West Coast of Paradise."[1]

The museum highlights the dual thrust of Jewish identity throughout the millennia. On the one hand, Jews desire to maintain a distinctive identity. On the other hand, Jews look forward to assimilating into the surrounding culture. As is typical in Jewish history, the borders of those distinctions are contested and in flux. The museum's architecture and collection is a fascinating modern, perhaps specifically American, reflection on those themes in Jewish history.

Rothstein's review uses the opening as a springboard for questions of Jewish identity. Pondering the museum's lack of emphasis on the Holocaust and Israel, Rothstein wonders whether Jews have moved beyond the borders and boundaries of both. If so, Rothstein wants to understand what this portends for the future.

For Rothstein, the museum seems stuck in a twilight reality. If the Holocaust and Israel remain central in the historical grounding of Jewish identity, the museum leaves both behind as a way of articulating that identity. Rothstein is left with a question that the Contemporary Jewish Museum raises but does not resolve: Have Jews moved forward or just avoided the difficult conundrum facing Jews as a people?

Rothstein uses the museum to explore interesting insights into the limitations and possibilities of contemporary Jewish identity. Rothstein's own limitations also provoke questions about Jewish identity in the twenty-first century and beyond. In both the Contemporary Jewish Museum and Rothstein's review, we appear far from the questions the Still/Former Jewish/

---

1. Edward Rothstein, "The Western Gates of Paradise," *New York Times*, June 9, 2008.

Israelis pose. Or, in their prophetic presence, are the Still/Former Jewish/Israelis the Jewish elephant in the museum/review room?

Rothstein begins by asking why the Contemporary Jewish Museum, like so many present-day Jewish museums, is "dedicated to a hyphenated American identity." He finds this especially curious in the San Francisco Bay Area, which ranks third among United States metropolitan regions in Jewish population. Jews have lived in San Francisco since its early boom days during the Gold Rush, so the Jewish presence in the area is longstanding. Still, Rothstein senses the museum remains tentative about Jewish belonging.

Rothstein speculates that in the Bay Area, as in the western United States in general, a particular style of American Judaism has developed. This style is highly assimilated; interfaith families are the norm. Judaism is treated more as a culture than a religion. So history, at least a particular interpretation of it, becomes less important than the concerns of the present. In its western American variant, Jewish culture is also closely associated with liberal values and leftist political leanings.

Because of this background, the Contemporary Jewish Museum is somewhat distinctive when compared to Jewish museums in other parts of the United States. For example, Rothstein finds the museum unconcerned with recounting the origins of the San Francisco Jewish community or even in chronicling its trial and triumphs. Absent in the museum are exhibitions about Levi Strauss, who began his clothing empire and became a noted Jewish philanthropist there. Nor are there museum exhibits about the broader historical dimensions of Diaspora life. A startling fact about the museum is that it lacks a permanent collection. Instead, the museum curates and hosts a broad array of exhibitions, among them "In the Beginning: Artists Respond to Genesis" and "From *The New Yorker* to *Shrek*: The Art of William Steig."

While other identity museums celebrate the particular identities they showcase, Rothstein finds it curious that the Contemporary Jewish Museum actively avoids subjects that are particular to Jews. Instead, the museum leaps into "aesthetic or cultural realms in which Judaism is an element or influence." Rothstein concludes that the museum is like its Jewish audience, primarily interested in assimilation to the surrounding culture and, as well, in the "ways in which the larger culture assimilates Jewish ideas and associations." Accordingly the museum "focuses not on the substance of Judaism, its laws, or history or ritual objects, but on perceptions of them."

Focusing on the perceptions of Jewish life rather than its substance presents an interesting challenge. Rothstein also finds it problematic, observing that there is something unsettled and unsettling about the museum in its focus on perception rather than substance—"as if something crucial was missing." His first problem is with Libeskind's architecture: "His San Francisco building is not particularly comfortable or reassuring." It seems that, for Rothstein, the difference between old and new in Jewish life may be materially more secure but psychologically confusing. Liberated from the old traumas of Europe, America may be introducing another kind of trauma in Jewish life, the trauma of being dislodged from a specific Jewish history.

To begin with, Rothstein finds Libeskind's "skewed geometries" to be unsettling. Its effect is "more vertiginous than harmonious." Instead of stability, Rothstein feels alienation. In addition, there is a self-conscious quality about the symbols being suggested in the building's architecture. Libeskind describes his building as being shaped to form two Hebrew letters spelling *chai*, meaning "life." But the physical rendering of the lettering is so abstract Rothstein has difficulty discerning its symbolism. For Rothstein, the abstraction renders the word almost invisible. When abstraction is taken to such a level, Rothstein wonders how meaning is to be derived or even struggled toward.

Rothstein is confused. For the interpreter to know what is being said "even the most elaborate interpretations of a text or tradition require more rigor and must begin with the literal." Moreover, the question of meaning is also challenged if we do not know where a symbol comes from and where else it is used. Yet, as Rothstein laments, those are the "types of questions—fundamental ones—that are not being asked or examined here about Judaism itself."

For Rothstein, multiple perspectives, open-mindedness, and diverse backgrounds can only be celebrated with grounding in knowledge, history, detail, object, and belief. Rothstein is uncertain if a museum can "serve its community without leading it into the unknown past as well as into speculative realms." He asks if "Jewish" can thrive without foundational knowledge of Judaism.

Rothstein is conscious of asking this museum—indeed, any museum—to be more than it is. No one can ask the architect or the museum's exhibits to do more than reflect an already articulated identity. The job of the museum is to inform and reveal understandings of identity rather than create them. "Right now the Contemporary Jewish Museum celebrates a vision of Judaism as a kind of freewheeling allegory, a *pardes* of open-mindedness and diversity and artistic enterprise," Rothstein concludes. "But for all the institution's considerable appeal, Judaism's fundamental, literal meanings—texts and laws and beliefs and history—are left outside the gates of paradise."

Indeed, this is where our exploration moves as well, though arriving from a divergent direction, or from a dissimilar originating point where Judaism's literal meanings, instead of being lost in abstraction, are being subverted and recovered. More than Judaism is in the mix, of course. Beneath and around Jewishness, and within the texts, laws, beliefs, and history of the Jewish people, the disturbing prophetic lies in wait.

The prophetic here is unlike Reform Judaism's light-unto-the-nations prophetic, where Jews are the vanguard people, the pioneers of democracy and inclusion, thought and science, movements for social justice, feminism, and civil rights. It differs from the abstract identity presentation that informs Rothstein's review. Both have their place. Neither move deep enough into the troubled waters of contemporary Jewish life.

The Jewish outreach to the world continues. Yet, in our time, it is being unmasked. Like any identity, Jewish identity can be self-serving, status seeking, empire building. It is not always that way, at least those trends are not always dominant. Like individual intentions, communal motives are frequently mixed. Still, earlier eras were filled with Jewish nobility in relation to the world. The best-kept secret is that, historically, Jews often had to leave the Jewish community in order to pursue this outreach to the world.

After the Holocaust, the trajectory changes and, with the increasing importance of Israel, the liberal sensibility, once the norm, shifts, too. True, a liberal sensibility remains, but neoconservatism vies for its place in the Jewish sun. Now it is the order of the day. This seemingly contradictory mix of liberal and neoconservative is confusing. Jews are liberal on most issues that are not intrinsically Jewish, neoconservative on almost everything that is. Few Jews recognize this schizophrenic reality even though it is defining of contemporary normative Jewishness.

The Contemporary Jewish Museum celebrates what it has difficulty analyzing. Obviously, the desire for assimilation is at the core even as there is a celebration of the Jewish distinctives that remain. This is Daniel Libeskind's vision—the difference between the old and new worlds of Jewish life, Europe burdened by tradition and the Holocaust and America unburdened by history and suffering. Rothstein sees this as too abstract, leaving Jews without a history.

This hardly means Jews and Jewish identity have left history. It may be that American Jews want to have it both ways, especially with Israel becoming more and more controversial within the Jewish and international community. The Holocaust and Israel remain essential but is out there, away from America's shores, out of sight, out of mind; America being a safe haven for Jews without recognizing that, especially in its empire formation, America has a history in which Jews are deeply involved. Rothstein is unclear as to what direction he wants Jews to take. True, he is unsettled by it all, but this may be because he, too, is unable to recognize the American empire history Jews want to benefit from and declare themselves above.

Rothstein asks whether Jewishness can survive without Judaism. When Jewishness is released from the boundaries of religion, is it properly Jewish? Or perhaps he is inquiring how Jewishness, released from the boundaries of religion, can be anchored.

What Jewishness is in relation to and even in rebellion against the boundaries of the past, which Rothstein identifies as Judaism, we now know. At least, that has been the Jewish trajectory over the past centuries. The tension has been robust and productive, startlingly so, even as its limitations have come into view. Rothstein's question is about the future. It is about the generations to come. In the museum's architecture and exhibits, at least in Rothstein's mind, that question has already arrived.

The museum's architecture—its "skewed geometrics"—says it all. As a skilled interpreter of images in Jewish life, Rothstein has trouble tracing the Hebrew letters inscribed in the building's design. How can ordinary Jews discern the significance of symbols that have become almost invisible?

Without boundaries, Rothstein understands Jewishness as already so diluted that museum signage is required to direct the viewer to the specific Jewish influence that the architecture and exhibits assume. Otherwise, Jewish visitors to the museum would be clueless.

Yet historical amnesia cannot be overcome through signage. Nor can signage assemble a Jewish identity that lacks internal coherence. Rothstein leaves open the implications for Jews who need to be told who they are. The historical amnesia may signal a further, as-yet-unnamed historical trauma of living a post-Holocaust/post-Israel reality where Jewish identity is too traumatic to be internalized and expressed.

Behind signage is authority. Those in the know tell Jews what should be going on within them. Besides the difficulty of internalizing the post-Holocaust/post-Israel trauma, this demonstrates that "Jewish" is less and less significant among Jews except as a recognizable, though vague, public distinctive. The museum experience is a moment of awareness. Jewishness is described for Jews by unnamed authorities who, in an interesting inversion, may or may not be Jewish. Tellingly enough, this is done in a museum, outside the confines of ordinary life or a specific Jewish place like a synagogue. The museum is a place where Jews and non-Jews mingle, so that non-Jews are likewise told by authorities what it means to be Jewish.

This same "telling" format is increasingly utilized for most Jews in relation to the Holocaust. Increasingly, the Holocaust serves as *the* symbolic reminder of Jewishness. Noting that the Holocaust is an event that the overwhelming number of Jews alive today did not witness or suffer in, this symbolic reminder will become progressively more important over the years. Because of ignorance and the struggle to define and control the message, Holocaust signage will intensify.

Already, Jews know few details about the Holocaust. Instead, the Holocaust is experienced as a grand emotion, a feeling of intense trauma and, paradoxically, as nostalgia. In a time when the Hebrew letters of the museum's architecture are imperceptible, the Holocaust, even and especially in an ahistorical format, is experienced as a place of solidity and clarity. Details are highlighted and described for Jews in museums to create predicable emotions. Holocaust emotion becomes the center of Jewish identity.

Israel was once like the Holocaust, as a twin-bill distinctive for American Jews. No community in America besides Jews can claim the destruction of their people in Europe in the middle of the twentieth century as a positive identifier. Nor can any community in America claim the rebirth of an ancient state in the place of its origins and this after the destruction of Europe's Jews, again in the middle of the twentieth century.

The combination of Holocaust suffering and Israel success, so closely tied in time, stands out, especially in a Christian culture that confesses its sins and makes its peace with an ancient and contemporary people. As well, this transpires in the West that is engaged, as it always seems to be, with spreading "light" to different, difficult, and "backward" peoples. Since Jews had been defined this way by the West—as different, difficult, and backward—it is an added bonus that Jews now join in the Western mission to others. In this joint crusade, Jews experience an enormous status, economic, and political upgrade, but, as the museum illustrates, at the expense of knowing who they are.

The Magnes Museum—(Mostly) Without Magnes

In his review, Rothstein suggests that the shortcomings of the Contemporary Jewish Museum might be addressed by partnering with the Judah L. Magnes Memorial Museum, popularly known as the Magnes Museum, which has an extensive Judaica collection. Unfortunately, an attempted merger of the museums failed. In 2010 the Magnes Museum closed and transferred its collection to the Bancroft Library at the University of California, Berkeley. The collection was renamed "The Magnes Collection of Jewish Art and Life". On the occasion of its opening in 2012, Rothstein wrote another review, aptly titled, "A Jewish Museum Shifts Its Identity."[2]

Yet, perusing the museum's website, which featured the museum's history and programs, it is notable how it replicated some of the same shortcomings Rothstein surfaced earlier. Perhaps Rothstein missed the issue at hand in both of his reviews. For without confronting the question of Israel and what it has done and is doing to the Palestinians, it is doubtful that Jewish identities portrayed in museums can actually address the substantive issues facing the Jewish people. How a museum named after the homeland Zionist, Judah Magnes, softened and sidelined the issue of Israel-Palestine—how Rothstein did as well—is instructive.

The Magnes Collection in the Bancroft Library continues this previous diversion. If anything, Magnes and his witness is even more diffuse there. In its shift from its original home, it is now located in a state university that carries no religious or ethnic identity. Has the life of Judah Magnes, like the design of the Contemporary Jewish Museum, become even more abstract now that the collection named in his honor is located at a "neutral" site?

The most prominent lacuna in the Magnes Museum and the university collection is the radical nature of its namesake's life passion. Both are named after Judah Magnes, an American rabbi and the first chancellor of Hebrew University, who we first discussed in chapter 1 as one of the principal founders of homeland Zionism and opponent of the creation of the state of Israel. Surprisingly, Magnes's commitment to homeland Zionism and vociferous arguments against state Zionism were minimized in the museum's original mission statement. They were similarly minimized in the original museum's official biographical statement about Magnes. This is coupled with an interesting side note that another, more famous, homeland Zionist, Martin Buber, once served on the museum's advisory council. As with Magnes, the museum's biographical information about Buber lacked attention to his life's passion. A committed homeland Zionist, Buber, too, actively opposed the formation of the state of Israel.

It is hard to judge whether this oversight is intentional or not. Either way, this testifies to a historical bracketing of the aspects of Magnes's vision most relevant to our time. At least some of the museum founders and board members had knowledge of the full range of the man whose museum bore his name. They even sponsored an international symposium in 1982 that covered some of Magnes's life and work in Palestine. Nonetheless Magnes's passion, when not completely absent, is downplayed and soft pedaled in the museum.

---

2. For a review of the collection now located in UC Berkeley's Bancroft Library see Edward Rothstein, A Jewish Museum Shifts Identity, *New York Times*, January 22, 2012. http://www.nytimes.com/2012/01/23/arts/design/magnes-judaica-museum-joins-berkeley-library-review.html?pagewanted=all&_r=0

Was this a retroactive attempt to rescue Magnes from his own controversial commitments?[3]

For contemporary Jews to identify with Magnes after learning of his opposition to the formation of the state of Israel would be difficult to say the least. If deemphasizing his steadfast opposition to the state of Israel by referring to it as a desire for Jewish-Arab cooperation was intentional, this would be an example of the kind of museum signage Rothstein wrote about. Here museum authorities pick, choose, highlight or minimize the biographical information deemed worthy—or possible—to share with Jews who have little knowledge of Jewish history.

Since the museum had non-Jewish visitors, cleansing Magnes of his homeland Zionism and opposition to the formation of the state of Israel may have been an attempt to keep the broader public ignorant of Jewish dissent as well. Or did the museum board deem it inappropriate or too difficult an issue to emphasize with non-Jews? It is hard to imagine Jewish or non-Jewish visitors to the museum encountering a well-known and important Jew who actively opposed the very creation of Israel on religious and ethical grounds.

Here is how the museum described the initial formation of the museum and the man for whom the museum was named. The year is 1961:

> Seymour Fromer and his wife Rebecca Camhi Fromer meet with Judah L. Magnes's widow, Beatrice Untermeyer, while on a trip to Israel. The Fromers gain her support to start a museum named after Judah L. Magnes (1877-1948), a former Oakland resident who became a renowned rabbi, lecturer, political activist, and the first Chancellor and subsequently the first President of The Hebrew University of Jerusalem. Martin Buber, the noted philosopher, agrees to serve on the advisory council.[4]

Then, in 1962, the first museum collection was obtained. Interestingly, it revolved around the Holocaust and Jewish ritual objects:

3. On the 20th anniversary of the museum's founding in 1982, the museum sponsored an international conference on Magnes's life which took place at the University of California, Berkeley. The proceedings were edited by William M. Brinner and Moses Rischin and published under the title, *Like All the Nations: The Life and Legacy of Judah L. Magnes* (Albany: SUNY, 1987). The way Magnes's vision and activism in relation to Zionism are handled in the papers published in the book is a subject in itself and worthy of further exploration with regard to the Magnes Museum.

4. The Magnes Museum website was found at http://www.magnes.org.

The Judah L. Magnes Memorial Museum is founded and is housed in one room in the Oakland-Piedmont Jewish Community Center. During its first year, the museum receives the Koretsky Collection of rare books and manuscripts. The Magnes also receives a collection of memoirs from Institute for Righteous Acts about the rescue of Jews by non-Jews during the Nazi persecutions. Its founding curator of Judaica is Ruth Eis, who guides the development of the Judaica collections and establishes the museum's international reputation with her scholarly publications covering the museum's Hanukkah lamps, Torah binders, and other objects.

In later years, the website served as the primary introduction to the museum. Reading through the extensive museum's programs and publications, including the ten-minute video introducing the museum, one finds little about Magnes's life and work. If there is any mention of his homeland Zionism, it is tempered. The final years of Magnes's life where he actively opposed the formation of a Jewish state is lacking. In 1948, just months before he died, Magnes personally lobbied Secretary of State George Marshall and President Harry Truman against recognizing the state of Israel. This is left for future historians to discuss and analyze.

The reserve is significant and relevant to the ongoing discussion on the future of Israel-Palestine, especially the lengths that Magnes went to oppose the birth of the state of Israel. Although a pacifist, Magnes recommended the establishment of a trusteeship in Palestine, backed by the United States. A trusteeship could have prompted an introduction of American armed forces in Jerusalem to maintain the unity of Palestine. Imagine today a high-profile Jew and rabbi lobbying the president of the United States to commit troops to regain Palestine's unity. Such a person would be accused of being a self-hating Jew. Any president who received such a visitor would be accused of antisemitism.[5]

Instead of focusing on the most controversial aspects of Magnes's life, the promotional video features Jews with a history in the Bay Area and who have donated memorabilia to the museum. The longest segment of the video is an

5. For a recent work on Magnes and his interaction with the Truman administration on the question of Palestine see John Judis, *Genesis: Truman, American Jews, and the Origins of the Arab/Israeli Conflict* (New York: Farrar, Straus and Giroux, 2014)

interview with a woman whose parents placed her on a ship to America as the Nazis came to power. In the trunk she stowed is a beautiful dowry dress, which ultimately finds a "home" at the museum. Interlaced with the display is the story of her new life in America, a life her parents, who were murdered in the Holocaust, never experienced.

These inversions are extraordinary. Magnes is noted as the first chancellor of Hebrew University and as a political activist, but the extent of his political activism is modified. It is drained of its essential content. Martin Buber is mentioned, again with his important work as a homeland Zionist occluded. It seems Magnes and Buber are significant figures recalled in the formation of the museum. Other than their names there is less of either than they deserve or that we need in the present.

In fact, Magnes spent the most important part of his life in Palestine. He organized and wrote on behalf of a shared Jewish-Arab configuration of Palestine and spent his last years fighting to forestall the mobilization and militarization of the Jewish world in Palestine and America. Although Magnes argued for increased European Jewish immigration to Palestine in light of the Nazi threat, his focus remained on a collaborative effort of Jews in Palestine and around the world to reinvigorate Judaism and Jewish life. Indeed, Magnes was very far away from the Holocaust memorabilia housed in the museum that carried his name.

Visitors to the museum were hardly aware of this. The more pressing issue, however, is whether they would understand Magnes's position on Palestine if the museum had emphasized it. The situation becomes worse or better, depending on one's perspective. According to Magnes's biographer, Daniel Kotzin, Magnes was a renegade Reform rabbi who came to believe that Reform Judaism had diluted Judaism of its religious and political content. Leaving for Palestine, he formed a divergent view of the possibility and hope of Jewish settlements in Palestine. Moreover, in Palestine and America, he actively organized against a Jewish state, always holding up the Jewish prophetic as the mirror of Jewish life there and here. As is true of the specificity of Magnes's commitment to a Jewish homeland rather than a Jewish state, Magnes's identifiable sense of Jewish particularity is correspondingly vague especially in a museum that covets his name.[6]

Magnes lived in the push and pull of Palestinian Jewish life. He actively promoted the idea that if Jews used military might to secure a state, Judaism and Jews would become like the Other Nations. For Magnes, this conquering

---

6. See Daniel K. Kotzin, *Judah L. Magnes: An American Jewish Nonconformist* (Syracuse: Syracuse University Press, 2010).

mentality was foreign to Judaism—or should be. To become like all the nations would be the travesty of travesties for Jews and Judaism. If Jewish life in Palestine moved in that direction irretrievably, Magnes advocated the abandonment of the Jewish experiment in Palestine.

As we have seen, a compatriot of Magnes's was Hannah Arendt, who wrote extensively about this trajectory. Her essay, "To Save the Jewish Homeland: There is Still Time," was written in the year of Magnes's death. It carries similar dire warnings of what would become of Jewish life if a Jewish state was created in Palestine. Arendt thought Israel would become a modern Sparta and that Jewish life in the Diaspora would be driven to defend the policies of the state in a way that did not comport with the Diaspora values of integration, inclusion, and democracy. Over the long run, Jewish dissent and intellectual life would degenerate into a false unanimity. No dissent would be tolerated.[7]

In the massaging of Magnes's biography, Arendt's predictions about Jewish life are realized. Arendt thought Jewish authorities would discipline Jewish dissent, as they have. She foresaw that once Israel was formed, Jewish popular opinion would also police Jewish dissent, as it has. Since Arendt was so close to the unfolding of Jewish history, she anticipated that the tradition of Jewish dissent would atrophy. The museum world of Jewish life was still in the future. That the final arbiters of Jewish history would be museum authorities who themselves have little knowledge of the subject was too far in the future for Arendt to visualize.

Magnes and Arendt foretold important aspects of a state-bound Jewishness. Still, neither understood that the other part of the Israel equation would be the Holocaust. Nor did they anticipate that Jewish life would revolve around the Holocaust and Israel in a way that, at the same time, distanced itself from both events. The possibility that both the Holocaust and Israel would be appropriated and Americanized was too distant, as was the later development of American Jews jettisoning Israel as it became too controversial. We have no idea what Magnes and Arendt would have thought about Jewish museums involving themselves with personalized stories from the Holocaust and memorabilia from family archives. I doubt they would have approved or even understood it.

This ahistorical inward-turning of American Jew happened quickly, in a matter of decades, and as the 1967 war and its aftermath turned sour. A major factor in this turning was the acceptance and affluence of the American Jewish community. Jews made it big in America. As part of the bargain, most American Jews increasingly accepted and enabled America's self-designated

---

7. Hannah Arendt, "To Save the Jewish Homeland: There is Still Time," in *Hannah Arendt: The Jewish Writings*, ed. Jerome Kohn and Ron Feldman (New York: Schocken, 2007), 388-401.

role in the world. Magnes and Arendt were nonconformists or, in Arendt's language, conscious pariahs. America became the land of Jewish conformity. Israel became the modern Sparta, Arendt predicted it would.

Magnes and Arendt came from different sides of the same coin. Magnes was an American-born religious Jew, heading toward Palestine. Arendt was a German-born secular Jew, arriving in America. Although far apart in background and temperament, their bond lay in refusing to accept prevalent cultural and political norms. Both traced their refusal to a Jewishness that traversed the American/European and religious/secular divide. Their bond revolved around repudiation of unjust power and violence, especially when Jews and the Jewish community were involved. In that repudiation, the divergence in outlook and geography collapsed.[8]

Both Magnes and Arendt saw Jews as a vanguard people. Magnes gained strength through his interpretation of the biblical witness. Arendt viewed Jewishness through the lens of the non-colonial history of the Jewish people. Neither could have imagined the assimilation away from these values that both the Contemporary Jewish Museum and the Magnes Museum represent.

The shame is more than the reduction of Magnes's life. Imagine having a museum in your name that virtually diminishes the radicality of your witness. It also collapses the history to which Magnes dedicated his life. Magnes was a major figure in Palestine, hardly a dissident on the sidelines. Buber was as well and, next to Albert Einstein, one of the most influential Jew of the twentieth century. As we have seen, Einstein was also a homeland Zionist. Like Magnes's proactive struggle against a Jewish state, Einstein's refusal to lend his prestigious name to the fledgling state as its president represented a strong statement about his conception of Jewishness in the world.

If we add to their witness the extraordinary time period in which they lived, then their witness is magnified. Recall that Magnes and Einstein, as well as Buber and Arendt, made their decisions about a Jewish state before the state was founded and during the Nazi period. They were hardly academic theoreticians of Jewish destiny. Einstein, Arendt, and Buber fled the Nazis. All four held to their views after the Holocaust and after the state of Israel came into being. None could be called armchair Zionists, either. As active promoters of homeland Zionism, they were fully aware of their reasons for supporting a Jewish homeland in Palestine and for rejecting a Jewish state.

In short, Magnes, Buber, Arendt, and Einstein, though operating from a strong sense of religious and secular Jewish identification, were internationalists.

8. A recent take on Hannah Arendt and her views on Jewish life is found in Judith Butler, *Parting Ways: Jewishness and the Critique of Zionism* (New York: Columbia University Press, 2012), 114–80.

Today we would call them global citizens. Their Jewish particularity grounded their universality. One cannot understand them and their contributions to the world outside of their Jewish particularity. Only since devotion to the memory of the Holocaust and uncritical support of Israel have become the essence of Jewish identity has the universality through particularity of Magnes, Buber, Arendt, and Einstein become suspect.

The Jewish path of universal outreach through the embrace of Jewish particularity is one casualty in the contested realm of Jewish identity. As exhibited in both the Contemporary Jewish Museum and the Magnes Museum, but also demonstrated in the United States Holocaust Memorial Museum in Washington D. C., another aspect of contemporary Jewish identity has quietly fallen by the wayside—Israel. This is a well-kept secret. More and more ordinary Jews identify less and less with Israel.

True, if Israel is challenged directly, there is a reaction, but this, too, is less so than in previous years. However, it is instructive how Israel is rarely featured in these museums that explore Jewish identity. When it was deemed appropriate years ago, Israel might be mentioned, but even then it was more as a sidelight, usually having to do with cultural matters. In these museums, Israel, if featured at all, is treated more like a small, out-of-the-way Diaspora community than an empowered and embattled Jewish state with a constructive mission to Jews and the world.

Israel is known, of course, and sometimes visited, though the percentage of Jews who visit Israel is amazingly low. For American Jews, the center of Jewish life is in America. Whether Jews are tired of the accusing images that now accompany Israel or there is an Israel fatigue factor, the museum narratives, holdings, and exhibitions paint an unmistakable picture. The decline in Jewish interest in Israel is alarming.

With the end of the narrative now being the Holocaust instead of Israel—or, rather, the Holocaust, America, and Jewish influences in culture and the arts (with the Holocaust inevitably lagging)—the erasure and reorganization of Jewish history is taking place. The news of the 1980s was that Israeli historians revised the history of the Jewish state, emphasizing its birth in the ethnic cleansing of Palestinians. As important, however, was that American Jews were disassociating themselves from the Israel narrative itself. It was at this time that the Former/Still Jewish/Israelis began to leave Israel and not join the Diaspora already in existence. In the decades to come there will be an acceleration of the movement toward a future beyond the Holocaust and Israel.

The not/joining of exiled Israelis and Diaspora Jews is mutual. Israelis in exile have little to do with Diaspora Jews. Diaspora Jews have little to do with

Israeli Jews, former or not. Neither group wants to see the other side of the Jewish coin. Perhaps there are too many accusing images—on both sides.

On the Israeli side, there is the perpetration of injustice and, on the Diaspora side, enabling that injustice as voyeurs. The Israelis who left "failed." They could not stand the injustice they were causing. American Jews also failed to keep those Israelis at their posts. Israelis in exile point to the hypocrisy of American Jews. They want Israeli Jews to do their dirty work for them.

Israelis remind Diaspora Jews that the Holocaust and Israel are real—that the suffering caused to Jews in the Holocaust is hardly summed up in memorabilia, museums and collections, and that Israel is less a dream than it is military boots on the ground that real Jews wear. Faced with the reality grounding of what has become important symbolic capital, Diaspora Jews have decided. The Holocaust and Israel are more easily dealt with conceptually.

When divorced from reality, symbolic capital dissolves. What happens when Jewish symbolic capital is infected with the blood and guts of occupation and atrocity? When one's fellow museum visitors see an Israel exhibit held up high by Jews as a hypocrisy that cannot be celebrated? When some Jews view the very same hypocrisy? The response is simple: the narrative changes. The presentations of identity through museums change. This may be the true lesson of the Contemporary Jewish Museum and the Magnes Museum.

What many Holocaust commentators refuse to appreciate is that Jews, when angered by Jewish behavior, distance themselves from it. Dealing with the behavior through critical evaluation is too onerous. Besides, ordinary Jews have little to say about how the American Jewish establishment and the Israeli government act in the world. When cajoling and threats lose the power they once had, Jews turn away from the now tainted historical signposts that previously carried positive symbolic power.

Both the Contemporary Jewish Museum, the Magnes Museum and its subsequent rebirth as a collection demonstrate that when events by which Jews are formed become confusing—when, say, Israel reflects back negatively on the meaning of the Holocaust—Jews distance themselves from both events as orienting for their lives. In the end, museums have to alert Jews to their past but in alternative ways Jews are willing to accept. Rather than centrally defining, the importance of the Holocaust and Israel take their place among others distinctives of Jewish history. Like the embroidery featured in the Magnes Museum video, the Holocaust becomes a place of nostalgic mourning.

Nostalgic mourning—is this yet another way to use the pain of the Holocaust and the early hope of Israel without having to dirty one's hands?

Does it allow Jews to move on to other conceptual identity formations when the previous ones no longer serve the community's interests?

Still, like beauty, moving on is in the eyes of the beholder. The museums in question are symptoms of retreat, a closing-down of Jewish identity and contact with the world rather than a movement forward into the unknown future. Abandoning Israel—indeed, as Israel abandoned part of its own value formation—and focusing on the Holocaust as it becomes more distant in time, is hardly moving into a future.

Focusing on esoteric contributions to culture, the arts, and the gathering of family papers is a leaving-taking of history, at least theoretically. As American Jews grapple with identity formations, however, they are safely ensconced in affluence and power, which have a history even if it is disguised in a different symbol structure. As well, a retreat into an almost nostalgic view of the Holocaust and Israel is fanciful. It is an infected nostalgia because a new culpability has arrived. Yet what is crucial here is that ordinary American Jews are losing their appetite for a sullied Jewish state. Designers of Jewish museums understand this.[9]

The ever-distant Holocaust becomes the Jewish safe harbor where questions about contemporary Jewish life are referred and buried. Since there are no questions allowed about the Holocaust, all questions referred there—whether the questioner wants them referred there or not—disappear into a void.

Insofar as Jews think of the Holocaust as a void, it makes sense for the questions—including the accusing images of what Jews are doing to Palestinians—to disappear in that void. The void into which they vanish is the same void where Jewish history disappears. Unbeknownst to Jews, the disappeared questions and history take their toll. What it means to be Jewish becomes amorphous. Is this yet another plan that Jews use to escape the demands of the Jewish prophetic?

To be unaccountable, one has to be ahistorical. At least, one has to pretend to unaccountability. Unaccountability is enabled by a sense of being outside of history. Possible responses to these issues, responses that might engage important questions and elicit a change of direction become, like the issues themselves, unappealing. They are downplayed. Soon they are unavailable. This is why few visitors to the Magnes Museum inquired as to what became of the central witness of Magnes's life. If Magnes's witness was moderated in

9. For a recent breakdown of the Israel factor in another direction—Jewish lesbian politics—see Sara Schulman, *Israel/Palestine and the Queer International* (Durham: Duke University Press, 2012).

the museum's narrative, does that mean its radical nature did not—and does not—exist?

The housing of the Magnes Collection at University of California, Berkeley may be symbolic of a further dissolution of Jewish identity. But for Judah Magnes's abiding life interest, the state university carries an interesting extension that was tempered in the Magnes Museum. Just over a year after the university opening of the Magnes Collection, the university's student senate passed a bill calling on the administration to divest its holdings in companies which profit from Israel's occupation of Palestinian territory. As might be expected, Jewish students were heavily involved in the debate about the resolution. Predictably, Jews were on both sides of the empire divide.[10]

THE BLOODLANDS CYCLE

As the portrayal of Jewish identity in the Contemporary Jewish Museum and the Magnes Museum illustrate, distance—and the negative trajectory of the state of Israel—is taking its toll on Holocaust memory. The number of Holocaust survivors dwindles with each passing year. On college campuses and the media in general, the accusing images facing the Holocaust's identity twin, Israel, increases with each year. In such a situation, Holocaust memorialization is used as a defensive weapon which encourages trivialization of the Holocaust. The end result is that the Holocaust functions as blunt instrument against dissent.

The Holocaust mobilizes the Jewish psyche. Antisemitic incidents are seen as cautionary notes about a future Holocaust. Criticism of the state of Israel is that cautionary note writ large. Yet the mobilization of the Jewish psyche has limits. Accusing images of Israeli soldiers occupying Palestinian land can only be portrayed as defensive for so long. American Jews want to get on with their lives, as do Israeli Jews. That is why the Still/Former Jewish/Israelis are so isolated.

Ordinary Israelis are not like the pioneers of the state, who knew their desire to build a state involved struggle. What the new generation wants is an ordinary life. That is why the short-lived Israeli Spring in 2011 was less about freedom from tyranny, as it was in the Arab Spring, than it was about economic reforms. Young Israelis want affordable housing. Yet as important as housing

---

10. See Nora Barrows-Friedman, "UC Berkeley student senate passes divestment bill," *Electronic Intifada*, April 18, 2013. http://www.bdsmovement.net/2013/uc-berkeley-student-senate-passes-divestment-bill-2-10909. For a letter from Israeli peace groups supporting the divestment bill see "Israeli Peace Groups in Support of UC Berkeley Divest Bill" at http://jewishvoiceforpeace.org/content/israeli-peace-groups-support-uc-berkeley-divest-bill

is, one wonders if the short-lived Israeli Spring was primarily about the larger issue that the Arab Spring ultimately failed to achieve—freedom for the new generation without being encumbered to a past that hangs like an albatross around their necks.[11]

The Holocaust unravels. Nonetheless, it remains an important public and political resource for establishment Jews, who bitterly oppose this unraveling. The race is to rescue a fading memory, and their anxiety is palpable. The Holocaust is a historical event that is re-presented continually to maintain its significance in the present. As an ongoing event, Israel is also re-presented to maintain its relevance in the present. But, unlike the Holocaust, Israeli actions in the occupied territories are reported daily. The Holocaust occurred in Europe and mainly functions as an important public signifier in the West. Residing in the Middle East, and with Jerusalem as its multi-faith capital, Israel's impact is global. Perspectives on Israel are diverse and increasingly severe.

Although the Holocaust has its interpreters, even its detractors, as a concluded historical event the Holocaust has a stability Israel lacks. Even Israel's supporters find it increasingly difficult to manage Israel's image. Israel has become a wild card in Jewish life. It threatens to turn up at every turn, and in an increasingly negative way.

The Jewish establishment wants silence on Israel, at least in public, as they work the political back channels to maintain Israel's political support. Besides, as Jewish interest drifts away from Israel, there are other empire enablers that have a more positive interest in Israel: Christian evangelicals. The arc of Jewish support for Israel lessens. Waiting in the wings and taking up the slack for waning Jewish support are evangelical Christians.[12]

The last line of defense for Jews is to hold on to the Holocaust. This is the way Jews maintain their innocence. The victims of the Holocaust are unable to speak. They cannot commit war crimes. Holocaust victims are not seen on television invading Palestinian homes or shooting Palestinian youth. Holocaust victims do not build the Wall around a dislocated and dependent people. In the end, the Holocaust is what American Jews have. If anyone tries to wrestle it away, they have a fight on their hands.

11. For an analysis of the Israeli Spring, see Daniel Bertrand Monk and Daniel Levine, "The End of the 'Israeli Spring,'" in Foreign Policy, September 12, 2011, at http://mideast.foreignpolicy.com/posts/2011/09/12/the_end_of_the_israeli_spring.

12. . On an important historical tracing of where this Christian support for Israel comes from and a commentary on its consequences see Robert O. Smith, *More Desired Than Our Owne Salvation: The Roots of Christian Salvation* (Oxford: Oxford University Press, 2013).

That some Holocaust survivors committed acts of theft and ethnic cleansing in Israel's origins and wars is safely buried, at least in the general discussion of the Holocaust. The threshold of innocence is too great. To suggest that survivors of the Holocaust did such things is considered heresy. Is this silence on the innocence of Holocaust survivors linked again to other silences, say the struggle of homeland Zionists against the birth of a Jewish state?

The Jewish retreat occurs within the context of security, power, and affluence. Those who suggest Jewish culpability and want a slice of the Jewish American pie are contested. After all, any person or group with affluence and power treats newcomers as undeserving interlopers. Like thieves in the night, they must be repelled, thrown to the ground, arrested, convicted, and jailed. Or if a deal can be struck that preserves that part of the pie, while also bringing in another who likewise has something to defend, a partnership forms.

This is how Jews ultimately succeeded in white Christian America. The Christian powers had their own material and theological interests at heart when they included American Jews at the elite levels of business and politics. Initially they allowed Jews to build their lives next store or in adjacent neighborhoods. Over the years, a mutual defense pact was agreed upon. Jews support American foreign and domestic policy and discipline the prophetic dimension of Jewish life. Christians allow Jews into the upper echelons of the American elite and support Israel without question. With this agreement in hand, their joint attention turned to others at the gates of affluence and power.

Israel is part of the anchor that Christian and Jewish elites jointly celebrated, though today this is less and less in public view. The other part of the anchor, the Holocaust, is still being commemorated. Here a joint solidarity seems more assured since the ties that bind Jews and Christians in the West is Christian culpability in antisemitism and overcoming it. Christians have a deep investment in Holocaust commemoration. The Holocaust is the gateway for Western Christians—now with Western Jews—to affirm that they are decent and civilized citizens of the world.

Antisemitism and the Holocaust throw the Christian assertion of decency and civilization into free fall. The only people who can rescue Christians are Jews. Finally recognizing the decency of Jews, with Jews affirming Christian repentance, the millennia-old blood-stained quarrel is cleared away. Christian antisemitism, and the violence that attended it, disappears from memory or, more to the point, remains highly visible as a way of disappearing present-day Jewish—and Christian—culpability in the oppression of Palestinians.

True, Christian history is replete with violence against other peoples and religion. Taking responsibility for the Holocaust, Christianity's other sins are subsumed under the Holocaust rubric. Recognizing the Holocaust and acceptance of Jews, therefore, act as a global cleansing agent for Christianity. In return, Jews assume a partnership role with their former enemies. This provides Jews with security from another Christian assault. It also prepares Jews to team up with Christians in contemporary assaults against others. Jewish-Christian teamwork is a security blanket for Jews. It is also an avenue for Jewish culpability in injustice.

Holocaust monuments and museums are the result. When the powerful publicize their sins, they assure their victory. What sins that victory promotes is for the next generation of critical historians to evaluate. Yet before the historians speak, the victory—and the cleansing of historical injustices—is accomplished in the public and identity-creating realms. Christians, who were guilty, become innocent, at least in their own minds. Jews, who were innocent, remain innocent, even in their assumption of power.

Then, seemingly out of nowhere, the wandering Still/Former Jewish/Israelis appear on the scene. They threaten to rain on this innocence-enthralled empire-forgiveness parade. Because, as they point out in their embodied way, the recovered Christian and maintained Jewish innocence are covers for empire extensions and creation.

The Western Gates of Paradise are assaulted by a history gone wrong. Ostensibly, these Still/Former Jewish/Israeli interlopers are only griping about an impasse in Israel's present-day policies. Things do not always go as smoothly as we want them to. Yet, on a more challenging level, they are witnesses to a malady much deeper than a state's checkered present. These Jewish exiles are like ghosts from the Holocaust. Their indictment moves back to the founding of the state of Israel.

Or are they ghosts from the Bloodlands? The Bloodlands is described by Timothy Snyder, professor of history at Yale University, in his book *Bloodlands: Europe Between Hitler and Stalin*. The outer core of Snyder's thesis is simple. The inner core is explosive.[13]

Although Snyder's book packs five hundred robust, fact-filled pages, his essential understanding of the Holocaust is clear and provocative. In short, Snyder believes that Holocaust remembrance reflects only part of the history of mass death in Europe during World War II, and a skewed one at that. Proposing a close examination of that history, Snyder neither denies the Holocaust nor does he, through sleight of hand, seek to minimize the suffering of Europe's Jews—far from it.

---

13. Timothy Snyder, *Bloodlands: Europe Between Hitler and Stalin* (New York: Basic Books, 2010).

In Snyder's exploration, the carnage of World War II and the Holocaust was as bad, indeed worse, than we remember. If anything, the suffering of individuals and collectives has been conceptualized to the point where the horror, though spoken and written about endlessly, has been diminished in its telling. Although inevitable and necessary, Snyder believes that conceptualization of suffering packages—and diminishes—what has yet to be rigorously thought.

In Snyder's view, packaging the Holocaust distorts what actually occurred. With suffering so immense, perhaps distortion was inevitable. However, when the distortion of a historical event like the Holocaust leads to a further distortion of what is to be done in the name of the Holocaust, historical analysis correcting the distortion is imperative. The obvious referent point is Israel and what it has done and is doing to Palestinians. Snyder thinks it is time to set the historical record straight.

In the Europe of the 1930s and 1940s, Jews suffered, but others suffered as well. After World War II ended a competition for who suffered most commenced. In the narration-of-suffering sweepstakes, Jews won handily, and Holocaust consciousness is the result. Holocaust consciousness narrates the story, featuring Jews as the people singled out for destruction.

Snyder does not dispute the monopoly Jews have established on narrating the Holocaust. Nor does he argue whether Jews might indeed qualify for this distinction. Instead, Snyder lifts up the others who suffered during this time period, for example Poles and Ukrainians. In doing so, Snyder shows that the singled-out condition Jews claim for themselves was shared in substantive ways.

Snyder is a historian rather than a theologian. As a historian, he aims to de-theologize the Holocaust. Snyder's first task is to restore the history of the time period, to get history right. In doing this, Snyder writes about non-Jews who perished by the millions. At least in the West, they have mostly been forgotten.

Snyder's subtext, though, is only announced in several paragraphs toward the end of his book. Snyder aims to deflect claims that certain groups and nations make on that time period, as the *raison d'être* for their existence and their innocence. This includes claims by Jews on the Holocaust in relation to Israel.

Jews should be alarmed by these paragraphs, but not for the reasons they might think. In Snyder's telling everything is worse—the barbarity of the war, the senselessness of the slaughter, the way the victims died, and, if they survived for a time, what survival forced upon them. In perhaps the most horrific twist, the places to which the living escaped were often the places they were subsequently killed.

Bloodlands is a tour de force. In the brutality of the slaughter we confront the meaninglessness of history. To escape the brutality of one's foe only to be murdered in your safe haven is to turn the order of life upside down. But then to be neither friend nor foe, to simply be caught between advancing and retreating forces, is to further invert the possibility of a moral universe. Such experiences render structures of meaning absurd. In Snyder's writing, the victims and the reader enter the realm of total dereliction.

Snyder's overall point, though, is that this total dereliction was shared by Jews and non-Jews alike. Antisemitism abounded in the Bloodlands. Snyder refuses to minimize Jewish suffering. But the animosity toward other communities was similarly high. The Nazis and Soviets craved empire. Anyone in their way was slated for destruction.

In the Bloodlands more than fourteen million civilian lives were lost. Most were savagely murdered. From the vantage point of the powers that sanctioned the killing, their purposes seem logical. For those caught in middle, the only logic was that of the killing machines. Few of the victims knew for what reason they died.

Today the search for the logic of victimhood spurs discussion and debate, but mostly derision. When ideology and theology dominate history, the meaning and destiny of humanity is up for grabs. So, too, is the presence or absence of God. The questions of meaning and God are of utmost importance but, as well, pale before the atrocities themselves. In focusing on meaning and God, especially when the questions are linked to the struggle to narrate and buttress power, history is often distorted. A critical history is the only way to rescue the history of suffering from becoming a tool of the powerful. Such a history holds the ideological and theological feet of the powerful to the fire.

Bloodlands is that fire. The scorched earth it revisits sears the powerful that narrate the Holocaust. Once history demythologizes the Holocaust, there is no way back.

Snyder's thesis is this: in the middle of the twentieth century, the Nazi and Soviet regimes engaged in a protracted and brutal struggle against each other for the spoils of empire. Caught in between their self-proclaimed destinies were tens of millions of people. In the process, millions were brutally murdered by both regimes. There was no escape. Those who would be murdered by one regime and escaped with their life turned on others who ultimately suffered the same fate by that or the other regime. If it was not the Soviets, it was the Nazis. If it was not the Nazis, it was the Soviets. Sometimes death came at the hands of both regimes.

The Bloodlands themselves extended from central Poland to western Russia, through Ukraine, Belarus, and the Baltic states. Snyder frames it succinctly:

> During the consolidation of National Socialism and Stalinism (1933-1938), the joint German occupation of Poland (1939-1941), and then the German-Soviet war (1941-1945), mass violence of a sort never seen before in history was visited upon this region. The victims were chiefly Jews, Belarusians, Ukrainians, Poles, Russians, and Balts, the people native to these lands. The fourteen million were murdered over the course of only twelve years, between 1933 and 1945, while both Hitler and Stalin were still in power. Though their homelands became battlefields midway through this period, these people were all victims of murderous policy rather than the casualties of war. The Second World War was the most lethal conflict in history, and about half of the soldiers who perished on all of its battlefields all over the world died here, in the same region, in the bloodlands. Yet not a single one of the fourteen million murdered was a soldier on active duty. Most were women, children, and the aged; none were bearing weapons; many had been stripped of their possessions, including their clothes.[14]

Snyder's Holocaust is inclusive of others without diminishing Jewish suffering. In the worldview of the Nazis, Jews held a special place of derision. Yet there is a caveat: Snyder believes that had Germany's war against the Soviet Union gone as planned, "thirty million civilians would have been starved in its first winter, and tens of millions more expelled, killed, assimilated, or enslaved thereafter." As for the ratio of Jewish and non-Jewish deaths, Snyder is clear: "The Germans murdered about as many non-Jews during the war, chiefly by starving Soviet prisoners of war (more than three million) and residents of besieged cities (more than a million) or by shooting civilians in 'reprisals' (the better part of a million, chiefly Belarusians and Poles)."[15]

So the Holocaust as it is narrated today is true—Jews died by the millions—but partial—non-Jews died by the millions, too. The mass murder of Jews tells only part of the story. As Snyder writes, the Bloodlands is a "history

14. Ibid., viii.
15. Ibid., ix-x.

of political mass murder." It is the clash of two empire hopefuls without a conscience and with a total disdain for life. This includes the life of Jews and non-Jews alike. Total disdain.

Despite his inclusive sensibility, Snyder retains the term *Holocaust* for the Jews who were murdered during the Nazi-Soviet war for empire. Nonetheless, understanding this history through Snyder's lens means that the story of the Holocaust itself is partial. Most often, the Holocaust is incorrectly narrated.

Of the many examples Snyder cites of this partial and incorrect understanding of the Holocaust, one stands out. Snyder disputes the often cited fact that the death camps—including Auschwitz—were the central arena in which the Holocaust took place. If only the death camps are factored in, Treblinka, Chelmno, Sobibor, and Belzec hold the dubious honorific of counting the most Jewish deaths. Yet, even so, Snyder writes that more Jews were killed over ditches and pits in occupied Poland, Lithuania, Latvia, Soviet Ukraine, and Soviet Belarus than in the death camps. "The horror of the twentieth century is thought to be located in the camps," Snyder writes, "But the concentration camps are not where most of the victims of National Socialism and Stalinism died." Snyder concludes that these misunderstandings of mass killing "prevent us from perceiving the horror of the twentieth century."[16]

The misunderstandings have at least two aspects to it, the first being that Jews were the only targets of the Nazis. Although Jews held a special place in the Nazi vision, if the Nazis had succeeded in their plans for global empire, Snyder believes that the numbers of others killed would have dwarfed the number of Jews. The second misunderstanding is that the murder of Jews was systematic and industrial, thoroughly modern in its barbarity. Snyder's analysis shows the opposite.

Mass killing in Europe is usually associated with the Holocaust, which, in turn, is associated with methodological industrial killing. Snyder finds this image too simple. At the German and Soviet killing sites, the murder method was rather primitive. Of the fourteen million civilians and prisoners of war killed in the Bloodlands between 1933 and 1945, Snyder cites statistics that more than half died because they were denied food. In the middle of the twentieth century, Europeans deliberately starved other Europeans to death in horrific numbers.[17]

---

16. Ibid., xii-xiii.

17. For further thoughts on starvation as a method of mass murder, see Snyder's review of a recent book on the subject, Lizzie Collingham's *The Taste of War: World War II and the Battle for Food* (New York: Penguin, 2012), in "On Their Stomachs: How Food Contributed to World War II: Its Origins, Its Outcome and Its Aftermath," *New York Times Book Review*, May 6, 2012.

After starvation as a method of murder came shooting, then gassing. Both have little to do with modernity. This includes the methods of asphyxiating Jews—hydrogen cyanide, a compound isolated in the eighteenth century, and carbon monoxide, which, according to Snyder, even the ancient Greeks knew was lethal. Instead, the Germans and Soviets "relied upon technologies that were hardly novel in the 1930s and 1940s: internal combustion, railways, firearms, pesticides, and barbed wire."[18]

Snyder displaces modernity as the engine of the Holocaust, though clearly modernity was present. Rather, Snyder relocates the dominant modern European characteristic of the Holocaust narrative, as the only or even its central thrust. While Snyder allows for the singularity of Jewish identity in certain conceptual frameworks, the deaths of Jews in the Holocaust was intertwined with the millions of others who died.

In the Bloodlands where most Jews died, Snyder considers that what happened to one group is "intelligible only in light of what happened to another." For Snyder, that is just the beginning of the connections we need to make: "The Nazi and Soviet regimes, too, have to be understood in light of how their leaders strove to master these lands, and saw these groups and their relationship to one another." Snyder concludes that a "description of Jewish life can include the Holocaust, but not explain it."[19]

Bloodlands reads like a mass indictment of humanity. This is especially true when nations mobilize for empire. Or *Bloodlands* is a mass indictment of empire and those who lead empires, regardless of their location or ethnic and religious designations. The empire here is Nazi and Soviet or German and Russian. The Bloodlands are their killing fields. The killing fields are created so that empire can be achieved.

As imperial powers, Germany and the Soviet Union unleash a bloodletting that ultimately involves everyone in the region. In an even more macabre scene, alternately it involves both sides within the other. So, for example, surviving an initial onslaught is little guarantee of survival in the long run. If individuals and communities survive the first onslaught, they are liable to be killed in the next. Surviving a German or Soviet onslaught in the Bloodlands was tantamount to buying time, and precious little at that.

Most horrifically, the Germans and the Soviets involved the ultimate victims in the killing fields as murderers themselves. Perpetrators, survivors, and the dead were all implicated in murder. Perpetrators murdered. In turn,

18. Snyder, *Bloodlands*, xiv, xv.
19. Ibid., xix.

they were murdered. Survivors who survived the perpetrators often became perpetrators and were slaughtered by other survivors/perpetrators.

In the Bloodlands at least, there were very few bystanders. Like Auschwitz and the other death camps, this is another category of Holocaust literature that Snyder displaces. To stand by was to die. But, then, to actively participate in killing, if only to survive, was ultimately a death sentence as well. The advances and retreats of the German and Soviet empire armies made the decision of individuals, even for survival, moot.

History's deconstruction is often painful. Our received and cherished understandings are challenged. For the victims and their surviving heirs, history is their only recourse. The judgment of history is like God's judgment on the abuse of power. In an era where God is silent, history is a force to be reckoned with.

Reading the *Bloodlands*, we are very far from the Western Gates of Paradise, as Rothstein described the Contemporary Jewish Museum. We are a long way from the dowry dress featured in the Magnes Museum, at least in the symbolic field of Holocaust commemoration that now envelopes it. As horrific as the story they narrate is, the Holocaust Memorial Museum and the panoply of other Holocaust memorials in the United States and Europe also diminishes the suffering of the Bloodlands..

With the Bloodlands in mind, Holocaust memorials stake their claim on an event that is much larger and more troubling. Exclusive Jewish rights to narrate suffering are undercut. Rather than a right asserted, narrating the Holocaust becomes a privileged entitlement. But who grants Jews this entitlement and whose suffering is silenced because of it? Is the tale of the suffering and death of others unmerited and therefore unwarranted?

In their objective circumstances, most victims of the Bloodlands suffered and perished like Jews did. That the Holocaust plotline is skewed Jewish because of the success and status of post-Holocaust Jewry in the West is obvious. But Jews also hold fast to the Holocaust as Jewish to assert the possibility of meaning after an event that, when expanded, makes meaning even more difficult to come by.

The Bloodlands is a geography that can be visited only on occasion lest we lose our faith in humanity. If one can contemplate such a possibility, the Bloodlands is worse than the Holocaust. However, that is far from Snyder's point. Snyder wants Jews and others to refuse to create another Bloodlands, anytime, anywhere. Like the shared suffering during the clash of World War II empires, Snyder understands that creating a future beyond mass death must also be shared. Jews did not suffer alone. Jews cannot create a future beyond suffering alone.

A SHARED SOLITUDE

The enclosed geography of Auschwitz, as horrible as it was—indeed, horrible beyond imagining—is shrinking. Even if we limit the causalities of the Holocaust to Jews and Poles, in Elie Wiesel's *Night* and in Holocaust museums, non-Jewish Polish inmates are virtually absent. In the Holocaust narrative, Auschwitz is defining. It is the place from hell where Jews from inside and outside of Poland were brought and murdered. The Polish claims of Auschwitz ownership, with tens of thousands of Poles murdered there, has to be reconsidered. Auschwitz as *the* symbol of the Holocaust has to be reconsidered. The Holocaust itself needs to be reconsidered.

Under the rubric of the Holocaust, the emphasis on Jewish singularity is the norm. No other emphasis is allowed. This singularity mirrors the biblical journey of the ancient Israelites into Canaan. Canaanites and others in the land, if they are noticed in the Bible, are on the periphery as shadowy figures. When they appear, they are menacing. In Holocaust literature, Auschwitz is even more isolated, as a people slated for murder dwelling alone. Solitude pervades *Night*, as does the rendition of Auschwitz in all of Holocaust literature. Snyder sees the Bloodlands in a different light. All are abandoned in the Bloodlands, even if at first loyalties are invoked. To be sure, at times, Jews experience an elevated level of abandonment.

Yet here Snyder notes the level of illusion among those non-Germans who helped the Nazis isolate, persecute, and sometimes murder Jews. Soon after, many received their reward from the Nazi or Soviet advancing/retreating empire forces—death. Persecuting Jews for their own status upgrade was often followed by their own isolation and death. When the advancing armies came, distinctions of who did what to Jews became unimportant. In the mayhem, whoever was in the way became a victim.

If the notion of singularity did not already surround our construction of Jews, it would be more difficult to disentangle the Jewish experience of the Bloodlands from the non-Jewish Poles or Ukrainians. It is only in retrospect, within the confines of Holocaust literature and theology, that Jews are so terribly isolated.

Even with this underlying thematic, Snyder has difficulties disentangling Jewish aloneness. After all, Snyder's book is important precisely because he challenges the appropriated Jewish singularity of the Holocaust. In the end, though, he is unable to escape the received Holocaust construction. Throughout *Bloodlands*, Snyder continues to employ Holocaust terminology for Jews, but he does not surface a specific name for the suffering others. The Bloodlands intertwines the experience of the people murdered in a shared geography. However, the Holocaust remains his only singular descriptive. In the shared solitude of the Bloodlands, Jews remain alone.

One waits for hundreds of pages before Snyder's drops his other historical shoe. Because of our "knowledge" of the Holocaust, however, the other shoe seems to be dropping throughout his book. In the end, the reader begins to wonder if Snyder will explicitly address this contention and name it as his own.

The build-up is excruciating. Once again, the point is delayed. Snyder cites abuses of the history of the Bloodlands in the present or, rather, the abuses of the history of suffering in World War II precisely because the history of the Bloodlands is either ignored or compartmentalized. "Our contemporary culture of commemoration takes for granted that memory prevents murder. If people died in such large numbers, it is tempting to think, they must have died for something of transcendent value, which can be revealed, developed, and preserved in the right sort of political remembrance." Snyder is approaching the central thesis of his book, albeit in vague terms.

When interpreted in transcendent terms, the bloodletting turns out to be national. "The millions of victims must have died so that the Soviet Union could win a Great Patriotic War, or America, a good war," Snyder writes, "Europe had to learn its pacifist lesson, Poland had to have its legend of freedom, Ukraine had to have its heroes, Belarus had to prove its virtue, Jews had to fulfill a Zionist destiny." But Snyder believes that the matter was simply that someone had the power and decided who would die: "Later on, someone else decides why. When meaning is drawn from killing, the risk is that more killing would bring more meaning." Snyder continues:

> Here, perhaps, is a purpose for history, somewhere between the record of death and its constant reinterpretation. Only a history of mass killing can unite the numbers and the memories. Without history, the memories become private, which today means national; and the numbers become public, which is to say an instrument in the international competition for martyrdom. Memory is mine and I have the right to do with it as I please; numbers are objective and you must accept my counts whether you like them or not. Such reasoning allows a nationalist to hug himself with one arm and strike

his neighbor with the other. After the end of the Second World War, and then again after the end of communism, nationalists throughout the Bloodlands (and beyond) have indulged in the quantitative exaggeration of victimhood, thereby claiming for themselves the mantle of innocence.[20]

Snyder concludes that meaning drawn from killing means more killing in the name of those who were killed. The decision about who will live and who will die is always with the powerful. This is true in history. It is true in the present. Destinies are then drawn from the dead—without their permission. Jews do this, but again, as in the Bloodlands, if Jews are not alone in this, neither are they exempt.

Did the Holocaust occur, is it remembered, so that Jews can fulfill a state Zionist destiny? For Snyder, the quantitative exaggeration of victimhood, or in the case of Jews, the qualitative exaggeration of being singled out, is problematic. The nationalism that emerges from the Holocaust and other events of mass death claims the dead and produces more dead. To do so "ethically," collectives exaggerate their position as victims and view the outside world as a challenge to the memory and the nationalism drawn from it. Once more, Jews are hardly alone in their claims. Jews are not exempt, either.

Snyder refers to this exaggeration as "competitive martyrology." Such martyrology, with the addition of power, ends as "martyrological imperialism." Again, Jews are one among many in this use of martyrs. Nonetheless, Snyder explores the Jewish emphasis on singularity in their use of martyrdom, using examples of those who died in the Bloodlands. He asks, for example, whether the Jewish girl who "scratched a note to her mother on the wall of the Kovel synagogue" belongs to Polish, Soviet, Israeli, or Ukrainian history. The girl wrote in Polish while other Jews in that synagogue on that day were Yiddish-speaking. Snyder also refers to a Jewish mother who urged her daughter in Russian to flee Babi Yar. Babi Yar is in Kiev, which is now the capital of independent Ukraine. Since, as Snyder knows, most Jews in Kovel and Kiev, as in much of Eastern Europe, were neither Zionists nor Poles nor Ukrainians nor communists, he asks whether they really can be said to have died for Israel, Poland, Ukraine, or the Soviet Union. For Snyder, "they were Jews, they were Polish or Soviet citizens, their neighbors were Ukrainians or Poles or Russians."[21]

20. Snyder, *Bloodlands*, 402, 401-402.
21. Ibid., 406.

The two Jews Snyder discusses belong to the histories of four countries, but then only insofar as the histories of these countries are separate. Snyder leaves the interconnectedness of these countries' histories for other historians of the period. Nonetheless, his point is that individual and collective identities are complex. Jews often gather multifaceted cultural, linguistic, and religious sensibilities under the generalized rubric "Jewish."

Snyder wants to recover the individuality of the victims. For him, generalized rubrics diminish individual existence and ultimately the worth of that existence. In Snyder's understanding, gathering Jews under the Holocaust banner, even as it seeks to raise the visibility of Jews, actually reduces them to a collective identity. This is how Snyder's comments on how the deconstruction of the Holocaust should be understood:

> Each record of death suggests, but cannot supply, a unique life. We must be able not only to reckon the number of deaths but to reckon with each victim as an individual. The one very large number that withstands scrutiny is that of the Holocaust, with its 5.7 million Jewish dead, 5.4 million of whom were killed by the Germans. But this number, like all of the others, must not be seen as 5.7 million, which is an abstraction few of us can grasp, but as 5.7 million *times* one. This does not mean some generic image of a Jew passing through some abstract notion of death 5.7 million times. It means countless individuals who nevertheless have to be counted, in the middle of life: Dobica Kagan, the girl in the synagogue in Kovel, and everyone with her there, and all the individual human beings who were killed as Jews in Kovel, in Ukraine, in the East, in Europe.[22]

Reading *Bloodlands* decades after the Holocaust and the establishment of the state of Israel, the Still/Former Jewish/ Israelis come to mind. When they leave Israel altogether, from what are they fleeing? Are they fleeing Israel only or a new Bloodlands, this time transported from Europe to the Middle East? If so, they are fleeing the new Middle East Bloodlands as many of their parents and grandparents fled the European Bloodlands, at least the ones that survived them.

One of the terrible truths found in Snyder's history is that fleeing one power often meant being trapped by another. Jews may have experienced this

22. Ibid., 407.

to a greater degree than others. Yet, as Snyder writes, the historical record suggests that the populations were thoroughly mixed. Nonetheless, a tragic irony remains. Did Jews who survived the Bloodlands and arrived in Palestine escape one Bloodlands to enter—and enable—another one?

The situation of Palestine during World War II and beyond was different to be sure, yet dangerous, nonetheless. Since that time, wars have followed wars. Between wars there are threats of wars to come. The dream of ending the cycle of violence and atrocity remains. That dream has yet to arrive.

If we take 1933 as the beginning of the Bloodlands in Europe, on the seventieth anniversary of Israel in 2018, Jews will have spent more than eighty-five years in what might be called the Bloodlands Cycle. By Joseph Massad's dating, the Palestinians will have existed more than 135 years in that cycle.

Conceptually, the years after the Holocaust have been less intense, at least on the order of mass murder. Yet the threat of mass murder and certainly murder in war continues. If we take seriously Snyder's admonition about how concepts like the Holocaust distance us from individual suffering, the Bloodlands Cycle has been harsh and unremitting. There seems to be no end in sight.

The Middle East as a region has become a Bloodlands. When the state of Israel was created, the Middle East was busy trying to free itself of European colonialism. Then, through the creation and expansion of Israel, the Middle East was caught there again, this time with more overt violence.

The concentration on what Palestinians have suffered in the Bloodlands Cycle is correct. Still, with the creation of the state of Israel, the Palestinian refugee crisis and the Arab world in general have been caught up in a post-World War II, post-Holocaust violence devastating to their internal development and self-governance. Although the Bloodlands Cycle is geographically situated in the Middle East, the former colonial powers that governed or coveted the Middle East have returned, this time as arms merchants and oil conglomerates. The Middle East Bloodlands Cycle has gone global.

Perhaps some of this was inevitable with the coming of the Cold War and the importance of oil, but the Bloodlands nationalistic claims of Israel, tied to Holocaust martyrdom, has contributed heavily to the region's woes. At least in America, we hear little about this expanding Bloodlands. In the global marketplace, at least from the perspective of the West, few claims compare to the powerfully articulated Jewish Holocaust martyrology.

Snyder's chilling term—martyrological imperialism—may be what the Still/Former Jewish/Israelis are enduring within Israel and fleeing from when they leave. The Bloodlands Cycle continues in Israel. So what Jews wanted to escape, they remain embroiled in. The Holocaust martyrs now fuel this cycle in, at least from the Middle Eastern perspective, a Jewish colonial intrusion from Europe. For the Arab world, Israel's empire, backed by America, exploits the Holocaust martyrs. This is because Jews, now empowered, view the Holocaust martyrs from a singular viewpoint. Forgotten are the millions of non-Jewish martyrs.

The haunting question remains: If the European Bloodlands is reframed and recognized for what they were historically, as a shared destiny of destruction and death, will Jews one day have to recognize the Palestinians and Arabs who have been dislocated, maimed, and murdered during Israel's existence in a similar way? It seems that the Still/Former Jewish/Israelis have already recognized this interconnection in their lives. It is only a matter of time before more and more Jews inside and outside of Israel acknowledge the same connection.

For now, the separation of the Holocaust martyrs is like the state of Israel—separated, at least in the Jewish perspective, from the Middle East. But, since Israel lives in the Middle East, the idea of separation, as if Israel exists somewhere in the trans-Atlantic North, is a nonstarter. Ultimately, Israel can be thought of alone in the Middle East only if the lens of a Jews-only Holocaust is employed.

Jewish identity has undergone a reversal after the Holocaust, over the years emphasizing more and more the singled-out condition of Jews. The pre-World War II trend of Jewish life was toward integration in Europe and America. The Bloodlands ended that experiment in Europe, though it continued in America. In Israel the trend reversed, building a religious-ethnic state against the tide of world history and Jewish life in the Diaspora.

Jews who integrated into America retained certain elements of Jewish particularity. However, they downplayed those traditions of Jewish life that concretely separated Jews from the broader society. In light of this Jewish-American experiment in integration, Israel's maintenance of an exclusive Jewish sensibility may seem odd. However, if American Jews can have their cake and eat it too—integration in America with a projected symbolism of separation in Israel—they can enjoy the best of both worlds, at least symbolically. Therefore, the seeming disjunction of Holocaust consciousness developing in America before it does in Israel is explained.

Holocaust consciousness is a projected symbolic separation for American Jews who flourish in an accepting non-Jewish society. Indeed, a public Holocaust martyrology develops in America before Israel and is sustained here in an almost uncritical way. Moreover, it often serves as a cover for a martyrological imperialism in Israel and, indeed, in America. Meanwhile, few

Jews reflect on what impact Jewish martyrological imperialism has on Palestinians and the Arab world.

Who in the West can question this Holocaust martyrology? There is no competition on the horizon, so it seems. This is because Holocaust martyrological imperialism has become institutionalized and empowered. Over the decades, the Holocaust has cleared the field of its competitors or driven them underground.

In America and around the world, there are other martyred peoples. From the perspective of Native Americans and African Americans, America is a Bloodlands in which the Jewish Holocaust narrative now reigns supreme. From the Native and African American perspective, the Holocaust museums around the country, including the Holocaust Memorial Museum, is viewed as the epitome of martyrological imperialism. Neither community can admit to their views or speak their story without being cautioned or ultimately disciplined as uninvited martyrological interlopers. It is difficult to know what non-Jews think about the Holocaust. The penalty for opening this question is the accusation of Holocaust denial. The middle ground of shared grief is cut away by an imposed hierarchy of suffering.

The solitude of the martyrs, if they are more than victims, is itself part of Snyder's history. Because, once we move from the individual murder to a collective counting, then we are already on our way toward imperialism of some over others. Those who call the shots of memory are usually those whose cards fall their way in the aftermath of destruction—that is, if they become empowered.

By then we are creating new martyrs, say the Palestinian martyrs, recognized as such by the unempowered Palestinians, but not, in the main, by Jews who are empowered. In a strange twist of martyrology, the Still/Former Jewish/Israelis do recognize the Palestinians in this way. Is that because they know that, with other Jews, they have created another martyrology?

Now we enter a different territory entirely, or perhaps it is similar, just logically extended. When another people are martyred by your own people, and is so recognized as a historical fact by the vanguard of the martyring people, a wild card is inserted into the martyrology deck. For Jews it is an old wild card, an indigenous one, the prophetic wild card. This prophetic wild card locates injustice to indict the destiny proffered by the recently martyred.

As we have seen, prophetic logic holds a strange inversion as its own. The oppressed are signposts of a storm on the horizon. By the time the prophetic wild card appears, it is almost too late.

The storm is the other side of the West Coast of Paradise. In Walter Benjamin's view, it is the storm from paradise. Benjamin, a German Jewish thinker who committed suicide during the Holocaust years, saw the prophetic inversion as a way of judging progress. Instead of advance, he saw debris and barbarism. Wherever it is, the Bloodlands is like Benjamin's storm from paradise. In the Bloodlands, the debris is corpses strewn about or buried in mass anonymous graves.[23]

It is the ultimate hypocrisy to murder in the name of the murdered, all the while using one's own murdered to narrate innocence and redemption. The powerful call the martyrs' roll as another people is driven pillar to post, as was the martyrs' lot, more or less. It hardly needs to be an exact replica to capture the attention of the prophet. Nor does the prophet need to know God or even believe that God exists to get the point. The prophet intervenes like God would—or should. The prophet intervenes where God does not. The prophet becomes God's voice on earth even, and especially, in an age where God's absence is defining.

This may have been what the great Jewish philosopher Emmanuel Lévinas meant when he wrote about the Jewish atheists and rebels of the nineteenth and early twentieth centuries. Many of them left the assimilating Jewish community to act and write for justice in the world. "Perhaps, from that age on, the Jewish presence manifested itself more in the Israelites' participation in liberal and social movements—in the struggle for civil rights and true social justice—than in the sermons to be heard in liberated synagogues," Lévinas writes. "All these denigrators of tradition, all these atheists and rebels, unwittingly joined the divine tradition of intransigent justice which expiates blasphemy in advance. With these rebels, Judaism, which had scarcely been absorbed into the surrounding world, already opposed it on one level."[24]

Writing in the middle of the twentieth century, Lévinas called on contemporary atheists and rebels to return to the Jewish community. Having left the Jewish community to pursue justice, Lévinas believed they adopted a foreign language. By this he meant European languages with their non-Jewish symbol structure. By returning to the Jewish community they would regain their "Jewish" language. For Lévinas, language is more than linguistic ability.

23. Walter Benjamin's "storm from paradise" can be found in his essay, "On the Concept of History," in *Walter Benjamin: Selected Writings*, vol. 4, 1938-1940, ed. Howard Eiland and Michael W. Jennings (Cambridge: Harvard University Press, 2003), 389-400.

24. Emmanuel Lévinas, "Ethics and Spirit," in *Difficult Freedom: Essays on Judaism* (Baltimore: Johns Hopkins University Press, 1990), 5-6.

Lévinas thought that the Jewish religious, cultural, and symbolic field returned Jews to their indigenous, the prophetic.

For Lévinas, the European languages that atheistic and rebellious Jews adopted were foreign to them. Ultimately, the Holocaust exposed these languages as morally bankrupt. Because of this moral bankruptcy, Lévinas believed that European languages could no longer fuel the divine tradition of intransigent justice that Jewish atheists and rebels entered. That divine tradition is housed in the Jewish community.

For Lévinas, Jews leave their tradition only when the Jewish community loses its way in the world. The Jewish community cannot find its way back, however, without these atheists and rebels returning to the fold. There is a mutual interdependence, a prophetic interchange, between individual Jews and the Jewish community. When they are separated for too long the individual and the community languishes.

Surveying Jewish history, it is hardly a coincidence that the very individuals whose grandparents and parents returned to the Jewish fold in its most intense form by coming to Israel as the state was being formed are now in internal exile or leaving Israel altogether. Using Lévinas as a guide, it is the Jewish symbolic/discourse field playing itself out once again in Jewish history. Jews leave the community when it has lost its way. They return to reconnect but are soon off again expiating blasphemy in advance.

Jews are on both sides of the empire divide, in the Diaspora and in Israel. Instability is a result of the prophetic, even when Jewish homecoming after the Holocaust mandates empowerment. This time, however, the empire divide is more noticeable. For the first time in modern history, Jews are assimilated to more than the bourgeois world. They are the captains of empire. Once again, non-Jews are suffering, but this time at the hands of an exclusive Jewish state.

Before, Jews may have ascended to positions of power; now they are power. Before, when non-Jews suffered, as a community Jews were innocent. Armed with a state, Jews now have direct responsibility for the suffering of others. In fact, Jews as a community too often enable that suffering. Jews benefit from that suffering.

Many Holocaust survivors came to live in Israel. From the Holocaust, Israelis know martyrdom intimately. Many of these Still/Former Jewish/Israelis come from families where martyrdom is present in recent history. Are they leaving Israel and Jewishness precisely because the tradition of martyrdom is expanding? The numbers of martyrs grow. Its growth is at the hands of those who claim the tradition as their own.

Martyrological imperialism has its own logic. It increases the numbers of martyrs. In fact, it often creates new martyr traditions. Joseph Massad's ongoing Nakba is important here, now looked at from the perspective of a developing martyr tradition. Displacement, occupation, ethnic cleansing, leads in this direction.

Did those who died and barely survived the Holocaust ever imagine that Jews, by their actions, would create such a tradition for others? It is the use of such power that limits the powerful from recognizing the martyr tradition it creates. Nonetheless, it was only a matter of time before some Jews would come to realize and then articulate the horror that surrounds contemporary Jewish power.

In the end, the newly created tradition of martyrs has an impact on the tradition of martyrs as narrated by the powerful. There is the obvious issue of trivialization—how to narrate an empowered tradition of martyrdom when that very tradition is creating a new tradition of martyrdom. As well, and more decisively, it is only a matter of time before the two traditions become interconnected.

In the long run, but sometimes suddenly, one tradition can hardly be spoken without invoking the other. That is when martyrological imperialism is humbled and understood for what it is. The discourse surrounding it is stripped naked. In relation to the Holocaust and the Nakba, the future is obvious. The Still/Former Jewish/Israelis join the Holocaust and the Nakba at their hips.

There is yet another level of engagement to be explored—when the martyrs of another people become your own—since they are martyred by your own people and interrupt your people's martyrological imperialism. The new martyrs announce judgment with their deaths. They announce the ethical doom of the powerful that use martyrological imperialism as their birthright.

Jews of Conscience are bound to break with the violence committed on behalf of the Holocaust martyrs. For in the end, everyone knows that, though the martyrs are invoked, there are other, more compelling reasons for imperialism: loot, land, domination. When a tradition of martyrdom becomes a cover for theft, everything, including memory, is up for grabs. Ethics loses its grounding. Lévinas's home "language" becomes bereft.

Whether announced or not, those from martyred peoples know the score. They know martyrs leave behind bank accounts, homes, property, jobs, art, and businesses. So, among other things, martyrdom abused is expropriation run amok. The victims are stripped of everything they inherited and possessed. Then the martyr tradition that abuses power is also stripped bare. Its only point of recovery is coming into solidarity with the tradition of martyrs it is creating.[25]

Those who awaken to the violence against the Other know how their people's martyrdom is often abused, spoken for, and adjusted for this and that political wind. They know when funds are collected in their name but are unseen by the martyrs themselves. They know when the politics on the right uses a nationalism that once helped do in their family members. They know the distance between real suffering and conceptualizing it. They know when suffering is being used against others and against their will—or what might have been their will, if the martyrs that are now used to martyr others had a voice.

So combine the indigenous prophetic with a people's martyrdom. Then add the knowledge that Jews are on both sides of the empire divide. Isn't it obvious that the Jewish language that expiates blasphemy in advance—always the language of justice—is destined to be turned inward?

25. For expropriation in the Holocaust, see Harold James, *The Deutsche Bank and the Nazi Economic War Against the Jews* (Cambridge: Cambridge University Press, 2001). For the expropriation in relation to Israel, see Nur Masalha, *The Palestinian Nakba: Decolonising History, Narrating the Subaltern, Reclaiming Memory* (London: Zed Books, 2012).

9

One State—One Future?

For decades, Jewish life and the perception of that life by non-Jews have been moving in different directions. The first romanticizes Jewish history: Jews are the great contributors and sufferers of history-only. The second renews the tradition of demonizing Jews and Judaism: Jews are intrinsically flawed and are prone to aggression and violence-only. A third reappraises Jewish history in a self-critical way, with a particular emphasis on contemporary Jewish links with empire. It explores the possibility of solidarity with all those who are suffering, including and especially the Palestinian people.

The first two directions are frequently on public display, with supporters and detractors arguing their cases. The third direction is nuanced, less obvious, and more complicated. For the most part this debate is hidden from public view and mostly internal. The reappraisal of Jewish history has first to deal with the previous directions, if only to set the stage for this other deeper and crucial discussion.

As we have seen, the discussion of Jews, Jewishness, Judaism, and Jewish history is fraught and framed by, yes, Jewish contribution and suffering and, yes, by Jewish abuse of power. All of this occurs within a mythic structure about Jews developed over the millennia.[1]

Public discourse about Jews enters a special historical district where Jews once inhabited and where Jews still reside in symbol and culture. Words about Jews carry layers of presumption, myth and hope. Negative and positive stereotypes abound. "Jewish" is rarely neutral. "Jewish" carries a large amount of baggage.

Increasingly Jews play around with language about Jews by bending negative stereotypes toward a badge of arrival. The twists are meaningful, sometimes with comic overtones, as in the British Jewish anarchist group,

---

1. One such take on Jewish baggage is Jean-Francois Lyotard, *Heidegger and "the jews,"* (Minneapolis: University of Minnesota Press, 1990).

which proudly carries the name *Jewdas*; or the online Jewish website, *Jewcy*; or the irreverent Jewish magazine, *Heeb*. These inverted name affiliations flourish along a proliferation of "Not in My Name" groups. Instead of claiming a slur against Jews and inverting it to the positive—in a sense, taking back the name and using it as a badge of honor as *Jewdas* and *Heeb* do—"Not in My Name" groups take back "Jew" from the state that uses its name and the establishment that pretends to innocence, both of which enable the oppression of another people.[2]

Inversion and reclaiming may be a coincidence in tactic and time, but certainly the simultaneous and unplanned synchronicity is important. It is yet another clue to a future beyond where Jews are today.

Inversion and reclaiming alert us once again that discussion of Jews is rarely neutral. So it is with the Holocaust and Israel. With the mythic framework surrounding all things Jewish, critical thought walks a fine line. Is that yet another reason that revising our understandings of the Holocaust and Israel is fraught?

Teaching the (Bloodlands-Revised) Holocaust

Although a history of the struggle between the Nazi and Soviet empires, in the end Timothy Snyder's historical exploration in *Bloodlands* is about how Jews and non-Jews alike perceive the Holocaust. An underlying theme Snyder addresses is Holocaust remembrance and memorialization, which has become a virtual industry in Europe and the United States.[3]

The output of materials relating to the Holocaust is enormous. Participants include, at one level, governments, the Jewish establishment, academia, publishing, Jewish and Christian religious houses of worship, and world-renowned architects. Other levels include informal, legal, and political levers of power that caution against criticism of the accepted Holocaust narrative. The established Holocaust framework influences public discussions, or lack thereof, about Israel, especially its policies relating to Palestinians.

Perhaps the biggest challenge *Bloodlands* poses to Holocaust remembrance and memorialization is the teaching of the Holocaust in Europe and America. Local and state governments across America are increasingly mandating teaching the Holocaust. For universities, teaching the Holocaust is a sign of

2. See the *Jewdas* website, http://www.jewdas.org. For an interesting biosketch of *Jewdas*, see http://en.wikipedia.org/wiki/Jewdas.

3. Timothy Snyder, *Bloodlands: Europe Between Hitler and Stalin* (New York: Basic Books, 2010).

prestige, as it combines elements of history with pedagogy acceptable to Jewish authorities. Like Holocaust remembrance and memorialization, teaching the Holocaust is a matter of public performance. Public standards are already in place and understood before the teacher is assigned the Holocaust to teach. They are to be adhered to. If not, penalties are applied.[4]

This mirrors the discussion of Israel in years past, where conformity in perspective was policed. Over the years, the ability to police thought about Israel has become more difficult. To some extent, though more in Europe than in the United States, the necessity to conform thoughts about Israel to a public standard has lessened. Today Palestinians speak for themselves in the public realm in Europe and America, whereas some years ago this was problematic, if not impossible.

Nonetheless, there are still strictures. In general, Palestinian leadership and especially Hamas remain no-go areas. Pushback continues in American politics and some universities, where penalties for "pro-Palestinian" speech remain in place. Policing dissent remains substantial. Nonetheless, space has opened. The landscape of public speech about Israel is changing.

Where arguing for a two-state solution to the Israel/Palestine crisis was once forbidden, now it is widely accepted, at least in a conceptual framework. However, other frontiers emerge. One example is Israel Apartheid Week on university campuses, where Israel's policies in the West Bank are linked with South Africa's previous system of separating races.

This raises the additional controversy as to whether boycott, divestment, and sanctions (BDS) should be applied to Israel as they were to South Africa. Another example is conferences arguing for a one-state solution, where Jews and Palestinians would live together in Israel-Palestine without privileging religious or ethnic status. BDS, Israel Apartheid Week, and the one-state conferences are deemed antisemitic by the Jewish establishments in America and Israel. Nonetheless they are thriving.[5]

---

4. For an important take on Holocaust memorialization in relation to gender and power, see Janet Jacobs, *Memorializing the Holocaust: Gender, Genocide and Collective Memory* (London: I. B. Tauris, 2010).

5. On the issue of BDS, see Audrea Lim, ed., *The Case for Sanctions against Israel* (New York: Verso, 2012). For discussion of the one-state option, see Hani Faris, ed., *The Failure of the Two-State Solution: The Prospects of One State in the Israeli-Palestinian Conflict* (London: I. B. Tauris, 2013). For a political rendition of equating BDS and antisemitism see an analysis of Prime Minister Benjamin Netanyahu speaking before AIPAC by Philip Weiss, Netanyahu mentions 'BDS' 18 times in denouncing movement and its 'gullible fellow travelers', *Mondoweiss*, March 4, 2014. http://mondoweiss.net/2014/03/netanyahu-denouncing-travelers.html

Perhaps it is a coincidence in timing, but *Bloodlands* deconstructs the Holocaust in much the same way that BDS, Israel Apartheid Week, and the renewed discussion of the one-state solution for Israel-Palestine deconstructs the framing of Israel as innocent and redemptive. *Bloodlands* is like *Jewdas* and *Heeb* in reverse. It ups the ante on what is perceived to be Jewish and whether the construct of Jewishness can be controlled by Jews—and what type of Jews will do the controlling. Add the Still/Former Jewish/Israelis who also engage in public discussion about Israel-Palestine. Taken together they are visible and confrontational deconstructions of Jewishness, Holocaust, and Israel.

Yet it remains that these movements are more complicated than most other deconstructions of identity in the public realm. After all, this involves an entire history and people whose very existence has been on the line, often because of the way Jews are perceived by others. At stake is whether Jews continue to be singled out and, if so, in what way, for how long, and with what consequences.

With contemporary identity deconstructions abounding, affirming a shared Bloodlands in Europe and now the Middle East, Snyder's cautionary note about martyrological imperialism undermines further the position to which the Jewish community has retreated. Posing significant issues regarding the public discourse about the Holocaust and, by extension, theologizing about the Holocaust, it is doubtful whether either can survive Snyder's rendering of the history of the Nazi/Soviet slaughter.

Example—A Shared Fate: This has to do with the more-or-less shared fate of the Bloodlands victims. Snyder makes it almost impossible to single Jews out of the larger story of destruction and death. In Snyder's analysis, the Holocaust loses its singularity. It now stands in parallel formation within the Bloodlands. To be sure, Jews are singled out within the overall catastrophe of World War II Europe, but in Snyder's view that is because the Bloodlands are populated by millions of Jews. Jews are caught in the middle of Nazi and Soviet imperial designs. Millions of non-Jews are caught there, too. Yes, Jews are singled out—within a shared catastrophe.

Example—The Question of God: On the theological level, the peoples of Europe may have similar questions that Jews have regarding God's presence. Clearly, there is a traditional and distinctive manner in which Jews ask questions about God. The drive to interrogate God is peculiar to Jews. Snyder avoids theological issues except through a back channel, and then perhaps without conscious intent. It could be that the Jewish way of doubting God's presence is singular.

Yet, through discrete ways of inquiry, we might find that the shared experience of slaughter joins Jews and others in a similar argument with God.

As well, communities that continue to affirm God after atrocity and mass death might have something important to contribute to the Jewish definitive sense of God's absence. Is it possible that listening to those who affirm God after the experience of the Bloodlands might expand everyone's view and make absolutes on the question of God seem out of place?

When turned away from solitary reflection, Jewish understandings of the Holocaust may have a renewed relevance to other communities. These reflections may then be shared by the surviving Bloodlands communities together—*after*. Even for Jews, *after* includes Auschwitz and beyond. The clarion call "After Auschwitz" may actually become "After the Shared Bloodlands."

Surely, the solitude of each community in the Bloodlands bears examination. Nevertheless, it seems a ghoulish enterprise to argue who was more abandoned. In the Jewish community this parsing has been assumed. The outcome—Jews were most alone—has been determined in advance. Yet, in the face of the Bloodlands, the assertion of Jewish singularity appears to be special pleading. Why emphasize isolation when a horrible togetherness was the order of the day?

Example—A Different Conception of Auschwitz: If the world stood silent when Europe's Jews were murdered *en masse*, the world also stood silent when the Bloodlands earned its horrific name. Moreover, according to Snyder, the Auschwitz conceptualization of the Holocaust needs a substantive reconfiguration for Jews:

Auschwitz was indeed a major site of the Holocaust; about one in six murdered Jews perished there. But though the death factory at Auschwitz was the last killing facility to function, it was not the height of the technology of death: the most efficient shooting squads killed faster, the starvation sites killed faster, and Treblinka killed faster. Auschwitz was also not the main place where the two largest Jewish communities of Europe, the Polish and the Soviet, were exterminated. Most Soviet and Polish Jews under German occupation had already been murdered by the time Auschwitz became the major death factory. By the time the gas chambers and crematoria complexes at Birkenau came on line in spring 1943, more than three quarters of the Jews who would be killed in the Holocaust were already dead. For that matter, the tremendous majority of all the people who would be deliberately killed by the Soviet and the

Nazi regimes, well over ninety percent, had been killed by the time those gas chambers at Birkenau began their deadly work. Auschwitz is a coda to the death fugue.[6]

Auschwitz as coda. Auschwitz as postscript addendum—to the Bloodlands. "After the Bloodlands" sounds strange, so familiar is the phrase "After Auschwitz." What can we say about God—*after* the Bloodlands? Or, rather, what is the Jewish conception of God—*after* the Bloodlands? Jointly considered with others, would the Jewish view be the same as it is now?

Where was God in Auschwitz? Though broadened it remains a question. Where was God in the Bloodlands? The same question in an expanded framework?

Jews ask the same question about humanity. Where was humanity in Auschwitz? The corollary, where was humanity in the Bloodlands? After the Bloodlands, what can we say about humanity?

This is similar to the question Hannah Arendt asked at the trial of the Nazi war criminal, Adolf Eichmann. Was Eichmann's crime directed primarily at the Jewish community or at the human community? In essence, Arendt asks, was Eichmann's crime against the Jewish people or against humanity?

Even in Auschwitz the question has to be broadened, since Auschwitz was also a camp for non-Jewish Poles who perished. In the Bloodlands, the broadening is fact. Jews were a minority of the Bloodlands population. Especially after so many years of emphasizing Jewish singularity, the particulars, if any remain, have to be disentangled and reinterpreted.

At the Eichmann trial, Elie Wiesel as a reporter emphasized the particularity of the Jewish catastrophe. Arendt, later to become a villain of Holocaust consciousness, was also a reporter at the trial and emphasized the universality of the Jewish catastrophe. Obviously, the Jewish community chose Wiesel's interpretation, which is how the Holocaust is thought, discussed, memorialized, and taught. Arendt was relegated to the sidelines. Their choices on Israel followed from their stances on the kind of crime the Nazis committed. Wiesel became an uncritical supporter of the Jewish state. Arendt was a homeland Zionist who opposed the Jewish state.[7]

---

6. Snyder, *Bloodlands*, 383.

7. For Elie Wiesel and Hannah Arendt at the Eichmann trial, see my *Encountering the Jewish Future—with Elie Wiesel, Martin Buber, Abraham Joshua Heschel, Hannah Arendt, and Emmanuel Levinas* (Minneapolis: Fortress Press, 2011), 145-57.

The Holocaust is primarily taught following Wiesel's interpretation. Having chosen the Holocaust as an exclusive affair, it leads students to affirm the need for the Jewish state of Israel. Through the Wieselian lens of the Holocaust, Jews were an unempowered people singled out for destruction. Therefore, Jews need a state of their own to protect them from being singled out for destruction in the future. The lesson of the Holocaust is "Never Again." The state of Israel guarantees that Jews will never face a future Holocaust. In this way, courses on the Holocaust join the historical event with the need for a state to protect Jews in the future.

Snyder's analysis leads far away from Wiesel's. It also moves far beyond the usual Holocaust curriculum, which often features Wiesel's *Night* as required reading. After Snyder's history, though, Wiesel's rendering of the Holocaust should be considered liturgical. But, then, much of discussion of the Holocaust is likewise liturgical.[8]

Liturgy is a story told in public with a cadence and rhythm that draws us into a story of depth and significance. Though we identify liturgy with overt religious symbolism, after the Holocaust religiosity has been thrown into doubt. Much of the public rendering of the Holocaust, however, may be an attempt to use the negation of faith through unmerited suffering as a way maintaining a dialogue with the absent God in the Holocaust.

As with any liturgy, liturgical renderings of the Holocaust serve more than one function. Especially with Elie Wiesel but similarly present in Holocaust remembrance ceremonies and Holocaust museums, the liturgical rendering of the Holocaust demands the attention of Jews and non-Jews. As the years pass the underlying theme of Holocaust liturgy is less about the historical event than it is orienting people around the importance of Jews, Jewish history and the significance of supporting the state of Israel.

Though facts and figures are featured in Holocaust textbooks, the trajectory of the Holocaust liturgical narrative is predictable. The trajectory runs as follows: isolated, with a history of antisemitism, the Nazis sought to end Jewish life on earth. There were collaborators and bystanders, to be sure, but in the end the world, too, was silent on the fate of Europe's Jews. The world would be silent if Jews were attacked today. What keeps history from repeating itself is Israel. Therefore, those who oppose the state of Israel desire a future Holocaust.

As a historian, Snyder is opposed to a liturgical rendering of any history, including the Holocaust. Emotional depth cannot substitute for a careful

---

8. For an example of this Holocaust liturgy, see Elie Wiesel and Albert Friedlander, *The Six Days of Destruction: Meditations Toward Hope* (New York: CCAR Press, 1988).

parsing of the historical data. Being drawn into an almost mystical realm through suffering may mystify, thereby dehistoricizing suffering itself.

Although Snyder gravitates more to Arendt's historically grounded oriented conclusions about the Holocaust, he also challenges several important claims found in her now-classic *The Origins of Totalitarianism*, published in 1951. After the Bloodlands, Holocaust liturgy must be interrupted on many levels; even Arendt must be read critically.

Snyder distances himself from Arendt's view of "people (victims and perpetrators alike) slowly losing their humanity, first in the anonymity of mass society, then in a concentration camp." Snyder points out that, though a powerful image, "it must be corrected before a historical comparison of Nazi and Soviet killing can begin."[9]

Again, Snyder concentrates on the Bloodlands where most of the civilians who died in World War II perished. Arendt's idea that the majority of Jews and others died in concentration camps is tied to her indictment of modern civilization. Arendt adds the additional warning that, even after the Holocaust, we dwell in modernity. For Arendt, the Holocaust is a preview. Mass death may be our future.

For Snyder, this line of reasoning is historically misleading. In analyzing the death of Soviet soldiers when they became German prisoners of war, he points to the interactive and relational ways Jews died as well. For Snyder, Arendt's analysis focuses attention on Berlin and Moscow as the "capitals of distinct states that exemplify the totalitarian system, each of them acting upon their own citizens." Yet, for Snyder, the Soviet prisoners of war died within the interaction of the two systems. Snyder writes that Arendt's "account of totalitarianism centers on the dehumanization *within* modern mass industrial society, not on the overlap *between* Germans and Soviet aspirations and power." True enough, but the fateful moment for the soldiers was their capture. There they "passed from the control of their Soviet superior officers and the NKVD to that of the Wehrmacht and the SS." Contra Arendt, Snyder concludes that the fate of millions in the Bloodlands cannot be understood as "progressive alienation within one modern society; it was a consequence of the belligerent encounter of the two, of the criminal policies of Germany on the territory of the Soviet Union."[10]

Holocaust literature—itself part of an ever expanding Holocaust liturgy—paints a devastating picture of life and death in the concentration

9. Snyder, *Bloodlands*, 380.

10. Ibid., 380, 381.

camps. Snyder feels this emphasis is misleading. It leads to a vast misunderstanding of Jewish death in the Bloodlands. Regarding Arendt's analysis of the concentration camps, Snyder concludes that the "vast majority of Jews killed in the Holocaust never saw a concentration camp." In a provocative conclusion, Snyder pointedly comments that the "image of the German concentration camps as the worst element of National Socialism is an illusion, a dark mirage over an unknown desert."[11]

Theologically speaking, and in liturgical renderings of the Holocaust in general, Snyder's dark mirage and unknown desert are sidelined. Reading and listening to reflections on the Holocaust, it is hard to imagine anything darker or more barren than Auschwitz. These images remain.

Yet the images that come from the Bloodlands are, if anything, more disconcerting. Holocaust literature describes Auschwitz as barbaric but in a thoroughly modern setting of mass death. Snyder contests the modernity of Auschwitz, as the ingredients of mass death used there were discovered generations earlier. Overall, Snyder's Bloodlands are barbaric without a modern lens. Whatever one says about the modernity of the concentration camps, Snyder marginalizes them. Most Jews were killed elsewhere, in towns and villages, in the cities and the fields, one by one.

What is the significance of Snyder's findings for Holocaust discourse, Holocaust liturgy and the teaching of the Holocaust? If taken seriously, the Bloodlands alters our sense of mass slaughter in the twentieth century. The concentration camp-centric teaching of the Holocaust has to change. Auschwitz, as the identifiable symbol of the Holocaust, demands reevaluation.

The historical weight Auschwitz carries is too heavy. Is the Holocaust narrative itself then displaced? If it is, what will replace it? Following Snyder, the Bloodlands—and the Holocaust—are much closer to the genocide in Rwanda.[12]

At first it might seem a terrible splitting of hairs to argue whether barbaric or modern factors should be emphasized in the teaching of the Holocaust. Why is it important to relate or separate Europe in the 1940s and Rwanda in the 1990s? Snyder alludes to but does not pursue the line of reasoning for this separation: that the Holocaust has becomes less a matter of history as it becomes central to producing and reproducing conceptions of Jews and Jewishness for Jews and non-Jews in Europe and America. Thus *Bloodlands* hints at a reckoning soon to come.

11. Ibid., 382.

12. On Rwanda, see Scott Strauss, *The Order of Genocide: Race, Power, and War in Rwanda* (Ithaca: Cornell University Press, 2008).

Teaching the Holocaust with the familiar tropes is more complex with the Bloodlands factored in. The patterns of life and death change. More and varied peoples are included, whose fates are intertwined. The spotlight on Jews dims, which means, for some, that Jews become less important.

What would it be like to alter the teaching of the Holocaust so it was no longer a stand alone? Imagine an announced curriculum change that cited Snyder's work and that henceforth courses focusing on the Holocaust would be replaced with courses that would include the Holocaust with Cambodia and Rwanda as examples of genocide in the twentieth century. The controversy would be enormous. It would also be instructive.

By returning the Holocaust to history, Snyder interrupts the Holocaust liturgy. By interrupting the Holocaust liturgy, Snyder returns Jews to history which makes Jews accountable after the Holocaust. Is an unstated but provocative challenge of Snyder's history that when Jews and others teach the Holocaust, Jewish culpability in the ongoing Nakba must be taught as well?

Re-connecting Our Jewish Atheists and Rebels

Importance is in the eye of the beholder. Anyone who speaks or writes onthe Israeli-Palestinian conflict is unwise to presuppose that Jews think of Palestinians as if they are on the same level with themselves. While most Jews admit that everyone, perhaps even Palestinians, have their own life and interests, an assumed, even if unannounced, inequality exists. However described, Jews perceive themselves as better, above, special.

No doubt some of this sense of being above has to do with Western perception of non-Western peoples. Nonetheless, there is a specific Jewish dimension to this sensibility. If truth be known, most people think of themselves and their community as first among equals. This involves material interests and self-involvement seemingly inherent in the human condition. Yet transcending or at least negotiating this stance is crucial to form society where people of different backgrounds coexist and, on the larger scale, where a global humanity can flourish. While admitting self-involvement, the rough edges of exclusive preoccupation require a thorough analysis if society and the world are to thrive.

Jews live in the same world as everyone else. Jews live with other peoples in close proximity. Yet the sensibilities demanded by living with others in a proximate and global setting are often expanded by religious claims. These expanded claims have to be disciplined. In the Jewish case, however, such discipline is sometimes hard to come by.

All religions have a particular view of their followers along with a universal outreach. This is true for Jews as well. Nonetheless, throughout history Jews have a dramatic self-involvement. This is where the Jewish contribution to the world comes from, though sometimes it is off-putting, as if the world revolves around Jews.[13]

Every generation struggles to determine precisely where the boundaries of the particular and universal reside. All religions, communities, and ideologies struggle with similar questions. Although symbolic fields and frameworks differ, the fundamental issues about our humanity remain.

The Jewish atheists and rebels of the nineteenth and early twentieth century that Emmanuel Lévinas wrote about chose the universal over the particular in the Jewish world of their time. The reason Lévinas cites for this choice and defection was that the Jewish community was assimilating to the broader, non-Jewish culture, a culture that was practicing injustice. Jewish atheists and rebels could not abide a Jewish community feasting at the table of injustice.

Since almost everyone who has the chance to so feast does so, especially those who as individuals and as a collective have watched others feast at their expense, why should Jews be prohibited from the table? One response is that injustice is wrong and therefore the battle must be joined. Yet few from other communities strike out the way these Jewish atheists and rebels did. Their intensity was missionary, as if a specific, quite important, destiny was at stake. Clearly, justice was part of their mission. As we have seen, though, the issue is whether the injustice of leaving others behind was central or whether that was less important than their largely subconscious struggle against the diminishment of Jewish distinctiveness. Was it injustice or the threat of assimilation that drove these Jewish atheists and rebels? It could be that, for Jews, injustice and assimilation are intimately interrelated. This means that assimilation to injustice is associated with the disappearance of Jewish distinctiveness.

Former/Still Jewish/Israelis face the same query. Is it only, or even primarily, the injustice that Jews have done to Palestinians that mandates their self-imposed exile? Or is it, as well, or even primarily, that in committing this injustice, Jews are joining—assimilating—to the Other Nations in their empire violence?

13. Judith Butler tackles some of these issues in her *Parting Ways: Jewishness and the Critique of Zionism* (New York: Columbia University Press, 2012). Her views of Jewishness, however, while not in opposition to mine, differ in significant ways. From the perspective of the prophetic, her views of Jewishness are too diffuse. In my mind, they can only approximate but not explain her own prophetic stance.

Substantial injustice was committed at the founding of the state of Israel. Since the uneasiness was there and most Israelis lived with it, why, with the passage of time, did the exile of Jewish Israelis inside and outside of Israel become more deeply felt? Perhaps Jews could tolerate injustice and the comparison with the Other Nations only up to a point. Jews could indulge in behavior that they knew others perpetrated as well—that is, until a certain boundary was crossed.

Where is that injustice boundary, Jewishly speaking? If the boundary is assimilation to injustice, then the crossing became obvious when the state of Israel became a permanent oppressor of the Palestinian people. Adopting the role of permanent oppressors, some Jews found that the empire violence of the world had become became intrinsic to Jewish identity.

If Jews work to correct injustice, does it matter for what reason or combination of reasons? The differentiation between being for others for their sake and being for others for one's own sake is difficult to discern in any individual or community. No doubt, it is usually a combination of concern for others and concern for self. Typically, the discernment is hidden or left to others to argue, if there is an interest. As we have seen, though, Jewish identity is a high-energy, high-stakes affair. And since Jews have been articulating and interrogating their drama since biblical times, it would be surprising if it was any different today.

As one would expect, Former/Still Jewish/Israelis deflect the "Jewish" question. They maintain that their stance, and exile, is only a matter of justice. They refuse to stand by silently when others are oppressed. Yet, in the countries in which they reside after leaving Israel, injustice also abounds. Although many are involved in the justice issues of their adopted home countries, they remain living there. The exile they experience in, say, Ireland, the United Kingdom, or America is real. But the exile at the center of their being is from Israel and from organized Jewish life. Opposing injustice everywhere, they reserve a special approbation for Jews who commit injustice. If "Jewish" is unimportant for the Still/Former Jewish/Israelis why the injustice fixation on the Jews of Israel?

So, despite the deflection, Still/Former Jewish/Israelis are more involved in Jewish destiny than they consciously think or admit. Likewise, they are more involved in Jewish destiny than their foes consciously think or admit.

Nonetheless, when Jewish destiny is up for grabs in the state of Israel, at least for the powerful, the safe harbor of retreat for their particular sense of Jewish destiny remains the Holocaust. If Israel is under assault from non-Jews, who from this perspective seem to hold Israel to a higher standard—even though these same Jews once touted Israel's higher standard to the world—the Holocaust remains a standard of Jewish suffering that is beyond reproach.

The Holocaust is contested by Holocaust deniers, who are few in number and languish on the margins of informed discussion. Yet the few are blown out of proportion in Jewish political and religious discourse. Instead of affirming their marginality, those in the Jewish establishment view Holocaust deniers as part of a broader assault against Jews and Jewishness. True, Holocaust denial is often twinned with antisemitism. Sometimes this is further paired with a particularly vehement anti-Zionism—as if Jews as a collective have no right even to a more just political sensibility. When the three are joined, they form a death wish for Jews. Here the symbolic projection of a future Holocaust gains ground.

No wonder many Jews hold the Holocaust as a sacred, untouchable arena, a holy of holies. In the biblical sense, the Holocaust translates into the off-limits Tent of Meeting where the sacred power of God abounds. Even if God is absent in the Holocaust world, an inverse holiness abounds. Yet if Holocaust deniers engage in their anti-Jewish fantasy, those Jews who make a fetish out of the Holocaust are living in their own empire dream world. As always, the challenge is to separate fact from fiction, critical thought from myth.

Truth is that the Holocaust is one of the most studied events in all of history. And considering the negative myths surrounding Jews through the ages, the percentage of the world population who recognize the Holocaust as a horrific event is astonishing. Concentrating on Holocaust deniers, then, must be critically evaluated. Whatever their intentions, are Holocaust deniers used as a tool of deflection to keep non-Jewish—and Jewish eyes—off the prize?[14]

The Bloodlands refocuses Jewish attention on the Holocaust. It does this by shifting the Jewish understanding of the Holocaust eastward. Here barbarism is less the advanced Western brand of modern violence, which Jews and others identify as an offshoot of modernity. In a strange and silent inversion—can it even be broached?—Jews in America and Israel prefer Jewish death in the Holocaust to be seen as unique and understandable in the Western framework.

Why is the Western framework prized? Such a framework is hardly straight forward. The West is where most Jews live or aspire to live. Jews, including many Jews in Israel, identify the West as their own geographic, cultural and political world. Logically, it would seem that Jews who live in and

---

14. On Holocaust denial, see Michael Shermer and Alex Grobman, *Denying History: Who Says the Holocaust Never Happened and Why Do They Say It?*, Updated and Expanded ed. (Berkeley: University of California, 2009).

identify so would want to project their violation outside the West. How can Jews be safe within the very same societies that condemned them to death?

The traditional interpretation of the Holocaust allows Jews to have it both ways. Jews critique the very world within which they demand security—and special leeway. The pariah within the gates can then use this critique as a path of ascendancy. In fact, the Holocaust serves as a status upgrade for Jews in the West. It becomes the ticket of admission to the West that in the past was frequently and violently denied them.

The eastern part of Europe, in Snyder's terminology, the Bloodlands, is where most American and many Israeli Jews trace their background. The post-Holocaust image has reserved this geography for a romanticized, albeit tragic, view of the Jewish past. It now serves as a backdrop that a thoroughly modernized Jewry can paint as they wish. If the first two legs of the Jewish stool are Holocaust and Israel, the third leg is a romanticized Eastern European hinterland. In the American and Israeli imagination, Jews no longer exist in Eastern Europe. Jews can mourn and romanticize at will.

Snyder's rendering of the Bloodlands leaves little room for romanticized images. After reading his account, it is hard to evoke descriptions of pre-Holocaust Jewish life beyond their senseless and brutal deaths. But, as well, these images of Jews are forever intertwined with others victims. Reading Snyder, it may be possible to combine images of pre-Holocaust Jewish culture and family life and the reality of a shared mass death, though now both the images before and during Jewish death are altered.

In any case, the Holocaust as a symbolic haven for Jews is coming to an end. If the Holocaust as a Jewish-only event is forever dissolved, the safe harbor of the Holocaust disappears. Without that safe harbor, there looms accountability for what has been done in the name of Jewish martyrs. The floodgates open. At least, the Jewish establishments in the United States and Israel can be indicted for the Bloodlands they helped create—and perpetuate—in the Middle East.

Romanticized martyrology is what the American and Israeli picture of Eastern European Jewry provides Jews. Martyrological imperialism is impossible without a romanticized martyrology. Nor, in the long run, is it possible without an innocent Israel. The Holocaust is typically narrated in the present; it has to narrate whatever is presently occurring.

In the halcyon days, when Israel was well received in the West, Israel was the contemporary event that justified commemorating the Holocaust. In today's environment, the Holocaust is thrown back onto itself. The question of questions is what the Jewish community in America and Israel would do if

Eastern Europe had a renewed, vibrant, and diverse Jewish community. Hints of this began occurring with the influx of Soviet Jews as the Soviet Union collapsed.

Recently arrived Russian Jews in Germany, especially, promises a renewal of Jewish life there. In general, though, the Jewish establishment looks askance at such a development. What is important for the memorialization of the Holocaust is Europe as a permanent graveyard. It might be, then, that a martyrological imperialism is more than dependent on a romanticized martyrology or that both are dependent on controlling European Jewish history in the present. Perhaps Holocaust martyrology itself is dependent on Jewish history never moving beyond the Holocaust. Yet is it really in Jewish interests to pretend that the movement of history beyond the Holocaust is restricted?

How much easier it is to place the image that others want on those who have no say in the image or what the image is mobilized for. As we have seen, this applies to the dead of the Holocaust. They are spoken for without the ability to add their voice. If there was a living Eastern European Jewish population of any size today, they could speak of their inheritance, from their own location, as well as about the future they are creating. Their voice would take priority. Indeed, their views might confirm the Holocaust and Israel narrative as it is. It might subvert it. The issue remains as to whether their voice would be honored. Would America and Israel's martyrological imperialism, dependent as it on romanticization on the victims of the Holocaust, also override their Jewish voice on the Holocaust?

European Jewry was decimated in the Holocaust. Thus the European image of Jews, especially the less affluent and educated segment of European Jewry, is gone or frozen in a romanticized visage. The unwashed, backward Jews, if they were so in reality, are no more. Or, rather, they exist in a cleaned-up, educated, and successful form in the United States, since most Jews in America come from precisely the regions where the majority of European Jewry lived and died. Even this image is complicated, since most American Jews of Eastern European origin immigrated to the United States well before the rise of the Nazis. It was their distant, mostly unknown, Jewish relations who were slaughtered in the Bloodlands.

Are the Former/Still Jewish/Israelis protesting the use of mobilized Jewish martyrs for empire but also, perhaps, refusing a romanticized martyrology that fuels violence? Because of their life experience of being under threat and violating others, they know that the cycle of violence and atrocity is fueled by empire-aided imperial and romanticized martyrologies. They understand that such martyrologies are entangled, that they feed off and fuel each other. They also know that the only way to break through one is to undermine the other.

The state of Israel is perpetrator and victim of this entanglement. We should not forget, however, that American Jews are in as fascinating and culpable position. American Jews claim and romanticize Eastern European martyrdom that, for the most part, they did not experience. They then project that martyrdom onto Israel, where the overwhelming majority of American Jews choose not live, let alone visit. For the Still/Former Jewish/Israelis, the projection of romanticization and empire is too much. In its service, they oppress others. In its service, they bury their friends and relatives. In its service, they, too, become martyrs.

ARGUING PALESTINIAN STATEHOOD AT THE UNITED NATIONS

The traditional Holocaust sensibility is so deeply ingrained that non-Jews often think and act as leaders of the Jewish community do or, indeed, as a liberal prime minister of Israel might. So it was that, in the days leading to the United Nations vote on the issue of Palestinian statehood in September 2011, President Barack Obama spoke to the United Nations General Assembly.

If one listens carefully, it is fascinating how President Obama portrays Jews and Israel. It is also instructive how he discusses Palestinians and Palestine. Obama attempts to be even-handed; at least, that is his stated intention. Yet how he frames Jews and Israel is quite different than how he frames Palestinians and Palestine.

How an issue is framed helps determine the logic of its resolution. Just as there is a structure in Holocaust discourse—where and how you begin influences where you end—so, too, the discussion of Jewish and Palestinian history determines how the resolution of the Israel-Palestine conflict is envisioned.

In President Obama's address, for example, Jews and Israel have a history that cries out for recognition and affirmation. Palestinians and Palestine are discussed as if they have no history; instead, they have needs. Palestinians require a state to meet those needs. For Obama, as for U. S. presidents before him, however, America's obligation to Israel moves well beyond Jewish needs. Israel is embedded in America's destiny.

In his U. N. address, President Obama plays America's obligation off against the Arab world's denial of Israel's right to exist. The Arab world's denial endangers Israel's existence, which America is obliged to preserve. Thus, in the president's understanding, Palestine deserves statehood only when that threat is eliminated. For President Obama, the threat to Israel's existence is longstanding and continues today. To buttress his argument, Obama cites the danger Israelis felt in the rockets coming from Gaza in 2008. However, the president is silent on Israel's subsequent invasion of Gaza, nor does he mention Israeli settlements in Jerusalem and the West Bank.

Is this highlighting on the Jewish side and silence on the Palestinian side determined by President Obama's sense that Jews have a history and Palestinians lack one? Does this mean that one people is more deserving of recognition, affirmation, and security than the other?

President Obama begins his address with a note of frustration. Middle East peace still eludes the world. Even his calling for an independent Palestinian state has failed to materialize. After reaffirming his desire to do the hard work of peace, the Obama affirms that ultimately Israelis and Palestinians are responsible to negotiate their future.

In President Obama's view, such negotiations must end with a Palestinian state. America is invested in such a state: "a sovereign state of their own, with no limits to what they can achieve." The need for a Palestinian state affirmed, Obama offers a series of caveats. To begin with, America's commitment to Israel's security is "unshakable." Again, reiterating past American presidents, Obama affirms that America's friendship with Israel is deep and enduring. Thus any lasting peace must acknowledge the "very real security concerns that Israel faces every single day." This is just the beginning of the story. As noted earlier, but now fleshed out in his dramatic oratory, Jewish history demands that security:

> Let us be honest with ourselves: Israel is surrounded by neighbors that have waged repeated wars against it. Israel's citizens have been killed by rockets fired at their houses and suicide bombs on their buses. Israel's children come of age knowing that throughout the region, other children are taught to hate them. Israel, a small country of less than eight million people, looks out at a world where leaders of much larger nations threaten to wipe it off the map. The Jewish people carry the burden of centuries of exile and persecution, and fresh memories of knowing that 6 million people were killed simply because of who they are.
> Those are facts. They cannot be denied.
> The Jewish people have forged a successful state in their historic homeland. Israel deserves recognition. It deserves normal relations

with its neighbors. And friends of the Palestinians do them no favors by ignoring this truth, just as friends of Israel must recognize the need to pursue a two-state solution with a secure Israel next to an independent Palestine.[15]

That is the truth as President Obama sees it which he continued to express in his visit to Israel in March 2013. There, he reiterated that, each side has legitimate aspirations, which is why peace is so hard to make. Obama believes that the "deadlock will only be broken when each side learns to stand in each other's shoes, each side can see the world through the other's eyes." Surely, the world should be encouraging and promoting this mutuality. Absent in Obama's addresses is the appreciation that the each other's shoes are quite different from the outset. If the shoes Obama constructs in his remarks are made of different materials, how can their shape be equal?[16]

If President Obama had spoken to both histories, speaking each side's different understandings of the past and present, then at least he could be seen as an honest broker. His admonition to stand in another's shoes would have substance. His statement—"Those are facts. They cannot be denied"—would become a challenge rather than a declaration. Standing in each other's real shoes would be a sign that the real negotiations could begin. Isn't that what the international community is waiting for from the president of the United States?

A further limitation is that the Jewish shoes Obama constructs are the Jewish establishment shoes. They are made with a certain kind of Holocaust/Israel stitching. Jews of Conscience see it differently. If Obama had signaled that that there are different Jewish shoes, some much closer, if not identical, to the Palestinian shoes that Obama fails to describe, the landscape of negotiations

15. For the full text of Obama's United Nations speech, see the Washington *Post* online, September 21, 2011, http://projects.washingtonpost.com/obama-speeches/speech/803/. President Obama's U. N. address and his speeches in Israel are in line with speeches he has delivered elsewhere and since, including during his visit to Israel after his reelection in 2012. His earlier speeches includet the annual convention of the pro-Israel lobby group, the American Israel Political Action Committee (AIPAC), just months before his UN speech. Obama's remarks are found in the *National Journal*, May 22, 2011, http://www.nationaljournal.com/whitehouse/text-obama-s-aipac-speech-20110522. Interestingly, the day after Obama's speech at the United Nations, the news leaked of further military aid to Israel. See "U. S Quietly Supplies Israel With Bunker-Busting Bombs," *New York Times*, September 24, 2011.

16. See President Obama's remarks during his visit to Israel in March 2013 see http://www.nytimes.com/2013/03/22/world/middleeast/transcript-of-obamas-speech-in-israel.html?pagewanted=all&_r=0 For my take on Obama in Israel, see http://mondoweiss.net/2013/04/prophetic-library-waiting.htm.

would change even more radically. Some Jews have tried to travel in Palestinian shoes. Isn't that important information to share with the international community?[17]

Not surprisingly, speaking the day after President Obama at the United Nations, the president of the Palestinian National Authority, Mahmoud Abbas, took a different approach. Known as a moderate and much criticized among Palestinians for giving over too much to the Israelis and Americans, President Abbas spoke in a strong voice. He filled in many of the details of Israel's behavior that Obama left out. Listening to Abbas after Obama, one is left wondering if they are describing the same Israel, let alone Palestine. Interestingly, Abbas cites Israeli research for his critical remarks:

> The reports of United Nations missions as well as by several Israeli institutions and civil societies convey a horrific picture about the size of the settlement campaign, which the Israeli government does not hesitate to boast about and which it continues to execute through the systematic confiscation of the Palestinian lands and the construction of thousands of new settlement units in various areas of the West Bank, particularly in East Jerusalem, and accelerated construction of the annexation Wall that is eating up large tracts of our land, dividing it into separate and isolated islands and cantons, destroying family life and communities and the livelihoods of tens of thousands of families. The occupying Power also continues to refuse permits for our people to build in Occupied East Jerusalem, at the same time that it intensifies its decades-long campaign of demolition and confiscation of homes, displacing Palestinian owners and residents under a multi-pronged policy of ethnic cleansing aimed at pushing them away from their ancestral homeland. In addition, orders have been issued to deport elected representatives from the city of Jerusalem. The occupying Power also continues to undertake excavations that threaten our holy places, and its military checkpoints prevent our citizens from getting access to their mosques and churches, and it continues to besiege the Holy City with a ring of

17. Much of President Obama's remarks were colored by his successful reelection bid in 2012. And in fact, he does know the other side of the Jewish story. For a take on Obama and the Jewish world he interacted with before becoming president, see Peter Beinart, *The Crisis of Zionism* (New York: Times Books, 2012), 79-99.

settlements imposed to separate the Holy City from the rest of the Palestinian cities.[18]

For President Abbas, the Israeli occupation is a race against time. It seeks to redraw the borders of Palestinian life and land so that it can impose a *fait accompli*. This is the Israeli policy of creating facts on the ground that it then argues cannot be changed. For Abbas, these policies are deliberate. They also undermine the realistic potential for the existence of a Palestinian state.

Even with the split between Hamas in Gaza and the Palestinian Authority, Abbas speaks of the situation of Gaza as part of Palestine's national patrimony. Once again, the picture of Israel Abbas draws is quite different from the one drawn by President Obama. This includes Israel's imposition of a blockade on the Gaza Strip, the targeting of Palestinian civilians by assassinations, air strikes, and artillery shelling.

President Abbas alludes to the Israeli invasion of Gaza right before President Obama took office, calling it a "war of aggression" that resulted in "massive destruction of homes, schools, hospitals, and mosques, and the thousands of martyrs and wounded." Shifting back to the West Bank, Abbas charges that Israel continues its "incursions in areas of the Palestinian National Authority through raids, arrests and killings at the checkpoints. In recent years, the criminal actions of armed settler militias, who enjoy the special protection of the occupation army, have intensified with the perpetration of frequent attacks against our people, targeting their homes, schools, universities, mosques, fields, crops and trees." And this, despite the repeated warnings of the Palestinian Authority: "The occupying Power has not acted to curb these attacks and we hold them fully responsible for the crimes of the settlers."

Offering these examples of the policy of the "Israeli colonial settlement occupation," Abbas notes that Israel's policies are responsible for the failure of the successive international attempts to jump-start the peace process. Abbas concludes that these policies destroy the chance of achieving a two-state solution, which is the international consensus for solving the Israel-Palestine crisis. Abbas cautions that this "settlement policy threatens to also undermine the structure of the Palestinian National Authority and even end its existence."

Predictably, Mazin Qumsiyeh, as a Palestinian commentator, responded indignantly to President Obama's speech. In his response, he replaces the bracketed applause insertions of the transcription of Obama's address with his

18. See *Ahramonline*, May 23, 2011, http://english.ahram.org.eg/~/NewsContent/2/8/22286/World/Region/-Mahmoud-Abbas-speech-at-the-UN--The-full-text.aspx.

own counter-commentary to highlight what he considers the cliché statements that Obama and the Jewish establishment usually make:

Let's be honest: Israel is surrounded by neighbors that have waged repeated wars against it. [False, Israel started all the wars except 1973]. Israel's citizens have been killed by rockets fired at their houses and suicide bombs on their buses. [Correct, but this should be balanced by explaining that 10 times more Palestinians were butchered]. Israel's children come of age knowing that throughout the region, other children are taught to hate them. [Israelis teach hate 100 more times than the other way around and hate of the colonizer to the colonized is not the same as the reverse]. Israel, a small country of less than eight million people, looks out at a world where leaders of much larger nations threaten to wipe it off of the map. [That is nonsense; Israel wiped Palestine including 530 villages and towns and now is the fourth strongest country plus having you Obama and Congress as its lackeys]. The Jewish people carry the burden of centuries of exile, persecution, and the fresh memory of knowing that six million people were killed simply because of who they were. [Irrelevant and highly emotional: just study the history of Nazi-Zionist collaboration to see how absurd to link Apartheid Israel with "The Jewish People", itself a mistaken term no more valid than concepts of "The Christian People" or "The Muslim People"]. These facts cannot be denied [They are regurgitation of Zionist myths, irrelevant facts, and half truths]. The Jewish people have forged a successful state in their historic homeland [A racist apartheid state based on land theft and ethnic cleansing; is that your definition of success?]. Israel deserves recognition [no it does not, Israel deserves to be faced with the truth and pressured to transform just like Apartheid South Africa] . . .[19]

At the same time, Qumsiyeh, usually a fierce critic of the Palestinian Authority, praised President Abbas for his address, calling it a brilliant speech that elicited continual applause from many of the United Nations representatives. From Qumsiyeh's perspective, Palestinian leadership has been

19. Mazin Qumsiyeh's circular on September 21, 2011 can be found at www.popular-resistanceblogspot.com/2011/09/international-day-of-peace.html

"unreasonably reasonable" for too many years. The hopes of peace and the Palestinian people have been "dashed on the rocks" of "Israeli expansionist, colonial and apartheid policies." [20]

Joining Qumsiyeh, Uri Avnery, the Jewish Israeli peace advocate, lambasted President Obama. Avnery starts out with irony: "A WONDERFUL SPEECH. A beautiful speech. The language expressive and elegant. The arguments clear and convincing. The delivery flawless." Avnery quickly moves to disdain: "A work of art. The art of hypocrisy. Almost every statement in the passage concerning the Israeli-Palestinian issue was a lie. A blatant lie: the speaker knew it was a lie, and so did the audience."[21]

For Avnery, it was Obama at his best—and his worse. Since, as Avnery believes, Obama is a moral person, he must have "felt the urge to vomit." But Obama is also a pragmatic person: "He knew that he had to do it, if he wanted to be re-elected." In Avnery's view, Obama "sold the fundamental national interests of the United States of America for the chance of a second term." Avnery is reminded that politics does this to morality. Should Obama be different? Avnery continues:

> It may be superfluous—almost insulting to the reader—to point out the mendacious details of this rhetorical edifice.
> Obama treated the two sides as if they were equal in strength—Israelis and Palestinians, Palestinians and Israelis.
> But of the two, it is the Israelis—only they—who suffer and have suffered. Persecution. Exile. Holocaust. An Israeli child threatened by rockets. Surrounded by the hatred of Arab children. So sad.
> No Occupation. No settlements. No June 1967 borders. No Naqba. No Palestinian children killed or frightened. It's the straight right-wing Israeli propaganda line, pure and simple—the terminology, the historical narrative, the argumentation. The music.

As for how Palestinians fared in President Obama's speech, Avnery is scathing. The Palestinians, of course, should have a state of their own—"but they must not be pushy. They must not embarrass America or come to the United Nations." Rather, they must sit with the Israelis, like reasonable people,

---

20. Ibid., September 23, 2011.

21. Uri Avnery, "Abu Mazen's Gamble," September 24, 2011, http://www.avnery-news.co.il/english/index.html.

and work it out with them like "reasonable sheep must sit down with the reasonable wolf and decide what to have for dinner."

We seem caught here, between President Obama's rendition of Jewish and Palestinian history—and his very practical military help to Israel—and Qumsiyeh's demands that the Israeli and American hypocrisy end before it is too late. Obama essentializes the Holocaust/Israel story as one of innocence and redemption. Qumsiyeh sees little in Israel or even a sense of Jewish destiny except platitudes that cover up the ongoing crimes against the Palestinian people.

President Obama denies Palestinians a real history and destiny. Can the same thing be said about Qumsiyeh regarding Jews and Jewish history? It bears repeating: when the broken middle collapses, there is very little left other than hagiography and denigration.

President Abbas is in the middle here, though his words at the United Nations are more pointed than the actions he has taken as leader of the Palestinians. It is clear that the middle of the Israeli-Palestinian conflict is quite different for Abbas than it is for Obama. Abbas narrates a history in the making from the Palestinian viewpoint. His address notes the ethnic cleansing of Palestinians and the catastrophe of 1948.

Like Joseph Massad, Abbas speaks about the continuing Nakba while focusing on Israel's "colonial" settlements. Most often, when referring to Israel in Jerusalem and the West Bank, Abbas uses the technical language of international law as the "Occupying Power." Unlike Obama, Abbas does not refer to the Holocaust or Jewish history.

As a Jewish Israeli who argues for a two-state solution to the Israeli-Palestinian crisis, Avnery is with Abbas. Avnery thinks Abbas has finally stood up to Israel. He calls Abbas's boldness a gamble, moving from a pliant to a defiant leader of the Palestinians. But notice as well in Avnery that though he supports a two-state solution to the Israel/Palestine crisis, in orientation and fundamental belief his critique of Israel contains radical elements.

As with his commentaries over the years, Avnery minces few words about his disdain for the kind of friendship America has for Israel. Instead, the United States is Israel's worse enemy, endangering Israel by feeding Israel's addiction to occupation. Israeli government officials are liars, fools, and criminals. They, too, are leading Israel into danger and demise, a black hole, ethically speaking. Avnery differs from most Progressive Jews who, though critical of the Israeli government policies, remain oblivious to the real history of Israel's creation and continuing expansion.

When Obama and Qumsiyeh are read side by side, it is difficult to catch a breath. Each side needs time and space to exhale. In the background at the United Nations was Prime Minister Benjamin Netanyahu. Historically, Netanyahu has worked to destroy every broken middle possibility in Israel-Palestine, starting with the Oslo Accords reached in 1993. Compared to Netanyahu, President Obama's approach is soft-gloved. Yet for the Palestinians suffering under occupation, the difference between them is minimal. Both Netanyahu's brass knuckles and Obama's soft-gloved approach are inimical to Palestinian aspirations.

President Obama clearly is aware of the realities Abbas spoke about. It is because Obama knows better that Avnery lashes out so vociferously. Yet, then beholden to the American Jewish establishment for his reelection bid in 2012, could Obama utter these words with reference to Israeli policy—1948, the Nakba, ethnic cleansing, and colonial settlements?

Avnery cuts Obama little slack. He cries out for Obama to speak the truth for the sake of Palestinians and for the sake of Jews. Let the American election cycle be damned. Palestinian and Jewish lives are at stake.

DEBATING ONE STATE

Listening to Qumsiyeh and, earlier, to Massad's comments on the ongoing Nabka, prompts the questions, Are they guilty of what President Obama outlines in his United Nations address and most Jews understand to be antisemitism? Is Abbas? Is Avnery?

Although the term itself is unmentioned in Obama's speech, the parameters are easy to survey. When Obama recites threats to Israel and pleads the historic sufferings of Jewish people, including the Holocaust, he lays out the parameters of antisemitism as he and many others understand them. But, as well, this understanding of antisemitism hides important parts of contemporary Jewish history. Emphasizing Jews under siege silences Palestinian history. In this recitation of Jewish achievements and fears, the ongoing Nakba continues as it disappears from view.

Because of the travails of Jewish history, anyone who objects to Israel as a state—more specifically, as a Jewish state—or acts to dismantle Jewish privilege within its boundaries, are considered antisemitic. Qumsiyeh and Massad no doubt qualify as antisemites under this definition. But so do the Still/Former Jewish/Israelis who no longer believe in a Jewish state of Israel.

Even if it means giving into the politics of nationality, Qumsiyeh, Massad, and the Still/Former Jewish/Israelis assert that for Israel to remain a state, it must become a state of all its citizens, Jewish and Palestinian alike—one person, one vote. This is what integration means—one person, one vote, and citizenship without regard to ethnic, racial, or religious background. President Obama trumpets this accomplishment when he speaks of the American civil rights movement. Is he unaware of the contradictions involved when his rhetoric and policies deny this possibility in Israel-Palestine?

In a civil-rights vision of Israel-Palestine, Jews are no longer privileged within the state of Israel and the lands Israel occupies. In a civil-rights vision of the future, Palestinian Israelis, for example, now comprising roughly 20 percent of Israel's population, would have citizenship, obligations, and rights equal to those of Jewish Israelis. Anything specifically Jewish about Israel—from its flag, anthem, property ownership, and military service—would be open to all without consideration of ethnic or religious status.

The truth, however, is that if equality took hold there the reason for a state of Israel would be undermined. Israel cuts Palestine physically in half and less. Palestinians argue that they, along with Palestinian refugees outside of Israel-Palestine, should have the right to live and flourish anywhere in the land. Jews would be granted the same rights. In this vision Palestine becomes whole again, albeit with an enhanced Jewish population. Some Palestinians and Still/Former Jewish/Israelis embrace a radical approach. They believe that Palestine should be reconstructed and that Israel as a Jewish state should disappear. Are they antisemitic?[22]

Does revisioning Israel/Palestine or Palestine alone also mean revisioning the definition of antisemitism? Historically, antisemitism means discrimination against and demonization of Jews. After the Holocaust, the urgency of the fight against antisemitism is recognized. Indeed, the very definition of antisemitism has changed because of the Holocaust. Many Jews believe that with the creation of the state of Israel, antisemitism now includes the critique of Jewish empowerment, say in the United States, but especially with regard to criticism of the state of Israel. Envisioning the end of Israel itself or demanding that it lose its character as a Jewish state is thus defined as antisemitic.

Although some criticism is allowed as political fair game, it is also monitored. When criticism crosses a red line, then the charge of antisemitism is leveled. But the concern is where the line is drawn and who draws it. Who defines antisemitism? Does the desire for Israel to become a state for all its citizens cross that line?

22. For Mazin Qumsiyeh's vision of a reconstructed Palestine, see his *Sharing the Land of Canaan: Human Rights and the Israeli-Palestinian Struggle* (London: Pluto Press, 2004)

Another red line on the issue of antisemitism is Holocaust denial. There are those who deny that the Holocaust occurred for reasons of historical "accuracy," but usually such denial has ulterior, Jew-baiting motives. Although many who deny the Holocaust say they have nothing against Jews per se, motives are rightly questioned. However, there seems to be a slippery slope of monitoring and accusations. Is the objection to Holocaust denial, the denial itself? Or are Holocaust deniers hunted with such ferocity as a way of deflecting other questions about Palestinian aspirations for freedom?

Obviously, there is no way to objectively measure the line that travels from Holocaust denial to criticism of Israeli policies against Palestinians. Yet the positive connection made between Holocaust denial and support for Palestinian struggles against Israeli power is powerful. So powerful that it is found in and around speeches and policies made by presidents of the United States.

In this heated political atmosphere, commentators query how the Holocaust functions in relation to support of the state of Israel. Too often, such queries are equated with Holocaust denial. As we have seen in *Bloodlands*, Snyder critically analyzes the Holocaust in its most specific historical sense. Snyder questions whether Jews were in fact singled out for slaughter. Although he continues to employ Holocaust terminology, in the end Snyder weakens the Jewish content of the Holocaust. What remains is Holocaust terminology that functions for political ends. Snyder judges the use of the Holocaust to be oppressive but, again, this is similar to other communities and nations that use suffering to justify power over others.

Snyder decenters the Holocaust. In his historical analysis, Holocaust terminology can still be used but the assertion of uniqueness is diminished. In Jewish terminology, Snyder places the Holocaust among the nations, as one among other tragic events that occur in history and as a shared, interconnected event at that. This has the parallel effect of decentering Israel as heir to the Holocaust. Without exploring this in detail, in Snyder's analysis Israel loses its special place among the nations. Israel should be judged like any other nation. Does Israel then lose it *raison d'être*?

On the political scene, after Snyder's account in *Bloodlands*, President Obama's argument is found wanting. If he accepted Snyder's analysis, much of his argument would have to shift precipitously. Perhaps Obama would then walk in Palestinian shoes, almost exclusively. At worst, he would have to reconstruct both the Palestinian and Jewish shoes in which he counsels everyone to walk.

Is a historical work like *Bloodlands* antisemitic? Placing the Holocaust among the tragedies of history, alongside other tragedies, and placing Israel among other nations that are judged for their policies without special exemptions, Jews are stripped of their singled-out status. Since Jewish power in the modern world is based, at least symbolically, on that singled-out status, does Snyder, and others who similarly decenter the Holocaust and Israel, play into the hands of those who want ill for Jews? In sum, if Snyder's work is not specifically antisemitic, does it, in other hands, lead there? If President Obama incorporated these understandings and reoriented American foreign policy to reflect them, would he and American foreign policy be antisemitic?

We return where we started—the question of Jewish identity. If there is such an entity as Jewishness, as distinct from other identities, is that identity tied up with a Jewish state in the Middle East?

There are Jews and Palestinians who deny that there is such a reality as Jewish particularity or at least a Jewish particularity that demands or should be allowed a collective political dimension. For them, the Palestinian struggle is simply to retrieve what was once theirs. Yet most often, Jews and Palestinians who seek a renewed Palestine do so in the name of human and political rights of the indigenous in the land. They see the Palestinian struggle as a universal struggle that anyone can join.[23]

The progressive universal struggle for Palestine is increasingly placed over against a backward-looking ethnic state of Israel. Because of the discrimination of the state of Israel toward dissenting Jews and against Palestinians, some universalists apply the apartheid label to Israel. Others go further. They see Israel's creation, present, and future as the epitome of ethnic cleansing and apartheid.[24]

When applied to Israel, the apartheid label cuts several ways. The first is the forced separation of Jewish Israelis and Palestinians, thus segregating one ethnic group from the other. The second is the attempt by others, using the model of white South Africa, to mythologize a settler colonial community as having a predestined right to the land cleansed of its indigenous population.[25]

---

23. For an extended discussion of particularity, see my article, "On Jewish Particularity and Anti-Semitism: Notes From a Jewish Theology of Liberation," *Human Architecture: Journal of the Sociology of Self-Knowledge* 7 (Spring 2009): 103-21. Also see my "Is the One State Discussion Relevant? Reflections from a Jewish Theology of Liberation," *Holy Land Studies* 12:2(2013): 161-180.

24. Obviously, many Palestinian commentators see it in this way. What is interesting is the shifting consensus among more and more Jews toward this understanding. I would count Judith Butler among them, at least in her book *Parting Ways*.

25. For an interesting comparison, see Amneh Badran, *Zionist Israel and Apartheid South Africa: Civil Society and Peace Building in Ethnic-National States* (London: Routledge, 2009).

Those who believe in one democratic secular state in Israel–Palestine view the issue as less about the political and economic inefficiency of two small and unviable states than about the injustice of according privileged rights to Jews. In an ever-expanding state that has a significant non-Jewish minority population in a non-Jewish region of the world the issue is one of justice. One-state objections use the examples of colonial enterprises that vexed the Middle East for centuries. After all, they say, no matter what justification some Jews want to provide Israel, the view from the Middle East is that Israel is a colonial settler state, pure and simple, like apartheid South Africa was. What is required is massive change, as in South Africa.[26]

Does the Bloodlands reconstruction of the Holocaust undermine the struggle to maintain a Jewish state of Israel? The Holocaust is an event so deep within the Jewish psyche that it defines contemporary Jewish particularity. If we accept the history of the Bloodlands and the possibility that the Bloodlands Cycle has also come to the Middle East via the Holocaust and an unjust Israel, it is a short step to calling for universalizing the state of Israel out of existence. Nonetheless, even if the Holocaust and Israel are to a large extent mythologized, aren't ethnic, religious, and national mythologies part and parcel of every nationality?

It is doubtful that any particularity can be held together without mythology. It is also doubtful that any new entity, no matter its claim to universality, can survive without developing a mythology that more or less succumbs to what it once saw as evident and detrimental hypocrisy in another's particularity. No doubt a free Palestine, comprising East Jerusalem, the West Bank, and Gaza, or a full and complete Palestine recovering all of what is now the state of Israel, would develop its own particular mythology.

To give a rationale for a history of displacement, struggle, and ultimate victory is the responsibility of leadership. It is essential to communal formation. This is yet to be set in place and, until then, another rationale will fill the void. There are few if any nation-states without national myths and ideologies, including, of course, the United States.

Because of this need for a rationale for the existence of a people, entity, or religion, mythology exists. As well, with its power to order and disorder a society, mythology is constantly contested. In every community, religion, and nationality, there are struggles over origins. There are struggles over direction. There are struggles over destiny. Jews are no different. In these matters, the state

26. On the one-state theme, see Hanis Faris, *The Failure of the Two State Solution: The Prospects of One State in the Israeli-Palestinian Conflict* (London: I. G. Tauris, 2013).

of Israel is the same as any other state, including, when it comes into being, a Palestinian state.

The struggle over Jewish identity regarding Israel is generational. The unraveling of Jewish identity is perennial. Aside from the Jewish claim of uniqueness, the overall method of Jewish identity formation may be far more similar to American, French, and Palestinian identity than Jews or others want to believe. On the religious side, Judaism's formation and reformation bears similarities to those employed in Christianity and Islam. There are struggles within each of these identities. All of these identities unravel, are reconstructed, and unravel again.

On the one hand, charges of antisemitism involve the denial of the right that Jews, as others, have to define themselves. There can be little argument with this. On the other, charges of antisemitism are too often used to keep Jewish identity and power from unraveling. If the latter is accepted, dissident Jews and Palestinians can be accused of antisemitism. They do want Jewish identity and power to unravel, at least how they are defined and exercised today.

Once more, the red line is crucial. Who defines the red line of antisemitism and for what purposes the line is chosen can be contested. In some forms and with certain intentions, the unraveling of Jewish identity is a form of antisemitism. In other forms and with different intentions, such unraveling may be the only way to penetrate to the heart of Jewishness. Disabling normative understandings of Jewish particularity may be the very essence of Jewish fidelity in the twenty-first century.

The issue, then, is not about whether each community, religion, or nation has a particular identity. Every entity has a sense of particularity and a way of expressing it. Rather, the issue is what a community's identity is at certain points in history. What is at stake in the definition of a particular identity will define how it is contested and where that identity formations ends up in a specific era. In addition, the issue of a community's identity has to do with whether or not it is trespassing on other identities—and lives—in pursuing its own.

Every community has a right to define their identity in the way they see fit. The issue is joined when one community trespasses against another community. If trespassed against, the transgressed have a right to dispute that self-definition and even disable it. In large part, this is what Qumsiyeh and Massad are doing in relation to Jews and Israel. Both promote their cause by undermining what mobilizes those who trespass against them. Still/Former Jewish/Israelis and Jews of Conscience in general do the same from inside the Jewish world. In this, some Palestinians and Jews work together. What are the limits of entities that claim particularity and destiny? What are the limits in using one's identity against others?

At issue, too, is what is fair game in the struggle of a weaker party against a more powerful one. Are there parts of the more powerful entities' identity that remain off-limits? Or, in the situation of defeat, is anything fair game? If the situation between the two parties is equalized, or if the weaker party becomes the stronger, do the rules change?

Historically, we know that what was once reviled in the oppressor in order to give succor to the oppressed has been affirmed when the situation on the ground is reversed. So it could be if and when justice is achieved between Israel and Palestine—mutual recognition of each other's particular history will become possible. If a joint journey commences, then the particularity of each community may, in part, be embraced by both.

Once the path toward justice commences, a mutual recognition of the Holocaust and the Nakba is achievable. That mutual recognition holds out the promise of healing that has eluded both peoples. Is it possible that only such a mutual recognition can provide the framework of healing for both Jews and Palestinians?[27]

If the Holocaust was not used against Palestinians, if the state of Israel did not aggress against Palestinians, the Holocaust and Israel should be left to Jews to sort out. Jews could choose to emphasize both, one aspect over the other, or none of the above. Jews would argue and decide. The world could look on or look away.

Is Criticism of Israel Hate?

President Obama is correct: the United Nations will not deliver a Palestinian state. He is also incorrect: Palestinians have a history. Israel is not innocent.

Qumsiyeh is correct: the Palestinians are the aggrieved party. He is also incorrect: Jews have a history beyond a synagogue Judaism where Jews gather to pray. Jews argue that they have a collective history. Jews are correct in that argument.

The Holocaust happened. The Bloodlands of Europe happened. The Bloodlands of the Middle East is occurring.

---

27. I raise this issue in "After the Holocaust and Israel: Can the Prophetic Heal Two Martyred Peoples?" in *The Case for Sanctions Against Israel*, 131-40.

No matter how it is argued with uniqueness at the fore or distorted in its use, the Holocaust is a seminal event in world history. At least Jews can claim this as true; others can affirm this claim or expand its horizons.

Palestinians who suffer from the aftermath of the Holocaust can do what they want with the Holocaust. Palestinians can ignore its occurrence. They can fold the Holocaust into other events of suffering, including their own. They can see the use of the Holocaust as a grand design to displace them from Palestine.

Massad is correct: the Nakba continues. The United Nations will not stop it. Europe will not stop it. The United States will not stop it. The Arab Spring will not stop it. The Still/Former Jewish/Israelis will not stop it. Flowery rhetoric aside, the endless peace processes will not stop it. The state of Israel will not stop it without being forced to.

As Qumsiyeh and Massad have offered—with concurrence from the Still/Former Jewish/Israelis—the challenge is to reverse the Nakba. Stopping it from continuing is not enough, since that would allow Palestinians only a truncated autonomy in a fake state. What would be left, what is left today, what is contemplated in peace process after peace process, is such a small percentage of its territory that it is almost impossible to envision rebuilding Palestinian society and projecting it into a future worth inhabiting.

"Land swaps," so prevalent in recent diplomatic speak and in President Obama's policies, is coded language. It means the inclusion of the large Israeli settlement blocs in the West Bank into Israel as a basis for a negotiated resolution to the conflict. Final status agreements on Jerusalem would then proceed with the same coded language. Palestinians would be allowed some symbolic sovereignty in East Jerusalem and guaranteed access to Islamic holy sites. The Jordan Valley, indeed all of what the Palestinians retain, would be occupied by foreign militaries. This is hardly enough. It is barely a beginning.

The Palestinians are on the other side of history. Historical, geopolitical, economic, and religious forces in the world have placed Palestinians in a quandary. This includes: the rise of Western power over the past centuries; the precipitous decline of the Ottoman Empire; the chronic weakness of the Arab world; the persecution of Jews in Europe culminating in the Holocaust; the reconciliation of liberal Western Christians with Jews after the Holocaust as a penance for their antisemitism; the recent rise of Christian evangelicals to power centers in the United States. Couple this with Jewish empowerment in the United States, and the outline of the Palestinian plight comes into focus.

Although history is not fate, historical context is crucial. What is needed is a negotiated settlement within these historical forces, but one that lays bare the realities of the dispossession of the Palestinians. Such a settlement demands that the historical forces arrayed against Palestinians be forced to retreat in a concerted fashion.

The negative forces impinging on Palestinian life must be disciplined and ended. Even with this viewpoint, one can still argue against the idea that the Palestinian cause is strictly based on universal grounds. The Palestinian assertion that the cause of Palestine has little to do with Palestinian particularity is wrong-headed and disingenuous. No cause is universal in and of itself. Even if we assert that issues like human and political rights are universal, they are viewed and applied through particular contexts.

This is true of every international body and protocol, including the United Nations. The United Nations' aspiration to universality is occasionally achieved. More often, the United Nations and, indeed, international law, represent a series confrontation among and between particular interests.

Perhaps better than the particular/universal dichotomy, competing interests can be seen as coming from inside and outside communities. What a certain community wants is not necessarily what another community wants. It is also true that these same particular/universal interests are found within communities. What one segment of the community wants, another opposes. Each part of the community may call on others outside of it to consolidate or even advance their position.

In its struggle for statehood, the Palestinian community calls on the United Nations. It appeals to Arab countries and beyond. Even so, there are those within the Palestinian community that reject this call for statehood, seeing a Palestinian state on part of the West Bank and with symbolic sovereignty in part of Jerusalem as effectively surrendering their patrimony. Across lines, Palestinians seeking statehood via the United Nations garner some Jewish support. As well, there are one-state Jewish thinkers who align with the Palestinian rejection of a truncated state. Both sides and alliances reach out to others for support. Palestinian statehood supporters look to the Arab world and Europe. One-state supporters look to South Africa and beyond.

For most of Jewish history, Jews lived as minorities in larger cultures and political configurations. The pressure within these Jewish communities and their need to align with or to survive outside forces was intense. In the age of Jewish empire, this pattern remains. Jews are a small minority of the population in America. The same is true of the Jewish population in Canada, France, the United Kingdom, Russia, and Argentina, the largest Jewish communities outside the United States and Israel. Of course today, though minorities, Jews are more empowered and live as equals with their neighbors.

If we look at Israel within the landscape of the Middle East, Jews are a minority. Even if we limit our view to historic Palestine, Jews and Palestinians are roughly equal in numbers. With the Palestinian birth rate far outstripping the Jewish birth rate, future numbers will skew Palestinian.

As a minority in the Middle East, Jews know well that history moves in a variety of directions. One direction is toward isolation and destruction. Another direction is toward negotiation and integration. In general, Israelis view their minority status as negative. Still, it is worth noting that the Jewish minority situation in the Middle East and even soon in Israel-Palestine is similar to the trajectory of the Jewish past. In some significant ways it is different, especially in relation to Israel's empowered self-governance and military capability. In other ways it is more of the same. Israel is dependent on outside entities to maintain its state.

Israelis are a militarized minority in the Middle East. Armed with nuclear weapons, Israelis are a nuclearized minority in the Middle East. In the end, though, it is doubtful that Israel's military, even its nuclear weapons, can protect it over the long run. As important, it is doubtful that Israel's nuclearized status will help its integration into the Middle East. Like presidents before him, President Obama has promised that the United States will always provide a military edge for Israel. What does such an edge mean in modern warfare? Does such an edge guarantee victory or even survival? When that edge diminishes or ends, for whatever reason, what then is Israel to do?

With modern armaments, victory may plant the seeds of defeat. All-out wars in the Middle East have gone Israel's way. But the fog of war is ripe for surprises. While American presidents guarantee Israel's military edge, victory in war is never guaranteed. What's more, can Israel, the Palestinians, and the rest of the Arab world continue to exist on the razor's edge without suffering a further decline in ethical behavior, political discourse and culture? In the long run, this is no way to live.

On another stage, Israel's political standing in the world continues to decline. The BDS movements in the American churches grow stronger. As well, the European Union and major international banks are becoming more insistent that Israel's continuing occupation and settlement policies be penalized in business, finance and scientific endeavors. Academic organizations like the American Studies Association have adopted their own boycott of Israeli institutions linked to the occupation of Palestinians.[28]

---

28. See Richard Perez-Pena and Jodi Rudoren, "Boycott by Academic Group Is a Symbolic Sting to Israel," *New York Times*, December 16, 2013.

Israel has power. It is also experiencing a deepening isolation from ideological and material forces arrayed against its policies. Though Israeli officials claim these initiatives to be antisemitic, the charge is too broad. Like crying wolf too many times, the plaintiff cry of antisemitism is beginning to fall on deaf ears.

Returning to the question of antisemitism and Jewish identity, let us stress: antisemitism is real. As well, charges of antisemitism function to bolster certain negative forms of Jewish identity against other more positive options. Once prejudice is in the human ecology, it rarely ends because culture and religions become more enlightened. In fact, prejudice separates from its original impetus and takes on a life of its own. So, regardless of how vehement retractions of antisemitism by mainline Christian denominations are, the antisemitism Christianity historically spawned remains alive. The same is true of Enlightenment antisemitism, itself beholden to Christian antisemitism. Though the Enlightenment prided itself independent of Christian prejudice, the reality is much more complex. Modernity, itself born of Christianity and the Enlightenment, carries its own variant of antisemitism.

Holocaust denial is clearly a form of antisemitism. Under cover of questioning the Holocaust, Jews are singled out for trumpeting their misery—as a way to power. With Holocaust denial, we are very near the Protocols of the Elders of Zion, the forged document from Tsarist Russia that proclaims an international Jewish conspiracy to control governments, the world economy, media, and public institutions.

However, to question how mainstream Jewish leaders and organizations use the Holocaust is fair game. For example, as a public and national institution, it is reasonable to ask why the Holocaust Memorial Museum commemorates an event that happened in Europe at such an important location in the American capital. The question is why this issue is raised in the first place. Is challenging the importance and location of commemorating the Holocaust done to denigrate Jews or to enlighten public opinion on how the Holocaust has come to function in American public discourse?

On the state of Israel, it is possible to affirm the need for Jews to be empowered and, at the same time, to ask if that empowerment has to be within a Jewish state in the Middle East. Some Jews and non-Jews believe that the most productive and secure form of Jewish empowerment is found in the integration of peoples and nations struggling together for an interdependent empowerment. There are non-nationalists of all stripes and in all parts of the globe. Should the state of Israel be a glaring exemption to this type of thinking?

Even if one decides that Israel is unique and necessary, does it mean necessarily that those who do not believe in such a state are antisemitic?

On the political front, the BDS movement with regard to Israel has been growing over the years. This movement is overtly political and comes from a variety of ideologies, institutions, and religious bodies. This movement is highly contentious and diverse. But, again, if such a movement became so strong in relation to apartheid South Africa that it contributed to the regime's collapse, it is reasonable to assume that the same tactics can be applied to Israel's occupation policies. To view BDS as a form of antisemitism is to paint with too broad a brush. So it is with the discussion of creating one state of Israel-Palestine with full equality between Jews and Palestinians. The end of a Jewish state is not in and of itself antisemitic. It is not a form of discrimination nor is it hateful to advocate for the transformation of Israel into a state of all its citizens.[29]

Yet it remains that some advocates for justice for Palestinians are relatively silent—others deny it outright—on the possibility and perhaps the need for Jews to have a political dimension that moves beyond individual citizenship. The individual citizen within the state as the be all and end all of identity is a modern sensibility to be sure, yet it cuts against the grain of Jewish history. It may that any collective that has suffered in recent history needs a collective politics to complement individual citizenship. Certainly Jews at least deserve the ability to explore this option within the movement toward and after justice with Palestinians is achieved. At the same time, Palestinians need access to a collective politics beyond their individual citizenship, lest they become prey to more powerful national and economic forces of Israel and their Arab neighbors. In one state who will guarantee protection and nurturance for Jews and Palestinians as members of a community?

These are only some reasons to favor a two-state resolution to the Israeli-Palestinian conflict. Unfortunately, because of its expansion, Israel has foreclosed this possibility. What is left is one state controlled by Israel and a truncated autonomy for Palestinians. This center will not hold. What is on the other side of the Israeli control and Palestinian autonomy is unknown.

The struggle over antisemitism often revolves around the theme of dream and reality. Or, better, myth and reality. The myth of Jews is wrong when applied in a wholly negative way—Jews as deceptive and controlling, bent on world domination. The myth of Jews is wrong when applied in a wholly affirmative way—Jews as eternal sufferers and victims whose needed empowerment is without culpability.

---

29. For a Palestinian take on the issue, see Omar Barghouti, *Boycott, Divestment, Sanctions: The Global Struggle for Palestinian Rights* (Chicago: Haymarket, 2011).

Jews as either/or, demonized aggressors or romanticized angels, is wrong. The difficulty is sorting myth and reality, especially with a history that has been unfairly demonized and now unduly romanticized.

Is there way forward through the complications of Jewish history and the complications of the Jewish present, including what is and is not antisemitism? There are so many levels surrounding Jewish life and Jewishness itself that only a negotiated settlement may be possible here as well. A resolution regarding Jews and the Jewish question, so present throughout history, is for now out of reach. This may be another singular aspect of the Jewish journey. Yet if we think about any identity, say African American or French or Islamic identity, they are continually contested as well. In each of these communities identity is asserted, contested, navigated, and, in the end, in doubt.

Even when it is announced as univocal and eternal, identity is always provisional. Territory, nationality, and religion, often showcases for identity, are provisional. When the Israeli government announces Jerusalem as the eternal capital of Israel for the Jewish people, history tells us this claim is provisional. More, when we look underneath and around this provisional claim, there are other variables at work. If Israel loses Jerusalem in a future war, does it remain the eternal capital of Israel? If Israel-Palestine becomes one state, does Jerusalem become the eternal capital of Israel-Palestine?

Looked at closely, announced identities are inconsistent and unpredictable. They are alterable. Usually, they are being altered as they are pronounced eternal. On antisemitism and on the Holocaust, on the state of Israel, on Jews and Jewishness, there is dream and reality, myth and reality, assertion and subversion, in a volatile and unstable mix that continues to journey through history.

This is the way it has been throughout Jewish history. Having so many variables, there is no quick fix. Nor is there a laboratory setting where measurements can be made and the proper equilibrium established. Rather, it is historical forces and the various movements which affirm and dispute certain configurations of Jewishness that will have their say. Whether done in a civil way or through verbal or even actual warfare, what it means to be Jewish is up for grabs, as it has always been.

10

The Jewish (Prophetic) Prison

The persistence of the prophetic is difficult to explain. Nor can it be defended with logical equations and data. Knowing that identity evolves and the deconstruction of identity claims is the order of the day, to declare that the Jewish prophetic is the root of the prophetic in the world, and that without it the global prophetic spirit would languish, seems outrageous. So we are told. So we believe.

Theory tells us that the ancient cannot appear in the modern except as disjointed and segmented fragments. We cannot travel from there to here without skipping many beats. Applied critically, history is as much about lacuna as it is about continuity. Eras are connected and disconnected from the past and present. The idea that the Jewish prophetic is the conscience of humanity is incredible, too self-involved, too particular.

We are experiencing an explosion of the prophetic in our time. All around the world the prophetic is in full bloom. And, it seems, at least with Jews, that the contemporary prophets have the same footprint as the ancient ones. No matter the deconstruction of Jewishness and Jewish history, there is continuity in the prophetic. The ancient Jewish prophetic is alive. It will never die.

Yet the survival and flourishing of the prophetic is dependent on an ancient tradition that is in deep crisis. In Jewish life, the prophetic is gathered in a tradition. There are always Jewish prophets on the way. The Jewish prophetic tradition is resilient.

The Jewish prophets are so pugnacious they sometimes work against the prophetic tradition itself, especially when it becomes mired in prophet-speak. Nor does the Jewish prophetic have much time for voices outside the Jewish community who advise Jews that the prophetic tradition needs to be upended and transformed into a universal outreach shorn of its particularity. Advising the Jewish prophetic tradition that it has to cease being Jewish is another long tradition.

Is there a difference between the prophetic and the prophet? The prophet stands at the origins of the prophetic, the singular individual who gives birth to others that follow in the prophet's way. The prophet is the birthplace of the prophetic community. Or, rather, the prophetic community gathers around the prophet.

One way of looking at the prophetic community is that it channels the prophet's heartbeat in eras beyond the prophet's death. The prophet's heartbeat is thus kept alive through prophetic commitment, and not just for the prophet's sake, as if the prophet might come back to life. Rather, the prophet's life is extended through the world within which the prophetic community lives.

The prophet and the prophetic community stand in the gap between deconstruction and affirmation, between discontinuity and permanence. They are a specific part of the human journey that accompanies history like a shadow companion. The prophetic community is the shadow companion of history touched by the prophets. Both are carriers of what is commonly called conscience.

A PROPHETIC EXORCISM

Many years ago the French postmodern philosopher Jean-François Lyotard proffered a distinction between "Jews" and "jews" that may be instructive. For Lyotard, "Jews" are real living beings, the Jews of history, individually and communally, the outsiders that continue to traverse history. Lyotard's "jews" are a conceptual, though real, counterpoint to living Jews. jews exist with and without Jews. Lyotard's analysis provides a fascinating beginning for an interpretive journey that explores the significance of Jew/jew for the future.[1]

For the most part, jews are those who live on the margins of societies and the world. Therefore, jews are symbolic Jews. Lyotard sees history as inscribed with Jewishness, a subversive memory of how the world should be and is not. Therefore, periodically the world wants to rid itself of Jews in a vain attempt to eliminate jews. Perhaps if Jews were eliminated calling attention to displaced, dislocated, and demeaned jews would become more difficult. If the real outsiders are eliminated, who will call attention to other outsiders?

In Lyotard's understanding, Jews are the Other of history—from which all others can be understood. Although they seem apart, Jews and the sufferers of history are joined as challenges to mainstream and often unjust societies.

1. Jean-Francois Lyotard, *Heidegger and "the jews"* (Minneapolis: University of Minnesota Press, 1990).

In some ways, Lyotard's vision of Jew/jew is parallel with Jean Daniel's understanding of the Jewish prison, though taken in a different direction. Daniel is an Algerian-born, French Jewish journalist. He is the founder and managing editor of *Le Nouvel Observateur*. As a Jew, Daniel wants out of the status of outcast, whether this status is dictated by the world or desired by Jews themselves.

Whereas Lyotard analyzes Jews/jews from the outside as a non-Jewish philosopher, Daniel sees Jewish self-definition as the chosen people as a prison he wants to escape. However, escape is challenging. The Jewish prison walls are high. It seems that the world outside Jews and Jews themselves seek to define Daniel's Jewishness regardless of his stated choice. The emergence of the Holocaust and the state of Israel has increased the pressure to self-identify as Jewish or to be so self-identified by non-Jews.[2]

Daniel asks why he and other Jews are not allowed to define themselves. Whereas in other eras in history identifying as Jewish was mandated by outside powers and internal communal pressure, today Daniel thinks it is also the fault of individual Jews who refuse to let go of their self-definition. If you no longer believe that God chose the Jews or that Jews as Jews have a particular destiny, then the meaning of "Jew" is meaningless. It is time to let go. When a Jew comes to that conclusion and is not allowed or refuses to let go, Jewishness becomes a prison without content. For Daniel, then, the only authentic life is to escape being self-defined or labeled "Jew."

Both Lyotard and Daniel make sense. Jews and Jewishness are defined identities, by Jews and non-Jews alike. Often those on the margins of societies are defined as the "Jews of," as in Chinese diaspora communities being referred to as the "Jews of Asia." From time to time, Palestinians are referred to as the "Jews of the Arab world." Some Palestinians employ this terminology to remind actual Jews of the role reversal inherent in the state of Israel. Are Palestinians the jews of Israel? If so, what does this mean for the Jews of Israel?

Identity inversion is part of the Israeli-Palestinian conflict. During the conflict, Palestinians have employed symbols from Jewish history to press Jews to reflect on what they are doing, specifically in light of Jewish history. So for example, at one point in Israeli prison camps, Palestinians spray painted "Auschwitz" on the outside of their tents.

Jews have inverted Jewish historical markers to refer their own reversal. One example is a Jewish Israeli physician, Marcus Levin, who reported to a prison camp for Palestinians in 1988 and asked what he was supposed to do.

2. Jean Daniel, *The Jewish Prison: A Rebellious Meditation on the State of Judaism* (Brooklyn: Melville House, 2005).

When another physician informed him that he would tend to Palestinians after they were tortured, Levin responded with a reference to an infamous Nazi doctor: "My name is Marcus Levin, not Joseph Mengele, and for reasons of conscience I refuse to serve in this place."[3]

When Jews experience Nazi inversions from Palestinians, it is a difficult experience. When they hear Nazi inversions from Jews, it takes on yet another dimension. What happens when such inversions are heard together? Does the distinction, Jews/jews, collapse? Does the Jewish prison open wide or close in on itself?

When these inversions are experienced together, a further component emerges. The issue is what is to be done with this inversion. On the Jewish side, for the most part, denial is the order of the day. Denial signifies refutation, as in what someone says is happening, is not. Too often, denial signals a deflection. What is supposedly unknown, is.

After entering the terrain of the Holocaust and even with the Bloodlands diminished sense of Jewish singularity in the Holocaust, Auschwitz-signed tents among Palestinian prisoners is clearly over the top. Or is it? When reasoned argument fails, symbolism comes into play. If the Holocaust is used by Israel and the Jewish establishment to justify the expulsion of Palestinians and the denial of their rights, Holocaust symbolism cannot be declared off-limits. Since the Holocaust and the state of Israel are now trumpeted as central to the Jewish drama, Jews should expect those on the other side of Jewish power to invert the Holocaust for their cause.

Inversion—a state in which the order, arrangement, or position of something is reversed. If the Palestinians are the jews of the Middle East, who are the Jews of Israel? Who are their Jewish enablers in the United States? It could be that the Palestinians are the Jews of the Middle East. Can jews become Jews?

If the Jews of Israel and their enablers in the United States are not Jews because of their unjust actions and because of their insider status and power,

3. Issa Nakhleh describes it this way: "Dr. Marcus Levin, a member of Kibbutz Matsuba, was called up for reserve duty in Ansar 2 prison. When he arrived at the prison clinic he met two of his colleagues and asked for information about the job of a doctor there. The answer: 'Mainly you examine prisoners before and after an interrogation.' When Dr. Levin asked, amazed, 'After interrogation?' his colleagues replied: 'It's nothing special. Sometimes there are fractures. Yesterday, for instance, they brought a 12-year-old boy with two broken legs.' After this, Dr. Levin met with the compound commander, a Lieutenant Colonel, and told him: 'My name is Marcus Levin and not Josef Mengele and for reasons of conscience I refuse to serve in this place.' One of the doctors present tried to calm Dr. Levin and said: 'Marcus, at first you feel like Mengele but after a few days you get used to it.'" See his *Encyclopedia of the Palestine Problem*, http://www.palestine-encyclopedia.com/EPP/Chapter22.

but are not jews either, who are they? The situation is further complicated if dissident Jews identify with Palestinian jews over against their Jewish counterparts. Are Jews of Conscience, real Jews, then remnant Jews? Many of these remnant Jews distance themselves from Jewish identity. Do they remain Jews without an identifying label? Since at least some Jews of Conscience seek to be released from Jewish identifiers, identifying remnant Jews as Jews may be depriving Jews of choice. In this way, Daniel's idea of the Jewish prison is reinforced.

We are left with the conundrum of the inverted Jewish condition. There are jewish Palestinians who cannot become Jews—officially. There are Jews who oppress Palestinians who are no longer Jews but are not jews, either. And there are many jews who do not want to be identified as such, who are not Jews, yet perhaps at the deepest level are Jews.

The Jew/jew conundrum is exaggerated further because, as we have seen, establishment Jews who abuse the privilege of being Jewish assert they are the authentic Jews, whereas dissident Jews have lost their way of identifying as Jewish. For the most part the outside world identifies establishment Jews as the real Jews. Jews of Conscience for example and the Still/Former Jewish/Israelis who do not fit the world's description of Jews are, for the most part, unknown to the general public. For the foreseeable future, Jewishness will be defined by the disguised empire-oriented establishment. The Constantinian framework of Jewishness prevails.

Constantinian Jews do not self-identify with empire. They prefer instead the Holocaust and an embattled state of Israel as their identifiers. Constantinian Jews compete on the same Jewish turf with Jews of Conscience without the substance of their commitment and from a very dissimilar social, political, and economic location.

Constantinian Jews seek to relegate Jews of Conscience to the periphery. They label Jews of Conscience as deluded, leftist, out-of-touch, self-hating Jews who encourage non-Jews in their antisemitism. Jews of Conscience struggle against Constantinian Jews and their powerful allies for space in the argument about what it means to be Jewish in our time. For Jews of Conscience though, the question is whether they should enter into a "authentic Jew" competition with Constantinian Jews. Is this fight the best use of their limited resources or is it better simply to let the public definition of Jewishness be, get on with justice making, and have the definitional chips of who is a Jew fall where they may?

Is the prophetic antisemitic? At first, this sounds like a strange question. How can the indigenous of the people Israel be seen as a form of antisemitism? After all, whatever one wants to make of the prophets, they are preserved and highlighted in Jewish canonical literature. When we listen to Ezekiel, a prophet and a priest, who was one of the Jerusalemites exiled to Babylonia in 597 bce, what do we hear? Ezekiel begins by recounting God's call on his life. Speaking to his people is going to be difficult, maybe even impossible:

> And He said to me, "O mortal, stand up on your feet that I may speak to you." As He spoke to me, a spirit entered into me and set me upon my feet; and I heard what was being spoken to me. He said to me, "O mortal, I am sending you to the people of Israel, the nation of rebels, who have rebelled against Me.—They as well as their fathers have defied Me to this very day; for the sons are brazen of face and stubborn of heart. I send you to them, and you shall say to them: 'Thus said the Lord God'—whether they listen or not, for they are a rebellious breed—that they may know that there was a prophet among them. And you, mortal, do not fear them and do not fear their words, though thistles and thorns press against you and you sit upon scorpions. Do not be afraid of their words and do not be dismayed by them, though they are a rebellious breed; but speak My words to them, whether they listen or not, for they are rebellious."[4]

Now listen to Gilad Atzmon, one of the Still/Former Jewish/Israelis, as he recounts his experience in 1984 as an Israeli soldier visiting Israeli bases inside Lebanon. Like Ezekiel, notice the historical reversals and his disdain for propaganda. Unlike Ezekiel, God is noticeably absent in Atzmon's vocabulary. Rather, Atzmon's calling comes from his encounter with the "enemy," which, as in Ezekiel's case, turns out to be his own people. Here Atzmon is being escorted around the infamous Israeli prison camp in Lebanon, Ansar:

> 'Who are these people?' I asked the officer.
> 'Palestinians,' he said. 'On the left are PLO [Palestine Liberation Organisation], and on the right are Ahmed Jibril's boys [Palestine Front for the Liberation of Palestine—General Command]—they are far more dangerous, so we keep them isolated.

4. Ezekiel 2:1-8, *The Jewish Study Bible*, ed. Adele Berlin and Marc Zvi Brettler (New York: Oxford University Press, 2004), 1048-1049.

I studied the detainees. They looked very different to the Palestinians in Jerusalem. The ones I saw in Ansar were angry. They were not defeated, they were freedom fighters and they were numerous. As we continued past the barbed wire I continued gazing at the inmates, and arrived at an unbearable truth: I was walking on the other side, in Israeli military uniform. The place was a concentration camp. The inmates were the 'Jews', and I was nothing but a 'Nazi.' It took me years to admit to myself that even the binary opposition Jew/Nazi was in itself a result of my Judeo-centric indoctrination.

While I contemplated the resonance of my uniform, trying to deal with the great sense of shame growing within me, we came to a large, flat ground at the centre of the camp. The officer guiding us offered more platitudes about the current war to defend our Jewish haven. While he was boring us to death with these irrelevant *Hasbara* (propaganda) lies, I noticed that we were surrounded by two dozen concrete blocks each around 1.2m in area and 1.3m high, with metal doors as entrances. I was horrified at the thought that my army was locking guard dogs into these boxes at night. Putting my Israeli chutzpah into action, I confronted the officer about these horrible concrete cubes. He was quick to reply: "These are our solitary confinement cubes; after two days in one of these, you become a devoted Zionist!"[5]

Atzmon ranges widely on the question of Jewish identity. Even the title of his book—*The Wandering Who?*—is a play on the ancient myth of the wandering Jew. Atzmon is not content to puncture contemporary forms of Jewish identity by reversing Jew/jew. Instead, he goes straight to the source, the Bible. In a chapter subsection titled "Swindler's List"—a play on the Holocaust-themed "Schindler's List"—Atzmon writes of the relation of the Bible to the contemporary ethnic cleansing of Palestinians:

Moses, his contemporaries and their current followers were and are excited about the possibilities that awaited them in the Land of Milk and Honey. Israel, the Jewish State has been following Moses' call. The ethnic cleansing of the Palestinian people in 1948, and the

5. Gilad Atzmon, *The Wandering Who? A Study of Jewish Identity Politics* (Winchester, UK: Zero Books, 2011), 6-7.

constant and total abuse of the Palestinian people since then, makes Deuteronomy 6:10-12 look like a prophecy fulfilled.

For more than sixty years, the Biblical call for theft has been put into legal praxis. The Israeli looting of Palestinian cities, homes, fields and wells has found its way into Israel's legal system: by 1950-1951, Israeli legislators had already approved the "Absentee Property Law," a racially-orientated law preventing Palestinians from returning to their lands, cities, villages, and allowing the new Israelites to live in houses and cities they "did not build."

The never-ending theft of Palestine in the name of the Jewish people is part of a spiritual, ideological, cultural and practical continuum between the Bible, Zionist ideology and the State of Israel (along with its overseas supporters). Israel and Zionism, both political systems, have instituted the plunder promised by the Hebrew God in the Judaic Holy Scriptures.[6]

"The Biblical call for theft"—it could hardly be stated more boldly. Clearly, Atzmon has placed the Bible on trial. "Put into legal praxis"—Atzmon brings his analysis to the present. If this is not enough, Atzmon believes that continuum goes further than just theft. He cites Leviticus 26:7-8 and Deuteronomy 7:1-2 as he recalls the devastating images of Palestinians being bombed in a United Nations shelter during the Israeli invasion of Gaza in 2008. Atzmon continues: "The IDF used lethal methods, such as cluster bombs and white phosphorus, against civilians as though its main objective was to 'destroy' while showing 'no mercy' whatsoever. It seems as though the Israeli military, in erasing northern Gaza in January 2009, were following Deuteronomy 20:16—they did indeed 'not leave anything alive anything that breathed.'"[7]

Without addressing the question directly, Atzmon confronts the persistence of the prophetic with the persistence of biblically sanctioned crimes. Here he is on familiar territory. Atzmon appears to be yet another example of Jews on both sides of the empire divide. Yet in calling out Moses and by extension the Bible as a whole, Atzmon reorients the empire divide's more obvious direction. The typical sides—biblical prophetic and biblical empire building—are both under indictment.

Although largely silent on the prophets, Atzmon's prophetic voice wants nothing to do with his biblical patrimony. It seems to him a contrivance

6. Ibid., 120-21.
7. Ibid., 122.

that leads to what Israel has become—and perhaps, more or less, always was. Harkening back to Daniel's prophetic prison, the very interplay within the Bible and Jewish history is a prison that exacts its revenge. The Bible, and by extension Jewish history, forces Jews and non-Jews, in this case Palestinians, into prison without chance of parole.

Atzmon is most poignant about the Bible when he visits Ansar prison. For Atzmon, the biblical narrative regarding the Promised Land is reprised in the state of Israel. Where he sees little if any continuity in Jewish life, thus throwing the entire understanding of Jewish history and Jewish identity up in the air, Atzmon does sees continuity between the Bible and the state of Israel. Atzmon compresses the immeasurably large spaces between real history and the claims of Jewish identity—so much so that he believes that Deuteronomy and the state of Israel are one. Atzmon announces and then flees this compression. For Atzmon, taking cues from the Bible to create a modern state is the height of idiocy. He is born into such a situation. Is there any choice but exile?

Contra Atzmon, there are other choices than geographic exile. Most people born into a certain geographic area remain there regardless of the ideologies of the state. One hardly needs to look far for examples. Take the United States, itself a settler nation, with competing myths of origins and governing principles, or the United Kingdom and its historic empire ideologies. No matter their critique of American and British history, most people born in either country live out their lives there. Besides, Atzmon cites both countries as among his favorite places to visit and live. Yet his thought is built largely of contrasting the open and engaging environments of the West with the restrictive and tribal nature of Israeli society.

Since both the United States and the United Kingdom are empire nations, how can Atzmon enjoy the fruits of their empires but rail against the biblical and contemporary Israel empires as inherently evil? How can he choose to live in non-Jewish empires but not in the Jewish one in which he was born? Having renounced his Israeli citizenship, how could he then apply for and receive British citizenship?

If this is not contradictory enough, Atzmon singles out Jews in America and the United Kingdom for special approbation. In an accusatory manner, Atzmon cites Diaspora Jews for constructing their identity through the Holocaust and the state of Israel. Since most Diaspora Jews were born after the Holocaust and do not live in Israel, Atzmon views them as voyeurs.

Atzmon finds Jewish identity outside of Israel to be as warped as Jewish identity in Israel. Or perhaps more accurately, Atzmon views Jewish identity inside and outside of Israel as a self-perpetuating fraud. Whether other identities contain the same fraud is left to the reader's imagination. For the most part, Atzmon is a one-act play, concentrating on Jewish identity in an overbearing way.

Atzmon does have a critical view of American and British politics. As an unapologetic leftist, his critique is wide-ranging. Yet, since there are problems all over the world, including in the less tribal and ostensibly identity-free zones of America and the United Kingdom, and since he protests injustice and idiocy in those zones as well, why not remain and protest in Israel? Although Israel is much smaller and has many more constraints, there are relative free zones in Israel, too. Jews like Atzmon can experience Tel Aviv as akin to, though on a smaller scale, New York and London. Why not visit the bigger cities and then return to home ground?

As importantly, if Atzmon is attracted to the cosmopolitan ethos of New York and London, why not take advantage of the opportunity to leave Israel and Jewishness and never look back? If there is no such thing as Jewish identity except its fabrication, why, after taking leave, write book after book about an identity that is imagined, fraudulent and restrictive?

In fact, Atzmon takes pleasure in the ire of Jews he antagonizes with his writing. He delights in calling attention to the restrictive Jewishness of Jews across the board. Atzmon recalls proudly that at one point in the United Kingdom he became known as "King of the Jews." This was because he had "achieved the unachievable, accomplished the impossible" by uniting Jews from all political, religious, and cultural stripes against him. This included Zionists, anti-Zionists, Jewish Socialists, Tribal Marxists, the Board of Deputies, and Jewish Trotskyites. As Atzmon writes: "Jews for this and Jews for that, for the first time in history all spoke in a single voice. They all hated Gilad Atzmon equally. 'Pretty impressive,' I thought to myself, 'I must have done something right.'" For Atzmon, this prompted a powerful insight and yet another reversal about antisemitism: "While in the past an 'anti-Semite' was someone who hates Jews, nowadays it is the other way around, an anti-Semite is someone the Jews hate." The other reversal goes unmentioned in Atzmon's description, this being the mocking title the Romans applied to the crucified Jesus.[8]

Atzmon's self-identification has led Jewish and Palestinian groups to publicly disassociate themselves from him. The lead has been taken by Palestinians themselves who struggle to separate Jews and Zionism. For these Palestinians, Atzmon muddles the waters since their dispute with Israel as a Jewish state is not with Jews themselves. By disassociating themselves from

---

8. Ibid., 54.

Atzmon, Palestinians want to set the record straight about their own views on Israel, Zionism and Jews.[9]

Atzmon views the accusation of being an antisemite as a last ditch attempt by Jewish groups of different viewpoints to insulate themselves against the deconstruction of Jewish identity. However, while protecting against the deconstruction of Jewish identity another projection of that identity comes to the fore.

For Atzmon, Jewish identity lacks a foundation. Therefore, ganging up on him becomes an agreed-upon foundation to deal with a group anxiety that there is little basis for Jewish identity at all. Why else would such diverse Jewish groups come together to denounce a fellow Jew with such vehemence? Perhaps, as well, Jewish group-think regarding Atzmon represents an anxiety that Atzmon himself voices and embodies: that the only foundation of Jewishness is injustice.

In a move that is intended to anger every Jew in Britain and beyond, Atzmon lumps together Jewish groups that see themselves as bitterly opposed to one another. From the Jewish establishment Board of Deputies to the marginal Jewish Trotskyites—"the Jews for this and that"—Atzmon sees it all as a giant scam. Hovering around the edges of his charge of group-think is the plundered Promised Land, whose very plunder Atzmon asserts is predicted by and connected to the Bible. Atzmon's book title, *The Wandering Who?*, could as easily be *The Promised What?*

Atzmon's motley Jews of the United Kingdom parallel the motley Jews of the state of Israel. Both parallel the motley Israelites as the Israelite settlers entered the land. How, then, does Atzmon hope to find redress in the motley cosmopolitan cities of New York and London?

Like so many Jews before him, Atzmon may be fascinated by the motley Other because he is anxious that Jews are motley, too. Perhaps subconsciously, Atzmon desires purity among Jews, which he does not find, and so prefers the mixtures of the Other Nations, which he assumes. This may be part of his indictment of the decidedly impure Bible.

Is Atzmon the quintessential Jew who demands an innocence among Jews that has never existed? If this is the case, life among the impure Other is a relief. His disappointment with the politics of the Other is expected. Atzmon is released from the prophetic demands that he imposes on Jews and Jewishness.

---

9. For more on this controversy with links to other material see Adam Horowitz, "Palestinian and Palestine-solidarity activists issue critique and condemnation of Gilad Atzmon," *Mondoweiss*, March 14, 2012. http://mondoweiss.net/2012/03/palestinian-and-palestine-solidarity-activists-issue-critique-and-condemnation-of-gilad-atzmon.html

Performing the Decolonized Prophetic

As in time past, today's exile geographies are dangerous for Jews. At least in the Biblical mindset, exile geographies are places where Israel loses its way, whores after strange gods, and, in a further rebellion, revels in being outside the restrictive confines of Jewish definition and power.

Exile in Jewish history is both loss and an assertion of power over against the demands of the land and God. New York and London function for Atzmon as a release from Jewish and God's authority where, paradoxically, he once again takes up his prophetic rap. So instead of disappearing in exile, Atzmon appears as the archetypally mocked Jew, King of the Jews. But then, if Jews are applying this title to Atzmon, a further denigration is applied. In short, who does this traitor think he is? Could it be that for Jews, like Jesus, Atzmon is a false messiah?

Atzmon wears this epithet with pride and responds in kind. He throws Ansar prison camp at Jews without distinction. No matter where they stand on the issues of Jewish empowerment, the Holocaust, or the state of Israel, Atzmon accuses Jews of being phonies. Jewishness itself is a sham. In Atzmon's mind, that is why Jews of every stripe seek to censor him. Like the ancient prophets, Atzmon exposes Jews. At the same time, Atzmon believes that the Bible, from which the prophets spring, is bogus. This is why Atzmon condemns even those Jews who espouse the Jewish prophetic as counterfeit heirs. Atzmon provides no hiding place for Jews anywhere.

Once again, Atzmon is moving the empire-divide goalposts. Perhaps this is because even the tradition of the prophets has gone stale. For Atzmon the prophetic voices within the Jewish community are too often, like the Jewish establishment, enablers or beneficiaries of empire. Hence, the claim to the Jewish prophetic is null and void.

Atzmon's judgment is extreme but, in his extremity, he is much like the biblical prophets. In the Bible, the prophets are often shadowed by competing prophets that the biblical prophets condemn as false. Deemed false prophets, they mislead the people. Here Atzmon ups the ante, not only by claiming to be the one and only Jew but also by refusing to place himself in the traditions of the recognized biblical prophets.

So what the biblical prophets did to top each other, Atzmon does to the entire prophetic tradition. Yet Atzmon is imprisoned within the tradition he desperately tries to escape. For how else can Atzmon be understood outside of the tradition he attempts to bury once and for all? Instead of King of the Jews, perhaps Atzmon should be recognized as the prophets of old. At least in his self-description and his outreach, this is the way he appears.

Atzmon complicates the Jewish–identity puzzle. None of the Atzmon puzzle pieces fit and no revised placement corresponds, either. Jews are (un)fit. Wherever they end up, they remain at loose ends. That said, for Atzmon, the Jewish puzzle has become too staid. Even those Jews who claim the prophetic tradition are pretenders.

In and around his text, Atzmon drives home the following point. Prophetic Jews have assimilated to the prophetic tradition, thus they have rendered the instability of Jewish life into a stability that denies the prophetic itself. Because of the stabilized prophetic, Jews are mirror images of the Jewish establishment. The Jewish empire mentality they ostensibly oppose they actually embody. When the chips are down, they coalesce with their "opposites," who are too much the same.

This general understanding may be shared by the Still/Former Jewish/Israelis in general—that even the Jewish prophetic tradition now conforms to power. Their opposition to unjust power has until now been half-hearted. Therefore, their Jewishness has been fake. In fact, any Jewish identifier is now, if not always, fraudulent because "Jewish" has become too stable. Being stable, it cannot enact what it professes. The prophetic has to embody instability to be what it is supposed to be.

When Atzmon looks on where Palestinians are held at Ansar and hears the Israeli soldier boast—"These are our solitary confinement cubes; after two days in one of these, you become a devoted Zionist!"—everything changes. Already on the left in Israeli politics, his foundations have been shaken. The Left looks on with its criticism, but it is too involved to be of use in dismantling the system that produces "devoted" Zionists. In fact, for Palestinians, much of the Israeli Left are devoted Zionists.

This, in turn, forces the prophetic to another level of intensity. For decades in Israeli politics and the Jewish world in general, the Zionist Left, known often as the Israeli peace camp, has been seen as the prophetic. For Atzmon, they are compromised to the core. Voting, organizing, protesting, even refusing to serve in the occupied territories is not enough. It is false protest, totally compromised. So, like the biblical prophets, Atzmon condemns the entire Israel enterprise, state, and people. But, unlike the biblical prophets, there is no path of repentance, except perhaps if everything, including Jewish identity and the land, is given over. After all, his family also returned to Israel. Now he is off into an exile without return.

What launches Atzmon on his journey into exile is, on the one hand, Ansar and all it represents, and on the other, his discovery of the saxophone, especially jazz and be-bop, derived from such classic African American musicians, Charlie Parker, John Coltrane and Miles Davis. Atzmon's exit from Israel, then, begins with his break with empowered Jewishness in the land and identification with the freedom struggle of Palestinian jews. It continues when he encounters the music heavily indebted to African American jews.

This dual identification with non-Jewish jews is important. Atzmon believes that the real Jews are the jews of this world, a name Jews no longer deserve. It might be that Atzmon is searching for his own recovered Jewishness among the non-real Jews of the world. Is it only among Palestinians and African Americans that Atzmon can be fully Jewish?

Atzmon the writer and musician is outrageous. He baits his opponents and leaves them without a place to turn. Nor does he leave himself room to turn. Unlike the biblical prophets, Atzmon's call to repentance leads nowhere—unless exile is always somewhere else. After all, exile is the only place left, now that the return to the land is such a disaster. Ansar is that disaster writ large, the place where the enemies of the Jews are imprisoned and dehumanized. Ansar is where Atzmon finds his prophetic voice. It is among the jews guarded by Jews that Atzmon finds his rage. His rage deepens in exile.

Like other Still/Former Jewish/Israelis, Atzmon performs the prophetic for our time. Like the biblical prophets he does not acknowledge, Atzmon believes we are at the end of Jewish history, a history, like the prophets, he no longer believe exists or, if it does, is not worthy of being carried forward. Irony of ironies, he witnesses to the continuity of both. Perhaps with Atzmon the designation of the Still/Former Jewish/Israelis should be enlarged. Still/Former Jewish/Israeli/Prophets?

We know little of the personal biography of the biblical prophets of Israel. In most cases, the biblical prophets are called by God and reluctantly accept their calling. The prophets deliver their message to the people who reject them and then often, but not always, escape the people's anger through subterfuge and divine intervention. After suffering intensely because of the message they deliver, the prophets disappear from view.

Once in a while, the screen is pulled back and we witness the anguish of the prophets' lives. The biblical prophets are often portraits of despair. Hope is in short supply. In the main, the biblical prophets announce that Israel's destiny is squandered, which throws the prophet's witness into question.

If anything, the prophets ponder the meaning of existence at the margins of our humanity. For if their reluctantly accepted, in truth, commanded, prophetic vocation goes nowhere, the sacrifice the prophets endure seldom goes anywhere either. The prophets probe the depths of history and witness the endemic corruption of their people and life in general. Which way do the prophets turn to maintain their sanity? When they turn to God, they are reminded of their initial trauma. When they turn away from God, they are reminded of the trauma they cannot escape. The prophets are left in the middle, between traumas, as it were, with both breathing down their neck.

In the Bible, the prophets perform. How else could they spread the words God has given them to speak in the land and among the people who are purposely deaf? Sometimes that performance is God against God, as in Pharaoh's palace. Other times, it is Elijah organizing a competition of prophets to separate the true prophets from the false ones.

A tradition develops around these performances, so that it is recognizable in different eras. Combining music and pronouncements, Atzmon stands in a very long line of those who have performed the prophetic. The depth, the very essence, of Jewish history is defined by these performances. The performed prophetic is exploding on the world stage, once again, in our time.[10]

Unlike the ancient prophets, the biography of contemporary Jewish prophets is accessible. Yet we seem uninterested. Instead, we prefer the bullet points of their accusations against unjust power and the accusations leveled against them. Indeed, like the biblical prophets of old, the Jewish prophets of our day are outrageous. Still, beneath their rage is a tenderness that is infectious and that one day when justice is established might lead us to another realm of exploration.

Surprisingly, the performed prophetic of our time contains a final reversal and, from the perspective of the Jewish establishment, a fatal one. Many of the Still/Former Jewish/Israeli/Prophets have an attachment to the Promised Land, though they dare not call it that. It is an attachment to the land of Palestine—sometimes noted as such—from which they are exiled and to which they long to return, but not before justice is instituted. Not a moment beforehand.

After living in London for some time, Atzmon pines for home. The outrageous prophet feels homesick. Rather than missing Tel Aviv, Haifa, or Jerusalem, Atzmon misses Palestine. Atzmon can do without the "rude and loud Israeli taxi drivers at Ben-Gurion Airport, or grimy shopping centres in Ramat Gan." Instead, he misses the "little place in Yeffet Street, Jaffa that served the

10. I am grateful to Aaron Ellis for this insight into performing the prophetic. His thoughts have come to me via conversations and emails. The application of his insight is my own.

best hummus money can buy and the Palestinian villages stretched across the hills amidst olive trees and *sabra* cacti."[11]

Whenever he becomes homesick in London, Atzmon ends up on Edgware Road, at a Lebanese restaurant: "Once I started to fully express my thoughts about Israel in public, it soon became clear to me that Edgware Road was probably as a close as I could get to my homeland." Atzmon is homesick for a land that he and his parents, along with millions of other Israeli Jews, have systematically settled and occupied. And yet, in the rubble and between the overdeveloped spaces, Palestine continues to live on. Palestine is on the run everywhere. Palestine can be found everywhere. Atzmon's exile ends where Palestine, "my homeland," exists, in the land or on Edgware Road.[12]

Here is Atzmon, a self-declared anti-Zionist, who discards his Israeli citizenship and refuses to return home because of his opposition to Israel, but who still longs to return to his homeland, which is Palestine. The closest he can come to the real Palestine is in London among Diaspora Palestinians or among Lebanese, who are also in exile.

Hoping to return to where one comes from is profoundly human. Yet the question remains: Where does Atzmon come from? As a Jewish Israeli, does Atzmon really come from Palestine?

In truth, Atzmon comes from an Israel built on Palestine, a Palestine that Atzmon hardly knew as a child. Growing up in Israel, Palestine was all around him. It was also invisible to him. Nonetheless, in Atzmon's prose, Palestine, the foundation that Israel is built upon, is Atzmon's Promised Land.

Like Moses, though with a twist, Atzmon is constrained from entering the land. In London, he views Palestine only from a distance. His experience of Palestine is now limited to the Palestinian Diaspora. But, unlike Moses, Atzmon, having been born in the land, has already entered and left it because of what Jews have done to its native inhabitants. Atzmon refuses to return until the Promised Land is liberated from the modern-day Israelites. In short, Atzmon's homeland is occupied by Jews.

Here, too, Atzmon is performing the prophetic—in a modern context. Whereas, in ancient times, the biblical narrative has few qualms about the displacement the Israelites will cause upon entering the land, Atzmon has experienced its devastating and ongoing effects. Using justice as his guide, therefore, the land Atzmon was born into is his homeland that isn't.

Before the modern state of Israel, Palestine existed. The land belonged to someone else. After Israel, Palestine continues to exist. The land belongs to

11. Ibid., 8.
12. Ibid., 8-9.

someone else. Atzmon desires to return to his homeland when it is restored to its rightful heirs.

Atzmon brings to bear his conscience in order to reverse the biblical narrative—and the modern Israeli and Jewish narrative—that sanctions ethnic cleansing. It seems that he, with other Still/Former Jewish/Israeli/Prophets, leave the state of Israel as a protest against the origins of the people Israel as they are being replayed in their lifetimes. Perhaps their stand is subconsciously a desire to stand up and be counted now, where in the biblical times, the ancient Israelites were unwilling to do so.

In real life, there are rarely do-overs. But in the long arc of Jewish history, the creation of the state of Israel is as close as it gets. This is yet another indictment of the biblical prophetic tradition as it is employed today. Do the heirs of the prophets go far enough in their condemnation of state of Israel as it replicates ancient Israel's original sin? For the Jewish establishment they go way too far. For Jews of Conscience, as they survey their own journey, it seems they go as far as any Jew could. Nonetheless, Atzmon remains dissatisfied. Even the outrageous demands of the biblical prophets is hardly enough for Atzmon's conscience. No doubt, he goes too far. Atzmon also exaggerates his distance from other Jewish prophetic voices in our time. After all, the biblical prophets provided the people Israel with license in the land as it regarded the indigenous peoples while the Still/Former/Jewish/Israeli/Prophets employ a conscious reversal of the indigenous/colonial paradigm. They, too, attempt to destabilize the Jewish prophetic tradition in order to purify it.

Standing at a remove from an ancient tradition, yet still tethered to it, attempting to purify what was impure, the contemporary Jewish prophets reinvigorate the prophetic by removing elements of the tradition that are either tied to unjust power or make it more difficult for the prophetic to address injustice. This may be a way of addressing yet another issue with the prophetic call—the prophet's relation to God. Claiming God's call in the modern world is too often associated with a reactionary politics that promotes injustice. After all that has been said and done with God historically, claiming God's call, even for justice, lacks credibility. So if God is out in this more radical prophetic stream, another element of the ancient prophetic has to be addressed. The colonial sensibilities of the prophetic tradition have to be jettisoned.

Since they are among the first Jews since biblical times to return as a political entity and the first Jews since that time to ethnically cleanse others, it could be that Atzmon and other dissident Jews are attempting to right the original sin of the Jewish people, to which they are now modern-day accomplices. This continues the prophetic tradition while standing it on its head. For without the promise of the land and its counterpart, the pollution of the land, the center of the biblical prophetic collapses. But, then, the biblical prophets likewise collapsed and recreated the promises ancient Israel inherited.

With performance being at the heart of the prophetic, the audience is central. Justice themes can entertain an audience and even convince them. With God as an ally, the voice for justice becomes supernatural. With the supernatural behind its claims, it is hard to dismiss the prophetic outright. Today, by jettisoning the its colonial claims, the prophetic tradition once again becomes compelling.

Although there is dispute from the beginning about the prophetic, since Jews have always stood on both sides of the empire divide, the prophet's audience is now a global one. For the global audience, justice in the modern world cannot be argued unless colonialism is left behind. More, it has to be actively countered. This means that the Jewish prophetic is less isolated and more connected than it previously has been and that the sticking point—Jewish colonialism in the past and present—has to be confronted. Otherwise, the Jewish prophetic will be dismissed from the international discussion on Israel-Palestine. The stage from which to perform the prophetic will be diminished since without a non-Jewish audience, the Jewish prophetic will be left with only a Jewish, mostly dismissive and openly hostile, one. Here we enter yet another fascinating twist in the journey of the Jewish prophetic. Is the Jewish prophetic now largely dependent on a non-Jewish audience for its survival and flourishing?

Today, the indigenous quality of the Jewish prophetic is tested in diverse waters. In order to perform the prophetic, the Still/Former Jewish/Israeli/Prophets have to reorient biblical prophetic thought in order to keep the prophetic message alive. Beyond purifying the prophetic, however, the contemporary anticolonial prophetic critique of the state of Israel might function to reclaim Jewish distinctiveness in its most distinctive component, the prophetic. This signals yet another Jewish struggle to keep reappearing on the world stage. For if the Jewish prophetic becomes irrelevant, what future is there for Jews in history?[13]

Atzmon and the other Still/Former Jewish/Israeli/Prophets are also adding another level of conscience to the ancient prophets, in a scriptural sense, reading with and against the prophetic grain. They extend the range of the prophets to a colonial project that the prophets could see from a particular and defining

13. Without focusing on the prophetic per se, the postcolonial view of Santiago Slabodsky is interesting in this regard. See his *Decolonial Judaism: Triumphal Failures of Barbaric Thinking* (New York: Palgrave Macmillan, 2014).

angle—the promise made to slaves to create a society different than the one they left in Egypt. Like the biblical prophets, Atzmon signals that "Egypt" in the biblical narrative has returned once again to the land. But this time a simple return of Israelites/Jews will not do the trick. It is only by undoing the original biblical colonial project - one that now continues in modern-day Israel—that Jews can once again claim an ethics worthy of their history.

If the Holocaust is factored in the biblical thematic as an extreme form of modern-day slavery, as the Israelites were enslaved in Egypt, then the birth of the state of Israel can be understood as a necessary entry into the Promised Land. Historically, the prophets railed against the injustices within Israelite society once Israel was in the land. They predicted and sometimes accompanied the exile that occurred because of injustice and idolatry. Modern-day Israelis who leave Israel enter into a voluntary exile because of injustice, this time to another people. Absent God, idolatry is injustice. They have returned and choose exile because of the nature of that return.

Conscience trumps need and in the end raises another disturbing question: Is there a reason for a Jewish state, even to right the wrong of the Holocaust? Modern-day Jewish prophets raise the issue of the nature of empowerment itself. Is empowerment in a state for an ethnic or religious group in and of itself an injustice that exacerbates historical wrongs and the trauma that comes within history? Should the state of Israel, as a Jewish state, be judged at its foundations?[14]

After the Holocaust, the possibility of an unempowered Jewish community is alarming to many Jews. Without power, who will protect Jews when danger presents itself? De-Judaizing the state of Israel raises deep questions about the safety of Jews in the Middle East.

Here contemporary Jewish prophets stand in concert with the biblical prophets. In the end, when it came to justice and idolatry, whether Jews lived or died was immaterial to the biblical prophets. Condemnation led wherever it led. After the Holocaust, can the Jewish prophetic likewise be unconcerned about Jewish security?

---

14. This is where the question of the Palestinian right of return resonates. International law enshrines the Palestinian right to return to the land they were expelled from. If such a return occurred, the very possibility of Israel remaining a Jewish state would be diminished, if not eliminated. Jews of Conscience are split on this right as an efficacious principle. Nonetheless, the Palestinian right of return accompanies the expanding discussion of the founding of the state of Israel in 1948. For Jews who believe in this right see Jews for Palestinian Right of Return at https://www.facebook.com/test1960

The Conscience of Humanity

Conscience is the prophetic embodied. It combines justice and compassion.

Conscience is prophetic solidarity, which often as not leads to prophetic brokenness. When the hope for justice is denied, conscience is prophetic mourning.

Conscience is discerning how to act justly, compassionately, in solidarity. Conscience is broken and in mourning with others, practicing what the world needs, does not want, and cannot do without.

Conscience is the human condition stripped bare, dancing to a primal beat.

Conscience is the interruption of history—for conscience's sake. Conscience says: "It does not matter where progress, ideology, or religion wants to takes us; it cannot go here, cannot go this way. There is another way we can find together."

Conscience says: "The innocence that power trumpets is criminality in disguise."

Conscience tells us what the powers to be in politics, religion, and ideology seek to divert. Conscience tells us that the powers that be spend their money/influence/teaching/militaries informing us that our gut sense for justice is wrong, that conscience needs to be redirected or jettisoned altogether.

Conscience is the inability to refuse a justice task that would be easier to turn away from.

Conscience is the refusal to be bought when being bought is our security as injustice continues.

Conscience says: "Even when the going gets rough, it is better to stand firm, whatever the consequences. There is nothing in history worth the violation of conscience. Especially when the stakes are high and the rewards are great, move toward those who are suffering."

Conscience says: "Give heart, soul, and body. Put it all on the line. Despite the absurdity and injustice of life, testify that nevertheless there is meaning.

Finally, conscience is a witness; the prophetic will never die. This does not mean that the prophetic remains static, or that the people who claim the prophetic as their indigenous can rest easy. Just the opposite is the case.

Although there is an explosion of the Jewish prophetic in our time, the prophetic is also exploding around the world. Just as it is atrophying in large parts of the Jewish world, remnant prophetic Jews are connecting with others who embody the prophetic. In concert with Jews of Conscience, these prophetic others advise the Jewish community in Israel and America that the hour is late. They know one day the sun will set on the Jewish empire. They also know that there is a way back and a way forward in a new prophetic coalition.

The Israeli siege of Gaza is decades old, despite various strategies to break the siege. Over the years, a series of flotillas filled with people from around the world have sought entrance to Gaza. This effort exemplifies this prophetic coalition. On the one hand, non-Jews and Jews join hands. On the other hand, there has been a vigorous debate on the Jewish and Palestinian Left about whether parts of the flotilla movement retain some vestiges of the past negative relations between Jews and others.[15]

Embarking from various ports, the Gaza flotillas attempt to break the Israeli blockade of Gaza and deliver much-needed medical supplies to the people there. The needs are immediate but the hope is greater. The flotillas demand that Gaza be free so that its people can flourish. As well, the flotillas directly challenge Israeli power that restricts goods and movement in and out of Gaza.

These flotillas re-present the prophetic challenge to the state of Israel and to the Jewish people at large. As the prophetic is disciplined and punished within the Jewish community by Jewish authorities, the prophetic appears on the horizon. The prophetic comes from outside the Jewish community, as a witness to the prophetic destiny of the Jewish people that is being squandered.

In November 2011, two boats carrying medical supplies and humanitarian relief attempted to enter Gaza. Like other flotillas before them, this effort was interrupted by power. As the Canadian boat *Tahrir* ("Liberation") came closer to Gaza, it was hailed by the Israeli navy commander and ordered to relay their destination. Ehab Lotayef, a Canadian activist of Egyptian background on board the ship, replied: "The conscience of humanity." When the commander again demanded to know the ship's destination, Lotayef replied: "The betterment of mankind."[16]

On first hearing, one wonders what Lotayef was signaling. Was the boat itself—the mission of the activists—the conscience of humanity/the betterment of humankind? This would make sense. But the question posed by the Israeli commander was one of destination. Where is the boat intending to dock?

15. For an interesting take on this issue see Larry Defner, "Free Gaza Movement: Anti-Semitic video in question is 'disgusting,'" *972*, March 6, 2012. http://972mag.com/head-of-free-gaza-movement-anti-semitic-video-in-question-is-disgusting/57188/

16. For a report on the Gaza flotilla, see "A4. United Nations Human Rights Council (UNHRC), Report by International Fact-Finding Mission To Investigate The Israeli Attacks On The Humanitarian Aid Flotilla Bound For Gaza, Geneva, 27 September 2010 (Excerpts)," in *Journal of Palestine Studies* 40 (Winter 2011): 178-87. See the "Free Palestine" communique of November 4, 2011, http://bsnorrell.blogspot.com/search?q=Free palestine.

The conscience of humanity/the betterment of humankind could reside in Gaza, among the dispossessed Palestinians. If this is the case, the activists were approaching humanity's conscience and betterment. Or this attempt to encounter the Palestinian people of Gaza could itself embody the difficult passage of conscience and betterment.

The declarative statements—the conscience of humanity/the betterment of humankind—speak volumes. Those on the ship were uninterested in providing an academic discussion on conscience. Nor did they seek to score political points only. True, the conscience of humanity/the betterment of humankind are intensely political. However, the assertion is deeper, even primal.

Conscience is the foundation from which a politics can arise. Conscience is the pre-political, political, before and after politics. Conscience is our humanity lifted up. It defines who we are. It defines who we are not. Or, better, the practice of conscience and how that practice is structured defines who we are as individuals and communities. It defines what our religions and nationalities are truly about.

Conscience is a strike against empire wherever it is found, including within us. Conscience is the foundation of community. Those who inquire of the conscience's destination are often empire enablers. They wonder what kind of destination the conscience of humanity/the betterment of humankind can be, since that destination is not found on empire's map. For empire, the destination of conscience is literally otherworldly, without nautical or land coordinates. Empire defines such otherworldly sensibilities as pie-in-the-sky, utopian delusions.

The newspaper accounts do not report the Israeli commander's response. Nor do they gauge his internal sensibility. In another setting, the Israeli commander might even utter the same words, or upon hearing them, recognize immediately where they come from, as in "Yes, good—I see—the conscience of humanity/the betterment of humankind—continue on your journey. Safe voyage!"

There will always be empires. There will always be those who bring relief to those in need. The two forces meet in turbulent waters. But here is the variation relevant to the prophetic: in the case of the Gaza flotillas, the conscience of humanity/the betterment of humankind are being brought to the attention of Jews who have often embodied that very conscience and betterment as the Jewish indigenous.

Jews have embodied the prophetic through adversity. Jews have carried the prophetic by crossing borders and boundaries of every shape and size. Ironically, it is Jews today who create the borders and boundaries they once transgressed. Jews create barriers to keep the prophetic at bay. The boats coming to Gaza tell us of a sea change in Jewish life and in Jewish history, that the conscience of humanity/the betterment of humankind have fled the Jewish scene or, at best, they reside among a remnant—Jews who, with others, ply the seas.

The great victims of empire, Jews, are now the empire. Empire Jews call the shots. It is hardly a surprise that Jews find it more difficult to locate the coordinates of conscience and betterment. Empire Jews have lost their own navigational instruments. In so doing, the Jewish community has lost its way.

In the death camps, most Jews did not speak German. They did not understand the language of the Nazi oppressor. Today, many Jews are losing their own language ability. They have difficulty understanding the language of conscience and betterment. Perhaps Jews retain that language ability on their own terms, so that when it applies to feminism or civil rights and religious liberty in America, Jews are there. When it comes to Palestine, however, their ability wanes. Because where Jews stand on Israel/Palestine is central to Jewish identity, the key that unlocks other issues of importance, the community's liberal stand on the other issues only serves as a deflection from this central issue.

Mainstream Jews think they are for justice, that they remain the conscience of humanity. The betterment of humankind is their credo. Yet the permanent occupation of another people's land makes this claim suspect. Armed with empire, such claim becomes an obvious hypocrisy.

The Jewish establishment asks: "How can you question our commitment? Isn't your commitment for the Palestinians some kind of twisted logic that sees our liberation in a Jewish state as a stain upon our character and a challenge to our justice?" The language that carries conscience and human betterment is always contested. Should we expect less when it comes to Jews and Jewish empowerment?

Over the years on these boats to Gaza there have been people of different faiths and secular folks, including Jews. There have even been boats where only Israeli and Diaspora Jews were present as a signifier that Jews are challenging Jewish empire and posing this question of questions: What does it mean to be Jewish? Which raises the question: What does it mean to be Christian, to be Muslim, to be modern? Since belief in modernity as the ultimate reality is also a religion, this issue may be the most important one of all. When we add the United States, Europe, and other entities that have geopolitical interests in the Middle East to the world religions, the Gaza flotillas pose the issue of conscience and betterment across the board.

Perhaps it is time to declare that the prophetic is wherever it is. That the prophetic has gone global. Having understood the global nature of the prophetic, it is also true that much of that global prophetic meets in Israel-Palestine. Is this a coincidence or does it once again testify to the centrality and connection of Jewish prophetic to the global prophetic?

Though this is rarely discussed it seems that a global unconscious is oriented in this direction. Otherwise, why is the world, including the voices of dissent, so focused on this small area of the world? The Jewish establishment see this focus on Israel-Palestine as a form of antisemitism but what is at stake is the ancient Jewish prophetic and its bonding with prophetic movements around the world. Along with the focus on Israel-Palestine, is it this prophetic bonding and the subversive power it portends that frightens the Jewish establishment?

Why, then, worry about the prophetic specific Jewish dimensions? Does endlessly parsing the Jewish empire divide go anywhere? Since the larger concern is the new and most powerful world religion of all—modernity—and the integration of the global prophetic, the Jewish prophetic question may be neither here nor there.

The more relevant subject is whether the prophetic, Jewish or otherwise, is up to the modern task and whether the prophetic of any and all stripes can successfully confront the empires of the world. Do empires wherever they are, whatever flag they fly, whatever religion they carry along for the ride, care where the prophetic emanates from if it lacks sufficient power to makes its voice heard?

The Jewish prophetic has indeed gone global. Jews/jews have as well. The task for every individual and community, religion and nationality, is to re-present the prophetic by embodying it. In this way, individuals and communities are confronted with the prophetic.

Although the prophetic is indigenous to Jewish life, within every culture, profession, religion, and ideology there is a prophetic core. Think of the prophetic core of the professions, medicine, education, and law as examples. Consider architecture and the arts. All are designed to serve humanity, with special attention to those on the margins of society. Yet how often a fundamental perversion occurs; instead of serving humanity, the professions are pressed into serving empire entities that exist to serve the powerful.

When President Dwight Eisenhower spoke prophetically of the military-industrial complex, he only touched one aspect of the problem that looms larger today than ever before. Think of the medicine-industrial complex, the agricultural-industrial complex, and the education-industrial complex. Now think of the information-industrial complex and its National Security

Administration global spying annex. There is a thin line between the prophetic and its perversion. The issue for the prophetic is what it says to these various industrial complexes that are more and more remote from our humanity.[17]

The prophetic is usually thought of as being outside, as in the restitution of land, fairness in the workplace, justice where there is injustice. We tend to see the prophetic—outward. As importantly, the prophetic is within all of us and at the heart of every human endeavor. Take medicine back—for those who need healing. Take architecture back—for a human scale of life and for the homeless. Take farming back—for the production of food, for sustainability, and for the hungry. Take education back—for the formation of life and society. All have to be taken back on the systemic level, to be sure. But can they ever be taken back without an intense ethical and spiritual refocusing as well? Railing against the machine is essential yet hardly enough. The prophetic has to look outward and inward at the same time. Without an inward turning, how will the prophetic community deal with the decades of failure that stretch into the distance?

There is no end to the prophetic within. Nor is there an end to the perversion of the prophetic toward greed and power. The prophetic is a continual engagement with possibility and its perversion. The Jewish struggle with Jews on both sides of the empire divide may simply be the root of the worldwide struggle with the empire divide. If this is the case, it is difficult to see how there can be a conscience divide. It is doubtful that conscience can itself be divided between Jews and others. Can conscience be partitioned between Jews and non-Jews or any other of the various identity divisions that have existed or exist today in world history?

The prophetic imperative of our globalized world may well signal the closing phase of particular identities themselves, at least as we have known and inherited them. Global issues like climate change and war are too massive to be divided among diverse groups, each one arguing how distinctive they are. Global systems simply use these various identities against each other. Divide and conquer is the strategy. The challenge is how to divide and conquer systems that run roughshod over people who are enslaved by these very systems.

This global challenge arrives as normative Jewish ethics are in deep decline. However, there may be more at play here. Historic identity formations all over the world are self-segregating into opposing forces. There are numerous identity civil wars in play. Empire divides exist in Islam and Christianity, in Hinduism, among many nationalities, even in modernity itself. It seems that

---

17. For a fascinating revisioning of Eisenhower and his views, see Evan Thomas, *Ike's Bluff: President Eisenhower's Secret Battle to Save the World* (Boston: Little, Brown, 2012).

the extremes of uneven development, systemic injustice and climate change are forcing a human reckoning unknown before in history.

The destination of the *Tahrir* relates to the Arab struggle, specifically the uprising in Egypt and its ongoing effects. Like the boat's journey, the Arab Spring's heyday was short lived. At the same time, another Spring phenomena, the Occupy movement, had burst onto the scene especially in the United States, eventually to slow and go underground. Both became stuck between prophetic hope and empire power.

When the *Tahrir* departed, the prophetic was on the move. When it was intercepted and boarded, empire seemed immovable. This was the plight of the Jewish prophetic writ large, though now inverted. The *Tahrir* was bringing the prophetic message home to Jews and Jewish power. It was intercepted by the Jewish powers that be. But so was the Jewish boat, *Irene*. It was bringing the same message. It was boarded by the same navy. Did it matter to the Israeli Navy how those boats identified?

Is the fate of the prophetic to be outside the gates of power boarded and escorted by the empire's navy? Empire thinks that the future is theirs. Often it seems that way. Even changes that appear responsive to prophetic criticism can be window dressing. Egyptians in Tahrir Square toppled Hosni Mubarak, but the army and the Egyptian elite have regained their footing. Even with changing faces, the solidity of empire is much in evidence. If anything the situation in Egypt is worse than it was before the Arab Spring. This leads to a cynicism about struggles for justice. What follows is an overestimation of empire's power and longevity. This leads to apathy. Empire power remains. Why struggle against them?

This is true in the seemingly endless game of brokering Middle East peace. What appears to be an advance, say the Oslo Accords in 1993, decades later leads to a worse fragmentation of Palestine, with a deepening Judaization of East Jerusalem and hundreds of thousands more Israeli settlers in the West Bank. The 2013-2014 peace process is the same, with frameworks of principles offered and accepted or not, with caveats on every issue. Meanwhile the expansion of Israel and ghettoization of the Palestinians continues apace.

Prophetic tactics include playing an insistent waiting game. Banging on empire's doors continues even as agreements are offered and the empire changes the faces of those in power. Initially, changing faces engenders hope. Some who had been on the outside come forward with the best of intentions. Others come forward to cash in. The prophetic weighs the scales. Even in the bleakest of situations, where are the opportunities to move forward? When does opportunity become assimilation to power?

The prophetic is constantly in danger of being seduced. What are the resources that will guide the Jewish prophetic as the ethical tradition of Jewish life becomes more distant? What will guide the universal prophetic as it struggles to help keep its eyes and mind open to the thin line that divides real and illusory change?

Israel-Palestine has its own particularities. Yet it is also ripe with universals coming from a world concern for Jerusalem. It is almost cliché to state that Israel-Palestine has an importance well beyond its size and location. Much of its importance derives from a symbolism inhering in Judaism, Christianity, and Islam. One can debate how that symbolism works and whether the exaggeration of Jerusalem makes it more difficult to live and flourish there. With so many real and presumed stakeholders of Jerusalem, irrational expectations and exaggerated importance burdens the city's history.

Because of this history, something well beyond the ordinary surrounds the future of Israel-Palestine. If peace with justice finds root there, other divisions in the world may be addressed more forthrightly.

Prophetic Shock Doctrine

This at least is the hope. Today the prophetic is more than Jewish. The prophetic is not only universal. The prophetic requires diverse resources of thought, politics, culture and theology that subvert and construct identities for justice making.

The prophetic needs constant nourishment and replenishment. It has to be kept honest to its own essence. More than ever, the intense interaction of the diversity of the prophetic is crucial to this task. Embracing people from different backgrounds and geographic locations who embody the brokenness and possibility of their particular histories may itself be prophetic. How can we hope to build bridges across the empire divide if the prophetic movements of the world have not already experienced the difficult struggle of embodying the diverse prophetic alive in the world?

The challenge is to deepen our particularity as we embrace others so that the universal in the particular is strengthened. Building bridges is less about abandoning where we come from than it is welcoming others into our lives and crossing the boundaries of others with respect and humility. Sharing the experience of suffering of others is crucial; it deepens our sensitivities and refuses the mobilization of one suffering against others. Sharing the possibility inherent in diverse identity formations enhances our own.

In sharing suffering and possibility we enter into a larger community and a broader tradition. While there is our own tradition of faith and struggle there is a broader one as well. Building bridges to one another, we enter a broader global tradition of faith and struggle. This tradition hardly promises victory. Often what is shared is an exile that deepens as the years pass. But, then, exile too has an extra dimension. We are not alone.

In this regard, two interesting Jewish bridge builders come to mind. The first is the Jewish Canadian political activist, Naomi Klein, whose books *No Logo* and *Shock Doctrine* provocatively engage the international globalization debate. *Shock Doctrine* especially has sparked debate about global capitalism and its response to natural and human-initiated disasters, what Klein terms "Disaster Capitalism." Klein claims that global capitalism increasingly uses disasters like September 11th, Hurricane Katrina, and the Southeast Asian tsunami to secure resources and penetrate markets.[18]

Kline analyzes the economic shock therapy that is applied to disaster areas in the wake of the public's disorientation as well as the weakness of governing authorities. Unfortunately, it is applied for the benefit of the few rather than reconstruction for the many. For example, in the wake of September 11th, the "War on Terror" benefited corporations like Haliburton and Blackwater. In the aftermath of Hurricane Katrina, public housing, hospitals, and schools were either destroyed or privatized. After the Southeast Asian tsunami, beaches were auctioned off to international tourist resorts. The 2010 earthquake in Haiti and 2013 Typhoon Yolanda in the Philippines may prove to be still other cases where natural disaster allows for military advancement, international profiteering and even expanded funding opportunities for NGO's that may or may not work to help the people struggling to rebuild their lives.

The shock doctrine, though dominated by economic motivations, is also promoted through military intervention and abusive paramilitary and police tactics. Here Klein analyzes how industries economically benefit from war. Klein cites the wars in Iraq and Afghanistan as two cases in point. In Klein's view, Disaster Capitalism increasingly functions as a form of domination within the United States and outside of it. Disaster Capitalism is disguised in forms of relief from natural disaster and toppled dictatorships. Thus relief involves financial profit more than service to others, while war is a thinly veiled economic grab bag.

18. Naomi Klein, *No Logo: Tenth Anniversary Edition* (New York: Picador, 2009); idem, *The Shock Doctrine: The Rise of Disaster Capitalism* (New York: Picador, 2008). On Haiti see Kathie Klarreich and Linda Polman, "The NGO Republic of Haiti, *Nation*, November 19, 2012. http://www.thenation.com/article/170929/ngo-republic-haiti#

Klein believes these disguises must be unmasked. Klein traces other interesting themes related to Disaster Capitalism, from Milton Friedman's and the Chicago School's economic theories and influence, to the CIA-funded experiments in electroshock and sensory deprivation in the 1950s. The latter informed the torture manuals the CIA used after September 11th.

In her writings about global capitalism, Klein rarely mentions her Jewish background. Born in Montreal, Klein's family has a history of peace activism. Originally Americans, her parents moved to Montreal in 1967 as resistors to the Vietnam War. Klein's paternal grandparents were communists, so her father's youth was surrounded by ideas of social justice and racial equality. Klein's father is a physician and a member of Physicians for Social Responsibility. Her mother is a documentary filmmaker best known for her anti-pornography film *Not a Love Story*.

The *Shock Doctrine* is about global economics and politics. Within the global, Klein has a chapter on Israel, especially as it benefited politically and economically in the aftermath of September 11th and the subsequent War on Terror. However, Klein analyzes the 1993 Oslo Accords, ostensibly an attempt to finalize peace between Israel and a new Palestinian state, as an opening for Israel to increase its exports to Palestinian society as well as relegate Palestinians to a cheap labor pool.

According to Klein, Israel capitalized on the September 11th moment in several ways. Citing security needs, Israel built the Wall around Palestinians in parts of Jerusalem and the West Bank. One of the benefits of the Wall was to confine Palestinians to certain geographic population centers. A ripple effect followed, which included the importation of cheap foreign workers to ease the resulting labor shortage. In the same time frame, the immigration of Soviet Jews swelled Israel's Jewish and European population. This provided a bulwark against expanding Palestinian demographics by diversifying Israel's cheap labor pool and enlarging its Jewish population. As important, after September 11th, Israel began to export homeland-security technologies to nations around the world. In the process, Israel became a "shopping mall" for homeland security technologies.[19]

In a world where instability is profitable and advanced nations attempt to cash in on disasters and turmoil, Klein believes that "Israel has crafted an economy that expands markedly in direct response to escalating violence." For Klein, Israel is "Exhibit A" of Disaster Capitalism and functions as a "stark

---

19. The following analysis is taken from Klein's chapter on Israel "Losing the Peace Incentive: Israel as Warning," in *Shock Doctrine*, 423-442.

warning" for the future: "The fact that Israel continues to enjoy booming prosperity, even as it wages war against its neighbors and escalates the brutality in the occupied territories, demonstrates just how perilous it is to build an economy based on the premise of continual war and deepening disasters." At the same time, Israel models what society comes to looks like when economic incentives for peace are lost and instead heavily "invests in fighting and profiting from an endless and unwinnable War on Terror."[20]

According to Klein, one part of this model looks like Israel, the other part looks like Gaza. Klein writes that as the South African, Russian, and New Orleans rich build walls around themselves, Israel has taken this "disposal process a step further: it has built walls around the dangerous poor."[21] The consequences of Israel's adopting Disaster Capitalism are immense. In the short term, Klein sees a political and economic victory for Israel, but her long-term predictions are more sanguine. Klein cites the deepening and debilitating economic and political divisions within Israel itself as a long-run threat to its vision of itself and its own stability. After all, thriving on economic and political discord carries the seeds of internal division and self-inflicted disaster.

For the Palestinians, Israel's Disaster Capitalism is both an immediate and long-term catastrophe. Since Israel thrives on continuing conflict, any prospect for a real and just settlement of the Israeli-Palestinian crisis is placed on hold. Politics aside, it is not in Israel's economic interest to end its domination of Palestinians. In a substantial sense, Israel's economy and society have become dependent on Disaster Capitalism. Meanwhile, the increasingly necessary occupation of Palestine grows stronger. For Klein, the future has already arrived. The West Bank and Gaza have been transformed into Israel's economic fiefdom. But, then, Israel has itself been transformed into an exemplar of the practice of Disaster Capitalism.

Several years after publishing *The Shock Doctrine*, Klein responded to the Palestinian call to support the movement of boycott, sanctions, and divestment (BDS) against Israel. As in her book, Klein called for action against Israel in relation to the global order and the flourishing of Disaster Capitalism. She also cited the example of apartheid South Africa as a model for her actions in relation to Israel. If apartheid South Africa was boycotted, why not Israel?

In her public speaking and writing, Klein plays down her Jewishness and her specific connection to Israel. Nor does she counsel any special pleading on Israel's behalf. However, Klein does note her hesitation and hesitation of other Jews to speak critically of Israel. Speaking and writing during the Israel invasion

20. Ibid.,428, 430.
21. Ibid., 442.

of Gaza in 2008, she felt the moment urgent. Her title says it all: "Enough: It's Time for a Boycott":

It's time. Long past time. The best strategy to end the increasingly bloody occupation is for Israel to become the target of the kind of global movement that put an end to apartheid in South Africa. In July 2005 a huge coalition of Palestinian groups laid out plans to do just that. They called on "people of conscience all over the world to impose broad boycotts and implement divestment initiatives against Israel similar to those applied to South Africa in the apartheid era". The campaign Boycott, Divestment and Sanctions was born.

Every day that Israel pounds Gaza brings more converts to the BDS cause—even among Israeli Jews. In the midst of the assault roughly 500 Israelis, dozens of them well-known artists and scholars, sent a letter to foreign ambassadors in Israel. It calls for "the adoption of immediate restrictive measures and sanctions" and draws a clear parallel with the anti-apartheid struggle. "The boycott on South Africa was effective, but Israel is handled with kid gloves. . . . This international backing must stop."

Yet even in the face of these clear calls, many of us still can't go there. The reasons are complex, emotional and understandable. But they simply aren't good enough. Economic sanctions are the most effective tool in the non-violent arsenal: surrendering them verges on active complicity.[22]

To the objections of others, Klein suggests that other tactics, including "constructive engagement," have been tried, and they failed. Citing her positions outlined in her book, Klein continues:

The world has tried what used to be called "constructive engagement". It has failed utterly. Since 2006 Israel has been steadily escalating its criminality: expanding settlements, launching an outrageous war against Lebanon, and imposing collective punishment on Gaza through the brutal blockade. Despite this

22. Naomi Klein, "Enough: It's Time for a Boycott," *The Guardian*, January 10, 2009. This statement is reprinted in Audrea Lim, ed., *The Case for Sanctions Against Israel* (Brooklyn: Verso, 2012), 175–78.

escalation, Israel has not faced punitive measures—quite the opposite. The weapons and $3bn in annual aid the US sends Israel are only the beginning. Throughout this key period, Israel has enjoyed a dramatic improvement in its diplomatic, cultural and trade relations with a variety of other allies. For instance, in 2007 Israel became the first country outside Latin America to sign a free-trade deal with the Mercosur bloc. In the first nine months of 2008, Israeli exports to Canada went up 45%. A new deal with the EU is set to double Israel's exports of processed food. And in December European ministers "upgraded" the EU-Israel association agreement, a reward long sought by Jerusalem.

It is in the context of economic reward that Klein believes Israeli leaders started the war on Gaza. Since Israel was confident that they would face no meaningful costs, why not pursue its policies of Disaster Capitalism? Indeed, Klein cites statistics that show that over seven days of wartime trading, the Tel Aviv Stock Exchange's index went up 10.7 percent.

"When carrots don't work sticks are needed," Klein writes. Strong calculation rather than emotion is needed. Details, applicable in any situation, are provided. Universal norms are applied to particular situations. In the end, they override special considerations. Importantly, Klein refuses even to catalogue the considerations she is now overriding, specifically her Jewish background. Is that because she no longer believes there are reasons to justify overriding justice-seeking, including her Jewishness? Is she simply stating the obvious so as to deflect criticism that might come her way? Or are the Jewish considerations her own but no longer arguable since the situation has become so dire?

Perhaps Klein is silent on what these "understandable" considerations are because it is too offensive to Palestinians who are suffering. It might also be generational, though Klein was born soon after the 1967 war. Growing up in a family with liberal Left leanings, Klein was oriented toward justice through human and Jewish considerations. Was Klein's family among the minority of Jews who consciously avoided the shift into the Holocaust/Israel modality that swept the Jewish world after the 1967 war? Or has Klein's exposure to the world scene, with her vaunted place as a critic of capitalism, left her little option but to speak on Israel-Palestine?

Shifting global discourse winds have made it more difficult for Jews to plead special consideration for Israel. This may give Jewish thinkers like Klein a freedom to express their frustration with Israel that would be more problematic without the international pressure. As well, "enough" may come from the place where Jewish identity and universal human rights intersect. Increasingly, Jews have to choose in which direction they will move. More and more, dissident Jews move from particularity toward universal human rights. In the present situation, Jews of Conscience have little choice.

Despite reservations, Klein has had enough. Klein writes succinctly that it is a "kind of cold business calculation that led many companies to pull out of South Africa two decades ago. And it's precisely the kind of calculation that is our most realistic hope of bringing justice, so long denied, to Palestine." She may also be naming the reason that she is over any Jewish reservation that holds her back from speaking truth to power—cold calculation. Notice that the usual disclaimer, that justice for Palestinians is crucial to save the Jewish soul or Jewish ethics, is absent. When "Jewish" appears in her work, Klein references Israeli activists, more or less like any activists working against an injustice in their society.

If the Israeli occupation of Palestinians is similar, perhaps worse, than apartheid South Africa was, are Israelis just like South African whites? In apartheid South Africa, the majority of whites enabled apartheid while a minority opposed it. Is Israeli society split in the same way, with Jews on both sides of the empire divide?

Thus, as in South Africa, in Israel the struggle is against the Jewish majority and the government that enables apartheid. Klein has been silent on this issue. Does she support, as she did in South Africa, the transformation of Israeli society into a democracy—one person, one vote? If this was extended to Palestinians in Jerusalem, the West Bank, and Gaza, the voting franchise might ultimately result in one state for Jews and Palestinians. Klein is silent on the one-state option or more accurately is adamant that she refuses to advocate any particular outcome of the Israeli–Palestinian conflict.[23]

The second bridge builder is the feminist poet Adrienne Rich, who died in 2012. Born of an assimilated "cultural" Jewish father and a religiously devout Episcopalian mother, Rich was baptized into the Christian faith as a youngster. Writing at the time of her death, Ryan Harper says that in her adulthood Rich became sensitive to the "subterranean presences and conspicuous absences of Jewishness in the home of her upbringing." It was during this time that Rich

---

23. For her refusal to take a stand on the issue of one-state/two-states see Philip Weiss, "Naomi Klein calls out an Israeli think tank for misrepresenting her views," *Mondoweiss*, March 14, 2010 http://mondoweiss.net/2010/03/israeli-thinktanker-says-naomi-klein-is-working-in-tandem-with-hizbullah-and-iran.html

chose to be Jewish. She realized her Jewishness would always be her choice as an "irresistible inheritance."[24]

Harper describes Rich's Jewishness as a dynamic interaction of the particular and the universal. "As a Jew, Rich claimed and was claimed by a vast, often internally-dissident tradition (she had the advantage of wrestling with a tradition that had wrestling in its marrow)," Harper writes. "She also insisted upon claiming and being claimed by a wider birthright than that tradition sometimes allowed." In Harper's analysis, Rich knew she had to claim her Jewish particularity because, whether she liked it or not, Jewishness was claimed her. For Rich becoming Jew meant being someone and not being someone else.

Rich lived with the "hope that, paradoxically, she could find something expansive in the particularity—something inside Jewish tradition that operated against that same tradition's more troubling parochialisms, something that connected her to all of humanity." That is why Rich proudly joined the time-honored tradition of being a non-Jewish Jew.

What did Rich mean by so identifying? In her own words, a non-Jewish Jew is not a Jew "trying to pass, deny or escape from the wounds and fears of the community." Rather, a Jew is "resistant to dogma, to separation, to 'remembering instead of thinking,' in Nadine Gordimer's words—anything that shuts down the music of the future—a Jew whose solidarity with the exiled and the persecuted is unrestricted. A Jew without borders."[25]

As a Jew without borders, Rich lived her life as a person bound by roots that expanded to include the world. If her roots cut her off from the wider world, she trimmed them. If the wider world tried to absorb her Jewishness, she resisted. As a Jew, she was non-Jewish. As a citizen of the world, she was distinctly Jewish. The interplay fascinated her. It also formed her distinctive witness to the world.

Rich's support for BDS combined the particular and universal. The title of her statement of support was phrased as a question: "Why Support the U. S. Campaign for the Academic and Cultural Boycott of Israel?":

Last week, with initial hesitation but finally strong conviction, I endorsed the Call for a U. S. Cultural and Academic Boycott of

24. Ryan Harper, "Split at the Roots: Adrienne Rich and (Religious) Identity," *Religion Dispatches*, April 3, 2012, www.religiondispatches.org/archive/culture/5852/.

25. Adrienne Rich, "Jewish Days and Jewish Nights," in *Wrestling With Zion: Progressive Jewish-American Responses to the Israeli-Palestinian Conflict*, ed. Tony Kushner and Alisa Solomon (New York: Grove, 2003), 165.

Israel. I'd like to offer my reasons to friends, family and comrades. I have tried in fullest conscience to think this through.

My hesitation: I profoundly believe in the visible/invisible liberatory social power of creative and intellectual boundary-crossings. I've been educated by these all my life, and by centuries-long cross-conversations about human freedom, justice and power—also, the forces that try to silence them.

As an American Jew, over almost 30 years, I've joined with other concerned Jews in various kinds of coalition-building and anti-Occupation work. I've seen the kinds of organized efforts to stifle—in the US and elsewhere—critiques of Israel's policies—the Occupation's denial of Palestinian humanity, destruction of Palestinian lives and livelihoods, the "settlements," the state's physical and psychological walls against dialogue—and the efforts to condemn any critiques as antisemitism. Along with other activists and writers I've been named on right-wing "shit-lists" as "Israel-hating" or "Jew-hating." I have also seen attacks within American academia and media on Arab American, Muslim, Jewish scholars and teachers whose work critically explores the foundations and practices of Israeli state and society.

Until now, as a believer in boundary-crossings, I would not have endorsed a cultural and academic boycott. But Israel's continuing, annihilative assaults in Gaza and the one-sided rationalizations for them have driven me to re-examine my thoughts about cultural exchanges. Israel's blockading of information, compassionate aid, international witness and free cultural and scholarly expression has become extreme and morally stone-blind. Israeli Arab parties have been banned from the elections, Israeli Jewish dissidents arrested, Israeli youth imprisoned for conscientious refusal of military service. Academic institutions are surely only relative sites of power. But they are, in their funding and governance, implicated with state economic and military power. And US media, institutions and official policy have gone along with all this.

To boycott a repressive military state should not mean backing away from individuals struggling against the policies of that state. So, in continued solidarity with the Palestinian people's long resistance, and also with those Israeli activists, teachers, students, artists, writers, intellectuals, journalists, refuseniks, feminists and others who oppose the means and ends of the Occupation, I have signed my name to this call.[26]

Rich's language is similar to Klein's, though in some ways it is harsher; her reference to Israel as a "repressive military state" is startling. For years, Rich worked with anti-occupation activists, but she is silent on the possibility that her condemnation of Israeli policies would have come earlier absent her Jewish identification. Rich identifies as a Jew in her call to action. Whether she does this to enhance her credentials to speak on this issue or it is important for her to self-identify as a Jew in her dissent is difficult to discern.

Is this the combination of the particular and universal that might become, or perhaps has already become, the future of the universalizing Jewish prophetic? In Rich, Daniel's Jewish prison is affirmed as an opening to the universal prophetic. Or, rather, the universal prophetic is so rooted in her Jewishness that Rich repudiates any assent on the universal scene without it having prophetic content.

Rich's Jewish particularity is the caldron out of which arises her universal affirmation. Thus, contra Daniel, Rich's Jewish prison roots and liberates her to be for others. Daniel's terminology and claim is inverted as Rich, in her own freely chosen way, affirms the Jewish (Prophetic) Prison.

Rich signs on to the boycott because of her critical embrace of Jewishness and her commitment to universal values. Her rooting in Jewishness is hardly accidental or ancillary. Being bound as a Jew is also her freedom to argue for humanity. For Rich, there is no contradiction between the two. Although Harper's essay on Rich is titled "Split at the Roots," it might be more accurate to define Rich as joined at the roots. Her roots were Jewish and human.

If Rich's Jewishness was an irresistible inheritance, she also chose to be Jewish. Looking at the rates of intermarriage and the ease of choosing identity in modern culture, Rich embodies the future of choosing the Jewish prophetic. But the choice will be made in light of the universal prophetic, rooting it in a particular prophetic, because, through birth or contact, a person is drawn that way.

Certainly, the future of the Jewish prophetic cannot be assumed within the norms of a Jewish identity that both looks askance at claiming Jewishness and its particular take on the prophetic and instead stresses only the universal. Rich's process may be similar for people from different religious and nonreligious

26. Adrienne Rich, "Why Support the U. S. Campaign for the Academic and Cultural Boycott of Israel?" *MRzine*, August 2, 2009, http://mrzine.monthlyreview.org/2009/rich080209.html.

backgrounds who may choose either the universal prophetic in and of itself or the universal prophetic through a rooting in a particular tradition.

The universal theme is furthered in Rich's declaration about freedom, censorship, and justice, which does not reference anything specifically Jewish at all. As a poet and a thinker, Rich's thought and feelings are multilayered. Her lesbian and feminist self-identification is also central to her reflections. It may be that these latter affiliations, being cross-cultural and cross-religious, help balance and even enhance her universal outreach, as when he writes: "When a woman tells the truth she is creating the possibilities of more truth around her."[27]

"A woman tells the truth." As with her Jewishness, Rich employs women as a particularity that reaches out to embrace others. Telling the truth to each other broadens the truth about women's experiences and, through their interaction with men, expands truth in the larger world. By enlarging the truth about women, truth about men also increases. It seems that, for Rich, ultimately the truth become truths. Truths move across female/male lines and works its way between women and between men and, then, among both.

Women as a particularity, with men, like Jews, stand on both sides of empire divide. Jewish and non-Jewish women on Rich's side of the empire divide stand together—with men who take a similar stand. Jewish and non-Jewish women, with Jewish and non-Jewish men, who stand on the other side of the empire divide, are also together. Perhaps this cross-boundary truth telling allows Rich to call for the boycott of Israel in stark language—as a repressive military state—without special pleading. Rich's Jewish, lesbian, and feminist identifications interact and deepen each other.

Her emphasis on truth telling leads Rich to an intense probing of censorship and freedom. For Rich, deprivation of knowledge within and across boundaries limits the depth of our rootedness and the reach of our universality. By restricting our search for truth, Rich believes that anything about everything is fair game. Without the freedom and knowledge to explore, how can we speak and share the truth which creates more truth around us? Rich writes poignantly: "Whatever is unnamed, undepicted in images, whatever is omitted from biography, censored in collections of letters, whatever is misnamed as something else, made difficult to come by, whatever is buried in the memory by the collapse of meaning under an inadequate or lying language—this will become, not merely unspoken, but unspeakable."[28]

27. Adrienne Rich, "Women and Honor: Some Notes on Lying (1975)," in *Adrienne Rich's Poetry and Prose: Poems, Prose, Reviews, and Critics*, ed. Charlesworth Gelpi and Albert Gelpi (New York: Norton, 1975), 200.

"Whatever is unnamed"–Rich lays out the foundation of the global prophetic. In the struggle to name the unnamed, no particular identity or route is laid out. How the unnamed becomes named in any particular culture or religion is honored. The contribution to the larger task of naming the unnamed is important and the particular route may have its importance, too. Yet that importance rests in the reminder that struggling to name the unnamable is shared across communities. It is only with that sharing that the unspeakable can become speakable.

Rich's statement ranges widely. Her prophetic thought encompasses our personal lives, but also includes history, economy, politics, religion, and national life. If one paraphrases and adds to her thought in terms of Jewishness, Rich's words move toward Jewish and/or universal: "Whatever is unnamed in Jewish life, undepicted in Jewish images, whatever is omitted from Jewish biography, censored in collections of Jewish letters, whatever is misnamed Jewish as something else, made difficult to come by, whatever is buried in Jewish memory by the collapse of meaning under an inadequate or lying language about Jews, Judaism and Israel—this will become, not merely unspoken, but unspeakable." The thrust of this paraphrase leads directly to the state of Israel. Whatever is unnamed or undepicted in Israel's history becomes "not merely unspoken but unspeakable."

Substitute other nations, the United States or France for example, and one sees how truth telling multiplies. For Rich, the prophetic is the concrete application of surfacing what is undepicted and unnamed. Rich's prophetic gets to the bottom of personal, institutional, religious, and national hypocrisy, where half-truths, and lies are the norm. No individual, concept, ideology, or flag can undergo Rich's rigorous examination and remain unscathed.

Rich's call for truth telling is seductive in its radicality. So incisive is Rich's language that it remains doubtful anyone, even the one who calls for it, can survive the result. The collapse of meaning Rich surfaces is the same collapse that leaves the truth unspoken and unspeakable. Indeed, the possibility of meaning may collapse under radical truth telling—that is, if we can get to the truth and speak it when we do.

Meaning is negotiated rather than posited. It is constantly threatened with collapse. This is the case when the truth is unspoken and when it is spoken. Since meaning is constructed, the threat of collapse is ever present. Meaning is a faith which asserts or holds fast to the hope that deconstructing every lacuna

---

28. Adrienne Rich, "It Is the Lesbian Within Us...." *On Lies, Secrets, and Silence: Selected Prose* (New York: Norton, 1995), 199.

in narrative, theology, and politics leads to more truth. Is this the essential faith of the prophet?

The defenders of withholding truth consider truth too vulnerable for the individual and society to withstand it. This is another way of viewing the two sides of the empire divide: those who believe that truth has to be withheld and those who believe that, no matter the consequences, truth must be told.

Paraphrasing and making Rich's imagery more specific is almost without limit. In Rich, we may have the major contribution of the Jewish prophetic. Although the prophetic is bound to a specific Jewish history, its universal applications and universalizing potential seem infinite. Still, there are a series of gambles inherent in Rich's evocation of the prophetic, most obviously, that there is truth or, in Rich's vision, more truth. Further, that more truth is available, it can be shared, and somehow individuals and peoples can embrace that availability/sharing in a life-enhancing way.

Rich's first gamble has to do with the prophetic we have already surveyed—that the instability at the heart of Jewish life, which paradoxically is its stability, is possible as a personal and communal foundation for others. Rich extends her gamble. She seems to believe that the instability at the heart of Jewish life is the instability at the heart of life itself. If this is the case, then a transcultural, transreligious, and transnational coalition can embrace prophetic instability at its very core.

Rich's second gamble relates again to instability. Instability is at the heart of the people Israel. It is also a chief characteristic of Israel's God. For Rich, truth, especially more truth, seems to be a substitute for God. Or is "more truth" Rich's name for God? Since Jews and non-Jews on the empire side of the empire divide desire a stable truth in life and a stable God which affirms that truth, Rich gambles that those on the prophetic side can do without that stability in the practical and philosophical areas of life.

Making life outside of more truth accountable is central to Rich's vision of the prophetic. She believes that the prophetic instability of more truth is the way to demystify institutional and state power, beginning with their patriarchal assumptions about what is and what is not truth. Clearly, Rich has little hope that institutional life will embrace more truth as its model for service. It is the prophetic nature of poetry and activism that places institutions of all types on notice.

Rich signals that the prophetic deconstruction of false truth, in the biblical sense of idolatry, must remain unstable. More truth is unstable because it is always evolving, becoming more. More truth needs instability to continue evolving. In parallel, the Jewish prophetic has to be continually deconstructed.

The "non" of the non-Jewish Jewishness is thus crucial to Rich's vision. But, as well, truth telling for another "non"—that is, non-Jews coming from other communities—is essential as well, even for Jewish truth telling.

Epilogue

Can a Jew be just? For that matter, can any person with a collective identity be just? It all depends, one might say, on a variety of variables. This includes the question: What is justice? What does commitment to justice mean?

If we simply assume for a moment that because of Israel's oppression of Palestinians, today's Jew cannot be just, where does that leave the prophet and the prophetic? If the prophet isn't just, who is?

Since this is not a book about speculative theory or academic definitions, the complicated issue of being just and the pursuit of justice is assumed in its most simple form. To be just is to seek engagement with others on the same playing field with equal power and possibility. To be just is to engage the complicated intersection of the person and society, and the structures that impact both.

Taking this definition, Jews, at least in America and Israel, are so intertwined with empire and injustice, and benefiting from both, that the initial response has to be: "No, in today's world, a Jew cannot be just." As for the prophetic and the prophet herself in relation to being just and justice, this, too, depends on definitions. Yet, again, using a plain sense of the category, and noting that the prophet and the prophetic are never pure, the initial response has to be: "Yes, in today's world, a Jew and Jews can pursue justice. Therefore, a Jew can be a prophet and Jews can be part of the prophetic."

That is, Jews—with others—within empire can struggle against empire, even as they benefit from it. The measuring rod is whether the struggle is real. This is why critical thought is honed within active participation for justice.

We know that justice is never fully realized. It is always partial. However, we can never be content with partial practice. There is always another step to be taken.

Whenever the prophetic is performed, we encounter impurity—and possibility. The prophet is invested in an identity that is both internal and external. The prophet is a boundary crosser—with boundaries. The prophet rails against the empire that is shared, wherever one is located in the socioeconomic and political hierarchy. The prophetic is about making choices. It is about vision. The prophetic embodies those choices and vision.

Impure Jews are not fake Jews, as Gilad Atzmon seems to suggest. Yet the prophetic glare exposes layers of Jewishness. It attempts to get to the heart of

361

Jewishness, to the indigenous prophetic. Whether Jews of Conscience claim the mantle of being Jewish or being prophetic is beside the point.

If the prophetic was easy, these layers would hardly be necessary. Most that cite impurity as an excuse do so as a protection against the prophetic call. The unsaid is that living the prophetic is almost impossible, in some cases suicidal.

Just weeks after the sixty-fifth anniversary of the birth of Israel and the continuation of the Palestinian Nakba, Mazin Qumsiyeh reflected on "Lenox Avenue Mural," a poem written by the African American poet, Langston Hughes. In the poem, Hughes asks what happens to a dream deferred: "Does it dry up like a raisin in the sun/or fester like a sore?" Later, he wonders if the dream deferred stinks like rotting meat or if it sags like a heavy load. Or, as Hughes suggests, does it explode?

Qumsiyeh quickly moves from his poem to his usual antisemitic rant or accurate analysis, depending on where one stands on the empire divide. The Palestinians are being herded into "concentration areas." Zionism is racism: "Zionism, built on notions of privilege and chosenness cannot help but spread racism." After traversing the culpability of the world powers, how various peace processes facilitate injustice, as well as the culpability of those Palestinian elites who benefit from the occupation, Qumsiyeh ends his reflection by paraphrasing Hughes with the Palestinian dream of freedom: "Does a dream deferred sag or does it explode?"

Langston Hughes, the African American poet of the Harlem Renaissance, via Mazin Qumsiyeh, the Palestinian Bedouin in Cyberspace. An unexpected combination. Or is it?

For Jews who affiliated with Hughes and the struggle for civil rights in America, the Palestinians affiliation can be troubling. It is also necessary. For some Jews the dream is Israel, the ancient Promised Land now contemporary. For other Jews the explosion is the prophetic, the ancient prophets come alive.

Where does the explosion lead? In America, lynching, dogs, and a vast prison population were used to fight against the struggle for African American freedom. The response of African Americans to oppression over the centuries featured long suffering, nonviolent resistance, and communal uprisings. Whites were there—on both sides of the empire divide.

Is Israel-Palestine, America's civil rights struggle reenacted in the Middle East? Are Jews, like American whites earlier, on both sides of the empire divide? Initially, one thinks the analogy interesting but ultimately misplaced. The civil rights struggle was located in the United States, contextually in one place with a specific history, therefore limited by its locality. Yet the black freedom struggle was also international. Movements for decolonization in Africa played a significant role in black consciousness. Other African Diaspora populations participated as well.

The expanding visions of Martin Luther King Jr. and Malcolm X regarding people of color around the world were symbolic of the widening struggle for human and political rights in America. There were links between the civil rights movement in America and the freedom struggle against apartheid in South Africa. All of these events, in turn, influence Jews of Conscience in how the state of Israel is perceived. Is this why linking apartheid and Israel is so highly charged? Movements around the globe come full circle. Jewish participation on behalf of the Other is ultimately destined to be applied within.

The embrace of Palestinians by Jews of Conscience may be similar in its effect. When Jews expand their view of human and political rights outward and then apply it in their own backyard, a global broadening of the Jewish horizon is inevitable. The struggle against that broadening, especially when it is more vigorously and repeatedly reapplied back home, is redoubled. Accusations fly on both sides. We are back with Jews on both sides of the empire divide.

For Jews, Langston's dream deferred is historically external—the Jewish desire to be free of oppression—and internal—the perennial issue of what Jews are to be about as a people with a particular destiny. In Jewish life, freedom from oppression and the prophetic call are intertwined. Jews may be free when they acquire power, but then the prophetic call for justice is invoked. If freedom and justice were natural bedfellows, this would be simpler.

One hesitates to rule out freedom and justice coexisting as a possibility in history. Yet looking at history, the two seem to be ideals rarely achieved or, if they are, that achievement is fleeting. The dream deferred is difficult to deal with. The dream of freedom achieved is often disillusioning.

The use of empire to maintain freedom is constantly undercut by the prophetic. Empire stability is buttressed by injustice. This the prophetic cannot abide. In the biblical world, injustice is instability personified. The Bible is clear on this. Stability through power is inherently dangerous. It cuts to the very fabric and purpose of Israel's existence. So what to do with this perennial issue in Jewish history, especially with the practical dilemma presented by Jewish empowerment in the United States and Israel?

After all of our explorations, we arrive where we started. Jewish empowerment is real and will remain for the foreseeable future. Dissenting Jews will continue and deepen their protests against the unjust use of Jewish power. Dissenting Jews are in exile. Their exile will deepen.

Although elements of the standoff are longstanding within Jewish history, there are new, more explosive ingredients. We are at a crossroads. The divisions of Jews on both sides of the empire divide have become permanent.

"Perennial" and "permanent" may be interchangeable terms. Then again, there can be a difference, at least with regard to Jewish history. The context of contemporary Jewish life, with its acceptance in the larger society and its assumption of power, has broken an underlying solidarity between Jews so necessary to survival in previous eras.

Over the last decades, the state of Israel functioned as a vehicle for Jewish solidarity. After the Holocaust and with the creation of the state of Israel, Jewish dissenters often censored themselves. With Jews in Israel on the line and with the Holocaust in the immediate background, the cost of speaking out was too high. Cautionary Holocaust flags were flown. Criticism of Israel could weaken the state to the point where it became indefensible. Criticism of Israel could cause Jews and others to abandon the Jewish state. If Israel weakened, what would happen to the millions of Jews within the state's boundaries?

For decades, solidarity of Jews on both sides of the empire divide held firm. After all, Jews live in a post-Holocaust world. That solidarity has frayed considerably in recent years. Whether that solidarity has broken down and is now irretrievable is the issue facing Jews around the world.

If solidarity among Jews is lost, are efforts to mend the divisions doomed to failure? One wonders if the desire on either side to bridge the widening solidarity gap still exists. For years, the Jewish community emphasized a post-Holocaust Jewish identity. There are few, if any, Jewish communities willing to confront the reality that Jews now come after the Holocaust and after the state of Israel.

How incredibly biblical this situation is. And how strange it is that after the suffering in the Holocaust in Europe and empowerment in the state of Israel—and amidst the heightening and seductive call of secular modern life—Jews find themselves once again biblically defined. Jews have been thrown into a pre-rabbinic sensibility, where metaphor and literary allusions, the parsing of biblical word order, silences in the text, and unanswered queries from the ancients suffice no longer. The embrace of the rabbinic sensibility by Progressive Jews has served as a deflection from the larger, more painful issues concerning an ever-expanding state of Israel.

The Holocaust rendered the rabbinic framework moot. The substitute proposed by the Jewish establishment was Jewish politics on the world stage, enabled and protected by the history of Jewish suffering. What the Jewish establishment did not account for was that eventually and, in historical terms quite quickly, the Holocaust would be overcome by the prophetic critique of Jewish power employed against the Palestinian people.

Holocaust theologians thought any objection to Jewish power would come primarily from outside the Jewish community. Of course, they knew well the possibility of the reemergence of the internal Jewish prophetic. Holocaust theology warns Jews against those who cannot abide Jews on the world scene, but the Jewish prophetic is equally cautioned against. Nonetheless, few Holocaust theologians predicted the ferocity of the Jewish prophetic that has emerged.

So, in 2012, when the former prime minister of Israel, Yitzhak Shamir, died, Jews wondered how to mark his passing. Born in Poland, and having lost most of his family in the Holocaust, Shamir fought the British and the Palestinians to help create the state of Israel. As prime minister in the late 1980s and early 1990s, Shamir ordered the crushing of the first Palestinian uprising. He also promoted Jewish settlements in the Israel-occupied West Bank.

Shamir was one of the founders of Israel. He was instrumental in foreclosing rapprochement with the Palestinian people. For those Jews on the empire side of the empire divide, Shamir should be celebrated. But those Jews who embrace the prophetic faced the question of how they should remember him. Should Shamir's passing be mourned with respect, even as political differences are maintained? Or should Shamir be lamented as an example of the existence of a criminal element in Jewish history?

The same issues where raised with the passing of Ariel Sharon in 2014. Like Shamir, Sharon served as Israel's prime minister. He lived his life in service to the state of Israel. Where did he lead Israel? In his policies within Israel, in Lebanon and in the occupied Palestinian territories, Sharon was a warrior. But in his death more than a few Jews inside and outside of Israel, considered Sharon a thug and a war criminal.

Israel's founders are passing into history. With each founder who dies, the judgment of history comes closer. Yitzhak Rabin was also a founder, a former prime minister, and, as a cabinet member in Shamir's government, pursued the policy of might and beatings that crushed the first Palestinian uprising. Many Jews hailed him as a hero for his late and controversial pursuit of peace with the Palestinians in the 1990s. Rabin's assassination in 1995 sealed his memory for many Jews as a seeker of peace. Yet, like Shamir and Sharon, Rabin was an ethnic cleanser of Palestinians in the 1948 war. Should Jews hold Rabin up as doyen of Jewish ethics or as a war criminal? Should Rabin be feted in public ceremonies today or retroactively be brought before the international bar of justice in The Hague?

Shamir, Sharon and Rabin's list of political assassinations, displacement of Palestinians, and settlements is long. On the empire side, they are impressive—one might say relentless. Yet their resumé is no more empire-impressive than that of Benjamin Netanyahu, who eulogized Shamir and Sharon as prime minister.

The continuity of the Israeli state's violence against Palestinians is clear, as is the colonialist sensibility of every prime ministers in Israel's history. The sense of "Arabs being Arabs" is hardly the exclusive province of right-wing Israelis. Rather, it is shared across the political spectrum of Israel. It is little different in the American Jewish community.

"Arabs being Arabs." "Jews being Jews?" Fixed identity structures they are, but also identity structures that continue to evolve in the Israeli-Palestinian conflict. The issue is whether Israeli and Diaspora Jewish identity will be frozen in this empire-colonial modality forever. At least for the part of the Jewish community around the world that cites a Jewish state and its imperatives for survival, this might be the case. It seems that Netanyahu and all the Israeli prime ministers before him share the same mission—to freeze Jewish identity, make empire mandatory for survival, so that the prophetic will be dispatched. Is that why Israel has added a new demand for Palestinians to be deemed worthy of a state—that Palestinians recognize Israel as a Jewish state—to permanently eliminate the prophetic from Jewish life?

In its present configuration, Israel demands that the Jewish prophetic voice be stilled. Yet as we have seen, the prophetic is alive. Where does it move? What decisions does it have to make? Where can the prophetic thrive?

These questions will be answered long into the future. For the prophetic, however, the time is always now. The tension inherent in the prophetic timescape is intense. Justice achieved at another point in time is always too late.

Mourning, too, is part of the prophetic. In the Bible, prophetic mourning is less for lost empire than it is for the people's lost moorings. Although Israel needs to survive, survival for survival's sake is way down the prophet's to-do list. Survival for survival's sake was Israel's undoing then—and now.

So the prophetic, under assault in its indigenous home, wanders to Other lands. This occurred in previous generations. Now the prophetic returns home to a communal landscape that is almost unrecognizable. Or perhaps it is the same home the prophetic left. Now the prophetic returns with eyes wide open.

In the end this is the prophetic—eyes wide open. Eyes wide open demands the courage or, rather, the obligation to name the unnamable, to speak what is witnessed and known. Naming and speaking thus, does the prophetic have to take into account that the Jewish community, let alone a Jewish state, cannot live by the prophetic alone? After all is said and done, does the prophetic have obligations beyond its appointed task, to reason with the exigencies of history, with antisemitism, with a state that has millions of Jews?

Some Still/Former Jewish/Israeli/Prophets have left the state of Israel. Some have left their Jewishness behind. The issue remains whether they are recognizable without either or both. Jewish history has marked them indelibly. The Jewish (Prophetic) Prison is theirs for life.

It is also ours, Jews of Conscience and Empire Jews, as well, but also Jews who are rarely heard from, the great majority of Jews who live out their daily lives primarily invested in ordinary life rather than Jewish politics. Jews are haunted by the biblical prophets because the Jewish prophetic is alive today. Brushing them off as malcontents simply demonstrates the hold the prophetic has on Jewish life.

As we have seen, Jewish life is filled with colonial mentalities. Does that mentality breed criminality? Since colonialism breeds criminality wherever colonialism exists, Jews cannot escape this fate.

Today, even the Jewish prophetic is tainted with colonial sensibilities. As part and parcel of Jewish history and contemporary Jewish life, the prophetic cannot escape—or transcend—the experience and thought patterns of the Jewish people. Nor can the Still/Former Jewish/Israeli/Prophets escape the contradictions of Jewish life as it is lived today. That is precisely their heroism, since, in many ways, the Still/Former Jewish/Israeli/Prophets embody the tension of colonialism and dissent. The Jewish prophetic struggles with its own demons.

So if the Jewish prophetic is itself compromised by its participation in the ongoing Palestinian Nakba, and yet refuses to be silent—if in fact the struggle of the prophetic against injustice is outward against the powers that be and inward against its own birth, educational, social, political, and military environment—then the prophetic must renegotiate its own flawed being in the world. With this acknowledgment of shared culpability, the prophetic renegotiates its witness to fellow Jews and the larger world.

The Jewish prophetic is one of the primal roots of the conscience of humanity. If it presents itself as innocent, the Jewish and universal complaint about its witness will have validity. The Jewish prophetic as innocent is hypocritical. By posing as innocent it takes on a dissenting empire manner. It competes with empire on its own turf of self-righteousness and power.

The contrast presented is a stark either/or. But in real rather than virtual life, the choice is rarely as stark. "My way or the highway" is hyperbole. We share the same byways and highways. Whether consciously or not, the fork in the road retains its original connection; it often meets up again sometimes in the least expected place. Think of the fork in the road Christians and Muslims took with regard to Jews. In the prophetic we meet again.

Choices have to be made. Lack of innocence does not let the prophetic off the hook. Instead, recognition of complicity ramps up responsibility. Yet other levels remain.

The Jewish prophetic is deeply wounded. Despite their bravado, the Still/Former Jewish/Israeli/Prophets are traumatized by their participation in injustice. They are also traumatized by their exile. The Still/Former Jewish/Israeli/Prophets represent the image of dissenting Jews as deeply wounded and traumatized.

The larger prophetic community, including and especially the Palestinian prophetic community, is wounded and traumatized. Being troubled and on the run hardly means a retreat from action. It does, however, demand serious reflection. Wounding and trauma penetrates the core of the prophetic. What does a wounded and traumatized Jewish prophetic have to say to the world? What does a wounded and traumatized global prophetic have to say to the Jewish prophetic?

The years ahead portend new challenges for the prophetic in the Israeli-Palestinian conflict. With an American-led peace process framework always in the works, Israeli and American-led NATO occupation forces proposed and ready to be deployed, only a virtual or outskirts presence in Jerusalem for Palestinians proffered, with Gaza nowhere to be found, and even the resultant scattered and organized Palestinian resistance that may develop in response—all of this may well drive the prophetic into darker terrain.

The prophetic has to keep its hand on the justice-wheel. High-blown rhetoric, economic packages, and Oslo Accords redos demand critical examination. Anything less than justice will not suffice for Palestinians or for Jews either. But, then, justice is hard to find anywhere. Should it be easier in Israel–Palestine?

The prophetic long haul knows that at times justice possibilities expand. At times, they narrow. Is the Jewish and global prophetic ready for the challenges ahead?

If the Palestinian Authority signs onto principles and agreements which effectively and permanently ghettoize the Palestinian people, the prophetic will be called upon to respond. Peace process rumblings are designed to alleviate the pressure on Israel in the international community and undercut movements for justice that are gaining traction in the international community. If this occurs, the Jewish prophetic will be on its heels. How can Jews of Conscience continue to argue for Palestinian freedom if Palestinian leaders throw in the towel? So, too, the global prophetic with its intense focus on the plight of the Palestinian people. What resources can the global movements of conscience galvanize if Palestinian leadership signs away its birthright?

Though few have analyzed its possible effects, worldwide movements for justice would be devastated. Israel-Palestine has become a galvanizing issue for the international community precisely because it joins the many diverse strands of the world's religions and the prophetic call within each of them.

The pressures attending even the rhetorical acceptance of such a framework might trigger another Palestinian uprising. The future is up in the air as the suffering deepens. There seems to be no way out of this conundrum—until there is.

In these pages, I have attempted to trace the outlines of the prophetic as it exists in our contemporary world. The prophetic witness will continue to unfold. Israel's ancient wisdom—the great gift of Jews to the world—remains steady. Today it is re-presented to the Jewish people by others. What we shall make of the prophetic together is the challenge before us.

This is where we end—for now. The prophetic witness is always before us. When Jews—with others—embody the prophetic, the worldly powers are placed on notice. What happens then we know from history. The struggle intensifies. The causalities mount. The empire, always on a war footing, intensifies the war against the prophetic. Yet history remains open. Perhaps this is ultimate message the prophets communicate to us throughout the ages. When we come to the end, against all odds, the prophet glimpses a new beginning on the horizon. When that hope will be embraced, when it will broaden so that the global community becomes prophetic, cannot be foretold in advance. The prophet is not a soothsayer. The prophet is the gatherer of light in dark times. Gathering light, hope on the horizon, justice around the corners of our lives. Eyes wide open, Israel's ancient wisdom, re-presented, reborn.

Index

CPSIA information can be obtained at www.ICGtesting.com
Printed in the USA
LVOW01s1905170414

382154LV00008B/11/P